QUALITATIVE
STUDIES OF
ORGANIZATIONS

Jennifer
Thackaberry

John Van Maanen
Editor

QUALITATIVE
STUDIES OF
ORGANIZATIONS

The *Administrative Science Quarterly*
Series in Organization Theory and Behavior

Administrative
Science
Quarterly

SAGE Publications
International Educational and Professional Publisher
Thousand Oaks London New Delhi

For information:

SAGE Publications, Inc.
2455 Teller Road
Thousand Oaks, California 91320
E-mail: order@sagepub.com

SAGE Publications Ltd.
6 Bonhill Street
London EC2A 4PU
United Kingdom

SAGE Publications India Pvt. Ltd.
M-32 Market
Greater Kailash I
New Delhi 110 048 India

Printed in the United States of America

Library of Congress Cataloging-in-Publication Data

Main entry under title:

Qualitative studies of organizations / edited by John Van Maanen.
   p.   cm. — (The administrative science quarterly series in
organization theory and behavior)
   Includes bibliographical references and index.
   ISBN 0-7619-1694-6 (cloth: acid-free paper)
   ISBN 0-7619-1695-4 (pbk.: acid-free paper)
   1. Organizational behavior.   2. Organizational change.
I. Van Maanen, John.   II. Series.
   HD58.7.Q35   1998
   302.3′5—ddc21   98-25344

This book is printed on acid-free paper.

98 99 00 01 02 03 10 9 8 7 6 5 4 3 2 1

Acquiring Editor:	Marquita Flemming
Production Editor:	Astrid Virding
Editorial Assistant:	Nevair Kabakian
Designer/Typesetter:	Janelle LeMaster

Contents

FOREWORD

We are delighted to inaugurate the *Administrative Science Quarterly* (*ASQ*) Series in Organization Theory and Behavior with this volume on qualitative research. Our aim in this book series is to identify topics, methods, or theories that have shaped the foundations and current direction of organizational theory and behavior and to compile a collection of published *ASQ* articles on the selected topic, in volume form, not only to make these articles more widely accessible to students and researchers but to focus and stimulate thinking on those areas of administrative science that have most profoundly shaped the development of organizational theory and behavior.

In this first volume, John Van Maanen has selected and introduced the compendium of *ASQ* articles on qualitative research. We feel extremely fortunate that a scholar of John's stature and expertise agreed to compile this volume. We admire John's integrity and accomplishments as a researcher, his passionate advocacy of unpretentious and penetrating scholarly analysis, and his ingenuous respect for shared learning, candid theoretical discourse, and methodological diversity. Like the compiled works in this volume, his own contributions have played a fundamental role in directing the focus and growth of organizational studies.

We express our sincere thanks to Marquita Flemming of Sage Publications, who encouraged us to develop this series and who has been extremely helpful throughout the process of launching this collaborative effort between Sage and *ASQ*. We also thank the *ASQ* staff, Gina Jackson, Jennifer Mitchell, and Sheila Sheehan, for their invaluable assistance and support. We are also indebted to all the authors, who allowed us to reproduce their enduring qualitative work in this volume. We owe a special debt of gratitude to Stephen Barley for his inspiration in conceiving the original idea for this volume and for his initiative in commissioning John Van Maanen's assistance. Although Steve's tenure as *ASQ* editor from 1993 to 1997 has concluded, Linda and I felt that Steve's designation as lead series editor was indispensable in symbolizing his true contribution to the series. We expect that Steve will care little for such a gesture, because his interests as *ASQ* editor were always for the journal, not for himself. Certainly, no such gesture can do credit to the success and contribution of his stewardship of *ASQ*, yet his innovative and rigorous intellectual leadership of *ASQ* is a legacy that the field of administrative science will enjoy for many years to come, and his initiative in launching this volume is just one of his many achievements as editor of *ASQ*.

We hope that you, the reader, will share our enthusiasm for this and future volumes of the *ASQ* Series in Organization Theory and Behavior and that you will be struck anew by the novelty and significance of what these authors, individually and collectively, have contributed to our understanding of organizational theory and behavior.

CHRISTINE OLIVER
Editor, *Administrative Science Quarterly*

LINDA JOHANSON
Managing Editor, *Administrative Science Quarterly*

DIFFERENT STROKES

Qualitative Research in the *Administrative Science Quarterly* from 1956 to 1996

John Van Maanen

The title of an essay, article, chapter, or book is part of the text. It is the first part of the text we encounter and therefore has some power to attract and perhaps condition the reader's attention. For the writer, choosing a title is something of a creative act, helping to bring into focus the piece of writing that follows. I jotted down thirteen possible titles for this essay—including the too frivolous but autobiographical "How I Spent My Summer Vacation" and the accurate but previously used "Varieties of Qualitative Research"—before settling (uneasily) on the rather whimsical lead phrase, which comes from the vernacular bon mot "different strokes for different folks." I settled on this title for several reasons.

First, this is an introduction to a collection of organizational studies produced by authors using a range of qualitative research methods. The plural is important, for it signals my concern with the grab bag of techniques and strategies used in qualitative research, including, for example, historical analysis based on archival materials, conversational analysis of closely edited snatches of naturally occurring talk, intensive interviews designed to ferret out native points of view and account for them, and living with and living like members of an organization so that ethnographic impressions of organizational life can be constructed. Each has distinctive information gathering and harvesting conventions to follow (and foil), and qualitative work, like quantitative work, comes in many different forms.

Second, my title indicates that the products of our research endeavors are ink stained. Whatever else we may do in the way of learning of organizational life, we must also write about it and convey our understandings to others through a publication process initiated by endless keystrokes. Narrative conventions associated with qualitative work are also varied, and writing styles followed consciously or unconsciously by authors are not perfectly correlated with methods. Thus, participant observation studies may take a realistic or confessional turn, just as historical studies might be given an objectivist or subjectivist wash.

Third, the intellectual field within which the "different strokes" that are my concern appear is an ambitious yet ambiguous one. Organizational studies rely on a strange brew of reference disciplines, including sociology, history, economics, psychology, anthropology, political science, and even literary, media, and communication studies.[1] Each discipline has humanistic as well as scientific wings, and qualitative work is undertaken, written, and read on both sides of the house. The scholarly circles within which qualitative work circulates are thus many. Some are relatively insulated, well armed with favored techniques and consensually approved reporting styles; others are emerging and eclectic, mixing parasitic and novel elements while shaping their aims and tricks of the trade by topical interests and pragmatic, on-the-fly concepts and concerns.

Such variety is neither a scandal nor (necessarily) a strength. It does suggest that equating qualitative research with ethnographies or case studies or historical descriptions is simpleminded. Qualitative methods are many, they are everywhere, and they do not easily boil down to formula. Moreover, qualitative work shapes and is shaped by numerous philosophical and theoretical traditions. Constructivist views of the world of the sort spun out of social and cultural anthropology or resting on the symbolic interactionist perspective in sociology inform a good deal of qualitative work but certainly not all. Nor is qualitative work restricted to the so-called individual or group levels of analysis. Powerful qualitative studies examine organizations writ large, as well as industries, societies, and the global character of contemporary political economies, capitalist and otherwise.

This leaves us with the question of just what distinguishes a particular work as qualitative. Elsewhere I have noted that we are perhaps best off thinking of qualitative research in terms of some of the organizing principles that mark the concerns and activities of those who do the work (Van Maanen, 1983). This is akin to Kuhn's (1970) celebrated definition of science in terms of what scientists do. Some principles that guide much qualitative work include a focus on meaning, the use of analytic induction, maintaining a close proximity to data, an emphasis on ordinary behavior, and attempts to link agency to structure through accounts based on the study of events (routine or otherwise) over time. But, as with most recipes for social practices, exceptions are the rule.

What makes qualitative research particularly difficult to pin down is its flexibility and emergent character. Qualitative research is most often designed as it is being done. It is anything but standardized or, more tellingly, impersonal.[2] As Becker (1993) pointed out, qualitative work allows for—indeed, insists on—highly contextualized individual judgments. It is a style of research that makes room for the unanticipated, thus focusing more on specific cases and exceptions than on abstractions and generalizations. In the end, qualitative researchers come to know a good deal about the specific social worlds they study and find it difficult if not impossible to reduce these worlds to a few representative and measurable dimensions.

This is another way of saying that qualitative work generally sidesteps the hypothetical-deductive research model in favor of an inductive, interpretive approach most often marked by a reliance on multiple sources of information. Data gathering or technique-dependent definitions of such work are faulty because they cannot absorb the diversity of methods subject to the qualitative label.[3] The aim of most qualitative studies is to produce a more or less coherent representation, carried by word and story, of an authorially claimed reality and of certain truths or meanings it may contain for those within its reach.

It is sometimes easier—although dangerous—to evoke qualitative work by looking at what it is not: A text stressing variables, operational definitions, and tests of propositions derived from a muscular theory that maps the world in terms of cause-and-effect forces is not a qualitative study; variable analysis marked primarily by examining arithmetic covariation is not a qualitative study. In quantitative research, the author attempts to interpose an intentionally standardized data collection process that operates between the social settings and situations studied and the analysis of those settings and situations. What is analyzed is not the setting or situation as it is experienced or represented more or less in the raw, but the data. Quantitative data can take many forms, such as answers to items on questionnaires or formalized observations of behavior but, in the end, such data must be amenable to frequency counts and statistical analysis. The products of such work are numbers, figures, and tables that summarize selected properties of the data.

Qualitative work produces narratives—nonfiction division—that link events to events in storied or dramatic form with beginnings, middles, and ends. Story elements are explicitly connected, thus *emplotting* a research report with an apparent causal structure that itself is made theoretically plausible through argument and analogy. There are many narrative forms available to qualitative researchers, but the idea is to create historically situated tales that include both highly focused portraits of what identifiable people in particular places at certain times are doing and a reasoned interpretation for why such conduct is common or not. The sociological specificity, historical particularity, and narrative form are distinctive features of qualitative work. The end result is its effect on the reader who, ideally, is both enlightened by the narrative and persuaded by the explanation the writer offered.[4]

We must not make too much of these distinctions, however, for they are heavy with evaluative freight and lead to rigid conceptual categories devoid of nuance and shared features. Quantitative research is not the evil twin of qualitative research. A problem in much of the methodological discourse and elsewhere is that dichotomies substitute for differences. Dichotomies produce sharp contrasts and thus sever, leading to a rather pat and pointless definition of qualitative research as everything that quantitative research is not. Dichotomies reflect a rigid, perhaps obsessive concern for opposition as expressed by the use of the structuralist's bold slash to mark loaded contrasts: A/Z, Good/Bad, Clean/Dirty, Right/Wrong, Truth/Fiction, Qualitative/Quantitative. Differences, however, as Jacques Derrida (1976, 1978) would have it, provide a comparison and thus point to relative, not absolute standards.

Such relative standards are evident in the matters of exploration and verification in research. Qualitative work is often characterized as exploratory, aiming at discovery, description, and theory building. Quantitative work, when set up as part of a dichotomy, is about justifying or verifying by test the empirical basis and generality of theory claims. The slash between the two, however, is anything but fat and wide, for exploratory work is never dreamwork or a leap into the dark; lots of reasoning enters, information gathering is always selective, and any exploration is governed in large part by theory that determines (at least partly) what counts as fact, evidence, story, and so forth. Nor is justification and the testing of ideas devoid of exploratory elements and novel analytic twists. Rather than a dichotomy, we have a difference whose particular shape varies from study to study.

Rigid dichotomies also obscure the inevitable interdependence of quantitative and qualitative work. Quantitative research is typically most interested in making general statements that take the form of defensible propositions about analytic classes or abstracted properties of social life. Qualitative work is usually most interested in coming to terms with specific instances of social phenomena and how broad principles or theoretical suppositions work out in particular cases. In this sense, the two imply (and deserve) one another, since any given case must display some general principle and the announcement of any general principle must assume that a specific case can be found for its illustration. While it appears rhetorically impossible to talk about research methods in organization studies without contrasting qualitative and quantitative work, neither approach can stand alone.

Finally, both qualitative and quantitative research confronts the dismal but stubborn fact that any given study—qualitative and quantitative—stands on shaky epistemological grounds. All methods are flawed in some way or another. Not everything can be examined at once, and limitations of scope and depth abound. Quantitative researchers must rely on their own experientially based understandings of social life to make sense of their findings, just as qualitative researchers must rely on all sorts of categorical and distributional data to locate their work. Like it or not, both must make use of data and methods that are questionable from their own epistemological orientation just to get on with the business of social research. It is, however, a business that shifts with the times.

We live now in an age of scholarly declassification. Blurred distinctions, fuzzy sets, and intellectual poaching all mark academic life, and theorists of many sorts avoid discrete, sharply delineated concepts set off from one another by empty spaces and turn instead toward continuous, overlapping concepts that slip and slide Escher-like into one another. The rise of Giddens's (1979, 1984) structuration theory provides a marvelous example of just such a move that has been taken up by a number of organizational researchers. But declassification extends well beyond the small worlds of organization research as scholarly disciplines intermingle, borders open, categories collapse, theories blend, authority disperses, voices multiply, and hodgepodge becomes the order of the day. Geertz (1983: 20), as scholar turned stand-up comic, surveys the scene and finds

> philosophical inquiries looking like literary criticism (Cavell on Beckett or Thoreau, Sartre on Flaubert), scientific discussion looking like belles-lettres morceaux (Lewis Thomas, Loren Eisely), baroque fantasies presented as deadpan empirical observations (Borges, Barthelme) . . . parables posing as ethnographies (Castaneda), theoretical arguments cast as historiographical inquiries (Edward Said), epistemological studies constructed like political tracts (Paul Feyerabend). . . . One waits only for quantum theory in verse or biography in algebra.

Scholars remain somewhat uneasy with such category scrambling in organizational studies, however, particularly on this side of the Atlantic. A good deal of our research talk—occurring in seminar rooms, corridors, taverns, tribal gatherings, and texts—reflects a discomfort with the expansion and diversity of our distinctly low-consensus field. Some of the talk pits high-flying theorists against in-the-trenches researchers. The former see the latter as dumb-as-a-post empiricists, while the latter think the former should be peeled from the ceiling and sent on their way. Some of the talk is framed by the professional debates (and status seeking) in the field as members of one theory circle try to boost their reputations, resources, and recruits at the expense of other circles. And, of course, some of the talk simply reflects the way a new generation in any research-dependent and self-defined scientific field is trained and comes to regard many of its forebears as little more than cognitively challenged plodders whose dated research styles and out-of-fashion ideas are a source of bemusement and ridicule.

A good example of such hostility is the current horror many students of qualitative methods develop for what they call, with spite, positivism. On occasion, the invective is deserved, as when some crude number-crunching device substitutes for thought. But students more frequently learn to use the term as an abusive catch-all for anything they don't like about theories, approaches, and findings coming from outside the theory and research circles with which they identify and are comfortable. This is particularly bothersome at the moment, because I can think of very few organizational researchers—qualitative or quantitative—who actually adopt the tag positivist.[5]

The problem here seems to be the familiar one of essentializing differences into dichotomies and then privileging one side of a dichotomy over the other. Such a process does not go unrecognized. In a pithy (and, in its entirety, rather droll) editorial statement appearing twenty years ago in the *Administrative Science Quarterly,* Karl Weick (1977: 138-139) took up these matters and noted that the journal "is not a sanctuary for the 'cute school' of organizational analysis . . . any more than it is a sheltered workshop for the 'opposite' group which presumably must be called the 'brute school.' "

A pose against privilege is struck in these lines and, while a dichotomy is put forth, it is simultaneously, if subtly, deflated by the judicious use of purposely snotty labels and quotation marks. How such a pose has played out in the journal is a matter of record and one I will soon take up. But before doing so, I offer some contextual remarks as an introduction and frame for my reading (and counting) of the qualitative research published in *ASQ*.

FORESHADOWINGS

The ideal reader of this book is a prospective, retired, certified, manqué, or practicing organizational researcher of either the qualitative or quantitative persuasion or both. Exclusivity is not my aim, for I am convinced that one form of research should inform the other. At any rate, a rigid compartmentalization between and among methods is impossible to maintain, since the differences are at best analogic, not digital, a matter of degree, not essence. More to the point, we seem to become obsessed with methods and insidious distinctions only when we have no story to tell.

Much storytelling, both manifest and latent, appears in the monographs and articles of organizational studies. Master themes embedded in the field at large concern the ways various forms of organization and administration alter the way we think, work, and live, as well as the ways organizations make us smarter or dumber, better or worse, freer or more enslaved. Such grand themes reflect the growing power of organizations to give shape to our lives, and researchers as authors often wind up telling of the kinds of paradise gained or lost as a result of such power.

There is certainly enormous variation in how these themes are realized in print. Research reports can bundle various compositional elements such as theory, methods, and evidence in many ways but, over time, reporting conventions emerge and help shape the stories that are told. This is evident in the presentational order and style of research reports in *ASQ*. Articles published in the early volumes of the journal—both qualitative and quantitative—show considerably less format standardization and language formalization than those of later volumes.[6]

Closer to my concerns here, method discussions attached to qualitative research articles in the first ten or so years of the journal's history are characteristically short and spare, sometimes consisting of a single paragraph or a footnote (occasionally less) and blissfully unconcerned with elaborating or even justifying a given approach. Similar work published from the late 1960s on carries in the text itself solemn, lengthy, detailed, and increasingly adroit rationalizations of the methods used to carry out a particular study. Convincing readers today that a given study is more or less safe for science takes up a good deal of journal space.

Changes in the appearance of qualitative work may also signal broader shifts. Particular field methods, theoretical interests, and analytic techniques all rise and fall in legitimacy and use. Such changes are not necessarily a mark of progress or advancement, although they are often accompanied by such claims. Method shifts may reflect changes in the availability or scarcity of research funds, just as theoretical moves may reflect the social organization of the field as subfields grow or decline in number and influence. Work published in a mainstream journal such as *ASQ* offers a convenient place to track such changes in the field over time.

Over the years, *ASQ*—like most other research journals publishing organizational studies—has come to present work that typically falls into an empiricist genre, with strong scientific claims for constructing reliable and valid knowledge about behavior in and of organizations.[7] The name and dedication of the journal speaks to this aim—"advancing the understanding of administration through empirical investigation and theoretical analysis." Across the journal's forty-plus years, organizational research discourse has been defined, refined, challenged, and amended in various ways. Controversy over what form a proper organizational study should take surfaced early in the journal's history and has never really gone away.[8] A part of this debate centers on the respective roles qualitative and quantitative research should play in the field at large. An early manifesto issued in the name of peaceful coexistence (and still one of the best) was put forth by Boulding (1958: 14-15), who, in a remarkably prophetic review of the first two volumes of *ASQ*, had this to say of what he called descriptive and historical work:

> It would be a great pity if a morbid fear of being "unscientific" were ever to lead to a suppression of this type of writing. The thing that distinguishes social systems from physical or even biological systems is their incomparable (and embarrassing) richness in special cases. Generalizations in the social sciences are mere pathways which lead through a riotous forest of individual trees, each a species unto itself. The social scientist who loses this sense of the essential individuality and uniqueness of each case is all too likely to make a solemn scientific ass of himself, especially if he thinks that his faceless generalizations are the equivalents of the rich variety of the world. I am not arguing of course that we should cease to make generalizations; this would be to abandon science altogether. I am merely urging that we should not believe them.

Whether or not blame rests fully on the morbid fear carried by solemn scientific asses, it is the case that at least some of Boulding's anticipatory anxiety was warranted. While qualitative work played a relatively large and prominent role in the journal (and the field) for a time, it went into a slump of sorts, from which it is slowly and sporadically recovering.[9] The slump cuts across the social sciences generally and is associated with particular historical periods, certain kinds of qualitative work, and the rise of quantitatively defined variable analysis emphasizing the formulation and testing of propositions drawn from existing theory and research circles.

This is a story that can be told best by looking at the publishing record of *ASQ* since its founding by James Thompson in 1956. While the story to be told is not so much about *ASQ* as about the relative place over time of qualitative research within organizational studies, an analysis of the journal is useful for examining that place, since it serves as something of a flagship for organizational scholarship as the field's oldest, most read, and quite possibly, most respected English-language journal now in circulation.[10]

FORTY YEARS OF *ASQ*

Looking across time at *ASQ* requires a number of classification decisions. Most critically, articles must be assigned categorical significance. The categories I use are but slight deviations of the four used by Boulding (1958) to type the content of volumes one and two of *ASQ*. The first is called "theory" and includes essays written to argue a given analytic, philosophical, or normative position into (or out of) existence. The category largely comprises writings that draw on other published writings (often the author's own) for empirical illustrations and theoretical exemplars. Little if any original data are presented in these articles beyond the anecdotal. A catch-all or general purpose function is served also by this category, for in it I dropped those articles I could not comfortably stuff into one of the other three categories. A good illustration is Mechanic's (1962) much cited treatment of the organizational power of lower participants. The article puts forward a series of interconnected theoretical propositions of which some are supported by previous (and published) research studies, some by personal experience, and some by plausible but hypothetical examples. While the work draws on qualitative research results, it does not, in the main, present original empirical materials and hence seemed to fit my theory category best.

The second category includes articles that take up methods. It differs from theory in that articles assigned to this category deal less with organizing or assessing a given body of work than in examining the ways in which selected research questions have been and might be addressed. The work in this category tends to be more exhortatory than critical. It contains the fewest number of articles of the four categories and would be fewer still were it not for three special issues of the journal, each dedicated to a methodological cause: "Laboratory Studies of Experimental Organizations" in 1969 (vol. 14, no. 2), "Evaluation of Change Programs" in 1970 (vol. 15, no. 1), and "Qualitative Methodology" in 1979 (vol. 24, no. 4).[11]

The third and fourth categories include original research articles of the qualitative and quantitative sorts, respectively. I have struggled to compare the two in previous sections and will not go beyond my earlier comments other than to note that narrative representations characterize the articles coded as qualitative, while numbers, statistics, and testing hypotheses mark the quantitative. The former generally eschews variable analysis, the latter embraces it. Qualitative studies are further broken down later in this section.

The assignment of a particular article to a given, singular category is, of course, a matter of judgment—in this case, my judgment alone. For this reason, my numbers, like all numbers, should be taken with a grain of salt. Coding is a troublesome business. My problems began with simply identifying what was to count as an article.

For the record, I did not count editorials, news and notes, book reviews, short comments on research or research methods, critical responses to specific authors, or authors' responses to specific critics. I did count articles appearing in special issues. Far more problems arose in assigning articles to categories for, in truth, many authors not only provide extensive theory and method discussions but also mix qualitative and quantitative evidence and argument. My four categories are therefore hardly pure types. My imperfect solution to case-specific coding dilemmas was not to drop ambiguous articles from the pool or to assign an article to multiple categories but to type each article in one and only one category according to what I judged to be its "dominant" character or emphasis. This said, however, I must also point out that my aim

TABLE I.1 Categories of Work Published in the *Administrative Science Quarterly* (1956-1996) by Decade

	Theory	Method	Qualitative	Quantitative	Total
Vols. 1-10 (1956-65)	53 (25%)	18 (8%)	61 (28%)	83 (39%)	215 (20%)
Vols. 11-20 (1966-75)	45 (14%)	27 (8%)	26 (8%)	234 (70%)	332 (31%)
Vols. 21-30 (1976-85)	47 (16%)	31 (10%)	35 (12%)	183 (62%)	296 (28%)
Vols. 31-40 (1986-95)	14 (6%)	4 (2%)	36 (16%)	178 (77%)	232 (22%)
Total	159 (15%)	80 (7%)	158 (15%)	678 (63%)	1,075 (100%)

was not to produce definitive and air-tight categories (an impossible task, to be sure) but merely to track in broad and comparative strokes the rough place of qualitative work in *ASQ*.[12] Table I.1 provides a summary glance at the kinds of work published in the journal since 1956.

Several trends are apparent in Table I.1. Most striking perhaps is the rise of quantitative studies and the decline of other types of work. Qualitative articles bottom out in the second decade (vols. 11-21) but come back over the next two. Theory and method articles shrink most noticeably in the past decade (vols. 31-40). Opinions will differ, of course, as to what the proper proportions in each category should be or whether the changes in proportions have gone too far and fast or not far and fast enough. As an admirer of qualitative studies, I lament its decline and applaud its recovery even if modest. But this is another story. My purpose is to convey the publishing history of qualitative work in *ASQ* as a representative organizational studies journal.

With respect to Table I.1, the reader should keep in mind that the numbers alone do not tell the story, and many stories are possible. One story, for instance, is that editors and referees in any given period are simply and quite properly doing their jobs, and while they may see, for example, many qualitative papers, most are without merit, poorly constructed, uninteresting, and thus rightfully rejected. More submissions will not change the distribution but better ones might. Another story, equally plausible, is that relatively few qualitative papers appear in a given period because few are submitted. After all, qualitative research in organizational studies may be uncommon at times. Or perhaps those who do it periodically seek other outlets for their work. Some may prefer to publish research monographs or chapters in edited books that allow for lengthier research products than is typical for journals. Colin Firebaugh (1997: 772), the current editor of the *American Sociological Review,* put this account forward in a recent and refreshingly direct plea to potential contributors to the journal:

> The *ASR* publishes more quantitative articles because we receive more manu-
> scripts of that type. The mix of articles reflects the mix in the manuscript
> pool. . . . The most recent data show that qualitative and theory papers are
> published at the same rate as quantitative manuscripts. If you want to see
> different types of articles published, please help us by submitting them.

TABLE I.2 Categories of Qualitative Research Published in the *Administrative Science Quarterly* (1956-1996) by Decade

	Vols. 1-10 (1956-65)	*Vols. 11-20 (1966-75)*	*Vols. 21-30 (1976-85)*	*Vols. 31-40 (1986-95)*	*Total (N = 158)*
Case studies	27 (44%)	15 (58%)	21 (60%)	13 (36%)	76 (48%)
Ethnographies	19 (31%)	5 (19%)	6 (17%)	11 (31%)	41 (26%)
Interview studies	13 (21%)	3 (12%)	3 (9%)	4 (11%)	23 (15%)
Linguistic studies	0 (0%)	0 (0%)	3 (9%)	4 (11%)	7 (4%)
Mixed (qualitative and quantitative)	2 (3%)	3 (12%)	2 (6%)	4 (11%)	11 (7%)
Total	61 (100%)	26 (100%)	35 (100%)	36 (100%)	

Both stories no doubt carry some truth, but neither addresses the temporal question: Why did qualitative articles drop off so precipitously during the mid- to late 1960s through the 1970s? In this regard, it is worth noting that this is the period in organizational studies when the influential Aston Studies were being published (in *ASQ* and elsewhere). It is a period marked by the popularity of contingency theories and the "discovery" of the environment as both an independent and dependent variable in the modeling of organization behavior. Comparative studies of organizations and organizational structures were on the rise, and such studies involved the analysis of large, standardized data sets and promised to put macro-organizational studies firmly on the scientific map. Not coincidentally, perhaps, this was also a period during which the IBM 360 computer became widely used, along with statistical software packages that made the analysis of large data sets considerably easier and more convenient than had previously been the case.

This was also a period of explosive growth of enrollments in American colleges and universities including, significantly, business schools. An enlarged supply of freshly minted Ph.D.s were needed to staff the teaching and research positions opening up. Jobs were plentiful. In this context, time-consuming, seemingly old-fashioned theory-building rather than theory-testing research techniques may well have fallen from favor among those pursuing research careers in organizational studies. That qualitative work would shrink during such a period seems, in retrospect, hardly surprising.

All this is speculative. These are not matters I can address with the materials in hand. What I can do, however, is look more closely at the kinds of qualitative articles published in *ASQ* to see just how qualitative research itself may have shifted over time. Table I.2 summarizes by decade the changing mix of qualitative work. I began with twelve categories for the work. Because this made for very small cell sizes, I kept recoding and cutting back on categories of qualitative research until I reached the magic number five, which seemed to me not too many, not too few, but just right. The five categories are case studies, ethnographies, interview studies, linguistic studies, and mixed qualitative and quantitative studies (with an emphasis on the qualitative materials).

While the numbers are small, the frequency, range, methods, settings, and compositional characteristics of the studies within the set are of interest. Case studies and ethnographies are by far the most common forms of qualitative research appearing in *ASQ* (about 75 percent of the total). Case studies concentrate on event sequences in particular locales and ethnographies on cultural portraiture and what it is like to be someone else. Various levels of analysis are represented in each category (e.g., groups, organizations, industries, states), and both include comparative works. Historical case studies, while few in number, are nonetheless present across all periods.[13]

Fieldwork of a continuous and intimate sort (i.e., reliance on long-term relations with so-called key informants) characterizes the ethnographies. Case study authors are more likely to rely on secondary data sources, brief rather than extensive forays into the field, and somewhat standardized (if open-ended) interviews with representative members of the particular unit(s) of study.[14] Induction—building concepts and theories from the ground up—is the favored (although not exclusive) mode of analysis claimed by authors of both ethnographies and case studies.[15] Ethnographers, however, are associated—sometimes closely, sometimes remotely—with given cultural theories and consequently tend to tell stories informed by the analytic traditions from which they come: materialist, symbolic, functional, linguistic, structural, cognitive, and so on. In both cases, however, authors emphasize local details, events, and members' perspectives. Conclusions are of a narrative sort and not easily detachable or decontextualized. Discipline-based theorizing tends to be light and used more to establish plausibility and invoke generality than to be tested. Boulding (1958: 5) considered such writings to be "travel over the field of study" and vital to organizational research:

> In every field there is a need for writing where the main objective is to extend the reader's field of acquaintance with the complex cases of the real world. Such writing does not have to be very exact or quantitative; it does not even have to formulate or to demonstrate hypotheses. It constitutes, as it were, travel over the field of study. Travel is certainly not enough, even for a geographer, but we would feel, I imagine, that a geographer who had never traveled would be under a serious handicap. Similarly the student of organizations who has never, even vicariously through reading, been in a hospital, a bank, a research laboratory, a large corporation, a Soviet factory, a revolution, an Egyptian civil service department, and so on, has missed something. His generalizations are apt to be based on too narrow a selection of the field.

The list Boulding rolls out specifies a number of delightfully diverse qualitative research sites plucked from articles appearing in the first two volumes of *ASQ*. The ethnographies and case studies that followed continued to honor Boulding's travel mandate of taking readers places they presumably had never been, but authors also began to attach more theory—both off-the-shelf and grounded—to their work than was true for the early period. Such explicit theorizing—no doubt nudged on by editors and reviewers—added to the specification of just what a given case or ethnography was about and thus sharpened (and limited) its focus and perhaps helped preserve a place for case studies and ethnographies in the journal.[16]

Comparing case studies and ethnographies, the former appear more frequently than the latter, but the gap between the two narrows considerably in the past decade, where ethnographies make up a little more than 30 percent of all qualitative work appearing in the journal. Part of this shift may reflect the slow but steady development of an organizational culture discourse within and across various research communities as well as the spread, and homecoming, of ethnographic research techniques. Ethnographers are as likely these days to be plying their trade in hospitals, research labs, tourist hotels, high-tech corporations, and the local public schools as in the remote villages of highland Burma or the urban neighborhoods of north-end Boston or southside Chicago (Clifford, 1997).

Interview studies are another form of qualitative research counted in Table I.2. My coding is stringent, since I included in the category only those studies that were primarily interview based. Such studies appear to have almost dropped off the research map at *ASQ*. Although interviews remain a much mentioned and more or less standard feature of qualitative work, particularly case studies, few research reports now rest on interviews alone, or so it is claimed.[17]

Linguistic (or language use) studies represent a relatively recent addition to *ASQ*. They rest on the researcher's interpretation of naturally occurring talk or the production of text taking place in and around (and usually about) organizations. This work is generally quite theory driven, informed by such related analytic fields as conversational analysis, linguistic anthropology, sociolinguistics, and narrative or literary theories. Interviews and ethnographic observations help frame such studies, but the researcher's interest is not with a case or culture per se but with matters such as speech acts, turns of talk, communication genres, and the interpretive practices of organizational members.

The final category of Table I.2 is called "mixed" and is filled up by articles that blend quantitative and qualitative methods, and like linguistic and interview-based studies, the number appearing in this category is small. The articles of this category exhibit a good deal of number mongering and crunching. However, as mentioned previously, to be assigned to this category, the qualitative orientation of the writing must (in my judgment) hold sway over the quantitative. This is occasionally difficult to discern. An example of the coding problems I produced for myself with this category is Elsbach's (1994) numerically dense study of talk in and about the California cattle industry. But her numbers serve largely to provide a context and topical frame for the account giving (and accepting) practices of members of the industry, which she uncovered through extensive fieldwork and content analysis. This I tagged qualitative (and mixed). A counterexample is my own study of police socialization (Van Maanen, 1975). In this article, a quick and glossy ethnography frames a longitudinal analysis of measured job attitudes treated as focus variables. This I coded quantitative.

That, in a numerical nutshell, is the place of qualitative research in *ASQ* over forty years. It is an up-and-down and (partly) up picture, with some period variation existing among the five types of qualitative work coded and reported. Taken as a whole, this work is conceptually diverse and of rather high quality and interest. Much of it is distinctive. Sobriety, attention to detail, care without obsession, a balance of the abstract and concrete, and (usually) an easy rather than relentless use of theory, imagery, and metaphor are integral to the continued legitimation and place of qualitative work in the journal.

Such matters are, however, set partly by fashion and the available genres of the time. Someone writing with Gusfield's (1958) literary sensibilities in "Equalitarianism and Bureaucratic Recruitment" or with Strauss's (1962) functional orientation in "Tactics of Lateral Relationship," or with Katz's (1965) disregard of method in "Explaining Informal Work Groups in Complex Organizations" might find it difficult to publish in *ASQ* today without attending to current methodological reporting conventions, changes in the theoretical interests of readers, and the apparent decline in the use of what Daft (1980: 623-624) called a particularistic but inherently ambiguous "high variety language." This is not to say such articles are without contemporary merit. To some, they are classics, having told stories that linger in the mind. But we should remember that texts do not remain the same over time, despite the fact that as written products they are fixed. From the point of view of their reception, research writings constantly change as readers reinterpret and redefine their merits (and demerits) in light of changing theoretical projects in the field and additional evidence coming from other studies. Of course, from the point of view of inception, styles of writing up (or down) qualitative studies change too in light of the continuous reinterpretation of past work. But some characteristics of qualitative research reporting have stayed the course. Three are particularly impressive.

First, I think much of the writing exhibits a relative freedom from analytic and technical jargon. Putting readers into the shoes of those studied continues to be a priority for most qualitative researchers, and this descriptive aim is best met through the use of a general rather than a specialized language. Theory is a must these days, to be sure, but theory seems more to animate than to motivate qualitative work, except perhaps in the linguistic domain. Authors still borrow concepts from broad public discourse (e.g., games, theater, politics, popular culture) and make much use of so-called native or member terms in naming, framing, and organizing research reports. For better or worse, Glaser and Strauss's (1967) thirty-year-old text, *The Discovery of Grounded Theory,* remains a source of inspiration to qualitative researchers and is still frequently cited.

Second, a good deal of qualitative work draws on fields that are somewhat removed from the mainstream of organization research and theory. Such areas include fieldwork-based sociology, semiotics, ethnomethodology, phenomenology, history, critical theory, and current streams of thought in cultural anthropology, symbolic interactionism, and narrative theory. This provides a distinctive conceptual landscape (and reading list) for both neophyte and experienced researchers. It also promotes what I regard as the slight but noticeable literary air associated with qualitative research writings, even in organizational studies, where loan words come mostly from science, not the humanities. Readers untutored in the research traditions, topical interests, or even theoretical questions central to a qualitative paper can nonetheless read and understand the work. Such writing is inviting rather than intimidating and, when well done, stimulating rather than boring. The voice reporting qualitative work is not always the omniscient voice of science (the voice from everywhere) but occasionally, and perhaps increasingly, the personal voice of a situated author with a story to tell. In this sense, narrative may well be the latent paradigm associated with qualitative work, rather than any of the manifest disciplinary, organizational, or research theories floating around and through such work.

Third, and finally, the methods of qualitative research, as critics gleefully point out, remain loose and unspecified. Any given study tends to be methodologically promiscuous. Even singular methods escape formalization. Interviews, for instance, carry situational properties that will not go away, and most experienced interviewers recognize that a "typical" qualitative interview is, at best, a construct known only in the ideal (e.g., Mishler, 1986; McCracken, 1988; Kvale, 1996). We know, too, that participant observation is always biographically shaped, and fieldwork guides still cannot get much past the simple cautionary tales of seasoned veterans recounting their experiences (e.g., Emerson, 1983; Sanjek, 1990; Lareau and Shultz, 1996). All this suggests to me a rather broad indifference (if not hostility) on the part of qualitative researchers for the endless efforts of other organizational scholars to define methodological rigor and, on its sturdy back, develop general and refined theory. In most respects, qualitative research reports continue to be improvised and crafted, inspired as much by artistic, aesthetic, and humanistic concerns as by social theory and research design. I am not unhappy with this steady state of the art. Yet such remarks border on ideological pontification. Some examples are needed. They take up the rest of this book.

COMING ATTRACTIONS

The following chapters present thirteen sterling illustrations of substantively focused and theoretically relevant qualitative research reports. All are articles appearing in *ASQ* sometime between 1958 and 1995. All are favorites of mine, and a few are rather famous across organizational research communities. Most important, however, they exhibit, as a group, a broad range of research styles and careful scholarship. They are models of qualitative research put forth in journal-length style. I regard each article in this collection as something of an exemplar and thus worthy of our field's highest reward, imitation. They are not the only exemplars I might have selected from the *ASQ* archives, nor do I maintain the illusion (or delusion) that other readers of the archives would make the same selections. For this collection, I deliberately sought variety in methods, topics, analytic style, level of analysis, publication period, and so forth. I also wanted to avoid celebrating work in which I had an acknowledged hand as a prepublication reader, however slight my hand and however much the work deserves celebration. Such criteria eased my task considerably.

The studies are spread across four sections. Each part of the collection is roughly distinguished by a topical concern rather than a particular level of analysis. Part I presents three studies of organizational processes. Part II includes three articles about groups in organizations. Part III offers four representations of organizational identity and change, and Part IV includes three depictions of the societal and institutional environment. These categories should not be taken as representative of the topics with which qualitative work is solely concerned. I used these categories to group the articles I had already selected as personal favorites of mine and hence candidates for inclusion in this collection. On my original list were about thirty articles, which I sorted into topical areas. I then eliminated those articles that seemed to form a class by themselves or closely resembled another article in the category that I happened to like better. I wound up with about twenty articles spread across the four categories and made the final selections subject to the criteria described above.

As the section heads denote, there is a considerable range of theoretical interests covered by the collection. There is substantive range as well, for the organizations studied in the collection include factories, churches, universities, engineering groups, fisheries, voluntary organizations, basketball teams, public organizations, pop music recording firms, and more. In terms of method, there are six case studies in the collection, four ethnographies, two mixed-method reports, and a single linguistic study. As for the historical periods represented by the readings, three come from the foundational era of 1956-1965 (vols. 1-10), two from 1966-1975 (vols. 11-20), three from

1976-1985 (vols. 21-30), and five from the recent period, 1986-1995 (vols. 31-40).

The authors of the works display a variety of disciplinary backgrounds, including sociology (the majority), political science, communications, management studies, and history. Some of the authors were graduate students at the time their articles were drafted (Robert Gephart, Nicole Biggart, Patricia Denton, and John Maniha). Others were well-established and well-known scholars (Burton Clark, Robert Cole, Richard Cyert, and William Dill). Many were relatively junior members of their respective guilds (Peter and Patricia Adler, Ann Langley, James Barker, Mayer Zald, Paul Hirsch, Reed Nelson, Petter Holm, Charles Perrow, and James March). Only one of the thirteen articles comes from a special issue (Cyert, Dill, and March); the rest went through the regular *ASQ* submission, review, and publication process.

Perhaps the most intriguing and engaging feature of this collection is the writing. Each piece can be read on its own with some pleasure even if the theoretical claims and substantive topics are remote from a reader's scholarly interests. Writing to inform as well as to please is no easy matter, and how to do it can only be insinuated, not preached. There probably are rules for writing the persuasive, memorable, and publishable qualitative research article but, rest assured, no one knows what they are. Examples must be our guide. In the end, all we can do if we are truthful is to tell a story. Such a tale will inevitably include certain nonrepeatable, particularistic elements side by side with authorially drawn analogies to stories of other fields and other times, both near and distant. The stories told here are of just such a sort. We need more.

ACKNOWLEDGMENTS

As always, this writing rests on a little help (and more) from my friends. Substantive and stylistic aid in straightening up a crooked tale came from Steve Barley, Linda Johanson, Karl Weick, Lotte Bailyn, Peter Manning, Wanda Orlikowski, Diane Vaughan, JoAnne Yates, and Ed Schein. The volume itself would not have been possible were it not for the organizational efforts and enthusiasm of Steve Barley and Linda Johanson, who kept this procrastinating editor on track if not on time. Asaf Darr provided me with an early reading list of qualitative work in *ASQ* gleaned from the journal's archives at Cornell University. Over the summer of 1996, Lyman Porter, Christopher Earley, Elaine Mosakowski, and Anne Tsui helped me with locating odd volumes and issues of *ASQ* missing or otherwise unavailable from the libraries at MIT, Harvard, UCLA, UCI, and CSU at Fullerton. I am grateful.

NOTES

1. Unlike organization studies in Europe, organizational studies in the United States stands on its own as a rather autonomous field, complete with internal rifts and divisions between and among those who are called macro- and micro-organizational theorists. It is a field that represents a growing assembly of rather diverse scholars frequently trained and/or working in business schools and held together largely by convenience, will, and a few summer meetings. For better or worse, organizational research in Europe, notably in the United Kingdom and France, is tied more closely to the reference disciplines mentioned in the text, especially sociology and psychology. Useful and recent discussions of these matters are found in Hofstede (1996), Koza and Thoenig (1995), Child (1995), Üsdiken and Pasadeos (1995), Guillén (1994), Chanlat (1994), Boyacigiller and Adler (1991), Cooper and Cox (1989), and Hinings (1988). The Atlantic, it seems, separates rather than connects the research worlds of Europe and English-speaking North America.

2. These are precisely the features of qualitative work many critics find most troubling. Because qualitative research is not impersonal and systematic but tries to take into account unfolding historical and situational detail, such work is said to be unable to produce the sort of objective and reliable knowledge necessary for prediction. Quantitative work, in contrast, tries to be systematic and impersonal but is faulted by other critics who say it leaves too much out and promises far more predictive power than it can deliver. Epistemological debates turning on these matters have been around for a very long time and are not likely ever to be settled. As critics of our research endeavors, epistemological theorists are necessary but annoying, since their job is to uncover and question all the taken-for-granted research conventions that make given lines of study possible. They are very hard to please. Becker's (1993: 227) advice for dealing with such Cassandra-like characters in our midst is to "listen to them, be polite, take what is usable and finesse the rest." This is good advice, and more of it can be found in Becker (1996).

3. A qualification is necessary here. Adherence to this or that method of data collecting does help to define membership in a particular theoretical school, and such an association can sometimes lead to a technique-oriented definition of qualitative or, for that matter, quantitative work. Symbolic interactionists are recognized, for instance, by the cult of participant observation surrounding their work, ethnomethodologists for their passion for audiotaping and videotaping anything that speaks or moves, status attainment researchers for their systematic use of path analysis, and network researchers for their use of matrix algebra and scaling techniques. How tight such conceptual linkages are is often brought home when several methods are combined in a single study and the work hailed as a breakthrough, a daring challenge to methodological monotheism—as when, for example, a discourse analysis is combined with an ethnographic description or a network study is grafted onto survey research. While virtually all qualitative studies are blends of various techniques, published method discussions usually acknowledge or imply that the work relies more on one method than others.

4. The narrative turn in qualitative work is perhaps most advanced in ethnography, where Clifford (1997: 67-68), among others, argued that a "literariness has returned." It has returned along with strong claims about the prefiguration and rhetorical nature of all social science data. More broadly, Ewick and Silbey (1995) pointed out that narrative in social research can serve as an object of study, a method of study, and/or a product of study. When narrative inheres in the scholarly production of books and articles, social researchers themselves serve as storytellers. It is worth noting, however, that narrative as a product of social research is not intended to be decorative or merely a way of making a work readable, palatable, and audience friendly. Narrative is a cognitive device, a way of ordering and interpreting the social world. Good things are now being said of narrative in many circles. See, for example, Mitchell (1980) and Bruner (1990), for broad discussions of narrative; Reissman (1993), for a look at some techniques of narrative analysis; and Czarniawska-Joerges (1997), for a study of organizational narratives put forth (thankfully) in narrative form.

5. The reverse is true as well, for much of what I consider quite sound qualitative work is labeled by my quantitatively oriented colleagues as undisciplined, soft, squishy, and lacking rigor. Some of the problems created by both quantitative and qualitative research bashing may stem from the way students are trained. For example, in a generic graduate course on research methodology, students are usually asked to examine various research strategies, techniques, and philosophies and report back, parrotlike, the advantages and disadvantages of each. Contrasts are emphasized, and students often understandably wind up preferring what their teachers prefer. Such courses seem to produce a learned incapacity to go out and actually do research of different sorts, for learning about the armed rival methodological camps in no way prepares one to face field data, which are far messier than any one camp is willing to admit. This is a point that comes through quite clearly in many of the selections included in the edited volume Frost and Stablein (1992) put together to honor what they considered exemplary organizational research projects.

6. In this regard, Davis's (1971) observations of what makes a given piece of research interesting (and publishable) are relevant. Among the reader-response propositions he puts forth is one suggesting that authors who deny weakly held assumptions of their audience will have their work noted (or, more exactly, footnoted), while those who deny strongly held assumptions will have their sanity questioned. The difference between the inspired and insane is located, according to Davis, in the strength and tenacity to which an audience holds onto its assumptions when they are violated or attacked. Such assumptions ground stylistic and representational conventions as well as substantive or theoretical claims. Assumptions surrounding the proper format, mode of expression, and rhetoric all appear to be strongly held among readers of and reviewers for established research journals—and are often inscribed as submission guidelines on the back pages of the journals themselves. This suggests that work challenging such guidelines and the assumptions on which they rest best look elsewhere for publication. On the role of rhetoric and style in science, see, for example, Gusfield (1976), Bazerman (1981), McCloskey (1983), and Locke (1992). See, too, Perrow (1985) for a wry treatment of what kinds of contributions are most likely to be welcomed by mainstream journals and why researchers of all ages and types should try—occasionally at least—to direct some of their work toward such fussy publications.

7. This is not to say that stylistic innovation and various forms of genre bending are absent from the journal. Superb examples of highly stylized writing from the very early days of *ASQ* include Richardson (1956), Presthus (1958), Gusfield (1958), Stinchcombe (1959), and Boulding's (1958) rogue and neglected essay cited throughout this introduction. Some of the same provocative (and evocative) playfulness shows up periodically across the journal's history. Editors, it seems, are willing to loosen the house strictures against an author's personal expressiveness now and then, with the apparent rule being the more eminent the author, the greater the loosening. Certainly, the field of organizational studies has its share of good writers and even a few powerful stylists with uncanny abilities to put forth gentle ironies, work with active grammatical constructions, and develop arguments supported by apt analogies and metaphors. Such relatively rare but felicitous trope deployment in *ASQ* beyond the foundational era is exemplified by Weick (1976, 1993), Brown (1978), March (1981), and, most recently, Leavitt (1996).

8. Challenges to what some claim is the "orthodox" research discourse promoted at *ASQ* sometimes appear in the pages of the journal itself. See, for example, protests lodged by Benson (1977), Morgan (1980, 1983), Astley (1985), and Astley and Van de Ven (1983). Several studies on the nature of this supposed orthodoxy exist. The most detailed and more or less affectionate is Daft's (1980) examination of the language used in the journal from 1959 to 1979. Boje, Fitzgibbons, and Steingard's (1996) much less affectionate appraisal took the journal to task for overlooking what they call "critical postmodern discourse." Weick (1985) also examined the character of the journal from the lofty position of a former long-term editor and, perhaps not unexpectedly, found things more or less in order, with few traces of a smothering orthodoxy at work. Recently, the editors have encouraged controversy in the form of personal thought, argument, opinion, and protest (of a mild and mannerly sort) through the publication of invited essays (and commentary) appearing in a stand-alone segment of the journal called the "*ASQ* Forum." See, for example, Sutton and Staw (1995) and Stern and Barley (1996).

9. Much article-length qualitative work in organization studies appears, as always, in journals off the mainline, such as the *Journal of Contemporary Ethnography, Qualitative Sociology, Human Organization, Human Relations, Organization Studies, Journal of Management Studies, Journal of Applied Behavioral Sciences,* and more recently, *Organization, Journal of Management Inquiry, Journal of Organizational Change Management, Qualitative Inquiry,* and *Studies in Cultures, Organizations and Societies.* A good deal of qualitative work is also published in monograph form and as chapters in edited volumes. Of most interest, perhaps, is that a good deal of qualitative work is cleverly brought into quantitative journal articles as an adjunct to variable analysis. Qualitative cases are often needed to put a numerically driven story into words by offering plausible examples of what a specific variable relationship might mean. My view on much of this is that the more qualitative work is tamped down, ignored, or marginalized in mainline journals, the more repression charge it accumulates and the more likely, as Freud might tell us, it will return, rebound, erupt in quite possibly unexpected but vigorous ways. This may be represented best by the specter of postmodernism hanging over the organization studies field and making many of us nervous (some cheerfully so). See, for example, Clegg (1990), Gergen (1992), Reed and Hughes (1992), Smircich, Calás, and Morgan (1992), Brown (1995), Friedland and Boden (1994), and Boje, Gephart, and Thatchenkery (1996).

10. This rather sweeping assessment is based not so much on *ASQ*'s circulation rates (holding steady at about 4,500 subscribers worldwide) but on its consistent placement among the top three to five most cited journals in the Social Science Citation Index (SSCI). As the SSCI figures make clear, *ASQ* articles are cited more frequently and live longer in academic communities than articles appearing in other organizational research journals. What is also clear is that a publication in *ASQ* bestows legitimacy on an up-and-coming organizational scholar, and it is probably the case that more than a few academic careers have been made (or broken) by publishing decisions made by the journal. For a somewhat different view on the ranking of organizational research journals, see Sharplin and Mabry (1985).

11. The effect of the fifteen special issues of *ASQ* published as of 1995, while tangential to my concerns, does raise intriguing questions. Special issues are put together to raise reader consciousness, which, like the Titanic, is deemed by an editor to be worthy of raising. As such, special issues are meant to increase scholarly interest in a particular area. Whether or not they do so is debatable. The 1971 special issue "Laboratory Studies of Experimental Organizations" (vol. 14, no. 2) edited by Karl Weick, seems, in retrospect, more an obituary than a tribute or call to action, for it marked the end of an era rather than a beginning. The 1983 special issue "Organization Culture" (vol. 28, no. 3) edited by Mariann Jelinek, Linda Smircich, and Paul Hirsch signaled the rise of a subfield in organization studies that is still going strong. Of particular interest to this volume is my own 1979 special issue "Qualitative Research Methods" (vol. 24, no. 4). The data presented in Table I.1 on the publication rates of qualitative research in *ASQ* are none too clear. Comparing all volumes prior to the 1979 special issue with all those that followed (vols. 25-40), there is no change—15 percent of the articles in the period preceding the special issue are qualitative and 15 percent following the special issue are qualitative. If I equalize the examined volumes between the pre- and post-special issue (vol. 9 to vol. 24, no. 3 and vols. 25-40), the percentage of qualitative articles appearing in the journal increases from 10 to 15 percent over the period. This cut of the publication evidence can perhaps be justified on the grounds suggested by Daft (1980), that the early years of *ASQ* were experimental or unsettled and therefore unhelpful when depicting publishing trends.

12. As an example of an exemplary quantitative content analysis, this motley, judgmental, count-and-classify approach of mine leaves much to be desired. It owes more to my daughter's Sesame Street calculator than to the Cadillac of a computer parked on my desk. It is, at best, a quick and personal glance at the journal's history. But, I hasten to add, such a glance required me to read forty years' worth of articles published in the journal. Some were read leisurely with pleasure, some were read carefully with annoyance. Most were read swiftly with coding on my mind. To gain a reliability estimate of my coding practices would require at least one other reader, but I could find no volunteers and had no budget for hired hands and eyes.

13. I include as historical case studies Dale's (1956, 1957) delicious biographies of Alfred P. Sloan and the Du Pont Company. With Dale's work, biography became extinct in *ASQ*.

14. Case studies can be quantitative as well as qualitative, representative as well as deviant or exemplary. In an important sense, however, all studies are case studies if only because all analyze social phenomena that are highly specific in time (by historical moment) and place (by group, organization, industry, nation state, or planet). The qualitative case studies of *ASQ* are close readings, put in writing, of certain specified social scenes and mix representational and interpretive elements. The worlds studied are generally seen as temporal sequences of events rather than sets of forces. The most important question is not so much "What is a case?" but, rather, "What is this case about?" Putting forth a distinctive, logical, and well-argued answer in terms that go beyond the case materials themselves is no easy task but separates the good from the not-so-good cases. Superb discussions of contemporary case studies are found in Feagin, Orum, and Sjoberg (1991) and Ragin and Becker (1992). An intriguing comparison of sociological case studies written by French (including French Canadian) and U.S. authors is provided by Hamel (1993).

15. Students are sometimes surprised and disappointed to discover that some case studies and ethnographies they regard as exemplars of inductive, bottom-up grounded theory are actually constructed on a rather tight, a priori conceptual framework in which field materials play only a minor illustrative role in telling a story driven by top-down, theoretical concepts. This is usually the reason why data and analysis are joined together so effortlessly by an author who produces a tidy and wonderful "just-so" story. To some extent, all fieldwork-based studies are subject to such a critique, for theory penetrates deeply and unavoidably into what we see, hear, record, and critically, write. The role of theory in contemporary fieldwork and qualitative research generally is taken up in several recent and sophisticated method texts. See, for example, Atkinson (1990), Emerson (1983), Wolcott (1995), and Silverman (1993). See also Manning's (1979) treatment of metaphor as a theoretical framing device underpinning fieldwork-based organization studies.

16. For better or worse, theory has worked its way deeply into qualitative work. "Having a theory" is today the mark of research seriousness and respectability. Theory is, of course, convenient and helps to organize and communicate unwieldy data and simplify the terrible complexities of the social world, matters that may well be more important to the field than whether or not a given theory is true or false. It also bestows rewards, since those who profess and publish theories that others find attractive are feted and promoted—or, if their theories prove unattractive, are unpublished, reviled, and fired. What is clear, however, is that the authors of case studies and ethnographies appearing in *ASQ* have increasingly tried to frame their work theoretically, making sure that the theories credited or discredited by their facts and stories are of current interest to readers. One can now be sure that when "travel over the field of study" makes its way to print, a theoretically informed guide will be along for the ride.

17. The hedge is important here, for no study represents a pure methodological type. As noted in the text, most qualitative studies appearing in *ASQ* mention interviews as one of several data sources, but few claim interviews as an exclusive or even primary source. This, as Table I.2 indicates, is more true today than yesterday. A few examples of splendid research articles that are primarily interview-based include Blau (1960), Wildavsky and Hammond (1965), Wildavsky (1972), Sutton (1987), and Vaughan (1990).

REFERENCES

Astley, W. Graham. 1985. "Administrative science as socially constructed truth." *Administrative Science Quarterly*, 30: 497-513.

Astley, W. Graham, and Andrew H. Van de Ven. 1983. "Central perspectives and debates in organization theory." *Administrative Science Quarterly*, 28: 245-273.

Atkinson, Paul. 1990. *The Ethnographic Imagination.* New York: Routledge.

Bazerman, Charles. 1981. "What written knowledge does: Three examples of academic discourse." *Philosophy of the Social Sciences*, 11: 361-387.

Becker, Howard S. 1993. "Theory: The necessary evil." In David J. Flinders and Geoffrey E. Mills (eds.), *Theory and Concepts in Qualitative Research:* 218-229. New York: Teachers College Press.

———. 1996. "The epistemology of qualitative research." In Richard Jessor, Anne Colby, and Richard A. Shweder (eds.), *Ethnography and Human Development:* 318-329. Chicago: University of Chicago Press.

Benson, J. Kenneth. 1977. "Organizations: A dialectical view." *Administrative Science Quarterly,* 22: 1-21.

Blau, Peter M. 1960. "Orientation toward clients in a public welfare agency." *Administrative Science Quarterly,* 5: 341-361.

Boje, David M., Dale E. Fitzgibbons, and David S. Steingard. 1996. "Storytelling at *Administrative Science Quarterly*." In David M. Boje, Robert P. Gephart, Jr., and Tojo Joseph Thatchenkery (eds.), *Postmodern Management and Organization Theory:* 60-92. Thousand Oaks, CA: Sage.

Boje, David M., Robert P. Gephart, Jr., and Tojo Joseph Thatchenkery (eds.). 1996. *Postmodern Management and Organization Theory.* Thousand Oaks, CA: Sage.

Boulding, Kenneth E. 1958. "Evidences for an administrative science: A review of the *Administrative Science Quarterly,* volumes 1 and 2." *Administrative Science Quarterly,* 3: 1-22.

Boyacigiller, Nakiye, and Nancy J. Adler. 1991. "The parochial dinosaur: Organization science in a global context." *Academy of Management Review,* 16: 262-290.

Brown, Richard Harvey. 1978. "Bureaucracy as praxis: Toward a political phenomenology of formal organizations." *Administrative Science Quarterly,* 23: 365-382.

———. 1995. *Postmodern Representations.* Urbana: University of Illinois Press.

Bruner, Jerome S. 1990. *Acts of Meaning.* Cambridge, MA: Harvard University Press.

Chanlat, Jean-François. 1994. "Francophone organizational analysis (1950-1990)." *Organization Studies,* 15: 47-79.

Child, John. 1995. "Guest Editorial." (Special issue: The European Perspective on Organization Theory.) *Organization Science,* 6: 117-118.

Clegg, Stewart. 1990. *Modern Organizations: Organization Studies in the Postmodern World.* London: Sage.

Clifford, James. 1997. *Routes: Travel and Translations in the Late Twentieth Century.* Cambridge, MA: Harvard University Press.

Cooper, Cary L., and Charles J. Cox. 1989. "Applying American organizational sciences in Europe and the United Kingdom." In C. A. B. Osigweh (ed.), *Organization Science Abroad:* 57-65. New York: Plenum.

Czarniawska-Joerges, Barbara. 1997. *Narrating the Organization: Dramas of Institutional Identity.* Chicago: University of Chicago Press.

Daft, Richard L. 1980. "The evolution of organizational analysis in *ASQ,* 1959-1979." *Administrative Science Quarterly,* 25: 623-636.

Dale, Ernest. 1956. "Contributions to administration by Alfred P. Sloan, Jr., and GM." *Administrative Science Quarterly,* 1: 30-62.

———. 1957. "Du Pont: Pioneer in systematic management." *Administrative Science Quarterly,* 2: 25-59.

Davis, Murray S. 1971. "That's interesting! Towards a phenomenology of sociology and a sociology of phenomenology." *Philosophy of the Social Sciences,* 1: 301-344.

Derrida, Jacques. 1976. *Of Grammatology.* Trans. by G. Spivak. Baltimore: Johns Hopkins University Press.

———. 1978. *Writing and Difference.* Trans. by A. Bass. Chicago: University of Chicago Press.

Elsbach, Kimberly D. 1994. "Managing organizational legitimacy in the California cattle industry: The construction and effectiveness of verbal accounts." *Administrative Science Quarterly,* 39: 57-88.

Emerson, Robert M. (ed.). 1983. *Contemporary Field Research.* Boston: Little, Brown.

Ewick, Patricia, and Susan Silbey. 1995. "Subversive stories and hegemonic tales: Toward a sociology of narrative." *Law and Society Review,* 29: 197-220.

Feagin, Joe, Anthony M. Orum, and Gideon Sjoberg. 1991. *A Case for the Case Study.* Chapel Hill: University of North Carolina Press.

Firebaugh, Colin. 1997. "Editorial statement." *American Sociological Review,* 62: 13-14.

Friedland, Roger, and Deirdre Boden (eds.). 1994. *NowHere: Space, Time and Modernity*. Berkeley: University of California Press.

Frost, Peter J., and Ralph Stablein (eds.). 1992. *Doing Exemplary Research*. Newbury Park, CA: Sage.

Geertz, Clifford. 1983. *Local Knowledge*. New York: Basic Books.

Gergen, Kenneth J. 1992. "Organization theory in the postmodern era." In Michael Reed and Michael Hughes (eds.), *Rethinking Organizations: New Directions in Organization Theory and Analysis*: 209-226. London: Sage.

Giddens, Anthony. 1979. *Central Problems in Social Theory*. Berkeley: University of California Press.

————. 1984. *The Constitution of Society*. Berkeley: University of California Press.

Glaser, Barney, and Anselm Strauss. 1967. *The Discovery of Grounded Theory*. Chicago: Aldine.

Guillén, Mauro. 1994. *Models of Management*. Chicago: University of Chicago Press.

Gusfield, Joseph R. 1958. "Equalitarianism and bureaucratic recruitment." *Administrative Science Quarterly*, 2: 521-541.

————. 1976. "The literary rhetoric of science." *American Sociological Review*, 41: 16-33.

Hamel, Jacques. 1993. *Case Study Methods*. Newbury Park, CA: Sage.

Hinings, Bob. 1988. "Defending organization theory: A British view from North America." *Organization Studies*, 9: 2-7.

Hofstede, Geert. 1996. "An American in Paris: The influence of nationality on organization theories." *Organization Studies*, 17: 525-537.

Katz, Fred E. 1965. "Explaining informal work groups in complex organizations." *Administrative Science Quarterly*, 10: 204-223.

Koza, Mitchell P., and Jean-Claude Thoenig. 1995. "Organization theory at the crossroads: Some reflections on European and United States approaches to organizational research." *Organization Science*, 6: 1-8.

Kuhn, Thomas. 1970. *The Structure of Scientific Revolutions*. Chicago: University of Chicago Press.

Kvale, Steinar. 1996. *InterViews: An Introduction to Qualitative Research Interviewing*. Thousand Oaks, CA: Sage.

Lareau, Annette, and Jeffrey Shultz (eds.). 1996. *Journeys through Ethnography*. Boulder, CO: Westview.

Leavitt, Harold J. 1996. "The old days, hot groups, and managers' lib." *Administrative Science Quarterly*, 41: 288-300.

Locke, David. 1992. *Science as Writing*. New Haven, CT: Yale University Press.

Manning, Peter K. 1979. "Metaphors of the field: Varieties of organizational discourse." *Administrative Science Quarterly*, 24: 660-671.

March, James G. 1981. "Footnotes to organizational change." *Administrative Science Quarterly*, 26: 563-577.

McCloskey, Donald L. 1983. "The rhetoric of economics." *Journal of Economic Literature*, 21: 481-517.

McCracken, Grant. 1988. *The Long Interview*. Newbury Park, CA: Sage.

Mechanic, David. 1962. "Organization power of lower participants." *Administrative Science Quarterly*, 7: 349-364.

Mishler, Elliot G. 1986. *Research Interviewing*. Cambridge, MA: Harvard University Press.

Mitchell, W. J. T. (ed.). 1980. *On Narrative*. Chicago: University of Chicago Press.

Morgan, Gareth. 1980. "Paradigms, metaphors, and puzzle solving in organization theory." *Administrative Science Quarterly*, 25: 605-622.

————. 1983. "More on metaphor: Why we cannot control tropes in administrative science." *Administrative Science Quarterly*, 28: 601-607.

Perrow, Charles. 1985. "Journaling careers." In L. L. Cummings and Peter J. Frost (eds.), *Publishing in the Organizational Sciences*: 203-215. Beverly Hills, CA: Sage.

Presthus, Robert V. 1958. "Toward a theory of organizational behavior." *Administrative Science Quarterly*, 3: 48-72.

Ragin, Charles C., and Howard S. Becker (eds.). 1992. *What Is a Case?* New York: Cambridge University Press.

Reed, Michael, and Michael Hughes (eds.). 1992. *Rethinking Organization: New Directions in Organization Theory and Analysis.* London: Sage.

Reissman, Catherine. 1993. *Narrative Analysis.* Newbury Park, CA: Sage.

Richardson, Stephen A. 1956. "Organizational contrasts on British and American ships." *Administrative Science Quarterly,* 1: 189-207.

Sanjek, Roger (ed.). 1990. *Fieldnotes.* Ithaca, NY: Cornell University Press.

Sharplin, Arthur D., and Rodney H. Mabry. 1985. "The relative importance of journals used in management research: An alternative ranking." *Human Relations,* 38: 139-149.

Silverman, David. 1993. *Interpreting Qualitative Data: Methods for Analyzing Talk, Text and Interaction.* London: Sage.

Smircich, Linda, Marta B. Calás, and Gareth Morgan (eds.). 1992. "New intellectual currents in organization and management theory." Special issue of *Academy of Management Review,* vol. 17, no. 3.

Stern, Robert N., and Stephen R. Barley. 1996. "Organizations and social systems: Organization theory's neglected mandate" [ASQ Forum]. *Administrative Science Quarterly,* 41: 146-162.

Stinchcombe, Arthur L. 1959. "Bureaucratic and craft administration of production." *Administrative Science Quarterly,* 4: 168-187.

Strauss, George. 1962. "Tactics of lateral relationship: The purchasing agent." *Administrative Science Quarterly,* 7: 161-186.

Sutton, Robert I. 1987. "The process of organizational death." *Administrative Science Quarterly,* 32: 542-569.

Sutton, Robert I., and Barry M. Staw. 1995. "What theory is *not*" [ASQ Forum]. *Administrative Science Quarterly,* 40: 371-390.

Üsdiken, Behlül, and Torgo Pasadeos. 1995. "Organizational analysis in North America and Europe: A comparison of co-citation networks." *Organization Studies,* 16: 503-526.

Van Maanen, John. 1975. "Police socialization: A longitudinal examination of job attitudes in an urban police agency." *Administrative Science Quarterly,* 20: 207-228.

———. 1983. "Epilogue: Qualitative methods reclaimed." In John Van Maanen (ed.), *Qualitative Methodology:* 247-268. Beverly Hills, CA: Sage.

Vaughan, Diane. 1990. "Autonomy, interdependence, and social control: NASA and the space shuttle *Challenger.*" *Administrative Science Quarterly,* 35: 225-257.

Weick, Karl E. 1976. "Educational organizations as loosely coupled systems." *Administrative Science Quarterly,* 21: 1-19.

———. 1977. "Editorial note." *Administrative Science Quarterly,* 22: 138-139.

———. 1985. "Editing innovation into *Administrative Science Quarterly.*" In L. L. Cummings and Peter J. Frost (eds.), *Publishing in the Organizational Sciences:* 284-296. Beverly Hills, CA: Sage.

———. 1993. "The collapse of sensemaking in organizations: The Mann Gulch disaster." *Administrative Science Quarterly,* 39: 628-652.

Wildavsky, Aaron. 1972. "Why planning failed in Nepal." *Administrative Science Quarterly,* 17: 508-528.

Wildavsky, Aaron, and Arthur Hammond. 1965. "Comprehensive versus incremental budgeting in the Department of Agriculture." *Administrative Science Quarterly,* 10: 321-346.

Wolcott, Harry F. 1995. *The Art of Fieldwork.* Walnut Creek, CA: Alta Mira.

PART I

STUDIES OF ORGANIZATIONAL PROCESSES

Fieldwork of the sort that characterizes a good deal of, if not most, qualitative studies is intended to be largely unobtrusive and, at least at the time it is being carried out, nonreactive. Researchers listen, observe, participate, converse, lurk, collaborate, count, classify, learn, reflect, and—with luck—understand. It is an unspoken methodological paradigm that is effective in not scaring away the phenomenon of interest and is more or less at odds with the no-nonsense discovery of truth by experimentation, survey, or highly formatted, call-and-respond interviews, which most fieldworkers believe ignore context and create reactions. Preserving the apparent naturalness and everyday character of what is being studied is the stock in trade of qualitative research on the ground and, critically, of qualitative research in writing.

The study of organizational processes puts these trade skills to the test. Such processes concern the ways members of organizations individually and collectively come to terms and cope with, but seldom solve, the recurrent problems and contradictions they face when going about their tasks. Organizational processes come in a variety of cultural forms, including routines, rituals, dramas, and games. Some are tightly scripted, rather predictable, and governed by well-established social rules and cognitive schemas. Some are not. Most processes probably fall somewhere in the middle, identifiable as a cultural form and tractable by a logic embedded in what people are trying to do, but always and forever subject to considerable situationally specific variation.

Three studies of organizational processes are presented in this section. The first, "The Role of Expectations in Business Decision Making," is something of a Carnegie School classic. The 1958 article by Richard Cyert, William Dill, and James March rests on direct observations, interviews, and the analysis of records in three organizations. The chapter begins with a review of the received wisdom of the day and then proceeds to offer up a strong ethno-graphic veto of such wisdom based on the details revealed by the close study of four highly particularized decisions. The four stories serve as empirical counterexamples to prevailing views and are framed as nothing less than instances of organizational decision making shaped by "satisficing" rather than profit-maximizing principles. The authors are, of course, modest about their theoretical claims, but such modesty typically accompanies attractive case-based work and, perhaps for many, adds to its persuasive appeal.

The second selection, "Intense Loyalty in Organizations," by the husband-and-wife team of Patricia and Peter Adler, takes up another organizational process. Five years of continuous participant observation provide the empiri-cal materials for this study, published in 1988, whose very title signals to readers the nonrepresentational or exceptional character of the story. Whether a matter of convenience, fascination, or luck (probably all three), the organi-zation studied—a successful NCAA Division I basketball team and program—is a letter-perfect site to examine the development of what the authors regard as uncommonly strong collective attachments. The alignment of certain structural features of the organization, akin to those associated with Goffman-like total institutions, are pushed forward in the account as key loyalty-induc-ing and loyalty-amplifying devices for team members moving into and through the program.

The third and last selection investigates the role that formal analytic techniques play in organizational problem-solving processes. Ann Langley sets up her 1989 article, "In Search of Rationality," with something of a compara-tive anthropological mandate: to discover from instances of studied native practice when, where, and why formal analytic techniques are used in three structurally distinct organizations. Quite aware that a study of what people say may not reveal what they do (and vice versa), Langley begins her search by developing and ordering an extensive set of occasions in which formal analytic techniques are used by organizational members. From this set, she then presents the reasons members provide for using a given analytic mode and connects these reasons to the social relations that obtain among those who initiate, those who accomplish, and those who receive the analysis. Her methods are mixed. They include some statistical hypothesis testing tucked inside a tightly packaged, taxonomically driven descriptive narrative. There is reflexive irony here, for Langley's formal analysis of formal analysis suggests that in the end, rationality—as displayed by the use of codified, numerical techniques—is largely and ordinarily a rhetorical category whose use and shape varies by circumstance and history.

Of the three studies, Cyert, Dill, and March provide the most detailed narrative and dramatic structure by virtue of their choice of specific decision situations to represent, and Langley the least. The Adlers' chapter examines one organization over a lengthy period, whereas the others look at specific occurrences in several organizations for considerably shorter periods of time. Each chapter makes a quota of formal generalizing remarks sufficient, I think, to satisfy all but the most obsessed of theory fans. Yet what is perhaps most memorable from these studies is not the theorizing or generalizing but the particularizing that occurs as authors report specific episodes that serve as small epiphanies to readers. A human logic attached to the processes being examined is thus made apparent, rather vivid and concrete. This is, of course, the trade and trademark of well-crafted qualitative research.

1

THE ROLE OF EXPECTATIONS IN
BUSINESS DECISION MAKING

Richard M. Cyert
William R. Dill
James G. March

Theories of organizational decision making have ordinarily made rather sharp distinctions between business and public organizations. Particularly striking is the contrast between the best-developed theories of business decisions—the economic theory of price and administrative theory—and the portrayal of public bureaucracies to be found in recent sociological and political theory. The contrast rests, rather explicitly, on two fundamental differences: the treatment of goals and the treatment of expected returns and costs.[1]

The theories of business behavior assume that an organizational goal is given: organizations attempt to maximize profit. They assume that the goal is operational: organizations know when they are and when they are not fulfilling that goal and what course of action will satisfy the goal. Although

AUTHORS' NOTE: The authors wish to acknowledge their indebtedness to C. J. Haberstroh and D. B. Trow, who, along with W. R. Dill, made the original empirical observations on which these analyses are based, and to H. A. Simon, who was also a member of the research group. They also wish to thank the firms in which the studies were made for their cooperation. The research was supported by grants from the research funds of the Graduate School of Industrial Administration and from funds provided by the Ford Foundation for the study of organizational behavior. Reprinted from *Administrative Science Quarterly,* 3 (Dec. 1958): 307–340.

we believe this conception of organization goals to be fundamentally wrong in some important respects, we consider it in this article only parenthetically.

We wish to examine here the treatment of expected return and expected costs in the classical description of business behavior and to consider in the light of the classical theory and some recently proposed revisions of it four specific decisions involving estimates of cost and return made by business organizations. Although the data are hardly conclusive, we think the case studies suggest rather strongly some important modifications in our views of the functions of expectations in organizational behavior.

EXPECTATIONS IN THEORIES OF BUSINESS BEHAVIOR

Theories of business decision making generally assume that estimates of cost and return *in some form* are made by the firm and that investment behavior depends heavily on such estimates. For example, the standard theory of price treats investment and internal resource allocation as hypersimple problems in maximization. The firm invests in each available alternative to the extent that the marginal return from each alternative will equal the opportunity cost. Except insofar as sunk costs are involved, the firm makes no fundamental distinction between internal and external investment; that is, all marginal returns are equal to the best alternative return available. Under these conditions, "efficiency"—the ratio of obtained to potential return—is equal to one.[2]

What conception of organizational decision making is implicit in such theories? They assume that the organization scans all alternatives continuously and just as continuously adjusts its portfolio of investments to changes in the pattern of alternatives available. They assume that firms have accurate information on the costs to be incurred and returns to be received from alternatives and that decisions are made on the basis of this information. As will be noted below, these assumptions have been attacked both by economists and by organization theorists.

Attempts to revise the standard theories have been designed primarily to modify these assumptions through the introduction of probability distributions and the substitution of expected profit (or utility) for the profit (or utility) originally specified.[3] The "modern entrepreneur" is probabilistically omniscient. He knows (with certainty) the probability distribution of outcomes from all alternatives. He can, therefore, compute the expected value of any particular alternative and equate expected marginal return with expected opportunity cost.

At the same time, the assumption of infinite search has been replaced by a theory of search that recognizes certain costs to search and thus makes allocation of resources for securing information on the investment decisions to be made. The modern entrepreneur does not scan all alternatives nor does he have all information about all alternatives. He invests in information only so long as the marginal expected return from the information gained exceeds the expected opportunity cost.[4]

There is general consensus that these theories, and specifically the economic versions of them, have been rather valuable in both normative and empirical analyses of aggregate behavior. Since this has been the major traditional interest of economic analysis, aggregate economic theorists have found no pressing reasons for re-examining the assumptions of the standard theories.

On the other hand, economists and others interested in the behavior of the individual firm have not been entirely satisfied with the classic assumptions, which have been subject to criticism on two major grounds.[5] As normative theory, they have been challenged for accepting too easily Bernoullian expected utility. Alternative formulations, arising primarily from game theory considerations, are preferred by a vocal, but apparently minority, group.[6] The normative uses of the theories, however, are tangential to our main interest here. We are more concerned with the challenges to these theories as explanations of business behavior. Because we wish to consider some empirical studies of business decision making, we will specify these challenges in somewhat greater detail.

There have been four major objections to the more or less "pure" theory of expectations insofar as it has been applied to the behavior of individual firms.

First, the theories assume continuous competition among all alternatives for all resources. As Coase has pointed out, the perfectly competitive market for internal resources is a major implicit assumption of the standard theory of the firm.[7] Such a description of organizational behavior is distinctly different from that implicit in many treatments of other organizations. For example, public administration models seem to emphasize local adaptation to specific problems; they stress problem solving much more than planning.[8]

Second, the theories make search activity (and thus information) simply one of the several claimants for resources to be evaluated in terms of calculable costs and expected returns. Simon and others have questioned this treatment of search behavior.[9] They have placed considerable emphasis on dissatisfaction as a stimulant to search, on the "conspicuousness" of alternatives as a factor in their consideration, on external effects on the generation of information, and on the sequential characteristics of alternative evaluation.

Third, the theories require substantial computational activity on the part of the organization. Shackle and others have argued that the theory grossly exaggerates both the computational ability and, more important, the usual computational precision of human beings.[10] A number of suggestions for constraining the amount of information that must be digested have been made.

For example, the heart of Shackle's theory (still completely untested) lies in the ϕ-functions by which the attention value of a particular outcome is determined.

Fourth, the theory treats expectations as exogenous variables. They are given, not explained. But such an eminently logical extension of certainty theory to the treatment of uncertainty ignores a major psychological aspect of uncertain situations, the interaction of expectation and desire. Quite aside from such an interaction, taking expectations as given in a theory of business behavior seems similar to taking the outcomes of all individual games as given in a theory of baseball championships.

Patently, it is not easy to test the validity of either what we have called standard theories or the proposed revisions we have mentioned. However, this article reports detailed studies of four major decisions in three firms. On the basis of an analysis of these four decisions, we arrive at some tentative hypotheses about the problems mentioned above with respect to the theories of investment and internal resource allocation. In particular we will raise some questions about the usual notions of the role of expectations in organizational decision making.

METHODS OF OBSERVATION

The three firms are all well-established, successful organizations: one a large, heavy manufacturing concern, another a medium-sized construction firm, and the third a medium-large manufacturing and retailing concern. Each of the firms gave the research group full access to files and to the activities of the organization. The decisions and the studies were made during 1953–1956. Three basic techniques of observation were used: (1) detailed analysis of memorandums, letters, and other written file material; (2) intensive interviews with participants in the decisions; and (3) direct observation of the decision process. The first two techniques were used in every case. All pertinent documents in the companies' files were examined. All participating members of the organization were interviewed at least once; key members were interviewed repeatedly. In two cases (the second and fourth below), an observer from the research team was present virtually full-time in the organization during the time the decision was being made. He was attached directly to a staff member in the organization and attended staff meetings. In the fourth case, the observer was permitted, in addition, to tape-record important meetings.

The data on the decisions are, therefore, as complete as the limits of memory (both organizational and personal), interview technique, and observer ability permitted. Since those limits can be surprisingly restrictive, some questions of detail could not be answered. Nevertheless, the case studies described below are based on substantial information, direct and indirect. For purposes of presentation they have been condensed considerably, and emphasis has been placed on one aspect of the situation—the role of expectations. We are well aware of the dangers in such an abstraction, and we scarcely hope that four case studies, however detailed, will allay the skepticism of critical readers. The justification lies in our belief that the key propositions we want to make are conspicuous in the data and in our hope that the data will provide a start for empirical research in an area of extensive ad hoc theory.

THE DECISIONS

Decision No. 1: A Problem in Accelerated Renovation of Old Equipment

The first decision problem we shall analyze arose in a branch plant of a heavy manufacturing corporation employing several thousand workers and divided into semiautonomous operating divisions—seven major divisions and several smaller ones. Auxiliary service departments such as safety reported to the plant manager and his assistants, but most such departments had liaison personnel assigned to the operating divisions.

An important goal of management was to achieve a better safety record than other plants in the corporation and in the industry. Particular stress was placed on eliminating fatal accidents and on achieving annual reductions in the frequency of "lost-time" injuries. Making the plant as safe a place to work as possible was more than a plant goal; it was a personal objective of most members of top management in the industry.

All the large divisions and most of the small ones made extensive use of overhead cranes. The movement of most cranes was governed by an old type of controller. Most cranemen and supervisors preferred magnetic controllers, a newer type that had been installed on many cranes in the plant. Because magnetic controllers operated on low-voltage control circuits, there was less danger of severe shock or of "flash"—visible arcing of current across contact points—than with the old type, which operated on full-line voltage. Magnetic controllers also allowed operators to direct crane movements more precisely: there was less danger of "drift," or unanticipated movements. Since they used less cab space than some older controllers, they offered the craneman better visibility and more work space. They were also supposedly cooler and less fatiguing to operate, as well as easier to maintain.

The actual safety benefits that would accrue from the replacement of old-type controllers with magnetic controllers were hard to estimate. Burns, shocks, and eye injuries resulted from "flash" in the older controller circuits, but they were infrequent and were not often disabling. Injuries caused by movements of cranes were more frequently attributable to human error by cranemen or ground crews than to mechanical failure of the controllers or to "drift."

Change-overs to magnetic controllers were being made only as the older controllers wore out, until a fatal accident in the plant triggered recommendations for an accelerated replacement program. A worker was killed when the unexpected movement of a crane load pinned him against a wall. Investigation by top management and by the safety department led to recommendations for a general review of problems of crane safety. The plant manager appointed a special committee to recommend steps that could be taken to improve a craneman's view of his working area and to give him better control over crane movements. The committee consisted of the director of safety, the superintendents of two operating divisions, and a man from the plant engineering department.

At the initial investigation of the accident, the craneman had been asked the type of controller with which the crane was equipped, but no links had been suggested between type of controller and the accident. Blame was assigned to the victim for standing in an unsafe position, to the craneman for moving a lift when his view was obscured, and to management for improper stacking of materials on the floor.

The special crane-safety committee did not mention magnetic controllers in its first report of recommendations for the division where the accident had occurred. Not until their seventh meeting, several weeks after the accident, while investigating conditions in a second division, did the committee discuss a suggestion for accelerated change-over of magnetic controllers. The change would "save space in the crane cab" and provide better control levers, but the committee feared initially that "the cost would be excessive."

Apparently the committee changed its evaluation of the costs of the change, although minutes of the meetings do not report any further discussion. In its final report to the plant manager, the committee recommended as one of several changes that the controllers then in use "should be replaced by magnetic controllers as quickly as feasible." The plant manager circulated the entire list of recommendations without change to the division superintendents and asked that they all be adopted and implemented promptly.

After the order for implementation, specific questions of cost were raised and searches for information were initiated. Most division superintendents individually made quick estimates of the minimum cash outlays required for purchase and installation of the new controllers and checked with the plant manager to see if these expenditures would be approved. Their estimates ranged from $27,000 to $50,000 per division and were described by the safety director as "an absolute minimum" since they did not cover all expected costs of installation.

To supplement the divisional estimates and to fit the accelerated replacement program into operating budgets, the plant manager asked the chief engineer to make a plant-wide survey of requirements and installation costs. Four months after the accident the chief engineer asked the special crane-safety committee to draw up detailed plans for the replacement program and suggested that the program be included in the following year's budget. He wrote, "It may be an expenditure between $150,000 and $200,000."

Seven months later, in another memorandum to division superintendents, the chief engineer was still asking for an itemized list of cranes that needed the new controllers and of the number of replacements each such crane would need. At this time he described the program as a five-year job with budgeted expenditures of $100,000 a year.

The chief engineer was not the only one exploring costs and benefits of the program. In the meantime one of the division superintendents had announced the program to a plant-wide conference of management personnel. He said that with the installation of magnetic controllers they would "virtually eliminate" injuries to cranemen from flashes and burns. Several other division superintendents prepared a memorandum summarizing their objections to the old-type controllers. The chief industrial engineer reported to management that for the new magnetic controllers "any increased costs in operation will be negligible." He mentioned the old-type controllers as a "cause" of the fatality which had initiated the program.[11]

Early in the second year of the program the plant manager asked the superintendent of maintenance to coordinate the replacement program over the next several years. By the ninetieth week after the accident the superintendent of maintenance had developed a revised plan for replacements. The estimated number of replacements had been decreased from 344 to 250, the estimated total cost increased from $500,000 to $600,000, and the estimated time for completion of the program increased from five to six or seven years. He reported costs in terms of the program's encroachment on men and facilities needed for other projects to which the maintenance division was committed. This was the first time in the written memoranda on the program that an estimate of available man power to install the controllers was cited as a limit to the completion of the program.

Initially, then, the program for accelerated replacement of controllers had been judged expensive but feasible. The original recommendation for the program had been promulgated along with a number of other suggestions for increasing crane safety that could be implemented less expensively in the short run.

The first year and a half after the program was approved by the plant manager were used to explore the scope of the decision and to plan for its implementation. Specific estimates of cost quadrupled in that time (rising from $150,000 to over $600,000); and the estimated time for completion changed from about two years to seven or more. Apparently the firm's commitment to an accelerated replacement program was made before the cost of new installations and the impact of the project on other commitments for maintenance and expansion were fully known. The development of cost information is summarized in Table 1.1.

In the end the commitment proved vulnerable, not to revised estimates of cost, but to short-run declines in available resources. At the end of two years two divisions stopped work on the program because a decline in operations had reduced their funds. One year later almost all divisions had reverted, for similar reasons, to the policy they were following before the accident; they were installing magnetic controllers only as the older control systems wore out.

Three major features of this decision process are particularly interesting from the point of view of the place of expectations in a theory of business decision making. First, it is clear that search behavior by the firm was apparently initiated by an exogenous event, was severely constrained, and was distinguished by "local" rather than "general" scanning procedures. Second, the noncomparability of cost expectations and expected returns led to estimates that were vague or easily changed and made the decision exceptionally susceptible to the factors of attention focus and available organizational slack. Third, the firm considered resources as fixed and imposed feasibility tests rather than optimality tests on the proposed expenditure.

The search behavior is difficult to interpret. The apparent sequence is quite simple: accident, concern for safety, and focus (among other foci) on magnetic controllers. As a view of top management, such a sequence seems to be reasonably accurate. Underlying this sequence, however, are a number of factors that make too simple a theory of organizational search unwarranted. Most conspicuous is the fact that the connection between the stimulus (fatal accident) and the organizational reaction (new controllers) is remote. There is no evidence that the fatal accident depended in any way on the type of controller used on the crane. At the same time there is little doubt that the accident had made members of management give greater priority to any device that would improve crane safety and that the possibility of new controllers was well known to parts of the organization. Thus organization search for safety alternatives at the level of top management can be viewed at lower levels as the promotion of favored projects under the impetus of a crisis. The alternative of magnetic controllers was discovered not so much because the organization at this time searched everywhere for solutions to a problem but because some parts of the organization were already (for whatever reason) predisposed toward the project and (a) thought of it as relevant and (b) were able to present it as relevant to the perceived problem in safety.

The decentralized characteristics of information gathering in this case are particularly striking in the pursuit of cost information. Cost information was not readily available, especially to the men who were charged with investigating crane safety. Each knew something about the costs of a single installation since some of these had already been made. But none of the four had the information needed for even a rough approximation of the over-all costs of an accelerated replacement program; and, as later searches showed, many people and much time would have been needed to gather such information. Even after the decision to make the plant-wide installations, when detailed cost and return data were sought, every new group brought in costs and advantages that other groups had not considered (see Table 1.1).

One of the reasons why detailed information on costs seems to play such an insignificant role in all but the final stages of the process is that at no time did the organization make a conscious calculation of costs and return in comparable figures. This feature of the decision is conspicuous in Table 1.1. Information about costs was not necessary to persuade members of management to order the installation of the controllers. All members of management apparently favored the new controls, and they were supported by noncompany technical literature. They had been putting the new controllers in as the old systems wore out. Statements made by the division superintendents indicated that they were placing strong positive emphasis on the safety advantages of the new controls. These gains were usually expressed in absolute rather than relative terms. None of the safety advantages and few of the operating advantages were ever formally expressed in dollar terms. There was consensus that the program would be beneficial and evidence that the benefits—whatever their size—would apply in several departments: safety, maintenance, and operating divisions.

Under these conditions it is not surprising that the early cost estimates were too optimistic (at least if we can assume later ones were more accurate). It is also not surprising to discover that variations in cost expectations had little impact on the basic decision until the focus on safety became less intense.

Measurable expectations entered in the decision only in the feasibility test. Do we have money for the controls? Initially agreement by various groups in management that the step was a good one and an estimate that costs—while unknown—would not be unreasonable were apparently sufficient to carry the decision. For costs to be reasonable under the standard theory of investment, they must be better (relative to the gain) than other available alternatives. This was not, however, how the issue was formulated here. Rather the question of "reasonableness" hinged on whether the expenditure could be made without appreciably affecting existing organizational arrangements adversely (e.g., profits, dividends, wages, output).

As long as estimated costs were modest and output high, the costs were reasonable. As the costs grew and business activity declined, accelerated installation of the magnetic controllers became less "reasonable." This was obviously not because they became suboptimal whereas they had previously been optimal but simply because the supply of uncommitted resources (one

TABLE 1.1 The Sources and Uses of Cost Information in Crane Control Decision

Time Since Fatality (wks.)	Evaluation Expressed in Available Correspondence	Source of Evaluation	Context of Evaluation
6–11	New controls would save space in cabs and offer better control levers; cost of plant-wide program might be "excessive"	Crane-safety committee	Series of meetings to find ways to increase the safety of crane operations
11	Accelerated, plant-wide installation of new controls is feasible	Plant manager	Directive to division superintendents to carry out such a program
13–19	"Absolute minimum" costs for purchase and basic installation would be $27,000 to $50,000 per division	Division superintendents	Individual requests to plant manager for approval of expenditures
20	Program will take at least a year and may mean expenditure of $150,000 to $200,000	Chief engineer	Guide to plant manager for fitting program into next budget
22	New controls will virtually eliminate injuries to cranemen from flashes and burns	Division superintendents	Speech at annual management safety conference on his division's progress
49	Program will take 5 years and will involve budgeted expenditures of $100,000 a year	Chief engineer	A request to division superintendents for more precise information on their requirements
52	Increased costs of operation with new controls will be negligible	Chief industrial engineer	Memorandum to the plant manager and division superintendents
55	New controls will be safer, easier to use, and cheaper to maintain	Group of division superintendents	Memorandum to inform others in management
95	Program will take 6–7 years, will require 250 installations, and will cost $650,000; rate of progress is limited by other maintenance commitments	Maintenance division superintendent	Report of plans to the chief engineer
106–112	Lack of funds prevents further work on program	2 division superintendents	Report to director of safety on progress of program

form of organizational slack) had been substantially reduced. The later stages of the decision were dominated by the necessity of making specific provision for the program in the plant budgets and of preparing tentative time schedules for installation. When, at this stage, there was not enough money for all of the approved projects, some comparisons of the relative merits were made. At that time the hierarchy of preferred projects seemed to reflect such considerations as the tangibility of their expected return, the importance of their major supporters, and the conspicuousness of the problem for which they were designed. It is of course possible that such a process would also generate the optimum set of investments. We will note only that the explicit decisions made by two divisions to abandon the program seemed to be timed specifically in relation to declines in their level of operations. When it became apparent that cash would not be available to meet more than the bare minimum of repair and maintenance commitments, the two divisions stopped work on the accelerated program completely and returned to preaccident policies.

Decision No. 2: A Problem of New Working Quarters for a Department with a Doubtful Future

The second decision was an attempt in a medium-sized construction firm to find new working and storage quarters for its Home Specialties Department, which held a unique and somewhat insecure position in the firm. Its customers were not often shared by other departments. It used union labor like other departments of the firm, but unlike most of its competitors; therefore, its labor costs were too high to enable it to bid successfully on many projects. Its labor costs and changes in style and technology in the construction industry were causing the department's market to shrink, though it had shared with other departments in the growth from new construction activity during and after the Korean War. Top management expected its sales to decline, and its members outside the Home Specialties Department had negative feelings toward the department for two reasons: (1) The head of the department was a senior man in the firm and his earnings under a profit-sharing contract were higher than the earnings of almost all other department heads. (2) Other departments were also expanding, and some of these were anxious to take over space that was being used by Home Specialties.

The problem of making a decision about the long-run importance of Home Specialties operations and of providing plant facilities to accommodate expanded operations had been current for at least two years. Management had long been aware of the need for some kind of action. However, there was no consensus about what the critical problem was or about what alternative would be satisfactory. The president, who believed centralized operations were most efficient, initially viewed the problem as one of finding a way to expand facilities at (or in the immediate vicinity of) the current site. The head of the Home Specialties Department wanted to move the department to a new location, where it would not be in conflict with the operations of other units. Some members of general management thought that the department should be dropped from the firm in order to release working capital for units that had a brighter future. The president and the branch manager had talked of maintaining the department but of limiting it to a size that fitted the existing site, of reducing the share of profits going to departmental personnel, and of forcing the head of the department to take a cut in earnings. Some years earlier, a few men had almost managed to force the department manager out of the firm.

The president's show of interest when a local plot of land became available, coupled with continuing pressure from departmental management to investigate possible new sites, resulted in a decision to concentrate on the search for a new site. Study of the feasibility of moving the department may have seemed timely, too, because of the president's independent decision to renegotiate profit-sharing contracts with departmental management. Since the department manager and his assistant wanted to move, a decision to support their search for a new location might have been regarded as an inducement to them to accept a cut in earnings. In addition, the move might make it easier to follow the cut in earnings with a later decision to curtail departmental operations or to ease the department out of the firm.

Requirements for the new site were set forth in a conference attended by the branch manager, the department head for Home Specialties, his assistant, and a specialist in estimation of costs of building alterations. The pressures on current facilities, at least, were not expected to increase greatly over the next year or two; and in fact, the space requirements of Home Specialties were expected to decline. The Home Specialties facilities were probably not grossly unsuited to their operations; in defining the requirements for a new site, the head men in the department were merely trying, on most measures, to find something that would be equivalent to what they already had. The assistant head of the Home Specialties Department initiated most suggestions for site requirements. He worked from a memorandum he had prepared earlier. The final set of requirements was drafted by the branch manager after the meeting. The key specifications are set forth in Table 1.2.[12]

The conference was notable for the absence of real debate about or explicit consideration of the relative importance of different kinds of requirements. The discussion was oriented toward making sure that the new site would offer the same facilities as the old one at no greater cash outlay for rent rather than toward determining what would be a "most efficient" site for the Home Specialties Department. The most intensive discussion for several requirements centered on reaching an agreement as to what facilities the department had in its current location. The question of the flexibility of various requirements was hardly raised, although it was unreasonable to expect to find a site that corresponded to all of the committee's specifications.

An intensive search for sites followed the conference and lasted for four months. The evaluation of each site about which information was received was a three-phase process. First, the branch manager or another member of the central management group looked at the initial information that was available from advertisements, phone calls, or cursory visits to the site to

TABLE 1.2 Selected Site Characteristics: Aspirations Versus Actions

Features of Site	Proposed Requirements				Characteristics of 3 Best Sites		
	Existing Facilities	Requested by Department	Agreed on in Meeting	Listed by Branch Manager	No. 2	No. 14	No. 10
Total space, sq. ft.	25,000	25,000 +	24,000	26,000	24,000 +	18,500	15,500
Yard storage space	8,850	8,850	8,850	9,000	Available	Not available	Available separately
Heating facilities	—	—	Work area to 60°	Work area to 60°	—	Will cost $150/yr.	Will cost $183/yr.
Location (minutes from main office)	0	—	10	10	9	More than10	About 10
Dock-height unloading space	—	Desired	Desired	Desired	Has	Has	Does not have
R.R. siding	—	Not mentioned	Worth $500 extra rent	Worth $1,000 extra rent	No	No	1 1/2 blocks from R.R.
Annual rent	$6–7,000	—	$10,000	$10,000	Bid of $10,000 submitted	Bid of $12,025 submitted	Bid of $17,000 proposed

decide whether the site was worth further inspection. As Table 1.3 indicates, at least 18 sites were rejected at this stage because they failed to meet one of a small set of requirements. The most important considerations at this stage were: (1) whether the site could be rented (the company did not want to purchase), (2) whether the site was located near the company's existing facilities (something within 10 minutes' driving distance was preferred), and (3) whether the site was approximately the right size (sites with 15,000 to 25,000 square feet were preferred). One or more of these three factors underlay the rejection of eleven of the eighteen sites in this early phase. (Of the remaining seven, one was rejected because of problems of access, one because of an unsatisfactory layout, and five for unknown reasons.)

The second phase consisted of a more detailed evaluation of the site's potentialities. Four sites were given detailed consideration. Members of the Home Specialties Department staff estimated the expenditures required to make the necessary heating, lighting, and ventilating installations. One of the four sites was rejected after the detailed inspection because the branch manager found it liable to frequent flood damage and because the company would have had to buy other leases on the property.

There were, then, three sites that management thought good enough to prepare bids on. Looking at the major criteria of space, price, and nearness to existing facilities, we note in Table 1.3 that management relaxed its requirements as time went on. Site No. 2, the first one for which a bid was prepared, had an area about the same as the specifications called for, but sites No. 14 and No. 10 were both smaller than the specifications required. Site No. 10 was at and site No. 14 was beyond the distance limits set by management. Management expected to get by on site No. 2 with a bid of $10,000 to $15,000 for 24,000 square feet of space; the bid on site No. 14 was $12,000 for 18,500 square feet. On site No. 10, the third one for which a bid was prepared, management considered offering $17,000 for 15,500 square feet of space (excluding yard space which had to be obtained separately).

The bids on sites No. 2 and No. 14 were turned down by the agents for the properties, but the bid on site No. 10 was never submitted. The president refused to approve the bid because he thought it offered too much money for too little space. The search for a new site for the Home Specialties Department apparently ended with the president's refusal to approve a bid for site No. 10.

Why were other sites not considered? Among the reasons for ending the search, the following were probably most important: (1) The branch manager and the others who had been most active in the search probably felt that they had explored most of the available possibilities. They had even resorted to driving around the neighborhood looking for "for rent" signs. (2) The earnings contracts of the departmental managers had been renegotiated— most of them successfully. Use of the search for a new location as an

TABLE 1.3 The Consideration and Disposition of Possible Sites

Site No.	Period of Consideration	Disposition of Site
1	June 14	Rejected: Inadequate access
2	June 20–Sept. 13	Bid upon: Bid of $10,000 + not accepted
3	June 23–July 12	Rejected: Considered in detail but too large and too liable to flood damage
4	July 6	Rejected: Too small, too far away
5	July 12	Rejected: Would have to be purchased
6	July 12	Rejected: Too far away
7	July 12	Rejected: Too far away
8	July 17	Rejected: Too large
9	Aug. 9	Rejected: Unsatisfactory layout
10	Aug. 18–Oct. 24	Rejected: Bid prepared but not submitted: considered too expensive by president
11	Aug. 24	Rejected: Reason unknown
12	Aug. 24	Rejected: Reason unknown
13	Aug. 30	Rejected: Too small (13,000 sq. ft.)
14	Aug. 30–Sept. 25	Bid upon: Bid not accepted by owner, who preferred commercial use of property
15	Sept. 7	Rejected: Too far away
16	Sept. 7	Rejected: Too far away
17	Sept. 12	Rejected: Would have to be purchased
18	Sept. 12	Rejected: Would have to be purchased
19	Sept. 12	Rejected: Too far away, wrong size
20	Sept. 17	Rejected: Reason unknown
21	Sept. 18	Rejected: Reason unknown
22	Sept. 21	Rejected: Reason unknown

inducement to counteract the negative effects of renegotiation was no longer of any importance, and, with renegotiation completed, one point of friction between Home Specialties and other departments had been eliminated. (3) Contrary to expectations, Home Specialties had continued to maintain a fairly high level of operations over the summer, while its most direct competitor for work space had suffered a decline in business.

The decision-making process here has some significant similarities to that connected with the purchase of automatic controllers. As before, search activity represented a response to some specific events rather than a form of continued planning. Second, detailed expectation data entered into the decision relatively late, after a conditional commitment to secure space had been made. Finally, most of the tests were primarily feasibility tests rather than checks on optimality.

From the present point of view, perhaps the most interesting aspect to this study is the fact that the organization focused on the problem of outside space for the department. Although the decision was contingent (and was in fact never executed because bids were rejected), it represented a commitment to a course of action. Yet the commitment was made not because it was shown to have the best return, in terms of organizational goals, of a number of alternatives. Quite the contrary, the decision to find new quarters was made because a number of important parts of the organization, for apparently quite different reasons, viewed such a step as desirable. Had there been agreement, for example, between the Home Specialties Department and other departments about the probable long-run consequences of this step, one or the other of those groups would probably have opposed the move. Since this was an important aspect of the decision situation, some of the more important expectations were not discussed in open meetings, and hopes and expectations appear to have become substantially intertwined. The role of ambiguity of expectations in securing agreement where there is a conflict of interests has previously been noted with respect to political and labor-management decision making. There is some suggestion here that it is also important for the formation of business policy.

Once the decision to secure additional space had been made, data on alternatives were organized around a set of more or less independent criteria. These criteria are interesting in two respects. (1) They represent for the most part a simple statement of current facilities. The adequacy of some aspects of these facilities was discussed, but the general question of what would constitute an ideal site was not raised. (2) With one or two exceptions (e.g., an attempt to place a rental value on the existence of a railroad siding) the specifications represented a check list. Sites that were unsatisfactory on one or more of the major criteria were rejected immediately. Only among the more or less "satisfactory" alternatives was there an attempt to compare the utility of an increment on one dimension of the criteria with a different dimension. And even at that point this comparison was somewhat halting and not always easily understood. Some of the sites rejected at an early stage might have been considered more thoroughly later, after management's aspirations declined.

In one conspicuous feature the site purchase decision was different from the decision to purchase the automatic controller. The search for alternative sites was much more exhaustive than the search for alternatives in the first case. The organization did not have a ready-made site alternative but had to look. Although it is conceivable that the organization did not discover all the alternatives that were within 10 minutes of the central office, it seems unlikely that they missed any that would have been suitable. To be sure, the use of the 10-minute criterion as a device for defining the range within which one would search made that criterion into an absolute one, in the sense in which the others (e.g., the size requirement) were not. But the difference between the number of alternatives considered in this instance and in the crane case is substantial. Similarly, the specific cost estimates reflected in proposed bids for sites and the decisions on whether to make the bids seem, in this case, to be more attempts to determine the intrinsic worth of the property to the organization and less a function of available resources than they were in the previous case.

Decision No. 3: Selection of a Consulting Firm

The third decision is part of a larger decision regarding the installation of an electronic data-processing system. It relates specifically to the selection of a consulting firm. The company, a medium-large manufacturing concern, had made some preliminary investigation of the problem and decided that a consultant was necessary. At the beginning of the process of deciding which firm should be chosen there was no clear program as to how many firms would be evaluated. A list of possible consultants was prepared, but a series of chance circumstances led to a meeting with Alpha, a relatively new consulting firm specializing in the design of electronic data-processing systems.

On February 21, consultants of Alpha discussed the problem of improving business methods with people from the company. By March 23, Alpha had submitted a step-by-step program that would survey and analyze the company's operations and data-processing procedures. Alpha stated that the objective of this program would be (1) the estimation of savings that could be realized through the use of electronic equipment and (2) the specification of the price class and characteristics of equipment required. The fee expected for this work was stated at $180 per man day (i.e., $3,600 per month assuming one man works a 20-day month). The initial consulting task was to be limited to 100 man days, and consequently the fee was limited to $18,000. Traveling expenses of some $4,000 would also be charged.

The report was well received by company officials, who generally agreed that Alpha would be retained until the question was raised whether it would not be appropriate to investigate other alternatives. As will be obvious, this was a crucial point in the process, but it is not clear what prompted the suggestion for additional search effort. The suggestion was rather quickly accepted, and a list of about a dozen potential consultants, which had been prepared earlier by a staff member, was presented. The controller decided that only one more firm should be asked to submit a proposal and that it should be Beta. Beta was more widely known, older, and larger than Alpha, although it did not so definitely specialize in electronic data processing.

Following analysis of the problem, Beta submitted a contract proposal covering an investigation of the company's problem. The stated objectives were two: (1) to reduce the costs of the accounting and clerical operation and (2) to improve the quality of information available for accounting and control. Beta stated in the contract proposal that employing electronic data-handling equipment was to be considered as a possible means of attaining these objectives. This contract outlined service charges that would not exceed $5,000 a month. The initial study was to be completed and a report submitted three to four months after active work began.

After Beta had submitted a report, it became necessary to choose between the two firms. At the request of the controller a staff member wrote a

TABLE 1.4 Comparison of Consulting Firms

Criteria	Alpha	Beta
Quality of personnel	Depth in quality of computer personnel	More experienced in business problems
Cost of services	$180 per man day ($3,600 per month); $18,000 max. charge plus traveling expenses	$5,000 per month max. plus traveling expenses
Commitment made	Committed themselves *primarily* to study of feasibility of application of E.D.P.E.	Will give consideration to both *methods* and *possibility* of using E.D.P.E., in order noted
Estimated time	100 man days maximum; possibility of doing work in 15 weeks	Longer time allowed because of greater commitment (actual time stated in contract was 3–4 months)
Availability and scope	No quantitative evaluation mentioned	
Geographic situation	Main office approximately 2,500 miles away from company's office	Main office approximately 500 miles away from company's office

memorandum that listed the criteria on which the decision should be based and also evaluated the two firms on each of the criteria. The results of this memorandum are summarized in Table 1.4.

The staff member who wrote the memorandum believed that on quality of personnel, cost of services, and estimated time the two firms were equal or could be made equal by negotiation. On the other criteria—commitment made, availability and scope, and geographic situation—he felt Beta had an advantage. He was supported in this opinion by an academician who had previously served as a consultant to the firm. An analysis of the memorandum seems to show, however, that the only advantage that can objectively be given to Beta is its geographic situation. Even here, aside from availability, it is difficult to see any advantage. The only possibility would be higher traveling expenses for Alpha, but presumably this would mean a reduction in some other part of the fee. Again, it should have been possible to negotiate on availability and scope, assuming that geographic proximity is divorced from availability. It is quite obvious that the commitment could have been negotiated, for Alpha as a new organization in the field was open to suggestion with respect to the kind of commitments it should make.

On the cost side (ignoring possible negotiation) there was a probable advantage accruing to Alpha. The approximate monthly charges were $1,400 less for Alpha than for Beta. The total charge for Beta to the company varied according to the length of time it would take. The estimated length of time for Beta was 3 to 4 months, which would mean a price between $15,000 and $20,000. Alpha on the other hand had a maximum price of $18,000. Exact price comparisons under the circumstances were difficult to make. However, Alpha gave a maximum total price whereas Beta used only a maximum monthly charge and no upper limit on the time. Thus what advantage there was in the cost situation probably was in Alpha's favor. However, the costs were close enough and the circumstances blurred enough so that relative cost was difficult to evaluate.

This fact was recognized by the staff members involved, who proposed that the decision be made on collateral grounds (e.g., geographic proximity, possible future uses). As noted above, the grounds specified seemed to favor Beta, and this preference of the staff was apparent almost from the moment that the decision to expand the search to Beta was made. That is, the staff members most closely involved seemed to view Alpha as a reasonable solution until the suggestion for further search was made. There is some suggestion that they interpreted the instruction to expand their search to include Beta and only Beta as a preference for Beta by their supervisors. The controller and assistant controller, on the other hand, felt that the final decision was based on the independent recommendations of their staff members and did not acknowledge the possibility that such an outcome was implicit in the decision not to accept Alpha until further investigation. The firm decided to hire Beta.

How did expectations with respect to cost and return enter the decision to hire Beta? First, the methods of search resulted in casual consideration of about a dozen possible firms, intensive consideration of two. Second, a comparison of the two firms finally considered was difficult. Expected costs and expected return were measured in a number of dimensions (e.g., fee, quality of personnel, convenience) that were not readily reduced to a single index. Third, given the difficulties of evaluation, there appears to have been substantial interaction between expectations and desires and between desires and perceptions of others' desires.

As in the case of the search for a new site for the Home Specialties Department there was some attempt here to be reasonably inclusive in searching for potential firms. Presumably if that original scanning had detected a firm that was conspicuously more appropriate than all others, that fact would have been noted. Since there were no conspicuous alternatives, it is not surprising to discover that not many were evaluated in detail and that the factors affecting the choice of firms to consider in large part determined which firm would be selected. Alpha was considered primarily because it was momentarily exceptionally visible to a key staff member when the organization needed a detailed proposal. Beta was conspicuous to the controller because it was well known in the business community and had apparently been considered as a potential consultant on other occasions.

In evaluating the proposal by Alpha and later in comparing it with the one made by Beta, the people involved in the decision seemed to have done two things. First, they asked whether the charges were within the range of what it was reasonable for the organization to pay for the services offered. There does not appear to have been any significant problem on this score. Second, they asked which of the two proposals offered the better return on investment. As the description of the two firms indicates, this was by no means an easy job. The simple comparison of the two consulting firms in Table 1.4 has some interesting features. Perhaps most conspicuous is the fact that the conclusion to be drawn from the comparison is not at all clear. Reasonable men could quite easily disagree as to its implications. It was not that part of the return was in intangibles; all of the factors explicitly considered were reasonably tangible. The problem was that they were not reducible to a single dimension (or at least were not reduced to one) and that neither firm was better on all dimensions.

The ambiguity in expectations that arose from the difficulty of making objective rankings of Alpha and Beta resulted in a decision process that seemed to be dominated in large part by nonexpectational factors. The final staff memorandum of the decision clearly recommended Beta. This recommendation was accepted by the controller. As he put it, "I asked the boys to set down the pros and cons. The decision was Beta. It was entirely their decision."

The staff members involved, on the other hand, seemed to have felt that the decision to search further rather than hire Alpha immediately reflected some bias in favor of Beta on the part of top management, and this was probably reinforced by the fact that the controller specified that Beta and only Beta would be asked to make a proposal. Since the differences between the two firms were not particularly striking, it is not surprising that these plausible assumptions about the attitudes of others were consistent with subsequent perceptions of the alternatives and the final recommendation.

Decision No. 4: Choosing a Data-Processing System

In November, six months after the original contract had been signed, Beta submitted a report which outlined some alternative proposals designed to improve the company's accounting and merchandising procedures. Essentially three alternatives were discussed in the report: (1) a centralized electronic data-processing center employing an IBM 705 or a Remington-Rand Univac; (2) an improvement on the current procedures requiring the addition of some Electrodata equipment; and (3) an improvement on the current procedures requiring the use of punched-card electronic equipment instead of Electrodata equipment. These alternatives were differentiated on the basis of projected savings and improved management control. In each, savings were to accrue from the elimination of personnel. Management control was to be

TABLE 1.5 Comparison of Savings of Alternative Proposals (per month)

Factors Considered	Centralized with IBM 705 or Univac	Decentralized With Punched Cards	With Electrodata
Direct savings			
Personnel reduction (savings)	$33,000	$8,570	$8,390
Equipment added (additional cost)	26,500	1,055	9,845
Space needed (additional cost)	1,500		
Net savings (cost)	$ 5,000	$7,515	$(1,455)
Less direct savings			
a) Reduction in cost of compiling physical inventory	$ 1,500		
b) Elimination of stock record personnel (20)	6,000		
	$ 7,500		
Net savings (cost)	$12,500	$7,515	$(1,455)

increased by additional reports, which would be more complete and more readily available.

The report shows a breakdown of the savings and reports provided under each system. A comparison of the savings for the three alternatives is shown in Table 1.5. The three alternatives have several significant differences. First, the decentralized system with punched-card equipment has a larger projected direct savings than either of the other alternatives ($7,515 savings for this system as opposed to $5,000 savings, and $1,455 additional cost for the other systems). Second, only when the less direct savings of $7,500 per month are added to the centralized system does this system become more attractive in price than the punched-card program. Third, the centralized system gives management six reports not provided by the other alternatives. On the other hand, the two decentralized alternatives give management four reports that are not provided by the centralized system. The centralized system has some additional advantage in that some of its reports are prepared daily. The other two systems require more time in the preparation of reports. Overall, there is a net advantage of two reports with the centralized system.

The savings of $7,500 a month for the centralized system noted in Table 1.5 are estimates for the time when the inventory is put on the machine. Since the estimates were rough and the time for converting the inventory was indefinite, no specific discounting factors were used. The consultants originally drafted a report which showed equal savings for a system using a computer and for a system which was basically a revision of the company's current practices with the addition of electronic equipment. When it was pointed out to the consultants that a recommendation was expected from them, the additional savings from converting inventory were added and the centralized system was recommended.

The implication of the foregoing should not be that cost and savings estimates were unimportant. During the six months of the consultants' investigations cost estimates played a prominent role in the analysis. For example, time and motion studies were made to derive time estimates, and the resulting estimates were closely scrutinized. Some time estimates were revised as many as three times. In the meeting of the management committee where the formal decision was made, the questions pertained primarily to costs. There was concern for the break-even point of the investment and the pay-back period.

Despite their explicit importance, however, costs entered into the decision in a way somewhat different from that anticipated by traditional theory. As in the previous cases, the first question apparently asked was whether the computer installation and/or the other installations studied would be economically *feasible*. The original report of the consultants as well as the analysis by management indicated that two of the three systems studied were feasible and preferable to the existing system. Given this basic conclusion, the use of cost data and the attitude toward that data became much more flexible than they probably would have been otherwise. Since two of the systems were defensible as replacements for the existing system, the choice between them seems to have depended less on an objective effort to assign meaningful values to intangible or uncertain advantages than on important individual preferences. Thus the controller was interested in a system that produced more information faster and with better control. He, and others, felt that the computer might become an important general managerial tool. Although they obviously felt constrained to justify the installation on comparative cost savings grounds, their attitude toward the hypothetical savings of $7,500 was undoubtedly more generous than it would have been if they had not been favorably inclined toward a computer or had not been persuaded that straightforward, tangible costs made this an "acceptable" solution.

In addition, the relation between the consulting firm and the organization points up some interesting features of the role of expectations. In this case, the organization relied on an outside source for information, but some of the behavior in the ambiguous situation of the third case also occurred here. The consultants made a detailed, careful, and responsible analysis of the proposed installations. Nevertheless, when asked to make a specific recommendation, they were able to change the summary figures on cost savings from a set that indicated indifference between two major alternatives to a set that indicated the clear superiority of the computer. The point is not that the consultants falsified their data. They clearly would have refused to do this, and the organization would not have countenanced it. But they had to make a judgment as to which uncertain costs and savings should be counted. And this judgment was almost certainly affected, as had been the earlier judgments of staff members within the organization, by their perception of management's attitudes and predilections.

DISCUSSION

The analysis of these four decisions suggests some problems with both the neoclassical conception of organizational use of expectations and some recent suggestions for revision. On balance, however, it suggests that each of the four criticisms of the conventional theory of decision making is warranted, at least in part.

Resource allocation within the firm reflects only gross comparisons of marginal advantages of alternatives. All the decisions were made within budgetary constraints and to that extent reflected any marginal calculations that entered into the formation of a general budget. When the rising estimates of costs for the crane controllers (Decision 1) and the decline of business created an internal problem of scarce resources, there were some attempts to compare the advantages of the safety devices with alternative investments. These attempts, however, focused on such considerations as prior commitment rather than marginal return.

In the other cases, there were distinct conceptions of "appropriate" costs or net return. Undoubtedly these were related in a relatively unsystematic way to the comparable statistics (e.g., "pay-off period") on other acceptable alternatives. Ignoring for the moment the problem of bias in estimates, the studies indicate that rules of thumb for evaluating alternatives provide some constraints on resource allocation even though it is substantially decentralized and there is no conscious comparison of specific alternative investments. Thus a theory that predicts grotesquely large deviations from a return on investment norm is probably not accurate.

On the other hand, it seems clear that the constraints do not guarantee very close adjustment, particularly where business conditions permit organizational slack. Any alternative that satisfies the constraints and secures suitably powerful support within the organization is likely to be adopted. This means that decision making is likely to reflect a response to local problems of apparent pressing need as much as it will reflect continuing planning on the part of the organization.

In a rough sense we can say that the first two decisions considered here arose primarily as responses to "crisis" situations, the last two as the results of planning. In the computer decisions the organization, and particularly the controller, had been alerted to the potential utility of electronic data-processing and had actually appointed a staff member to be responsible for continuing attention to possible applications. In the other cases the organization was stimulated to search for solutions to conspicuously unsatisfactory conditions. In every case, once an alternative was evoked, it was accepted if it satisfied the general cost and return constraints and enjoyed the support of key people in management. The support in turn came about through a rather complex mixture of personal, suborganizational, and general organizational goals. In Decision No. 2 the support came for mutually contradictory reasons from two or three different parts of the organization. In Decision No. 1 the support from top management came for reasons that were not directly relevant to the events that had triggered the search. In Decision No. 4 the support from top management came in considerable part from collateral expectations about the action.

Search activity is not viewed as simply another use of internal resources. In general these studies suggest that there are several stages to motivated search activity on the part of an organization. If a problem area is recognized, there is ordinarily a search for possible alternatives. At this stage only rough expectation data are used to screen obviously inappropriate actions. In each case considered here this early scanning generated only a few suitable possibilities, which were then considered in greater detail. In most cases a rather firm commitment to an action was taken before the search for information proceeded very far, but the search became more and more intensive as the decision approached implementation. This was particularly obvious in the case of the crane controls.

One major reason why this seems to be true is that organizational "search" consists in large part in evoking from various parts of the organization considerations that are important to the individual subunits, and the relevance of such considerations, and the impetus to insist on them, are not manifest until the implications of the decision are made specific through implementation. An obvious corollary of such a conception of the search process is the proposition that search will be much more intensive where organizational slack is small than where it is large. Where there are enough excess resources in the organization, the interdependence of allocation decisions is uncertain; search consequently becomes relatively routine.

At the same time a conspicuous factor in these cases is frequently ignored in search theory. Whether in its classical form or in the level of aspiration form, the theory of search is basically a prospecting theory. It assumes that the objects of search are passive elements distributed in some fashion throughout the environment. Alternatives and information about them are obtained as a result of deliberate activities directed toward that end. Not all information comes to an organization in this way, however. Many of the events in these studies suggest a mating theory of search. Not only are organizations looking for alternatives, alternatives are also looking for organizations. In the computer decisions the intensity of search activity by the organization would scarcely have generated as much information as it did if the manufacturers of electronic data-processing equipment and the consulting firms had not been pursuing as well as pursued. In Decision No. 1, too, many efforts had presumably been made by producers of magnetic controllers to "sell" management on a change. In fact, the timing of the major spurts of activity on those decisions was as much a function of the pressure from such outside groups as it was from internal factors.

The *computations* of anticipated consequences used by the organizations seem to be quite simple. Although there is no particularly strong evidence for Shackle's specific concept of what computations are made, at most only a half-dozen criteria were used explicitly in making the decisions. There appear to be two main reasons for the simplicity. First, in one form or another the major initial question asked of a proposed action was not how it compared with other alternatives but whether it was feasible. In the decisions discussed here there were two varieties of feasibility. The first was a budgetary constraint: Is money available for the project? The second was an improvement criterion: Is the project clearly better than existing procedures? In one form or another these questions were extremely important in all of the decisions discussed here. In some cases they were rather hard to answer, but they were almost always considerably easier than the question required by the classical theory of expectations: Does the expected net return on this investment equal or exceed the expected return on all alternative investments?

The second apparent reason for simplicity in establishing decision criteria was the awkwardness of developing a single dimension on which all relevant considerations could be measured. In each of the decisions described above costs in dollars were factors; so were dollar savings. But so also were such considerations as speed and accuracy of work, safety of personnel, distance from railroad transportation, quality of performance, and reputation of company. Unless one is prepared to make explicit the dollar value of such diverse factors, and none of these firms did do so to any great extent, they must be treated substantially as independent constraints. Detailed expectations on these dimensions seemed substantially irrelevant to efforts to estimate costs because the organization had no way of using such information.

Expectations were by no means independent of such things as hopes, wishes, and the internal bargaining needs of subunits in the organization. Information about the consequences of particular courses of action in a business organization are frequently hard to obtain and of uncertain reliability. As a result, both conscious and unconscious bias in expectations is introduced. In each of the cases there is some suggestion of unconscious or semiconscious adjustment of perceptions to hopes. The initial estimates of cost for the crane controllers appear to have been fairly optimistic. The expectations about the consequences of moving the Home Specialties Department seem to have been substantially a function of subunit goals. The evaluation of consulting firms seems to have shifted before detailed expectations were formed; subsequently, the expectations supported the evaluation. Expectations about net return from alternative data-processing systems apparently were influenced by some feelings of a priori preferences.

In addition, there is some evidence of more conscious manipulation of expectations. The classic statement came from a staff member involved in one of the decisions. He told a group of men outside the company: "In the final analysis, if anybody brings up an item of cost we haven't thought of, we can balance it by making another source of savings tangible."

It would be a mistake to picture the biases introduced in either of these fashions as exceptionally great. In almost every case there are some reasonably severe reality constraints on bias. But where the decision involves choice between two reasonably equal alternatives, small biases will be critical. Consequently, research on selective perception and recall is of substantial importance to an empirical theory of business decision making.

NOTES

1. Compare, for example, G. J. Stigler, *The Theory of Price* (New York, 1946) and J. M. Gaus, *Reflections on Public Administration* (Birmingham, Ala., 1947).

2. Stigler, *op. cit.*

3. M. Friedman, *Essays in Positive Economics* (Chicago, 1953).

4. B. O. Koopman, The Theory of Search I, *Operations Research*, 4 (1956), 324–346.

5. For a thoughtful recent statement, see T. C. Koopmans, *Three Essays on the State of Economic Science* (New York, 1957).

6. D. Luce and H. Raiffa, *Games and Decisions* (New York, 1957).

7. R. H. Coase, The Nature of the Firm, *Economica*, 4 (1937), 386–405.

8. E. Devons, *Planning in Practice* (Cambridge, Eng., 1950).

9. H. A. Simon, A Behavioral Model of Rational Choice, *Quarterly Journal of Economics*, 69 (1955), 99–118.

10. G. L. S. Shackle, *Expectations in Economics* (Cambridge, Mass., 1949).

11. If this had been the case, it definitely had not been brought out in the detailed records of the inquiries following the accident.

12. Other specifications were discussed initially, but they did not figure explicitly in the later evaluations of actual sites.

2

INTENSE LOYALTY IN
ORGANIZATIONS
A Case Study of College Athletics

Patricia A. Adler
Peter Adler

———

The concept of organizational loyalty has inspired considerable interest in the organizational sciences, although much of the resultant research has been widely divergent in its approach and conclusions. We define organizational loyalty here as a bond formed either to an organization or to some person or group within it that can be either individually or collectively forged. It consists of feelings of attachment, of belonging, of strongly wanting to be part of something; it involves the readiness to contribute part of one's self; it incorporates trust, the voluntary alignment of self with the group, and a willingness to follow faithfully the leadership or guidelines of the organization.

Proponents of the capital value approach have suggested that the organizational loyalty bond is fundamentally economic in its base and is evoked by a favorable exchange of workers' skills, labor, and productivity for earnings

AUTHORS' NOTE: We would like to thank Jean Blocker for help during the data-gathering portion of this research and Charles Gallmeier, Peter Manning, John Van Maanen, and the editors and anonymous *ASQ* reviewers for their comments on earlier drafts of this article. Reprinted from *Administrative Science Quarterly,* 33 (Sept. 1988): 401–417.

(Barnard, 1938; March and Simon, 1958; Marsh and Mannari, 1971; Parsons, 1972; Becker, 1975; Mortensen, 1978; Jovanovic, 1979; Bielby and Baron, 1983). The workplace authority model conceptualizes organizational loyalty as a function of workers' perceptions of the legitimacy of their employers' exercise of authority, focusing on such factors as structurally derived value codes, centralization of authority, formalization of rules, span of subordination, and the normative dimensions of the loyalty bond (Blau and Scott, 1962; Ostrom and Brock, 1968; Morris and Steers, 1980; Halaby, 1986). Finally, adherents of the job-satisfaction-occupational-commitment (JSOC) approach see it as fundamentally an individualistic factor lodged in the personal costs, benefits, and intrinsic rewards inherent in work (Kanter, 1968; Porter and Steers, 1973; Buchanan, 1974; Locke, 1976; Kalleberg, 1977; Mowday, Porter, and Steers, 1982; Oliver, 1984; Lincoln and Kalleberg, 1986).

While these researchers have shed light on some aspects of loyalty, we still know very little about the development of intense loyalty toward organizations, such as that sometimes observed in attachments to religious organizations (such as Jonestown) or as might be expected for organizations in which members are highly interdependent and in which performance might require unswerving commitments from members. Examples of such organizations might be combat units, complex and intensive surgical teams, astronaut work groups, and high-performing athletic teams, to name a few. The loyalty required by these organizations surpasses the fairly mild attachment engendered by good pay and benefits, acquiescence to authority, or the expression of professional creativity. Rather, these organizations evoke the devotional commitment of their members through a subordination that sometimes borders on demanding subservience. Our purpose was to examine the development of intense loyalty in one such organization—a college basketball team in the south-central United States. Through this case study we describe and analyze the structural factors that emerged as most related to the formation of intense organizational loyalty.

METHOD

Over a five-year period (1980–1985), we conducted a participant-observation study of a major college basketball program. Much like in the classic socialization study of medical students, *Boys in White* (Becker et al., 1961), we followed several classes of student-athletes through their college years. We used team field research strategies (Douglas, 1976) and differentiated roles to enhance our data gathering and analysis. Peter initially gained access to the team because the coaches perceived him as an "expert" who could provide valuable counsel on interpersonal, organizational, and academic matters. Although college and professional sport settings are generally characterized by secrecy and an extreme sensitivity to the insider-outsider distinction (Jonassohn, Turowetz, and Gruneau, 1981), he gradually gained the trust of significant gatekeepers, particularly the head coach, and was granted the status and privileges of an assistant coach (the "team sociologist"). Through this "active membership role" (Adler and Adler, 1987) he became especially close to the athletes, whom he counseled when they came to him with their problems, worries, or disgruntlements. Thus, although he, like Barley (1984), initially defined his role in the setting, it was similar to what Schein (1987) has called the "clinical" ethnographer.

Patti assumed a more peripheral membership role, interacting with participants as both a coach's wife and as a professor in the school. She "debriefed" Peter when he returned from the setting and looked to understand and unravel the member's perspective he was developing. These differential roles helped us to experience both the involved passion of the member and the detached objectivity of the outsider.

Throughout the research, we carefully made field notes at the end of each day, based on our observations. We recorded the events of the day, the reactions and comments of each participant as close to verbatim as possible, and discussed the emergence of possible patterns. Often, we tape-recorded these sessions to preserve our exact memories as freshly as possible. As the research progressed we also conducted a repeated series of intensive, taped interviews with members of the coaching staff and with all 38 members of the basketball team who were associated with the program during these five years. During these interviews we asked respondents to give us a life-history account of their experiences with sport. We then asked them to describe their view of the significant aspects of college athletics. Using Glaser and Strauss's (1967) grounded theory, we let significant patterns and concerns emerge from the data. We triangulated (Denzin, 1970) the perceptions and generalizations of various members by cross-checking them against other accounts, our own observations and experiences, and hard data wherever possible (team records, media accounts, scouting reports) (Douglas, 1976).

We then analyzed the data according to Glaser and Strauss's grounded theory model. We began by generating categories and their properties through clustering respondents' observations around particular themes. Examples of these included the stripping down of the self, the role of the peer culture, the loyalty contract, and learning loyalty. Each of these categories had subgroups that described how they operated, including both structural components and processes. We then searched our field notes and the transcribed interview tapes for instances that represented these categories and their properties, examining them to check further on the validity of our conceptualizations.

Once certain patterns had emerged, we began to ask about them more routinely in our interviews, searching for the limits and variations of their applications and parameters. We also looked for relations between different patterns and concepts, seeking to understand how they arose and influenced each other. As some of them yielded more fruitful data we began to delve into them further and to center our thinking around them as analytical concepts. At this point, we abandoned some of the earlier concepts that seemed routine or theoretically uninteresting. The result of these searches were what Wiseman (1970) has called total patterns, or collective belief systems held by the group, and data clusters, or combinations of events and occurrences that coalesced in the group we studied. These included such broader concepts as self-engulfment and glory, as well as more routine but mundane occurrences such as "puffing" and "snapping." These careful and rigorous means of data collection and analysis were designed to maximize both the reliability and validity of our findings.

The Setting

The research was conducted at a medium-sized (6,000 students), private university (hereafter referred to as "the University"), in the mid-south-central portion of the United States. Most of the students were white, suburban, and middle class. The University, which was striving to become one of the finer private, secular universities in the region, had fairly rigorous academic standards. The athletic department, as a whole, had a very successful recent history: the University's women's golf team had been ranked in the top three nationally, the football team had won its conference in each of the previous four seasons, and the basketball program had been ranked in the top forty of Division 1 NCAA schools and in the top twenty for most of two seasons we studied them. The basketball team had played in post season tournaments every year, and in four complete seasons, they had won approximately four times as many games as they lost. Players were generally recruited from the surrounding regional area, were predominantly black (70 percent), and ranged from the lower to the middle classes. In general, the basketball program was fairly representative of what Coakley (1982) and Frey (1982) have termed "big-time" college athletics. Although it could not compare to the upper echelon of established basketball dynasties or to the really large athletic programs that wield enormous recruiting and operating budgets, its recent success compensated for its size and lack of historical tradition (the University's basketball program could best be described as "up and coming"). Because the basketball team (along with other teams in the athletic department) was ranked nationally and sent graduating members into the professional leagues, the entire athletic milieu was imbued with a sense of professionalism and purpose.

INTENSE ORGANIZATIONAL LOYALTY

From our in-depth research experiences and insights into this college basketball organization, five conceptual elements have emerged as critical to the development of intense loyalty in organizations: domination, identification, commitment, integration, and goal alignment.

Domination. Organizational members develop loyalty through the experience of domination by a strong leader. The leader's control over all facets of their lives (both directly and indirectly involved with organizational activities) causes them to recognize their position of subordination. Domination is most effectively achieved in situations in which the organization reshapes individuals, stripping away the unique aspects of their selves and molding them into role-enacting organizational members.

Identification. Organizations can also effectively enhance the loyalty of their members by fostering individuals' identification with both the group and its leader. This can be done by casting them into a position of representing the group and then rewarding them for it. The leader can further inspire their personal loyalty by encouraging a familial atmosphere, offering loyalty to group members, and serving as a personal role model. By fusing organizational members' conceptions of their selves with those of the group, organizations are more likely to inspire meaningful interest and devotion.

Commitment. Mechanisms that foster the commitment of members to their organizations are also likely to encourage their loyalty. This includes organizational characteristics or activities encouraging members' feelings of performance and investment.

Integration. Organizations characterized by a high degree of group cohesion, or integration, are also likely to elicit the loyalty of their members. This is usually dependent on harmonious in-group relationships, combined with isolation from or an adversarial attitude toward outsiders.

Goal alignment. The final component fostering organizational loyalty is goal alignment. When individuals perceive their ultimate ends to be best served by fostering organizational goals, they will sacrifice immediate gratifications and strive for the good of the whole.

An organization's ability to instill in people the kind of loyalty that is collectively forged and transcends a particular circumstance or relationship varies. The strongest loyalty bonds are forged by organizations that are able to generate all five of these conceptual components. Similarly, individuals who meet the criteria of all five components will develop more intense loyalty bonds. Loyalty can thus vary from person to person and group to group depending on the individual's and organization's correspondence to this model.

Domination

A significant factor influencing the development of loyalty among college athletes was their domination by the head coach through both his institutionally derived structural authority and his personal leadership.

Subordination

Structurally, college athletic programs are hierarchical organizations characterized by an extreme centralization of authority. By virtue of their position of authority, power, and superordination, coaches wield enormous influence over the lives of players. In their subordinate positions, players at the University were dependent on the coach for almost all their daily needs and responsibilities. Their food, lodging, sense of well-being, and future careers were controlled by him. With little recourse against his superior power, they had to accede to his rules or withdraw from the program. Thus, in spite of the modern tendency toward a progressive liberation of the individual from the bonds of exclusive attachment (Simmel, 1956, 1959), college athletics remains an arena of low social differentiation. They thus represent what Coser (1974) has called "greedy institutions," organizations that exert inordinate pressure on individual members to weaken or sever ties with any person or institution that might make successful competing demands on their loyalty and commitment. Players at the University experienced a limited span of subordination, being subordinate to a relatively small and concentrated rather than a numerous and diffuse group of individuals (the head coach and his assistants).

To reinforce his domination and solidify his firm grasp on players, the coach occasionally used displays of power. In one case, he indefinitely suspended a star senior player who had attempted to punch an assistant coach. After a week the dispute was resolved, the player apologized, and he was reinstated, but not before he had to endure the embarrassment of a media scandal. His humbling retreat from his earlier arrogant and aggressive position was not lost on his teammates, who sensed and shared his feelings of powerlessness and servitude.

While subordination brought the negative feelings of resentment, anger, powerlessness, and engulfment, it could also induce loyalty. Athletes' subordination in status and power (not to mention age) increased their feelings of awe and respect for the coach and, hence, their loyalty. They also undoubtedly saw instrumental value in giving their loyalty to such a powerful superordinate.

Control

While the coach's control began with his role as the gatekeeper to the organization, he maintained this control on a daily basis by staying abreast of the flow of information. He would then use this knowledge to intimidate players by surrounding himself with an aura of omniscience. One player described how he was awed by the coach's knowledge and insight:

> Coach finds out what you do, some kind of way. Like he was out of town recruiting and there was a fight in the gym — he found out. Or like, I was unhappy and thinking about going home, and I didn't really tell nobody. He called me in and he said, "What you sulking about?"

The coach also sought to regulate players by controlling their time and location (see also Raney, Knapp, and Small, 1983). His assistants arranged players' schedules, requiring them to be at classes, practices, study halls, team meetings, banquets, and booster functions. As one player exclaimed in exasperation: "Oh man, they can really control your time! If they want to keep you 24 hours on the schedule they can do that. . . . Because you are on the clock once school starts." Between curfews, two practices on weekends, games, films, entertaining recruits, and booster functions, players had little time to themselves. When they did, the coach often interfered:

> He tries to control your whole life. That's one of those parts that I know a player hates, when he gets into that aspect of your life—your girlfriend, who to hang out with, where you can hang out—and he gets into all those things.

Thus, while the players accepted the coach's authority over them to a certain degree, they had a collective feeling that there should be limits to the extent of his control. When he overly encroached on their social lives, his behavior violated their intuitive sense of the legitimate norms governing his authority and became a detriment to their feelings of loyalty. These norms of dominance suggest the existence of an implicit loyalty contract: Upon joining the program, players understood that they would accept the coach's authority over them and return it with their loyalty. When he tried to extend his domination into illegitimate arenas, however, this breached their sense of appropriateness and disrupted the loyalty contract.

Simmel (1950:193) has suggested that while people resent and oppose a leader's domination and control over them, on some level they also seek it; they both want it and need it to protect themselves against the outside world and their own selves. This allowed them, at times, to place an almost blind faith in him and to follow his directives loyally.

Finally, loyalty was enhanced by the reciprocal need of the coach and players for each other. The players recognized that the coach held the key to their future careers, since professional scouts and potential employers went to him for information about them. In turn, their successes and failures reflected back onto him and affected his future recruiting and reputation. Turner (1970) has suggested that such longitudinal involvement fosters the development of "crescive bonds," the accumulated products of the unique history of a relationship that promote loyalty.

Resocialization

A third dimension of athletes' domination came through the process of resocialization they underwent. This parallels Berger and Luckmann's (1966) view of resocialization as secondary socialization, a nihilation of the old reality and legitimation of the new reality. The athletes' entry into college athletics led to a stripping down and rebuilding of their selves, such as occurs in many total institutions (Goffman, 1961). Simmel (1950:181) has noted that this form of domination goes beyond external control to break people's internal resistance. It aims, moreover, for the reduction of individuality and the "de-selfing" of initiates by forging them into members of the group, dischargers of predetermined roles (Simmel, 1950:373).

The stripping down began soon after athletes' arrival, with a sobering introduction to the realities of college basketball. They were no longer high school stars, able to play as long as they wanted, to engage in all aspects of the game (shooting, passing, rebounding, dribbling), and to play in a loose, undisciplined manner. Instead, they were freshmen, "riding the bench," waiting for their turn. They went through a rigorous training process in which they abandoned their old style of play, completely relearned the fundamentals, and learned the team's offense and defense. Throughout this process, the coach drilled the individualistic, "hot dog" qualities out of them and shaped them into team players (i.e., specialized, role players), into a group whose members could integrate well with each other on the court. This involved a transition from the mechanical solidarity of doing it all to the organic solidarity of specialization and interdependence. One sophomore described what this meant to him:

> Right now I'm in a stage, I'm working on becoming a complete player. I'm pretty sure I'm gonna be before I leave here. I don't care who shoots, I'm gonna get the ball when I can; I'm gonna dive for it when I see it. When I say complete player, I mean a team player. When you come in as a freshman you don't think they're gonna stress on your being a complete player. You think they're gonna stress on your being an individual. . . . In college ball, you learn that you have to rely on so many people.

The changes in their style of play were reinforced by changes in their selves. Here the stripping down began with a series of private talks held in the coach's office. He pointed out the negative aspects of each player's self, while at the same time encouraging the development of other aspects. One player recalled these talks:

They cut you down, they find out what you really like. You're a pretty good guy. But if you got one of them ole Billy-bad-ass attitudes in the background, they goin' break that first. They goin' to get to that good guy and they goin' show you how to go with it.

The coach's private talks were reinforced by individual and collective shaming rituals. During these degradation ceremonies, he would openly denounce players in front of the whole team. He would rant about the attitudes or behavior of "certain parties" or "hopeless cases" and threaten them with ineligibility, benching, suspension, or nonrenewal of their scholarships. No players, even the "candy-asses," were immune from these tirades. These sessions were intense and caused all players, even just by association, to feel shame, fear, and embarrassment. Gross and Stone (1964) have suggested that such instances of deliberate embarrassment may be intended as both displays of power by the perpetrator and as negative sanctions against the embarrassed. In their structural resemblance to military hazings and humiliations, they symbolize rites of passage into an established social world. These public and private assaults on their selves jarred athletes into dislodging from their old self-centeredness and made them ready for molding into team loyalty.

Identification

A second main component integral to the development of loyalty was the players' forging of self-conceptions in which they identified with both the organization and the leader.

Identification with the Organization

According to Cooley (1962:38), "In so far as one identifies himself with a whole, loyalty to that whole is loyalty to himself." Thus, to the extent that people identify with a group or institution, every act supporting the whole is one of self-realization. Loyalty to the whole is equivalent to loyalty to one's self.

In much the same way that people identify with and feel loyalty to their country (see Bell et al., 1983), these college athletes identified with and felt loyalty to their team and its program. The value of loyalty and identification was expressed in the commonly heard saying, "Get with the program." The coach and his assistants repeated this phrase often, exhorting players to put themselves fully into internalizing the ideals and realizing the goals of the organization. College athletes identified their selves with the program not only when they were wearing their uniforms, traveling together, or hanging around the coaching offices and gym, but whenever they went out in public. Early on, the coach impressed upon them the responsibilities and restrictions they carried whenever they left the protected enclave of the University. As one player stated:

> I was in the public eye. A college basketball player has to represent not only himself but the University, because you've got to think about the media, what they can do if they see you drinking a beer in public, or getting into a fight, how that make your school look, how that make your coach look, how that make your team look.

They thus realized that wherever they went they represented the program. At times this involved considerable sacrifice. They had to spend time with boosters when they would rather be spending time with friends. Any time they were in a public setting, they were likely to be approached by autograph seekers. At these times they had to relinquish their privacy and take on the role of the athlete. While this was bothersome, it also made them feel good, it gave them a sense of prestige and pride. As one player explained: "I love signing autographs for people. If somebody is interested enough in me and my team to want my name on a piece of paper I'll sign 50 of them for him. I'm proud." These feelings reinforced athletes' identification with and loyalty to the program.

Identification with the Leader

The athletes' degree of self-identification with the head coach also influenced their feelings of loyalty. Just as they represented the program, so, too, did they represent the coach; their behavior, both good and bad, reflected on him personally, in much the same way that children's behavior is a reflection on parents' competence as socializing agents (Denzin, 1979).

The coach sought to enhance players' personal loyalty and identification with him through the paternalistic character of his program. While some coaches structure their organizations bureaucratically and adopt a rational-legal style of leadership, this coach administered his team in a charismatic, patrimonial manner. He created a familial atmosphere by symbolically extending his family bounds to include the players: "I had them at my house every Saturday and Sunday to feed them. We became closer from getting to know each other better. That way it became like a family."

Some players felt more like a part of his family than others, and, hence, identified with him more strongly. This varied by the two social groups that made up the team. Members of the "straight" group spent more time at the coach's house, called him nicknames like "Pops," were close with his wife and children, and gratefully accepted his paternalistic demeanor. The "partyers," however, tended to look on him as more of an employer, one of just another series of bosses they would have throughout their lives. In failing to accept the paternalistic relationship offered them by the coach, members of this latter group developed weaker feelings of organizational loyalty and identification with their leader.

Another means used by the coach to build athletes' self-identification with and loyalty toward him involved the principle of reciprocity. He taught them to extend him their loyalty by offering his loyalty to them: "When you need me, I want to be there. If I can help you, I will help you. That's what loyalty is about."

Finally, he fostered their identification with him by presenting himself as a role model they could emulate. He accentuated his humble origins, hard work, and struggle to reach his coaching position. He spoke of his own aspirations and dreams at their age. He related their problems to his experiences in suggesting ways that they could overcome them. This approach helped players empathize with him, strengthening the bond between them.

Commitment

Another key component integral to the development of loyalty was commitment. Both personal and institutional factors encouraged and sustained athletes' feelings of commitment to the organization.

Signing

As high school ballplayers, future college athletes included both the highly touted and recruited superstars and the unknowns, hopeful of making a major college squad. Except for a brief period in the fall, NCAA rules require colleges and high school athletes to refrain from committing to each other for the following year until the spring. Much anticipation built up in these athletes over the winter of their senior year, especially for those having to choose among a number of suitors. When "signing day" finally arrived, most of the top picks signed letters of intention announcing their choice of program. While these letters placed only limited restrictions on players' ability to rescind later, they were treated with utmost seriousness. One player described the pervasive attitude toward signing: "When you sign it's almost like you're taking an oath that you're gonna follow this man, do what he tell you for four years, play on his team. It feels like signing your life away."

For players, then, the signing represented a symbolic loyalty oath wherein they swore allegiance to the coach and his program. Usually the signing ceremony was conducted in the presence of the coach or one of his assistants and was accompanied by local media hoopla, with the player being given a piece of team equipment bearing the insignia of the school. This encouraged the athlete to adopt symbolically the identity of the team. At the same time, it forcefully launched their feelings of self-investment in the program.

Transfer Rules

Not only were there personal factors committing athletes to the team but, through the NCAA rules of eligibility and transfer, institutional factors as well. According to these rules, athletes were eligible to play, assuming they qualified academically, during four of their first five consecutive years following their entry into the University. If they wanted to transfer they had to sit out a year before they could play again. NCAA regulations thus functioned as a "side-bet" (Becker, 1960) or secondary investment, making it difficult for athletes to leave and hence enhancing their feelings of permanence and long-term commitment to the program. The rules also brought stability and security to their careers, since these cut down the number of transfers and lengthened an athlete's stay at any one program.

Integration

Another major conceptual component fostering the development of loyalty was integration. Integration refers to the coalescence of discrete individuals into a cohesive unit such that they work well together, they feel they can count on each other, and they can anticipate and understand much of what the other members of the group are doing. But unlike the more abstract self-identification with the whole, integration into a group grows out of the intimacy of face-to-face cooperation and from a group acting and interacting together (Cooley, 1962:38). Two modes of integration, unification in opposition to the leader and group solidarity, are relevant to the development of loyalty.

Unification in Opposition

Simmel (1950:190) has pointed out that "the subordination of a group under a single person results, above all, in a very decisive unification of the group." The characteristics or behavior of the leader, however, may also cause the group to fuse in opposition to him or her. Even more than harmony, discord causes the group to unite and become motivated to cling together (Simmel, 1950:193). The coach recognized this fact and used it to integrate his players into a cohesive unit:

> The pressure is on them every day to compete against each other to impress me for the starting jobs on the team. Now when I come out and start running them and screaming, they're not trying to impress me anymore; I'm the real enemy right there. That's how you make a team become closer together: by them hating the coach. Once I become the enemy I take the pressure off of them.

Group Solidarity

Other aspects of athletes' experiences caused them to develop group solidarity and feelings of cohesion and belonging. This began with their earliest impressions upon arrival at the campus. Unlike other students, athletes were required to move into the dorms at the beginning of the summer. During the subsequent three months they worked at summer jobs provided by boosters, practiced in the gym daily, and hung around with other athletes—the only other students living on campus. By the end of that time they had already jelled into an integrated group. As one freshman described it:

> By the time the three months were over I felt like I was there a year already, I felt so connected to the guys. You've played with them, it's been 130 degrees in the gym, you've elbowed each other, knocked each other around. Now you've felt a relationship, it's a team, a brotherhood type of thing. Everybody's got to eat the same rotten food, go through the same thing, and all you have is each other. So you've got a shared bond, a camaraderie. It's a whole houseful of brothers. And that's home to everybody in the dorm, not your parents' house.

These feelings of belonging were heightened, once school began, by athletes' divergences from other students on campus and their overlaps with each other. Demographically, for the most part, they were of a different race and class than the rest of the student body. Spatially, they lived in an athletic dorm located on the far side of campus, away from the other students. Temporally, they had little time to socialize with other students because their mornings, afternoons, and evenings were scheduled with classes, practices, and team functions, respectively. Physically, many students found them intimidating because of their size, race, and musculature. They thus were separated and isolated from other students at the same time as they were thrust, once again, together. Their shared outlook and status further legitimated and reinforced the athletes' intensive associations and integration. Team members thus developed "task bonds" and "person bonds" (Turner, 1970) based on their shared experiences, time spent together, propinquity, and concomitant isolation from other students.

Sponsorship

A final factor related to team cohesion and integration was the sponsorship exhibited by older players toward younger ones. When the new freshman class arrived on campus, the veterans gravitated toward those they liked and helped them adjust to the scene. One senior described his experiences:

> When I was a freshman a couple of the older players took me under their wings. They told me what the coach was like, how to get by when the coach is on you, gave me tips on my game, helped me with my algebra class, told me to dress

nice for games, how to get by with the boosters and stuff. . . . It was some of these things they told me that right now I catch myself telling the other freshmen.

This kind of reaching out to newcomers who were strangers to the scene and who were having trouble adjusting to its often unexpected and overwhelming characteristics caused immediate and close-knit relationships to form. Not only did players' sponsorship generate intimacy and camaraderie, but it generated interpersonal loyalty.

Goal Alignment

The final element fostering the development of loyalty involved the affiliation, or alignment, of individuals' goals with those of the group. By alignment we refer to the fitting together or unification of individuals' aims for their present happiness and future careers with the organizational goal of achieving a winning program. When this occurred, team members cooperated with the coach about the means to strive collectively for their mutual ends. Without this alignment the relationship between players and coach could disintegrate into competition and conflict.

In this setting the players and the coach had overlapping, albeit not identical, goals. The players wanted many things: to have fun and enjoy their college years, to graduate so they could get good jobs, to achieve fame and glory on the playing field, and, most importantly, to keep alive their dream of making it in the pros. The organizational goal, directed by the coach, was to build a winning program at the University. As one player expressed it:

> Coach's main goal is to keep producing quality basketball teams. He wants to maintain his winning reputation, pull in more money for the school, keep his job, and build his chances of getting a better job. His job isn't to produce accountants or NBA athletes—it's to have a winning program.

These two sets of goals overlapped and became aligned around the principle of winning. One player showed his understanding of the importance of aligning his goals with that of the team:

> For me to make it, we need to go to the Final Four. I know I can perform good, but we've gotta win some games for me to go high up in the draft. And we have two other guys who can score good on this team. So I can't average over 25 points a game. So when I go out there I just concentrate on getting the job done for the team.

When the team had a winning season, not only did the coach achieve his objectives, but the players achieved a variety of intrinsic and extrinsic rewards. Extrinsically, they acquired clothes and other little gifts from the boosters; they improved their long-term chances at an athletic, booster, or business career; and their social lives were enhanced due to their improved social status. Intrinsically, they felt proud to go out in public, they felt a sense of achievement that accompanied the symbolic material possessions of winning (i.e., a ring, a watch, a letterman's jacket), and they derived a feeling of satisfaction from facing a series of challenges and performing well. As one player explained, winning enhanced the structural opportunities for players to achieve all their goals:

> Winning is as important to me as it is to him [the coach]. To me, if you're a winner you're gonna develop your skills, you're gonna get seen nationally and develop a national rep so you can get high in the draft, get an education, get a social life, meet people—like boosters for getting a job—'cause all those things go with winning.

Most of the players aligned their goal with the coach's and concentrated on achieving team wins. This was the most significant thing to them, and they perceived that achieving this goal enhanced the attainment of all their secondary goals. There were some, however, who did not feel this way, who felt that the group goal would not benefit them individually. These individuals cared more about bolstering their own playing statistics to enhance their pro chances and, thus, did not make the same sacrifices for the team. As one individual expressed his feelings:

> Thinking about scoring is in the back of my mind, and in the middle of my mind, and in the front. I have to look out for myself because nobody is going to look out for me. Coach isn't going to say this guy should be a first or second round draft pick. He might back me a little, but not like what he done for others.

Players who took this attitude neither gave their loyalty to the organization nor believed that the organization would be loyal to them.

The importance of goal-orientation to social organization thus emerges clearly. When members of the organization subjugated their selves to the collective and "jointly aligned their actions" (Blumer, 1969) to work toward team goals, they achieved cooperation, harmony, loyalty, and success. When their individual lines of action became disaligned, as this negative case shows, they created an atmosphere of jealousy, mistrust, competitiveness, and conflict that damaged their cohesion, camaraderie, and collective achievement.

CONCLUSION

The type of loyalty we have discussed here, as noted earlier, is different from that found in most other organizations. College athletic teams generate an intense loyalty that surpasses the more bland forms of organizational commitment commonly found in ordinary organizations. Other organizations that generate this kind of intense loyalty, such as combat units and religious cults, are frequently groups with highly interdependent members that function at a high performance level. The question arises, then, what kinds of organizational characteristics foster this intense kind of loyalty, and how do these organizations differ structurally from those without it?

The first way to answer this question is to examine the organization's format and leadership. Drawing on Weber's ideal types, paternalistic organizations with traditional or (most especially) charismatic leadership are more likely to promote intense loyalty than bureaucratic organizations with rational-legal authority forms. Worker-employer relationships that are personal or familial in character are more likely to evoke strong feelings of loyalty than impersonal bureaucracies, as Hodson and Sullivan (1985) found in their comparisons of worker commitment among large, nationally recognized corporations and locally based firms. Concomitantly, charismatic and traditional leaders or employers inspire greater allegiance through their appeals to workers' hope and excitement or because workers are comfortable with this style of leadership. In his study of worker subordination in a Southern textile plant, for example, Leiter (1986) found that employees readily acquiesced to accepting low pay and poor opportunities for advancement without diminishing their loyalty to the firm because the family-oriented and religious character of their community reinforced the traditional mode of plant leadership.

Second, most traditional work organizations recruit not only on the basis of ability but on individuals' style, or how they will "fit in" the organization (Gouldner, 1954). College athletic teams overwhelmingly seek out new members on the basis of talent, with significantly less attention paid to other factors. The result is a greater need to subject these recruits to an intensive socialization experience so that they may be shaped into the type of individuals who behave themselves appropriately off the court, project the optimal team image to the media and public, and perform during games in a manner that facilitates the highly interdependent team play. Military units and religious groups are similarly undiscriminating about the nature of their recruits (Rochford, 1982), collecting a wide assortment of highly undifferentiated new members who must be programmed to fit into the new environment.

Third, organizations that engage in controlling the extraorganizational behavior of their members are more likely to evoke intense loyalty. This domination over members leads them to subordinate all their other interests to the organization's and focuses them more unilaterally on their relationship to the organization. Just as the coach sought to limit the span of acquaintances and control the time, living arrangements, and course selection of his basketball players when they were not playing or practicing, so do military units have strict rules for their members' recreational location and behavior, and religious groups have dogma that prescribes appropriate and proscribes inappropriate thoughts and deeds.

Fourth, organizational loyalty is more likely to arise in organizations where the central life interest (CLI) of the members revolves around work (Dubin, Champoux, and Porter, 1975). Most organizations are role segmented and exclude the core aspects of individuals' selves from their domain. Organizations able to capture that core and involve the CLI of their participants will evoke greater organizational loyalty. Organizational studies have shown, for example, that white-collar and managerial professionals have a greater CLI in their work than do blue-collar and clerical workers (Parker, 1965; Maurer, 1968) and that religious groups capture the CLI of their members more often than do secular ones (Dubin, Champoux, and Porter, 1975). Organizations desirous of evoking intense loyalty in their members must go beyond merely involving individuals' CLI; they must compel that role that commands members' most salient self-identities (Stryker, 1968) and generates their master statuses (Hughes, 1945), thereby not only dominating over the central aspect of these individuals' lives but engulfing them entirely.

Another dimension in which we can differentiate the structural components separating intense-loyalty-generating organizations from their more ordinary counterparts is the area of subordination versus autonomy. In traditional work organizations, employees, even at the management level, resist subordination. When their individuality is subverted through the substitution of their personal for organizational values they react with defensiveness, resistance, and retrenchment (Katz, Sarnoff, and McClintock, 1956; Ostrom and Brock, 1968; Buchanan, 1974). Members of intense-loyalty-generating organizations, however, accept subordination, ranging from the physical subordination of the military, to the spiritual and behavioral subordination of religious groups, to the social and behavioral subordination of college athletic teams.

The structure of the work group is another factor enhancing or diminishing the likelihood of intense loyalty. Organizations in which productivity is achieved on a group basis generate greater loyalty than those characterized by individual achievement (see Oliver, 1984; Rothschild and Whitt, 1986). On teams, individuality must be removed and obedience built. This fosters a commitment to the group and the leader over individual recognition. Thus military squadrons, athletic teams, and workers' cooperative groups foster more intense loyalty than academic departments, sales forces, or agents. This is due, partly, to the emergence of strong loyalty bonds between coworkers, in addition to those they form to their employer and organization (Miller and Labovitz, 1973), and to the symbiosis of the teammate relationship.

A final dimension involves the alignment of organizational (group) and professional (individual) goals. Traditional analyses of organizational loyalty and professional commitment have explicitly assumed that the individual had to choose one over the other (Shepard, 1956; Gouldner, 1957; Merton, 1957). Professional commitment draws individuals toward personal achievement at the cosmopolitan level, while organizational loyalty has been seen as holding them more closely tied to the concerns of the local corporation. More recent works, however, have shown that these factors can be independent or aligned (Friedlander, 1971; Berger and Grimes, 1973; Flango and Brumbaugh, 1974; Jauch, Glueck, and Osborn, 1978). To the extent that an organization is able to engineer the alignment of individuals' professional goals with those of the organization, it will have a greater likelihood of producing intense loyalty in its members. Thus, organizations such as team sports or military units that are structured so that individuals are dependent on the success of the group for their own success will be more likely to produce intense loyalty. Future research could profitably build on this analysis by examining intense loyalty in other organizations, thus providing a comparative base on which to test these structural propositions.

REFERENCES

Adler, Patricia A., and Peter Adler. 1987. *Membership Roles in Field Research*. Newbury Park, CA: Sage.

Barley, Stephen R. 1984. "The professional, the semi-professional, and the machine: The social implications of computer imaging in radiology." Unpublished doctoral dissertation, Sloan School of Management, MIT.

Barnard, Chester I. 1938. *Functions of the Executive*. Cambridge, MA: Harvard University Press.

Becker, Gary S. 1975. *Human Capital*. Chicago: University of Chicago Press.

Becker, Howard S. 1960. "Notes on the concept of commitment." *American Journal of Sociology*, 66: 32–40.

Becker, Howard S., Blanche Geer, Anselm Strauss, and Everett Hughes. 1961. *Boys in White*. Chicago: University of Chicago Press.

Bell, Wendell, Walker Connor, Joshua Fishman, and Louis Snyder. 1983. "Collective sentiments and their social hierarchies." *Canadian Review of Studies in Nationalism*, 10: 267–270.

Berger, P. K., and A. J. Grimes. 1973. "Cosmopolitan-local: A factor analysis of the construct." *Administrative Science Quarterly*, 18: 223–235.

Berger, Peter, and Thomas Luckmann. 1966. *The Social Construction of Reality*. New York: Doubleday.

Bielby, William T., and James N. Baron. 1983. "Organizations, technology, and worker attachment to the firm." In R. Robinson (ed.), *Research in Social Stratification and Mobility*: 77–113. Greenwich, CT: JAI Press.

Blau, Peter M., and W. Richard Scott. 1962. *Formal Organizations*. San Francisco: Chandler.

Blumer, Herbert. 1969. *Symbolic Interactionism*. Englewood Cliffs, NJ: Prentice Hall.

Buchanan, Bruce. 1974. "Building organizational commitment: The socialization of managers in work organizations." *Administrative Science Quarterly*, 19: 533–546.

Coakley, J. J. 1982. *Sport in Society*, 2d ed. St. Louis: Mosby.

Cooley, Charles H. 1962. *Social Organization*. New York: Schocken.

Coser, Lewis. 1974. *Greedy Institutions*. New York: Free Press.

Denzin, Norman. 1970. *The Research Act*. Chicago: Aldine.

————1979. "Children and their caretakers." In P. Rose (ed.), *Socialization and the Life Cycle:* 36–51. New York: St. Martin's.

Douglas, Jack D. 1976. *Investigative Social Research.* Beverly Hills, CA: Sage.

Dubin, Robert, Joseph E. Champoux, and Lyman W. Porter. 1975. "Central life interests and organizational commitment of blue-collar and clerical workers." *Administrative Science Quarterly,* 20: 411–421.

Flango, Victor E., and Robert B. Brumbaugh. 1974. "The dimensionality of the cosmopolitan-local construct." *Administrative Science Quarterly,* 19: 198–210.

Frey, James. 1982. "Boosterism, scarce resources and institutional control: The future of American intercollegiate athletics." *International Review of Sport Sociology,* 17: 53–70.

Friedlander, F. 1971. "Performance and orientation structures of research scientists." *Organizational Behavior and Human Performance,* 6: 169–183.

Glaser, Barney, and Anselm Strauss. 1967. *The Discovery of Grounded Theory.* Chicago: Aldine.

Goffman, Erving. 1961. *Asylums.* New York: Doubleday Anchor.

Gouldner, Alvin. 1954. *Patterns of Industrial Bureaucracy.* New York: Free Press.

————. 1957. "Cosmopolitans and locals: Towards an analysis of latent social roles." *Administrative Science Quarterly,* 2: 281–306.

Gross, Edward, and Gregory Stone. 1964. "Embarrassment and the analysis of role requirements." *American Journal of Sociology,* 60: 1–15.

Halaby, Charles N. 1986. "Worker attachment and workplace authority." *American Sociological Review,* 51: 634–649.

Hodson, Randy, and Teresa A. Sullivan. 1985. "Totem or tyrant? Monopoly, regional, and local sector effects on worker commitment." *Social Forces,* 63: 716–731.

Hughes, Everett C. 1945. "Dilemmas and contradictions in status." *American Journal of Sociology,* 50: 353–359.

Jauch, Lawrence R., William F. Glueck, and Richard N. Osborn. 1978. "Organizational loyalty, professional commitment, and academic research productivity." *Academy of Management Journal,* 21: 84–92.

Jonassohn, Kurt, Alan Turowetz, and Richard Gruneau. 1981. "Research methods in the sociology of sport." *Qualitative Sociology,* 4: 179–197.

Jovanovic, Boyan. 1979. "Job matching and the theory of turnover." *Journal of Political Economy,* 87: 972–990.

Kalleberg, Arne. 1977. "Work values and job rewards: A theory of job satisfaction." *American Sociological Review,* 42: 124–143.

Kanter, Rosabeth M. 1968. "Commitment and social organization: A study of commitment mechanisms in utopian communities." *American Sociological Review,* 33: 499–517.

Katz, Daniel, Irving Sarnoff, and Charles McClintock. 1956. "Ego defense and attitude change." *Human Relations,* 9: 27–45.

Leiter, Jeffrey. 1986. "Reactions to subordination: Attitudes of southern textile workers." *Social Forces,* 64: 948–974.

Lincoln, James R., and Arne Kalleberg. 1986. "Work organization and workforce commitment: A study of plants and employees in the United States and Japan." *American Sociological Review,* 50: 738–760.

Locke, Edwin. 1976. "The nature and causes of job satisfaction." In M. Dunnette (ed.), *Handbook of Industrial and Organizational Psychology:* 1297–1349. Chicago: Rand-McNally.

March, James G., and Herbert A. Simon. 1958. *Organizations.* New York: Wiley.

Marsh, Robert M., and Hiroshi Mannari. 1971. "Lifetime commitment in Japan: Roles, norms and values." *American Journal of Sociology,* 76: 795–812.

Maurer, John G. 1968. "Work as a central life interest of industrial supervisors." *Academy of Management Journal,* 11: 329–339.

Merton, Robert. 1957. *Social Theory and Social Structure.* Glencoe, IL: Free Press.

Miller, Jon, and Sanford Labovitz. 1973. "Individual reactions to organizational conflict and change." *Sociological Quarterly,* 14: 556–575.

Morris, James H., and Richard M. Steers. 1980. "Structural influences on organizational commitment." *Journal of Vocational Behavior,* 17: 50–57.

Mortensen, Dale T. 1978. "Specific capital and labor turnover." *Bell Journal of Economics,* 9: 572–582.

Mowday, Richard T., Lyman W. Porter, and Richard M. Steers. 1982. *Employee-Organization Linkages: The Psychology of Commitment, Absenteeism, and Turnover.* New York: Academic Press.

Oliver, Nick. 1984. "An examination of organizational commitment in six workers' cooperatives in Scotland." *Human Relations,* 37: 29–46.

Ostrom, Thomas M., and Timothy C. Brock. 1968. "A cognitive model of attitudinal development." In R. P. Abelson et al. (eds.), *Theories of Cognitive Consistency:* 577–589. Chicago: Rand McNally.

Parker, Stanley R. 1965. "Work and non-work in three occupations." *Sociological Review,* 13: 65–75.

Parsons, Donald O. 1972. "Specific human capital: An application to quit rates and layoff rates." *Journal of Political Economy,* 80: 112–143.

Porter, Lyman, and Richard Steers. 1973. "Organizational, work, and personal factors in employee turnover and absenteeism." *Psychological Bulletin,* 80: 151–176.

Raney J., T. Knapp, and M. Small. 1983. "Pass one for the Gipper: Student athletes and university coursework." *Arena Review,* 7: 53–59.

Rochford, E. Burke. 1982. "Recruitment strategies, ideology, and organization in the Hare Krishna movement." *Social Problems,* 29: 399–410.

Rothschild, Joyce, and J. Allen Whitt. 1986. *The Cooperative Workplace.* New York: Cambridge University Press.

Schein, Edgar H. 1987. *The Clinical Perspective in Fieldwork.* Newbury Park, CA: Sage.

Shepard, H. 1956. "Nine dilemmas in industrial research." *Administrative Science Quarterly,* 1: 340–360.

Simmel, Georg. 1950. *The Sociology of Georg Simmel.* Translated and edited by K. H. Wolff. New York: Free Press.

———.1956. *Conflict and the Web of Group Affiliations.* Translated by K. H. Wolff and R. Bendix. New York: Free Press.

———.1959. "The problem of sociology." In *Georg Simmel, 1858–1918: A Collection of Essays.* Translated and edited by K. H. Wolff. Columbus: Ohio State University Press.

Stryker, Sheldon. 1968. "Identity salience and role performance." *Journal of Marriage and the Family,* 30: 558–564.

Turner, Ralph H. 1970. *Family Interaction.* New York: Wiley.

Wiseman, Jacqueline P. 1970. *Stations of the Lost.* Chicago: University of Chicago Press.

3

IN SEARCH OF RATIONALITY

The Purposes Behind the Use of
Formal Analysis in Organizations

Ann Langley

INTRODUCTION

Management teachers, writers, and researchers spend a good deal of time advocating more formal, more systematic, more logical, and more analytical approaches to decision making. However, in spite of all this normative emphasis on the use of formal analysis, surprisingly little is actually known about how it is used in practice in organizations, especially at the top-management level. Is it in fact used at all? And if so, when and why?

Much of the management writing and teaching aimed at practitioners emphasizes the use of formal analysis for informational purposes. Yet, anyone who has ever worked in a complex organization knows that other types of motivations for doing analysis are also common. Many have in fact been noted in the scholarly literature. For example, Dalton (1959) suggested that staff

AUTHOR'S NOTE: The author is grateful to Christiane Demers, Jean-Louis Denis, Cynthia Hardy, Gilbert Laporte, Louis-André Lefebvre, Henry Mintzberg, and Jean-Marie Toulouse, Gerald Salancik, Linda Pike, and four anonymous *ASQ* reviewers for assistance and advice on various aspects of this work. Reprinted from *Administrative Science Quarterly,* 34 (Dec. 1989): 598–631.

people in the firm he studied often served a control function. Others (e.g., Bower, 1970; Kerr, 1982; Meyer, 1984) have noted that a great deal of formal analysis is more concerned with the justification of decisions already made than with a need to know. Quinn (1980) suggested that formal analysis and planning may have an important role to play in focusing the attention of others on issues, raising comfort levels, and gaining commitment. Lindblom and Cohen (1979), Porter, Zemsky, and Oedel (1979), Prince (1979), and Wildavsky (1979) have suggested that formal analysis is often used as a tool in adversarial debate. Brewer (1981) and Meltsner (1976) described how analysis may be used to deflect attention away from issues by giving the impression of action. Edelman (1985), Feldman and March (1981), Meyer and Rowan (1977), and Pfeffer (1981) drew attention to the symbolic and ritualistic uses of language and information in conveying messages of rationality and thus legitimizing organizational actions. However, these contributions are fragmented. There has, in fact, been very little empirical research that has examined the purposes behind formal analysis in any systematic way. This article describes some of the results of an exploratory empirical study in which the purposes behind the use of formal analysis in three organizations were systematically identified and a typology was developed.

Biases in favor of considering formal analysis mainly as a source of information have also led to another frequent conception: that an organization in which formal analysis is very common is also an organization that has adopted a "rational/comprehensive" mode of decision making and one in which political and social interactive modes of decision making are relatively less important. For example, this assumption partly underlies Fredrickson's (1984) definition of the "comprehensiveness" construct. And Mintzberg (1979c) explicitly associated formal analysis with the "machine bureaucracy" structural type, in which political modes of decision making are relatively unimportant as compared with other structures. In the study described here, it is noted that, far from being antithetical, formal analysis and social interaction are inextricably linked in organizational decision making. Several propositions concerning the relationships between the use of formal analysis and its social interactive context are offered.

As the subject of this research had been very little studied in the past, a qualitative research approach, emphasizing richness of the data base, seemed appropriate: description, concept development, and hypothesis generation were more important than hypothesis testing at this stage. I therefore decided to focus on understanding the role of formal analysis in strategic decision making in three organizations in depth. The general approach taken reflects that proposed by Glaser and Strauss (1967) for the development of "grounded theory" and the "direct research" approach advocated by Mintzberg (1979b). A very rich data base was therefore developed, with the use of multiple data sources providing some assurance that a complete and accurate picture of the decision-making processes was obtained. However, the study does suffer from the familiar and somewhat inevitable limitations usually associated with this kind of qualitative research. One of these limitations is related to the small sample size: caution is required in generalizing the results, especially those in which the three organizations are compared. The second limitation of this type of research is perhaps more serious: data analysis relies greatly on the perceptions of one researcher. The problem is aggravated by the data themselves, which are verbal and therefore ambiguous. Two measures have been taken in an attempt to alleviate this problem at least partially. First, within the limits of available space, I have tried to expose the reader directly to the flavor of the raw data by examples and by using quotations from interviews to illustrate my points. Second, where possible, for certain key variables, two coders were involved in evaluating the data and an attempt was made to verify the reliability and the robustness of the results.

METHOD

The three organizations studied were deliberately chosen to represent three different structural types, according to Mintzberg's (1979c) typology: one machine bureaucracy, one professional bureaucracy, and one adhocracy. Given that several authors have suggested that different organization structures may produce different types of decision-making processes (e.g., Mintzberg, 1979c; Shrivastava and Grant, 1985; Fredrickson, 1986), three types of organizations were chosen for study, to enrich the data base, to provide exposure to as many different types of uses of formal analysis as possible, and also to enable me to make some preliminary comparisons between the different structures. The machine bureaucracy (Mintzberg, 1979c) is a type of organization in which coordination is principally achieved by the standardization of work processes. Operating work in these organizations is stable, predictable, and well understood and is carried out by relatively unskilled personnel. The machine bureaucracy chosen (called here "Servico") operated a public service that satisfactorily filled this description.[1] The "professional bureaucracy" and the "adhocracy" are structures in which operating work is complex and must be carried out by highly trained professionals (Mintzberg, 1979b). However, while work in the professional bureaucracy is relatively routine and repetitive, the adhocracy is oriented toward innovation, and its professionals work in multidisciplinary teams to produce one-time outputs. The sample professional bureaucracy was a hospital (called here "St. Gabriel's Hospital," while the sample adhocracy, (called "the CAC") was involved in a form of artistic production. The three sites chosen were medium sized (between 500 and 5000 employees) and were all under some form of public sector control.

At each site, from eight to ten current or recent strategic issues were selected for in-depth study. The issues were chosen through discussions with the CEO (chief executive officer) and through the review of the minutes of top-level management committee meetings for the past two years. An attempt was made to choose a range of different issues, while ensuring that the most important issues for the organization were included. In all, 27 issues were chosen. The topics covered a wide range, including diversification, market development, restructuring, vertical integration, closure of services, capital investments in equipment and facilities, overall productivity, and strategic planning.

The next task was to identify all incidences of "formal analysis" carried out on the 27 issues. This required some kind of operational definition of the concept of formal analysis itself. Paradoxically, given the precision and accuracy conveyed by the idea of formal analysis, such a definition is not easy to develop. While conceptual writers (e.g., Lindblom and Cohen, 1979; Mintzberg, 1979a; Pondy, 1983) freely talk about the role of "formal analysis" in the abstract as any kind of systematic approach to decision making, most empirical researchers have restricted their investigations either to a specific type of formal technique (e.g., Greenberger, Crenson, and Crissey, 1976; Frénois and Chokron, 1982) or more commonly to work done by staff specialists of a particular kind (e.g., Meltsner, 1976; Kerr, 1982; Prince, 1983; Feldman, 1983). But the concept of formal analysis means more than any specific technique, and formal analysis can surely be carried out by anybody. To understand the role and purposes of formal analysis in general, I generated an operational definition of it that was broad enough to cover most of what the conceptual writers were talking about. Although the definition adopted is not as clear and easy to apply as methods focusing on specific techniques or staff groups, it is more general and could be operationalized sufficiently to be useful. The approach used focuses on written documents reporting the results of some systematic study of a specific issue.

For every strategic issue in the sample, all documents related to this issue were collected. This set of documents formed the raw material for identifying individual formal analysis studies and classifying them according to a number of criteria. Documents that were merely descriptive reports of events (e.g., minutes of meetings) were rapidly excluded from consideration. The remainder were examined in more detail. Gradually, a set of conventions was developed by which individual formal analysis studies could be circumscribed and identified in a fairly consistent way across the three organizations. Eventually, a total of 183 individual incidences of formal analysis were identified for the 27 issues in the three organizations. Then, as some of these studies were clearly more analytically sophisticated than others, content analysis was used to place the studies in four different categories. The criteria for classification, described in Appendix A, were quantitative content, length of report, time input required, the number of alternatives considered, and the

TABLE 3.1 The Number and Frequency of Studies in Each Category of Analytical Sophistication by Organization

	Servico		St. Gabriel's		CAC		Total	
Studies	*N*	*%*	*N*	*%*	*N*	*%*	*N*	*%*
Armchair	2	4.3	4	10.0	30	31.3	36	19.7
Short	4	8.5	8	20.0	27	28.1	39	21.3
Medium	15	31.9	15	37.5	15	15.6	45	24.6
Major	16	34.0	11	27.5	14	14.6	41	22.4
Unclassified[a]	10	21.2	2	5.0	10	10.4	22	12.0
Total	47	100.0	40	100.0	96	100.0	183	100.0

a. Insufficient information.

complexity of the methodology used. The four categories were labeled, in order of increasing analytical sophistication, armchair studies, short studies, medium-sized studies, and major studies. While the armchair studies were generally rather short and unstructured, involving the development of an argument based on relatively little data, the major studies usually required considerable quantitative data, multiple research methods, and a great deal of time. The distribution of the entire sample of studies between the four categories is illustrated in Table 3.1. This shows that very few lower-category studies were found for Servico, while a very large number were found for the CAC. St. Gabriel's Hospital falls somewhere in between. In fact, the absolute number of studies identified at the CAC was more than double that of each of the other organizations, although the number of issues examined was of the same order of magnitude. The difference is largely made up of reports of low sophistication.

Three data sources were then used to examine the role of these formal analysis studies: documents, interviews, and direct observations. Documents were of crucial importance in identifying the individual studies, in tracing the chronological development of issues over time, and providing a fact base for later interviews with decision participants. Over 80 formal interviews were carried out with senior managers, analysts, professionals, and line managers who were in one way or another involved in the development of the issues. In addition, I was present at 26 senior management meetings across the three organizations and was thus able to observe directly how people interacted with one another and how formal analysis might be used for some of the more current issues.

At the first stage of data analysis, I viewed the data as a large sample of 183 individual formal analysis studies, regardless of the issues to which they were related or the organizations in which they were carried out. Patterns were sought in the ways studies were used, and a typology of purposes behind formal analysis was derived. Later, comparisons were carried out to determine whether different patterns tended to be associated with different organizational contexts.

THE PURPOSES BEHIND FORMAL ANALYSIS

Interviews with people in the three organizations and conversations in meetings were the most important sources of information concerning the purposes of formal analysis. The interviews were loosely structured to allow respondents to answer in their own words. However, usually, when any individual study was under review in an interview, I asked the question, "Why was this study done?" or more pointedly, "Why do you think X initiated this study?" Other information about the purposes of formal analysis was available from documents, and this was used to complement the verbal information.

In developing a typology of purposes, a number of a priori factors (e.g., my knowledge of previous literature and my previous work experience both as a consultant and as an internal analyst in two different organizations) suggested possible categories. I was also concerned to be as exhaustive as possible, while producing a parsimonious classification with a small number of components, each suggesting a distinct reality. The main objective, however, was to reflect the data accurately. To do this, in my first passes through the material, I generated a large number of purposes, sometimes using terms taken directly from interviewees: e.g., "education," "assistance," "side-tracking," etc. These were combined together into internally consistent groups. The typology that eventually emerged consisted of four broad categories of purposes: (1) information, (2) communication, (3) direction and control, and (4) symbolic purposes. Within each of these broad categories, the original, more specific categories survive as variants. These are listed in Appendix B and are described below. Clearly, no classification is perfect, and another researcher might group purposes differently. The information and communication groups seemed self-evident in the data and correspond readily with other researchers' distinctions between instrumental and justificatory uses of analysis (e.g., Kerr, 1982; Meyer, 1984). Symbolic purposes for analysis were immediately very striking as a group during contact with the CAC, and they too have support in the literature (Meyer and Rowan, 1977; Feldman and March, 1981). The direction and control group has been less frequently distinguished by other authors. However, there were several important studies in the sample in which the main motive for analysis seemed to be to stimulate other managers to get something done by asking for a report. This seemed both distinct from other categories and important, and elements of it have been suggested by Dalton (1959) and Quinn (1980). Various definitions and labels (e.g., "attention focusing," "action") were examined before the final choice of a label was made.

It should also be emphasized here that it was not always possible to associate a single type of motivation with each analytic study. Formal analysis has a number of obvious characteristics: it generates information, it is a vehicle for communicating ideas, it focuses attention on problems, it symbolizes rationality, and it consumes time and energy. When people choose to initiate formal analysis, they are choosing a "gestalt"—not one particular characteristic of the whole. People may have several reasons for choosing to do an analysis. In coding the data, therefore, the four categories were not viewed as mutually exclusive. In fact, in the final coding, 55 percent of studies were associated with one broad type of purpose, 39 percent were associated with two types, 5 percent were associated with three types, and 1 percent of studies were found to involve all four types of purposes.

A special "purposes" data file was created for each study. This file included the following raw data items extracted from the complete data base: (1) extracts from all interview transcripts referring to reasons for initiating the study, (2) notes taken in meetings in which the reasons for doing a given study were discussed, and (3) all references to study objectives or purposes taken from the report itself or from other relevant documents (e.g., minutes of meetings, correspondence, etc.).

On average, each file coded contained information from 2.34 interviewees and from 1.34 documents. Twenty-one studies were excluded from the analysis because the information obtained was inadequate to make an assessment of the purposes behind the study. It is difficult to assess the effect of these exclusions on the overall results. However, the absence of adequate data on a given study is often symptomatic of the low importance accorded to it by people interviewed. Purposes were then assigned to individual studies by reading carefully through the special files to determine whether each of the types of purposes described in Appendix B was relevant to that study, based on the information contained in that file. The quotations from interviews given in the next section provide examples of the types of statements that were seen as indicating the presence of different kinds of purposes. Studies were classified solely on the basis of the information in the special files: the purpose had to be specifically indicated in documents or in the interview or meeting transcripts. Thus, the results on the relative frequencies of different purposes may be biased toward those purposes that were considered most presentable or legitimate in organizational terms and against those purposes that were less easily admitted.

To improve the classification and examine its reliability, a second coder reevaluated all the studies according to the same classification scheme. Disagreements were then discussed and resolved by requiring each coder to carefully justify his or her assessment. In their initial independent assessments, the two coders concurred about the presence or absence of the information, communication, direction and control, and symbolic purposes for 78 percent, 85 percent, 84 percent, and 88 percent of studies, respectively. Some significance tests were carried out on comparative frequency data on the purposes behind analysis (presented below). Given the imperfect reliability of the classification, the tests were carried out using the three different codes (two coders' ratings and an agreed code). Many of the conclusions are strong enough to be insensitive to changes in the coder. A similar approach was used by Staw, McKechnie, and Puffer (1983) in their study of justifications for organizational performance in annual reports.

The four groups of purposes identified for formal analysis are described below in more detail. Quotations from interviews are used liberally to illustrate the kinds of purposes identified, and qualitative observations are used to enrich the description.[2]

Information

Formal analysis studies are often carried out to obtain information to gain a better understanding of issues. As one interviewee put it, "I have to do an analysis, have all the information . . . as much information as possible." This corresponds to the view purveyed by much of the prescriptive literature on management, which presupposes that the person who initiates the study is in a state of uncertainty. Because information seeking is seen as a very legitimate motive for formal analysis, people tend to be very willing to cite such reasons in interviews. Moreover, most analyses generate some sort of information, whether this was the main purpose or not. Information collected is often later used to justify a proposal to others (a communication motive, discussed below), and it is rarely certain, even to internal people, to what extent the same information might have been collected anyway in order to take the decision and to what extent the initiator of the analysis was merely trying to construct a convincing case. For these reasons, the frequency of information-seeking motives may be overestimated here. However, it remains clear that this was an important motive for analysis. Fifty-three percent of the studies in the sample were classified as involving this purpose, based on the data obtained.

Information seeking via analysis could occur in various ways. Sometimes, the initiator of the study was seeking new knowledge open-mindedly: "It's very simple. I've always thought that to manage was to look ahead. So we absolutely have to install a system which focuses on what we want to do next year and brings together all the information in the organization." But information seeking can also be less open-minded, as people seek to confirm a tentative opinion: "We had data which led us to come to this conclusion. And a study like that, coming from outside, could help us validate and confirm our ideas."

Further information-seeking activity, especially at top-management levels is oriented toward the verification of other information sources reactively. This seemed to be particularly necessary when issues were highly technical and understanding required specialized expertise that was not readily available to senior management: "We're prisoners of the technicians, and they're not objective. At one point, we got the engineers involved simply to obtain an independent view."

Cases were also noted in which top managers asked for analyses, not so much to obtain hard factual information but at least partially in order to sense the feelings of a wide range of organization members, what might be called "pulse taking." In fact, at the CAC (though not in the other two organizations), the "call for papers" seemed to be an accepted way of simply finding out how organization members viewed issues: "I insisted that each and every one of that group write a paper on his own concerns. Then we'd meet for lunch and then swap the papers around and discuss what our points of view would be. . . ."

Communication

Formal analysis is also often initiated by people who have very few doubts about what should be done. They are already in a state of conviction and use analysis simply to communicate this conviction or to bring other people over to their point of view. "I prepared the report because I knew we had to justify the project," as one interviewee stated. This should come as no surprise—the phenomenon has been noted by many people (e.g., Bower, 1970; Feldman and March, 1981; Kerr, 1982; Meyer, 1984). In fact, there is a perfect duality between the information-seeking and communication motives for analysis. However, while information seekers are likely to try to maximize the number of independent sources of information they receive, we can expect that communicators would like to minimize this number—and retain control over as many of them as possible. Overall, it is estimated that 57 percent of the analyses in the sample were at least partially initiated with some kind of communication motive in mind.

Analysis used for communication takes several different forms. Often it is simply used as a means of direct persuasion by a line manager who has a project for which he or she desires approval from senior management. The manager writes up a study him- or herself or delegates a subordinate to do the work. There is often no pretense here that information was a motive for the analysis, and the communicator's own criteria for the decision may be openly quite different from that of the principal target: "We didn't really do it for the profitability but for other reasons. The study . . . that was just because we had to have economics of it for the Board. We had to have something to support the decision. . . ."

Sometimes, instead of doing the study him- or herself or delegating it to a subordinate, the initiator of a study asks an outside consultant or a staff person from a higher level to do the analytical work. Obviously, the communicator has seen that the credibility of his or her case will be enhanced if it is supported by an independent source. This manifestation of the communication motive could be called indirect persuasion: "Well . . . we were chicken—we knew that if we came with a study as important as this done internally by a couple of sparrows, our chances of getting it through would have been less. And also, we wanted to confirm that our ideas were O.K. It was half and half." This kind of communication activity overlaps with information-seeking motives, especially at the level of self-confirmation.

In other cases, the most important communication targets for formal analysis may not be at the top, but among subordinates or colleagues. In fact, although top managers often have on paper all the formal authority necessary to impose their wills, they are aware that things will go more smoothly if everyone is convinced that the directions chosen are the right ones, or at least that they are inevitable. Several interviewees used the word "education" to describe this phenomenon. I identified two approaches to the use of formal analysis for the education of subordinates and colleagues. Sometimes, information was generated (i.e., statistics illustrating the phenomena in question) and a direct appeal was made to the "pupil's" intelligence: "We're doing studies on this. That should help to convince certain people." In the second approach, emphasis is placed on participation in the decision-making process and developing commitment to decisions reached "collectively." "Education" in this mode may appear somewhat manipulative:

> We said, "O.K.—nothing is decided yet—we'll set up a task force to look at alternatives." And we did put forward some ideas. . . . Naturally, we favoured option A. But if we suggested that, they would have all sorts of arguments—we had to get them to bring it up themselves. So we came in and said we wanted option B . . . those were our "alternatives." . . . And so gradually through the discussion, they came round to saying O.K. to option A.

In another variant of the communication motive, sometimes people use analysis to communicate their points of view ("positioning"), even though they know there is little chance of influencing the organization's decisions in any immediate way. This is the communication counterpart of "pulse taking." This kind of motive was very common at the CAC and seems to account for a large proportion of the "armchair analyses" found in this organization. People seemed to feel a great need to tell others where they stood, or did not stand: ". . . there has been no attempt to consult with us about this. This is a vacuum I'm working to fill. I'm writing a paper on it. . . ."

Direction and Control

One interviewee explained, "They have to meet their objectives. . . . When they didn't do that, well, they had other people looking over their shoulder, and they didn't like it. . . ." In this research, cases were encountered in which managers initiated formal analysis not so much because they needed information, nor because they needed to convince anyone of anything, but because they wanted a specific problem solved or a particular decision detailed and implemented. Analysis was used for direction and control to focus subordinates' attention on issues and to ensure that actions were taken. It is estimated that 25 percent of the sample involved this kind of motivation, which obviously overlaps with information seeking and may also occur in different ways.

Line managers have responsibility over certain areas and often solve problems and initiate changes themselves. However, sometimes problems are first identified or major changes are initiated from above. In this case, senior management often delegated work to line managers by initiating a formal study and reporting process (direct delegation): "There are programs and activities which must be specified to reach the ultimate objective. Human and financial resources are required. Even if these have been identified in a macro way before, I think decision-making must be delegated." The details of major decisions had to be worked out so that they could be implemented and action could be taken. Requesting a formal analysis report describing in detail what was to be done was a way of ensuring that the line was responding adequately.

But what happens when direct delegation fails to produce the desired results—when line management lacks the skills or the inclination to ensure that the desired action is taken or that the given problem is solved? One answer to this is to send someone to "help" them—usually a staff person—in another manifestation of the direction and control motive for analysis: "It wasn't a question of spying or anything like that —it was mainly to help them. If they couldn't do it themselves, they were helped."

Symbolic Purposes for Analysis

Several writers (e.g., Edelman, 1985; Meyer and Rowan, 1977; Feldman and March, 1981) have suggested that societal norms of rationality encourage organizations to adopt formal analysis procedures in order to legitimize their activities and enhance their survival prospects, even though these procedures may not serve any immediate instrumental purpose. More specifically, because it is often used to obtain information, to rationally justify positions, and to prepare for action, formal analysis has come to symbolize information use, rational decision making, and willingness to act. And when many people are involved in a study process, analysis may also symbolize participation and concern with other people's views. However, the fact that formal analysis is carried out does not ensure that information will be used, that rational arguments can influence the decision, that action will be taken, or that anyone's opinion will be listened to. Analysis may therefore also be used to convey a message that is purely symbolic—to impress others within or outside the organization or to hide another less laudable motive. The following quotations illustrate various facets of the symbolic uses of analysis:

> **Symbolizing rational decision making:** The project would have gone ahead anyway. If we had wanted to use the analysis to say "No"—we could have done some more work, but it would have gone ahead anyway. It was a question of principle . . . you have something which goes through with no authorization or discussion—that scared me. That must not happen because tomorrow, it'll be something else. . . .

> **Symbolizing action:** Well, it was a way of making a decision to go ahead without making a decision to go ahead. So it was possible to say "We're moving to a new phase. . . ."

> **Symbolizing participation and concern:** . . . I think it was part of his campaign strategy to get support for his candidacy as CEO . . . but that's a cynical view. I'd also like to believe he was looking for ideas and genuine input.

Certain authors (e.g., Beyer and Trice, 1982; Meyer, 1984) have tended to use the term "symbolic" in a broader way than I have done in this study by including all noninformational uses of formal analysis in the symbolic category (in particular, those I have described under "communication"). However, when analysis is used for persuasion, the implicit message, "Here is what I want and here is why you should approve it," is not inherently "symbolic." It becomes so only if it is transmitted to a target who really has very little power to decide on the issue. The analysis may then allow the target to believe that he or she participated in the decision and/or took the decision rationally. Such cases did occur in the sample, and there is therefore some overlap between communication and symbolic purposes, but all uses of analysis for communication are not necessarily symbolic.

As several writers have suggested, symbols serve a very useful function in organizations, and skilled managers are masters of them (Meyer and Rowan, 1977; Peters, 1978; Pfeffer, 1981). But the symbolic studies identified in my research sometimes left people rather angry: "I'd much rather someone would say to me, 'Look, Dick, old boy—this is it. . . . Don't give me that crap.' " In fact, when symbolic uses of analysis were mentioned by interviewees in general, it was often either in a derogatory way (notably by targets of the symbolic message) or with a hint of conspiratorial complicity with the interviewer (by participants in the creation of the symbol): they were viewed as slightly underhand. All this may seem paradoxical, given that symbols are intended to enhance legitimacy. The explanation lies in the fact that a symbol loses most of its value as soon as people suspect that it is a symbol—and not the real thing (see also Pfeffer, 1981). It is conceivable that the studies identified explicitly as having symbolic purposes in my sample may be biased toward the less successful symbolic uses of analysis—less successful because their nature has been revealed explicitly (to the respondent, to the researcher, and therefore probably to others). Other studies, whose role is also symbolic, may not have been identified as such by participants because they have succeeded so well in their symbolic function that this may be hidden, perhaps even from those who participated intimately in their development. As suggested by Pfeffer (1981: 47), "management and politicians fool themselves as well as others with their symbolic acts." Moreover, if the illusion is preserved, such studies are also more likely to begin to serve substantive functions as well as symbolic ones. As Feldman and March (1981: 181) suggested, the dynamics of symbols are such that symbolic uses of information can be gradually transformed into instrumental ones as "individuals who request information are likely occasionally to find it useful, even to come to believe in the general utility of information gathering." The best symbol is of course the real thing, which makes empirical identification of symbolic uses of formal analysis rather difficult. Because such purposes are less easily recognized and admitted, they are also less easy to detect. Thus, although only 19 percent of studies were associated with this purpose through the classification process, this may be an underestimate. I believe that the results obtained here are nonetheless revealing. They demonstrate the existence of symbolic motives and provide indications of their perceived prevalence in each of the three organizations.

One other characteristic of formal analysis is that it consumes time and energy. Normally, one would view this as the cost of doing analysis. However, it can sometimes become an end in itself: analysis is used for procrastination. Formal analysis may postpone the moment of truth when a decision must be taken or may divert attention until problems resolve themselves. At Servico and at St. Gabriel's, this type of motivation was mentioned only rarely. But Brewer (1981) placed great emphasis on it in his evaluation of the role of analysis in government, and at the CAC, this motivation was suggested by several interviewees: "All I wanted was to be able to gain time. . . . " Other formal analysis studies would probably never have taken place but for the serendipitous occurrence, more or less unrelated to the issue at hand, that someone was available with a particular kind of expertise waiting to be used:

Then I bumped into Ivor by accident—I know him well because we used to work together. I said, "What are you up to these days?" And he said, "Nothing much—I've left my old job and I'm looking for something else. . . ." So we had a drink together and I said, "I have this problem . . ." and I gave him a small contract.

Not all human activity is purposeful—not even the initiation of a formal analytic study in a fairly large organization. Organizations of this size have analysts permanently on staff, and these people must keep themselves (or be kept) occupied in order to justify their existence. Because the use of analysis for procrastination or to keep analysts occupied is not generally perceived as legitimate, the symbolic aspects of formal analysis noted above are crucial to disguise such behavior, so these motives are grouped together in the same broad category.

THE PURPOSES FOR ANALYSIS AND ITS SOCIAL INTERACTIVE CONTEXT

The use of formal analysis has often been associated with the classical rational actor model of decision making and thus viewed as somewhat incompatible with political and social interactive processes. But from the above discussion, it should be clear that far from being incompatible, formal analysis and social interaction are closely related. Formal analysis would be less necessary if everybody could execute their decisions themselves, and nobody had to convince anybody of anything. In fact, one could hypothesize that the more decision-making power is shared between people who do not quite trust one another, the more formal analysis tends to become important. Formal analysis is often done to obtain information, but people also use it for communication, direction and control, and for its symbolic value in conveying messages of rationality, concern, and willingness to act. Even when they use formal analysis for information purposes, they may be checking up on other information provided by other people— because they do not quite trust it. To understand the role of formal analysis in organizations, it is necessary to understand how it is related to its social interactive context.

In the remainder of this article, the relationship between the use of formal analysis and its social interactive context is explored, and six interaction patterns are identified. I examine how the nature of the hierarchical relationships between the participants in the analysis process may help to predict how it is used. The frequencies of different purposes for analysis in the three organizations are then compared and these results are related to the nature of the organizational structures involved.

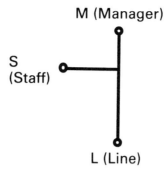

Figure 3.1   The Elemental Interaction Triad

Interaction Patterns

   To characterize the social interactive contexts surrounding the individual formal analysis studies inventoried, I identified, for each incidence of analysis, the "initiator" of the study (the person who first requested or suggested it), the "executor" of the study (the individual or group responsible for carrying it out), and the main "targets" (the individuals or groups to whom the study was principally addressed). By examining the hierarchical links between these three participants in the process, most incidences of analysis could be mapped onto one or more of six interaction patterns, built around the elemental interaction triad shown in Figure 3.1. This consists of a mini-organization chart connecting three types of people: a manager (M), a line person reporting to M (L), and a staff person (S). This staff person may be an internal analyst, reporting hierarchically to M, or an independent consultant. When the initiator, executor, and targets of any incidence of analysis are identified and linked on this skeleton organization chart, the interaction pattern for the analysis is obtained. Each interaction pattern is summarized by three letters identifying sequentially the relative hierarchical positions of the initiator, the executor and the main target(s) of the study. For example, interaction pattern "L-L-M" indicates that a study is initiated by line management (L), executed by line management (L), and sent up the hierarchy to top management (the target—M). By combining the three roles (initiator, executor, and target) with the three points in the triad, one could theoretically obtain $3 \times 3 \times 3 = 27$ possible combinations. However, many of these are either unlikely or seem to be minor variants of others. In order to create a meaningful but relatively parsimonious classification, a certain number of conventions for identifying line and staff people, for telescoping the hierarchy, and for combining targets were developed. This resulted in the six main interaction patterns described below and illustrated in Figure 3.2. Ninety-five percent of the studies for which sufficient information was available could be classified in this way, although some studies were placed in more than one category (see Appendix C).

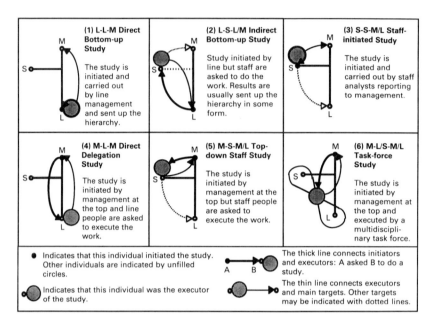

Figure 3.2 The Six Interaction Patterns

The frequencies of each of the major categories of purposes for each interaction pattern are presented in Figure 3.3. As indicated, several key differences between the patterns are statistically significant, both for the agreed purposes and for those suggested by the two coders separately. Moreover, the same key differences tend to emerge when the three organizations are considered separately, even though these organizations were structurally very different. The data used to construct the figures and to carry out the tests are presented in Appendix D. I now summarize briefly the implications of each of the six interaction patterns as suggested by the research results, using qualitative descriptions of the types of behavior observed, supported by quotations from interviews to build on the quantitative comparisons in Figure 3.3.

It was suggested earlier that when an individual chooses to initiate a formal analytic study, he or she is choosing a "gestalt" that has a variety of different properties. The data presented here suggest that different interaction patterns may correspond to different gestalts, grouping together somewhat different sets of purposes. Moreover, each pattern seems to have its own political dynamics related to the different hierarchical positions of participants, their diverging motivations, and their different knowledge bases. In the discussion of each pattern, I put forward propositions concerning the purposes behind this type of study. These propositions are supported by the data presented in Figure 3.3, although because of small sample sizes, I have limited statistical tests to grouped data. I also provide some examples of the kinds of political

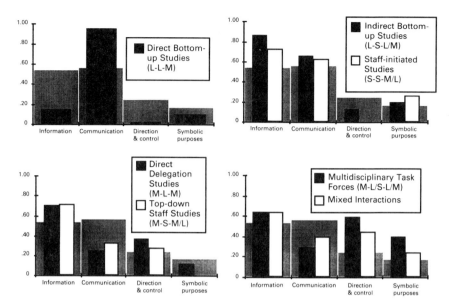

Figure 3.3   Frequencies of Different Purposes for Formal Analysis by Interaction Pattern

NOTE: The shaded background area shows the frequency of the four types of purposes across the entire sample.

Statistically significant differences between interaction patterns, controlling for organization:

Interaction patterns are often grouped together in this analysis to create sample sizes large enough for statistical tests, e.g., direct bottom-up (L-L-M), indirect bottom-up (L-S-L/M), and staff-initiated (S-S-L/M) interaction patterns are all "bottom-up." Direct delegation (M-L-M), top-down staff studies (M-S-M/L), and multidisciplinary task forces (M-L/S-M/L) are all "top-down." Mixed patterns are both bottom-up and top-down. The total number of cases associated with each interaction pattern is 47, 15, 11, 24, 18, 20, and 20, respectively (see Appendix D).

1. *Information motives are less frequent with direct bottom-up studies (L-L-M) than with the other pure interaction patterns.* Differences in proportions significant ($p < .01$) for overall sample (Coder 1, Coder 2, and agreed codes). Differences significant ($p < .01$) both for St. Gabriel's and the CAC taken separately using chi-squared test (sample sizes too small for test of differences in proportions). Differences in the same direction for Servico, but not significant. The Cochran-Mantel-Haenszel general association statistic controlling for organization is significant ($p < .01$).

2. *Communication motives are more frequent for bottom-up interaction patterns (i.e., direct bottom-up studies, indirect bottom-up studies, staff-initiated studies, and mixed studies) than for other interaction patterns.* Differences in proportions significant for overall sample ($p < .01$) (Coder 1, Coder 2, and agreed codes). Differences significant ($p < .05$) for St. Gabriel's and for the CAC ($p < .01$) using chi-squared test. Differences significant ($p < .05$) for Servico using Fisher test (expected cell frequencies too small for chi-squared test). The Cochran-Mantel-Haenszel general association statistic controlling for organization is significant ($p < .01$).

3. *Direction and control motives are more frequent for top-down interaction patterns (direct delegation, top-down staff studies, multidisciplinary task forces and mixed studies) than for other interaction patterns.* Differences significant ($p < .01$) for overall sample using chi-squared test (Coder 1, Coder 2, and agreed codes). Differences significant ($p < .01$) for the CAC using chi-squared test. Differences significant for Servico ($p < .01$) and St. Gabriel's ($p < .05$) using Fisher test. The Cochran-Mantel-Haenszel general association statistic controlling for organization is significant ($p < .01$).

4. *Multiple types of motives are more frequent for interaction patterns involving more actors (multidisciplinary task forces and mixed patterns) than for others.* Differences in proportions significant ($p < .01$) for overall sample (Coder 1, Coder 2, and agreed codes). Differences significant for the CAC ($p < .01$) using chi-squared test. Differences in the same direction for Servico and St. Gabriel's, but not significant ($p > .10$).

issues raised by each of the patterns, based on qualitative evidence obtained from interviews.

Pattern L-L-M: The Direct Bottom-Up Study

This interaction pattern applies to studies in which the initiation and execution of a study is under the hierarchical control of a single line area (L), while the main target is at a higher hierarchical level (M). The content of the report sent up the hierarchy is thus fully controlled by line-area management. People with independent access to top management have had no input, and the initiative lies not with top management but with the line area itself. This interaction pattern was often present in combination with others. For example, a senior manager might ask a staff subordinate to study an issue within the domain of a line subordinate (M-S-M/L, the top-down staff study). This report, or some version of it, is then sent by this senior manager to his or her hierarchical superior (i.e., pattern L-L-M, the direct bottom-up study). Only "pure" L-L-M studies (about 30 percent of the sample) are identified as direct bottom-up studies in the graphs in Figure 3.3. Those involving more than one set of interactions are classified as "mixed."

As illustrated in Figure 3.3, direct bottom-up studies are firmly and consistently associated with communication purposes. This interaction pattern was associated with attempts to obtain approval for desired projects in all three organizations (direct persuasion) and with less focused "positioning" by professionals and managers, especially at the CAC. Pure bottom-up studies were also on average less analytically sophisticated than studies using other interaction patterns. The differences were significant ($p < .01$) and consistent across the three organizations. Because their authors have a clear message they want to communicate, these studies tend to compare fewer alternatives and are clearer about the actions recommended than others. Moreover, because they are often carried out by line people, rather than staff analysts, simpler methodologies are used.

Given that the people who initiate and execute bottom-up studies are usually already in a state of conviction about an issue, and often have a personal interest in championing it, one would expect this kind of study to be received with a good deal of skepticism by its targets. In fact, bottom-up studies done by professionals (doctors at St. Gabriel's and especially artists at the CAC) were particularly likely to be ignored, as many were done for positioning purposes—there was little expectation that influence would be very high. It was also clear that for some professionals, perhaps more than for other managers, formal analysis was often only one relatively minor element in their strategy for getting what they wanted: "I prepared the report because I knew we had to justify the project. But on its own, it wouldn't have worked. I had to take other steps. . . ."

"Mixed" studies involving both bottom-up and top-down patterns are much less clearly associated with communication (see Figure 3.3) and tend to be more analytically sophisticated than pure bottom-up studies (differences were significant at $p < .01$ over the whole sample). In these cases, the bottom-up process was preceded by a top-down phase in which initiators of studies used analysis for information or for direction and control. It was noticeable, however, that when such studies were sent up the hierarchy in the bottom-up mode, uncertainty tended to be absorbed along the way (as suggested by March and Simon, 1958): the number of alternatives was reduced, and a more decisive tone was taken in the report. Reasons for adopting the course of action proposed were multiplied, and those for adopting alternative courses of action were suppressed.

Pattern L-S-L/M: The Indirect Bottom-Up Study

Here, the study is initiated by the line but executed by staff people who are not under the direct hierarchical control of the initiator. The study may be used locally, but it is also sent up the hierarchy in some form. The staff people used may be hierarchically responsible to top management, or they may be outside consultants, as in fact occurred with most of the cases encountered.[3] Here, the line controls the mandate of the study but has less control over its content than with the direct bottom-up study. This assumes that external consultants are usually more independent of study sponsors than internal analysts under the hierarchical authority of the line (L) may be. This assumption may not always be true but was clearly shared by people interviewed: "Well, coming from the outside and not being under the CEO . . . I had greater liberty of expression than other team members." Ten percent of the sample of studies used this pure pattern.

Indirect bottom-up studies are clearly associated with both information and communication purposes, as shown in Figure 3.3. Outside analysts are used to obtain access to expertise unavailable internally (information) but also to make the conclusions more credible to targets at higher levels (communication): "We didn't know. And when we don't know, we get someone from outside . . . and at the same time, that gives Board members confidence." For several instances of the interaction pattern, the initiator was in fact clearly looking for support for a preconceived idea. People in this position are torn between two more or less incompatible objectives: to control the content of the information sent to their superiors and to maximize the credibility of this information by making it appear to come from an independent and objective source. If line managers really do control the information contained in these studies, then it will be difficult to make them appear independent: "I didn't even read that report—I just filed it, because it was simply a commission—the consultants just wrote what he told them to write." And if the source is really independent, then control over the information is at least partially lost and there is a risk that the analysts will fail to come to the desired conclusions. A trade-off has to be made between the risk that the analyst will not confirm one's ideas and the potential return if he or she does. With pattern L-L-M (the direct bottom-up study), the risk is zero, but the potential return may also be low. With L-S-L/M (the indirect bottom-up study), the risk is higher and so is the potential return—with the level of risk and potential return increasing as the analyst moves further away from the initiator in terms of perceived independence and credibility with the management target.

Indirect bottom-up studies were typically more analytically sophisticated than those using other interaction patterns (significant at $p < .01$). However, several studies were also rather unclear about their recommendations. One reason for this is that there were sometimes discrepancies between the analysts' personal conclusions, based on their own expertise, and what the sponsoring client wanted the study to demonstrate. Typically, these studies went through many discussion drafts as sponsors objected to certain conclusions and tried to persuade analysts to modify their report. The result was usually a compromise: a report that made few precise recommendations and left much of the interpretation of the data to the reader: "So a firm of consultants was called in to do this study which . . . they didn't really recommend anything. . . . And the report was tabled, and it was a very iffy sort of a situation really. . . ." Deliberate vagueness to disguise differences of opinion occurred in at least three cases, all of them major studies, of three different issues. In his research on the use of operations research in the British Ministry of Defense, Kerr (1982) identified the same phenomenon.

Pattern S-S-M/L: The Staff-Initiated Study

In this pattern, staff people (i.e., those with no formal authority concerning the issue) initiate and carry out the study, which may be sent to line colleagues and to management superiors. Staff control the definition of the problem, the work carried out, and the destination of the report. The initiating staff person may do the study him- or herself, delegate a subordinate, or hire an outside consultant. The sample size is small here (11 cases), so the conclusions are tentative.

Staff-initiated studies are particularly associated with information and communication purposes. They may also be done by analysts to symbolize activity and usefulness. Staff analysts view their jobs as suppliers of information, and this is reflected in the motivation profile in Figure 3.3. But some analysts also became personally very committed to certain specific ideas. Their analysis activity became oriented toward exploring and advocating these ideas. Also, when analysts initiate studies, it may be partly because they have time and skills available that they must use to justify their existence. This explains the higher than average frequency of symbolic purposes for this configuration in Figure 3.3.

Consistent with the conclusions of other researchers (Alter, 1978; Wedley and Ferrie, 1978), few staff-initiated studies in the sample ultimately led to the implementation of what was recommended. In fact, this interaction pattern was used for some of the most spectacularly unsuccessful incidences of formal analysis observed. The pattern seems to go something like in this analyst's account:

> Well, so we initiated the process—and it was a pretty complex process I must admit, which quickly caused reticence amongst managers . . . because we entered a bit into their areas of activity. We questioned established ways. And they were ill at ease with that. And this resulted in all kinds of normal reactions . . . well, you get us to work on this but these deadlines are impossible . . . we don't have the time, etc., etc. . . . So there was some insecurity about the whole thing. . . . and the last point, which was the main point really because if we'd had it on our side we would have completed the process, it was the lack of the CEO's support. He said "Yes"—but when it was time to say, "Yes, and that's how it's going to be," he didn't say it. And from that moment on, nothing worked.

Of course, line-staff tensions occur in almost any analysis activity in which staff are involved in studies that overlap line responsibilities. However, the consequences are perhaps more strongly felt with staff-initiated studies, because, while the analyst usually has senior management's consent for the initiative, the senior manager concerned may not necessarily have internalized the analyst's driving motivations for the study. In the face of line resistance, his or her support may crumble rather easily. The analysts involved in the most dramatic staff-initiated disasters were clearly "intrapreneurs." They mobilized considerable resources and energy in the face of skepticism, opposition, and even (so I'm told) sabotage. However, they needed executive power to make changes of the order they envisaged. In the two most important cases (one at Servico and one at the CAC), full top-management support of the analyst and the success of the analysis effort would have implied initiating drastic action, including major structural changes that might have involved firings and demotions. The senior managers concerned clearly felt railroaded. Through their activities, entrepreneurial analysts tended to invade the territory not only of line people at lower levels, but also that of their management superiors. Staff-initiated studies seem to be risky. In my study, the risk never paid off— although based on a sample of 11, I can by no means claim that it never will.

Pattern M-L-M: The Direct Delegation Study

Here, the study is initiated by a manager, and the work is delegated to a line subordinate. The manager at the top controls the definition of the mandate, while the line fully controls the response to it. Independent staff people are not involved, although the line may use subordinates to help respond to the request. About 19 percent of the sample used this pure interaction pattern, sometimes in combination with a bottom-up pattern.

As shown in Figure 3.3, direct delegation studies are associated with information and direction and control purposes. They represent the use of "normal" formal organizational channels for carrying out analysis. This pattern expresses top-management confidence in the line's expertise and ability to implement decisions: "The analyses were done by the different functional areas . . . we said to ourselves, 'We have to have confidence in each other—we receive the studies and they are accepted.' " For these reasons, this pattern tends to be rather uncontroversial. It leaves full control of the content of the study to the line manager. However, if senior management is not satisfied with the information provided or with the actions taken, the situation could become more threatening. Persistent failure to satisfy management requirements would result in mandates being given to outside people—creating a much more tense situation: pattern M-S-M/L, the top-down staff study.

Pattern M-S-M/L: The Top-Down Staff Study

Here, management initiates a study and asks staff people to carry it out. Management therefore controls the mandate of the study, the staff control the content, and line people have virtually no control at all. This was a fairly common pattern, representing about 18 percent of the sample, sometimes in combination with other patterns.

As with direct delegation, two types of purposes tend to occur more frequently than average for top-down staff studies: the need for information from an expert source or the need for some kind of control with respect to line management (see Figure 3.3). Staff people were sometimes asked to provide expert opinions, information, or suggestions to managers that involved no contact with or intrusion into the domain of line people lower in the hierarchy. Sometimes, however, the motivation had definite control elements. Staff analysts could be used because senior management had been unable to obtain what it required by direct delegation to line management, and sometimes they were used to check out information provided by the line (reactive verification).

Certain staff analysts seemed to be particularly valued for their creativity and ability to challenge established ways of doing things, in spite of the fact that some or all of the time, their ideas were too "way out" to be given serious consideration or too theoretical to be applied directly: "His ideas can be a bit shocking—but they force you to think." This idea of the top-down staff study as a "challenge" appears particularly strongly when analysis was used for "assistance"—to stimulate action and problem solving on the part of the line (a direction and control motive). As one analyst put it: "I would say that 90 percent of consultant studies are not implemented. It has to be this way. If I was a manager, I wouldn't implement them either. The manager has to use his own judgment—he has to live with the thing—analyses only serve as a challenge."

Sometimes this type of study could present a particularly strong "challenge" to line managers. In at least one case, the line person involved was demoted as an indirect result of the study. Usually though, the line manager's job was not so seriously threatened and, in fact, staff people faced a difficult dilemma in handling the situation. To obtain the information they needed, they had to maintain good relations with the line, but they were often there to make recommendations that might reflect badly on the individuals concerned. Failure to maintain good relations would mean difficulty in obtaining information and a report that had little credibility. Excessive concern with good relations could, however, defeat the purpose of the exercise—to take an objective look at the situation.

The difficulties of maintaining objectivity also arose when top-down staff studies were used for "reactive verification," for example, to evaluate a project proposed by somebody else. Sometimes the line people proposing the projects were in fact more expert in the area than the analyst: "When the administration realized the problem, they asked me to take a look at it. But it is difficult to get the credibility. I wasn't really an expert—I had just arrived. What was missing was a really objective analysis." Moreover, over the long term, analysts would develop personal relationships with certain line managers, which made independent evaluation very difficult. In one of the three organizations, analysts were deliberately rotated round the organization in a conscious attempt to overcome the staff's tendency to develop loyalties that compromised their independence.

Pattern M-L/S-M/L:
The Multidisciplinary Task-Force Study

Studies in this category are initiated by managers and carried out by multidisciplinary task forces or ad hoc working groups. These task forces may include both line and staff people, or they may include line people from different functional areas (and no people in staff positions). The manager controls the definition of the mandate, and control over execution is shared by many people, with no one having absolute authority over the others. Seventeen percent of the sample used this pattern, sometimes in combination with a bottom-up pattern.

A combination of information, communication, direction and control, and symbolic purposes tends to lie behind multidisciplinary task-force studies, as illustrated in Figure 3.3. Task forces are ideal mechanisms for obtaining input and information from a wide variety of people concerning issues (an information purpose). They are also seen as an ideal mechanism for developing involvement and therefore commitment to proposals. Some task forces seemed more oriented toward top-down "education" of line managers and/or professionals (a communication purpose), rather than being pure study and decision mechanisms. Other task forces, notably at the CAC, where management was undergoing a crisis, seemed to be set up to gain time and give people the impression that they were participating in decisions (a symbolic purpose). Finally, others were established so that coordination could take place between various functional areas over the implementation of certain well-defined projects (a direction and control purpose). Often several purposes were involved simultaneously. As indicated in Figure 3.3, significantly more types of purposes per study were associated with this pattern than with others. The wide participation of organization members allows scope for many different motives and for many different political phenomena to occur.

In consonance with this, almost all task forces were the scene of interpersonal tensions of some kind. This was particularly true when there was ambiguity over the leadership and mandate of the study. Ambiguity over leadership was very common. Task forces were often set up with nominal "coordinators," but without formal hierarchical authority, power usually flowed toward the person with the greatest expertise, energy, and interest in the issue under study. There was a clear difference between the nominal and real leaders of task forces in at least six cases in the sample: "The problem was that the project leader didn't know anything either. So she was dependent on Bill and hating it." Another interviewee commented: "I was the one who wrote the report. He took the position of mediator mainly."

In fact, because of this ambiguity over leadership, task forces often provide a secondary battleground for career rivalries, even if people are not too far apart on substantive issues: "Everyone on the task force was hoping that he would be the one to take over this new unit." This kind of ambiguity and rivalry over leadership could be constructive if it encouraged people to be creative and gave them an opportunity to demonstrate their skills and leadership potential. However, when ambiguity over leadership was combined with ambiguity over the mandate for the study and conflict over substantive issues, the results could be disastrous. This occurred for one issue at the CAC. Management apparently felt that if everyone was put into the same room together they could come up with a consensus and that consensus would decide what should be done. In fact, the opposite occurred: "There were about 200 different viewpoints but there was no institutional viewpoint. We spent days and days arguing about various options . . . all sorts of technical details . . . but nobody stated what kind of thing we were really trying to do." Coordinated action across functional areas seems to require clarity of purpose on the part of senior managers who ultimately have to act as referees whether they participate directly or not. The wide literature on small groups (Collins and Guetzkow, 1964; Cartwright and Zander, 1968; Bradstätter, Davis, and Stocker-Kreichgauer, 1982) tends to support these conclusions.

COMPARISON OF THE THREE ORGANIZATIONS

The relationship between the purposes behind analysis and its social context is now examined at a more macro level by comparing the three organizations. Given that these organizations had different structural configurations (Mintzberg, 1979c), one would expect the overall social interactive context also to be different in the three organizations, generating different patterns of purposes. This expectation is confirmed, as shown in Figure 3.4. Although not all the differences observed are statistically significant, the CAC apparently used analysis less for information and more for communication and symbolic purposes than the other two organizations. Servico is the most information oriented, the most control oriented, and the least communication oriented, while St. Gabriel's Hospital generally falls in the middle but is the least control oriented of the three.

With a sample of only three organizations, it is impossible to draw firm conclusions about the causes for these differences. However, they do not seem inconsistent with the nature of the organizational structures represented, and it is therefore hypothesized that the patterns in the purposes behind formal analysis may vary depending on the organization's structural configuration. For example, the relative importance of information and direction and control purposes at Servico seems consistent with the machine bureaucratic nature of this organization—a structure in which decision-making power is concentrated at the top and where the technostructure is very important. In fact, the CEO here was well-known for defining in very clear terms exactly what was required in analyses. This insistence on detail at the top was transmitted down the hierarchy, because people knew that their proposals would have to be well documented: "You really had to be on your toes when you presented something at management meetings . . . he always had the right questions." If people did not produce information satisfactory to the CEO, they would be sent back to the drawing board until they did. Repeated failure to respond as required might ultimately affect a manager's career path within the organization: the direction and control orientation of analysis was very evident here.

At St. Gabriel's Hospital, the CEO was also an avid consumer of information and seemed very concerned that decisions should be taken rationally. However, although this organization could function in a similar way to Servico for administrative-type issues, it was not possible to operate this way for some

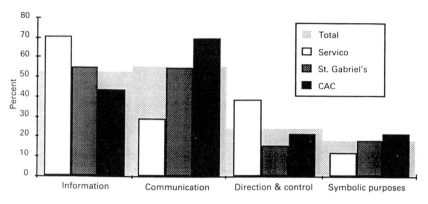

Figure 3.4 Frequencies of Different Types of Purposes by Organization (percentage of studies associated with each type of purpose based on agreed classifications)

| | Statistically Significant Differences in Proportions (one-tailed tests)[a] | | | | | | | | |
| | Servico vs. St. Gabriel's | | | St. Gabriel's vs. CAC | | | Servico vs. CAC | | |
Purpose	C1	C2	A	C1	C2	A	C1	C2	A
Information	NS	*	*	**	***	NS	**	***	***
Communication	***	***	***	NS	NS	*	***	***	***
Direction & control	**	**	**	NS	NS	NS	**	NS	**
Symbolic purposes	Values too small			Values too small			Values too small		

a. C1 = coder 1, C2 = coder 2, and A = agreed score. $N = 41$ for Servico, $N = 38$ for St. Gabriel's, and $N = 83$ for the CAC.
*$p < .01$. ** $p < .05$. *** $p < .01$.

of the most crucial issues in which medical staff were involved. Some of these issues were necessarily initiated by the medical staff members themselves, making bottom-up communication an important purpose for analysis. However, even when initiatives came from the CEO, it was not easy to use analysis in a direction and control mode as at Servico. Most physicians were not even on the payroll and could not be forced to comply with management requests. But although doctors could not be directed, they might be "educated" through involvement in decisions and exposure to relevant information. This contributes to explaining the relative infrequency of direction and control purposes and the relative importance of communication purposes here. This phenomenon is directly related to the professional bureaucratic nature of the organization, accentuated by the modes of remuneration used for medical staff.

The results from the CAC also seem consistent with its organizational structure as an adhocracy, but they are probably also influenced by the fact that this organization was undergoing a major crisis around the time of the research. I have already noted the large number of minor analyses generated here as people volunteered their views on major issues. This generates a high frequency of the communication motive in this organization. This exchange of opinions in writing was partly stimulated by professionals' anxiety concerning the organization's future. But although the organization's problems were certainly an important causal factor, such behavior also seems more likely to occur in an organizational structure like the adhocracy, which involves wide participation in issues and relatively weak authority relationships (Mintzberg, 1979b). Figure 3.4 also suggests more uses of formal analysis for symbolic purposes at the CAC than at the other two sites. In fact, as many more studies were done overall at the CAC, the relative frequency data in Figure 3.4 translate into about three times as many studies per issue done for symbolic purposes at the CAC than at the other sites. This was accompanied by a pervasive and overwhelming cynicism about its role. The following comments from people in three different jobs illustrate this:

Top manager: Studies—for me, they're nothing but a sidetrack. . . .

Professional: It's not necessary to write so much if you want to decide. If the objective is to avoid deciding, well studies are good for that.

Top corporate analyst: Most of the studies I have been involved in were not used to make decisions. Studies are used to support political decisions already taken.

Perhaps symbols may be more necessary in a structure in which many people are involved in decisions. However, given that my methodology may more easily identify the less successful incidences of symbolic analysis, another contributing factor may be the breakdown in organizational legitimacy that accompanied the crisis noted above.

A final question concerns the degree to which the interaction patterns explored in the previous section can explain all the differences observed between the three organizations. The question is, to what extent are these differences due to different relative frequencies of the interaction patterns, and to what extent are they due to other factors? To test this, linear models were fitted to the data shown in Figure 3.3. For example, to examine the importance of interaction pattern and organization in determining the frequency of communication purposes, the entire sample of studies was subdivided into six populations, classified by organization and by whether or not they involved bottom-up patterns (direct, indirect, staff-initiated, or mixed). The dependent variable was defined as the proportion of studies involving the communication motive, while the nominally scaled independent variables were "organization" (Servico, St. Gabriel's, or the CAC) and "interaction pattern" (bottom-up or not). When a simple linear model was fitted using weighted least squares estimation (SAS Institute, 1985: 173), both interaction pattern and organization emerged as significant variables (with $p < .001$). In fact, it appeared that studies at Servico seemed to be consistently less communication oriented than elsewhere, even within the same interaction pattern group. For information and direction and control purposes, only the interaction pattern variable emerged as significant when similar linear models were tested. In the case of symbolic purposes, sample sizes were too small to draw useful conclusions. An inspection of the results for communication purposes suggests that the way in which the data were grouped in order to create sufficiently large sample sizes for statistical analysis partially influenced the results. Communication is logically much more consistently associated with direct bottom-up studies than with indirect or staff-initiated studies. However, the pure direct bottom-up pattern represents only 15 percent of the Servico bottom-up sample, while it is 60 percent of St. Gabriel's bottom-up sample and 66 percent of that for the CAC.

A more conceptually interesting element of explanation for the differences might be that the professional status of the people involved in analysis may change the dynamics and purposes behind it within the same interaction-pattern group. For example, it could be hypothesized that for top-down patterns (direct delegation, top-down staff studies, or task forces) in organizations involving professional operating staff (St. Gabriel's and the CAC), top-down communication (education) may replace direction and control as a purpose of analysis. But, given the small sample sizes and the small differences (not significant) observed for direction and control purposes, firm conclusions cannot be drawn.

The study seems to indicate that different types of organizations may use formal analysis differently, in ways consistent with the nature of the structural configurations. Machine bureaucracies, with their top-down decision-making style, may use analysis most for information and direction and control purposes, to determine the substance of decisions, and to ensure that decisions made at top levels are detailed and implemented. Professional bureaucracies, in which strategic initiatives often come from the bottom up, may require analysis most for communication (direct persuasion) and information (reactive verification) as proposals move toward approval. Finally, in an adhocracy, the wide participation of individuals in decisions and the ambiguity surrounding formal authority may generate even greater uses of formal analysis for communication purposes (especially positioning and direct persuasion). However, other factors besides structural configuration could affect the relative frequency of different types of motives for formal analysis. The crisis situation at the CAC has already been mentioned as one possible factor explaining this organization's pattern of use for analysis. Other organizational variables with a potentially significant role could include leadership style, ownership (public vs. private), size, or industrial sector. Clearly, much larger samples of organizations are needed to distinguish these different effects and to verify the relationships between structural configuration and uses of analysis.

DISCUSSION AND CONCLUSION

Implications for Theory and Research

The study presented in this article was exploratory and inductive. The objective was to examine empirically the purposes behind the use of formal analysis in organizations as perceived by organization members and to determine the circumstances under which different types of purposes might emerge. Few links have so far been made with existing trends in organizational theory, practice, and research, although the results are relevant to four very different research streams.

Organizational decision making. Beginning with Lindblom's (1959) classic article, many researchers have effectively demolished the idea that strategic decision making can be accurately described as a comprehensive rational analytical exercise (e.g., Cyert and March, 1963; Allison, 1971; Mintzberg, 1979a; Quinn, 1980) and have suggested that formal analysis has only a partial or "incremental" role to play in decision making. However, very little systematic empirical attention has been devoted to determining exactly how this incremental use of analysis works. Most treatments of organizational decision making still use variants of the stage-based model (e.g., Mintzberg, Raisinghani, and Théorêt, 1976; Simon, 1977; Nutt, 1984; Fredrickson and Mitchell, 1984). But these appear to have limited usefulness for describing the incremental contribution of analysis to decisions, because they de-emphasize the social interactive aspects of the process that are seen here to be critical to an understanding of its role. Some writers focusing more on the political and social interactive aspects of decision making have become interested in the role of formal analysis (e.g., Pettigrew, 1973; Meyer, 1984), but this has rarely been the principal focus. My results suggest a framework for examining the different ways in which the incremental (rather than comprehensive) use of analysis may occur. In another article (Langley, 1990), I examined specifically how formal analysis studies intervened incrementally in the development of the 27 issues studied in this research, using the typology of purposes for analysis presented here. It was found that different dominant patterns in the sequencing of formal analysis studies tend to emerge for different issues and different types of organizations, confirming the suggestion made above and also put forward by several other writers (Fredrickson, 1986; Shrivastava and

Grant, 1985; Hickson et al., 1986) that structural configuration may be an important contingency factor affecting decision-making processes.

Information and principal-agent relationships in organizations. There has been growing interest recently in applying ideas from agency theory to the internal workings of organizations (e.g., Fama and Jensen, 1986; Eisenhardt, 1989; Allaire and Firsirotu, 1990). In fact, the organizational hierarchy can be conceptually viewed as a cascading nested set of principal-agent relationships in which superiors (principals) and subordinates (agents) have diverging goals, and agents tend to be better informed than principals. Agency theory deals with the ways in which appropriate incentives and information systems may be developed to reduce opportunistic behavior on the part of agents. This approach is complementary to that taken by organizational researchers adopting a political perspective (e.g., Crozier, 1964; Pettigrew, 1973; Newman and Rosenberg, 1985), who have shown that control over information is an important source of power. The results presented here clearly fit into this type of framework. They suggest that agents (Ls in my terminology) can be expected to try to retain control over information, while principals (Ms) initiate formal analysis partly to reduce their information disadvantage, sometimes via the use of staff analysts (Ss). In the mean time Ss are also agents for M, with other diverging goals and other types of information asymmetry. Moreover, they too may suffer from information asymmetry with L and may sometimes be induced to align their goals partly with those of L in order to obtain access to the information they need to satisfy their contract with M. This suggests that a useful and interesting unit of analysis in the study of principal-agent relationships within organizations might be the elemental interaction triad introduced here: Under what circumstances do such triads succeed in reducing information asymmetry and in aligning agents' goals with those of principals, or vice versa? The agency implications of these triads merit further study.

Implementation and the role of staff analysts. This study is also of some relevance to a large body of work on implementation, notably that which examines the factors enhancing or inhibiting the implementation of staff recommendations. Most of this work has focused on the implementation of management science or large computerized information systems (e.g., Doktor, Schultz, and Slevin, 1979; Schultz and Ginzberg, 1984; Ginzberg and Schultz, 1987). However, the key issue of how staff analysts can best achieve acceptance and implementation of their advice seems of interest to people in a variety of advisory roles, from management scientists to strategic planners to policy analysts in government agencies. As Ginzberg (1978) has noted, the literature has consistently identified two factors that enhance implementation prospects in this situation: top-management support and, most important, participation of line managers in the project. However, with some exceptions (e.g., Newman and Rosenberg, 1985), most of the implementation literature ignores the fact that staff people very often play a control role of some kind, even if this is not made explicit. In fact, as indicated here, the value of staff analysts to managers lies not only in their expertise but also in the fact that this expertise is independent of other sources of information—such as the line manager responsible for the area concerned. This suggests something that tends to be glossed over in the implementation literature, where emphasis is placed on the importance of participation, good line-staff relations, and the avoidance of line-staff conflict: The effectiveness of the staff-line dichotomy depends on the maintenance of a certain amount of tension between the two. When the tension disappears, the staff may not be doing its job. In fact, overemphasis on the importance of achieving implementation of recommendations may lead to a situation in which it is in the analyst's interest to allow him- or herself to be co-opted by the line. This study suggests that all staff recommendations do not have to be implemented for them to play a useful role in challenging line management. Other ways need to be found of evaluating their usefulness.

Institutional versus rational explanations for the use of formal analysis. In this article, I asked initiators, executors, and targets of formal analysis why it was carried out, and I obtained a series of answers. But perhaps I did not go far enough. There is always another why: Why was it so important to obtain information? Why would analytic information convince anybody? and Why do people bother so much about rationality or the appearance of it? Institutional theorists would respond that generally accepted norms force organizations to adopt procedures that are viewed as rational in order to be perceived as legitimate (Meyer and Rowan, 1977; DiMaggio and Powell, 1983; Zucker, 1987). They would further suggest that the public nature of the three organizations concerned would enhance these forces, because organizational survival in the public sector is more likely to depend on public perceptions that management is responsible and that procedures are "rational" than on objective efficiency, which may be difficult to measure. Institutional theorists have also suggested that when institutional pressures are present that force an organization to do things that are not consistent with technical efficiency, then the organization will tend to "decrease internal coordination and control in order to maintain legitimacy" (Meyer and Rowan, 1977: 340). The question is, To what extent did these organizations adopt formal analysis because of institutional pressures—or because of pressures for effective decision making? My research was not designed to test institutional versus rational theories of organizing. However, it is interesting to examine how these theories might apply to the three organizations studied.

All three organizations sometimes did formal analysis studies for external consumption: to persuade government agencies to release funds or to symbolize action or rational decision making. They were thus all to some extent subject to institutional pressures for rationality. However, only at the CAC, where symbolic purposes for analysis seemed most common, could the decoupling process suggested by Meyer and Rowan (1977) be clearly observed:

> Before, planning was done merely to present a certain image to the government. It was decided what image to present and a text was invented to go along with it and some figures were put in it. But it didn't bear any relationship to reality. It wasn't done to guide action. The results diverged more and more from reality and things became more and more untenable.

At Servico, institutional pressures for rational procedures were accompanied by very real economic pressures: This organization's outputs were more easily measured than those of the other two organizations, and its board included private as well as public shareholders whose concern was clearly with the bottom line. St. Gabriel's Hospital was a different and rather interesting case. At the time of my study, its adoption of formal analytic procedures seemed to precede institutional requirements rather than to follow them. The CEO had arrived in an organization fraught with problems and had turned it around. But, at the time, government organizations seemed out of step with his new, more rational approach: for example, the organization's first ventures into formal planning were viewed with some anxiety and disapproval by government officials, and the CEO expressed great frustration with government-controlled incentives surrounding health care delivery, which in his view rewarded bad management. The positive results obtained from this internal emphasis on rationality, however, ultimately enhanced the organization's perceived legitimacy both internally and externally, and this organization's use of formal planning and rational methods later became something of a model for others in the health care sector. Like Tolbert and Zucker's (1983) early adopters of civil service reform, St. Gabriel's Hospital was a source of institutional innovation, rather than a follower of institutional rules, at least insofar as the use of formal analysis was concerned. Given the above, neither purely rational nor purely institutional explanations seem sufficient to explain all uses of formal analysis in the organizations studied.

Conclusion

This study represents an attempt to determine empirically how formal analysis is used in practice. The study was exploratory and based on a limited number of organizations. However, it does suggest a number of avenues for further theoretical development and research. Most important, this research emphasizes that formal analysis and social interactive processes in organizations must be viewed as being closely intertwined rather than as mutually incompatible. At the micro level, it is noted that formal analysis studies are carried out within specific social contexts involving different people linked together in hierarchical relationships: some people request analysis, some do it, and some receive it. This study suggests that the purposes of analysis and the political dynamics surrounding it depend on who does what for whom, and, at a more macro level, it appears that the types of uses of formal analysis favored by an organization may depend on that organization's structural configuration. Given the methodological limitations of this study, these propositions need elaboration and verification using larger samples and different methods. It seems clear, however, from this research that a good deal of the formal analysis carried out in organizations might not be necessary if decisions were taken and implemented by single individuals rather than by groups of them interacting with one another. In its use for communication, direction and control, and symbolic purposes, formal analysis acts as a kind of glue within the social interactive processes of generating organizational commitment and ensuring action. Organizations that undertake a great deal of formal analysis may not necessarily be more rational—but they are likely to be more pluralistic.

NOTES

1. These names are fictitious to protect the anonymity of the organizations participating in the research.

2. Names and certain other details in the quotations have been disguised to protect anonymity, and some quotations have been translated from the original French by the author.

3. Because of this, a dotted line rather than a full line is used to connect "S" to the hierarchy in the diagram representing this interaction pattern in Figure 3.2.

REFERENCES

Allaire, Yvan, and E. Mihaela Firsirotu. 1990. "Strategic plans as contracts." *Long Range Planning,* 23(1): 102–115.

Allison, Graham T. 1971. *Essence of Decision: Explaining the Cuban Missile Crisis.* Boston: Little, Brown.

Alter, Steven L. 1978. "Development patterns for decision support systems." *MIS Quarterly,* 2: 33–42.

Beyer, Janice M., and Harrison M. Trice. 1982. "The utilization process: A conceptual framework and synthesis of empirical findings." *Administrative Science Quarterly,* 27: 591–622.

Bower, Joseph L. 1970. *Managing the Resource Allocation Process.* Homewood, IL: Irwin.

Branstätter, H., J. H. Davis, and G. Stocker-Kreichgauer. 1982. *Group Decision Making.* London: Academic Press.

Brewer, Garry D. 1981. "Where the twain meet: Reconciling science and politics in analysis." *Policy Sciences,* 13: 269–279.

Cartwright, Dorwin, and Alvin Zander. 1968. *Group Dynamics: Research and Theory.* New York: Harper and Row.

Collins, B. E., and H. Guetzkow. 1964. *A Social Psychology of Group Processes for Decision Making.* New York: Wiley.

Crozier, Michel. 1964. *The Bureaucratic Phenomenon.* Chicago: University of Chicago Press.

Cyert, Richard M., and James G. March. 1963. *A Behavioral Theory of the Firm.* Englewood Cliffs, NJ: Prentice Hall.

Dalton, Melville. 1959. *Men Who Manage.* New York: Wiley.

DiMaggio, Paul J., and Walter W. Powell. 1983. "The iron cage revisited: Institutional isomorphism and collective rationality in organizational fields." *American Sociological Review,* 48: 147–160.

Doktor, R., R. L. Schultz, and D. P. Slevin. 1979. *The Implementation of Management Science.* Amsterdam: North Holland.

Edelman, M. 1985. *The Symbolic Uses of Politics,* 2d ed. Urbana and Chicago: University of Illinois Press.

Eisenhardt, Kathleen M. 1989. "Agency theory: An assessment and review." *Academy of Management Review,* 14: 57–74.

Fama, Eugene F., and Michael C. Jensen. 1986. "Separation of ownership and control." In Jay B. Barney and William G. Ouchi (eds.), *Organizational Economics:* 276–298. San Francisco: Jossey-Bass.

Feldman, Martha S. 1983. "Policy expertise in a public bureaucracy." Unpublished Ph.D. dissertation, Stanford University.

Feldman, Martha S., and James G. March. 1981. "Information in organizations as signal and symbol." *Administrative Science Quarterly,* 26: 171–186.

Fredrickson, James W. 1984. "The comprehensiveness of strategic decision processes: Extension, observations, future directions." *Academy of Management Journal,* 27: 445–466.

————. 1986. "The strategic decision process and organizational structure." *Academy of Management Review,* 11: 280–297.

Fredrickson, James W., and Terence R. Mitchell. 1984. "Strategic decision processes: Comprehensiveness and performance in an industry with an unstable environment." *Academy of Management Journal,* 27: 399–423.

Frénois, Jean-Pierre, and Michel Chokron. 1982. "Les déterminants de l'emploi de méthodes scientifiques en gestion financière: Observation de deux décisions d' investissement." Rapport de recherche No. 82-06. H.E.C., Montreal.

Ginzberg, Michael J. 1978. "Steps towards more effective implementation of MS and MIS." *Interfaces,* 8: 57–63.

Ginzberg, Michael J., and Randall L. Schultz (eds.). 1987. Special issue on Implementation, *Interfaces,* vol. 17, no. 3.

Glaser, Barney C., and Anselm L. Strauss. 1967. *The Discovery of Grounded Theory: Strategies for Qualitative Research.* Chicago: Aldine.

Greenberger, M., B.L. Crenson, and B. L. Crissey. 1976. *Models in the Policy Process: Public Decision Making in the Computer Era.* New York: Russell Sage Foundation.

Hickson, David J., Richard J. Butler, David Cray, Geoffrey R. Mallory, and David C. Wilson. 1986. *Top Decisions: Strategic Decision Making in Organizations.* San Francisco: Jossey-Bass.

Kerr, R. M. 1982. "The role of operational research in organizational decision making." *European Journal of Operational Research,* 14: 270–278.

Langley, Ann. 1990. "Patterns in the use of formal analysis in strategic decisions." *Organization Studies,* 11: 17–45.

Lindblom, Charles E. 1959. "The science of 'muddling through.' " *Public Administration Review,* 19: 79–88.

Lindblom, Charles E., and David K. Cohen. 1979. *Usable Knowledge.* New Haven, CT: Yale University Press.

March, James G., and Herbert A. Simon. 1958. *Organizations.* New York: Wiley.

Meltsner, Arnold J. 1976. *Policy Analysts in the Bureaucracy.* Berkeley: University of California Press.

Meyer, Alan D. 1984. "Mingling decision making metaphors." *Academy of Management Review,* 9: 6–17.

Meyer, John, and Brian Rowan. 1977. "Institutionalized organizations: Formal structure as myth and ceremony." *American Journal of Sociology,* 83: 340–363.

Mintzberg, Henry. 1979a. "Beyond implementation: An analysis of the resistance to policy analysis." In K. B. Haley (ed.), *O.R. '78:* 106–162. Amsterdam: North Holland.

———. 1979b. "An emerging strategy of direct research." *Administrative Science Quarterly,* 24: 582–589.

———. 1979c. *The Structuring of Organizations.* Englewood Cliffs, NJ: Prentice Hall.

Mintzberg, Henry, Duru Raisinghani, and André Théorêt. 1976. "The structure of 'unstructured' decision processes." *Administrative Science Quarterly,* 21: 246–275.

Newman, M., and D. Rosenberg. 1985. "Systems analysts and the politics of organizational control." *Omega,* 13: 393–406.

Nutt, Paul C. 1984. "Planning process archetypes and their effectiveness." *Decision Sciences,* 15: 221–238.

Pettigrew, Andrew. 1973. *The Politics of Organizational Decision Making.* London: Tavistock.

Peters, T. J. 1978. "Symbols, patterns and settings: An optimistic case for getting things done." *Organizational Dynamics,* Autumn: 2–23.

Pfeffer, Jeffrey. 1981. "Management as symbolic action: The creation and maintenance of organizational paradigms." In L. L. Cummings and Barry M. Staw (eds.), *Research in Organizational Behavior,* 3: 1–52. Greenwich, CT: JAI Press.

Pondy, Louis R. 1983. "Union of rationality and intuition in managerial action." In S. Srivastva and Associates (eds.), *The Executive Mind:* 169–191. San Francisco: Jossey-Bass.

Porter, R., R. Zemsky, and P. Oedel. 1979. "Adaptive planning: The role of institution specific models." *Journal of Higher Education,* 50: 586–601.

Prince, Michael J. 1979. "Policy advisory groups in government departments." In G. B. Doern and P. C. Aucoin (eds.), *Public Policy in Canada:* 275–300. Toronto: Macmillan.

———. 1983. *Policy Advice and Organizational Survival.* Farnborough: Gower.

Quinn, James B. 1980. *Strategies for Change: Logical Incrementalism.* Georgetown, Ontario: Irwin-Dorsey.

SAS Institute Inc. 1985. *SAS User's Guide: Statistics,* version 5 ed. Cary, NC: SAS Institute Inc.

Schultz, Randall L., and Michael J. Ginzberg (eds.). 1984. *Management Science Implementation.* Greenwich, CT: JAI Press.

Shrivastava, P., and J. H. Grant. 1985. "Empirically derived models of strategic decision making processes." *Strategic Management Journal,* 6: 97–113.

Simon, Herbert A. 1977. *The New Science of Management Decision.* Englewood Cliffs, NJ: Prentice Hall.

Staw, Barry M., Pamela I. McKechnie, and Sheila M. Puffer. 1983. "The justification of organizational performance." *Administrative Science Quarterly,* 28: 582–600.

Tolbert, Pamela S., and Lynne G. Zucker. 1983. "Institutional sources of change in organizational structure: The diffusion of civil service reform, 1880–1935." *Administrative Science Quarterly,* 28: 22–39.

Wedley, W. C., and A. E. J. Ferrie. 1978. "Perceptual differences and effects of managerial participation on project implementation." *Journal of the Operational Research Society,* 29: 119–124.

Wildavsky, Aaron. 1979. *Speaking Truth to Power: The Art and Craft of Policy Analysis.* Boston: Little, Brown.

Zucker, Lynne G. 1987. "Institutional theories of organization." *Annual Review of Sociology,* 13: 443–464.

APPENDIX A

Classification of Formal Analysis Studies
by Analytical Sophistication

Table A.1 summarizes the scoring scheme used to classify studies as more or less analytically sophisticated. Each criterion was scored on a scale of 0 to 3, and the individual scores were summed to obtain a total from 0 to 15. The rationale behind these items was simply that studies that are more quantitative, produce longer reports, require more time, evaluate more alternatives, and use more sophisticated methods can be considered more analytically sophisticated. The scoring approach was validated by selecting three random samples of 31, 16, and 16 studies, respectively, and asking another judge to rank these studies in order of analytical sophistication. The Spearman rank correlation coefficients between the independent rankings and that developed using the scoring method were 89 percent, 93 percent, and 95 percent, respectively. The total scores from 0 to 15 were then divided into four equal categories, as described in the text.

TABLE A.1   Scoring and Criteria for the Classification of Formal Analysis Studies by Analytical Sophistication

	Criterion				
Score	*Quantitative Content*	*Length of Report*	*Time Input (estimated)*	*Number of Alternatives*	*Methodology*
0	At most one table, graph or figure and at most one page with quantitative data	<10 pages	< 1 person-week	1 with only minimal evaluation	Almost none: "armchair" analysis, formalized intuitive argument
1	At most one table, graph or figure and from 2 to 5 pages with quantitative data	10-24 pages	1 person-week to 1 person-month	1 alternative with substantial evaluation	Simple "soft" approaches only e.g., internal opinion surveys
2	2 to 4 tables, graphs and figures, or 1 table, graph or figure and over 5 pages of quantitative data	25-49 pages	1 to 6 person-months	2 or 3 alternatives or scenarios	Simple "hard" techniques: e.g., budgeting, cost estimates, etc.
3	At least 5 tables, graphs and figures	At least 50 pages	Over 6 person-months	many alternatives (>3)	Complex or multiple techniques, e.g., statistics, computer models, data from diverse sources

APPENDIX B

The Four Categories of Purposes Behind Formal Analysis

The following guide was used to classify formal analysis studies into the four main categories:

1. Information: Analysis initiated to obtain information useful in decision making includes (a) *new knowledge:* seeking information about an issue in an open-minded fashion; (b) *self-confirmation:* seeking information to verify a preconceived opinion or idea; (c) *reactive verification:* seeking backup information in order to check out or complement information provided by another or the same source; or (d) *pulse taking:* seeking input and opinion of others within the organization.

2. Communication: Analysis initiated to communicate ideas to others. This includes (a) *direct persuasion:* using analysis done internally (by oneself or subordinates) to justify or support a given project one wishes to promote with superiors or external influencers; (b) *indirect persuasion:* attempting to persuade superiors or external influencers by using an independent outsider (i.e., not a subordinate) to write an analysis on an issue; (c) *education:* using an analysis process to bring peers or subordinates over to one's point of view; may include use of analysis as "trial balloon," sensitization to issues through analysis, introducing information into a debate to attempt to educate other participants; may also involve participative analysis done in order to try to bring people on board; (d) *consensus building:* use of an analysis process to build a consensus on a given issue through exchange of views; or (e) *positioning:* writing a report to establish one's position on an issue or to structure one's thinking.

3. Direction and control: Analysis initiated to ensure action on the part of subordinates. This includes (a) *direct delegation:* delegating analysis to line managers, technical experts, or task forces for detailing or elaborating major decisions or to ensure action on specific problems; or (b) *outside investigation/assistance:* use of staff analysts, consultants or management outside area most concerned by an issue to investigate problems, ensure that actions are being taken, or to check on what is going on in line areas; may be used when management is dissatisfied with performance or when staff suggestions could be helpful.

4. Symbolic purposes: Analysis initiated for symbolic purposes includes (a) *symbolizing action:* analysis done to give the impression that action is being taken, that a manager has the situation under control, or done to impress others with the manager's dynamism; (b) *symbolizing rationality:* analysis done to send a message that a decision was taken rationally, or done "in case"—for security, to be sure that one can respond to any questions that might be asked now or in the future; (c) *symbolizing participation:* analysis done to give the impression that management is interested in line concerns; (d) *procrastination:* analysis done to gain time or to postpone decision making; or (e) *serendipity:* analysis done because of chance occurrence, e.g., the availability of analytical skills at a given time or done by analysts to keep themselves occupied.

APPENDIX C

The Identification of the Interaction Patterns

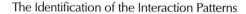

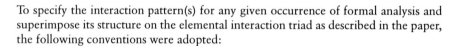

To specify the interaction pattern(s) for any given occurrence of formal analysis and superimpose its structure on the elemental interaction triad as described in the paper, the following conventions were adopted:

Definition of major actor types. "Line" people (L) are people who are either formally responsible for or deeply concerned by the issue under study. "Managers" (M) are hierarchically responsible for the line. "Staff" people (S) are individuals who have no formal authority over any aspect of an issue. They may be analysts reporting to managers, or they may be outside consultants hired by anyone. They could also be peers of the line, as long as their formal responsibilities are unrelated to the issue in any way. Obviously, the identification of who is a line person and who is a manager may shift up and down the hierarchy depending on the level at which analysis is carried out and the identity of the ultimate target. In addition, analysts reporting hierarchically to people classified as line are not considered to be staff but are members of the line group, as are all other subordinates of the line. Outside consultants are considered to be staff, whomever they ostensibly report to. The key assumption here is that external consultants are more independent of their clients than internal analysts, as is evident in the indirect bottom-up study.

Mixed interactions. When two different targets are involved in an analysis in sequence, two different interaction patterns of quite different appearance can sometimes be generated for the same analysis. For example, a senior manager may ask a staff subordinate to study an issue within the domain of a line subordinate and to report to him on it (M-S-M/L—the top-down staff study). The report, or some version of it may then be sent to the senior manager's hierarchical superior (L-L-M—the bottom-up study). Studies in which more than one interaction pattern must be used to fully describe the social context surrounding it are labeled "mixed" in the text: they involve the combination of a top-down configuration with a bottom-up configuration.

Interaction pattern M-L/S-L/M (multidisciplinary task forces). This interaction pattern was used to describe studies done by task forces involving combinations of line and staff people or line people from different functional areas and no staff people. If the line participants were all from the same functional area, and were directed by someone with formal authority over all participants, this situation was treated simply as M-L-M (direct delegation).

Several attempts to characterize the social context surrounding analysis were made before the approach presented here was adopted. The advantage of the current method is that social contexts are classified parsimoniously and fairly accurately without losing too much information. When this approach was applied to the analyses in the sample, it was found that six basic patterns could be used to account for 95 percent of all interaction patterns observed. The exceptions were not frequent enough to be of great interest. In other attempts at classifying the social context, an effort was made to avoid mixed interactions, but this tended to generate interaction patterns that were too complicated. Distinctions between different levels of analysts and managers and between managers and professionals were also included in earlier efforts. These distinctions may have some value as contingency factors affecting the interaction patterns (as suggested in the text), but when used as part of the definition of the concept, they tended to obscure similarities between situations and make the model more complicated than necessary.

APPENDIX D

Absolute Frequencies of Purposes by
Organization and Interaction Pattern (agreed codes)

TABLE D.1

Pattern	Information	Communication	Direction & Control	Symbolic Purposes	Number of Studies
Servico (8 issues)					
Direct bottom-up	2	3	0	1	4
Indirect bottom-up	7	3	1	0	7
Staff-initiated	2	1	0	1	2
Direct delegation	2	0	1	2	3
Top-down staff	5	1	2	0	7
Multidisciplinary task force	3	0	4	0	4
Mixed	8	5	7	1	13
Unclassified/other	0	0	1	0	1
Total	29	13	16	5	41
St. Gabriel's (10 issues)					
Direct bottom-up	2	12	0	1	12
Indirect bottom-up	2	1	0	0	2
Staff-initiated	1	1	0	0	2
Direct delegation	4	1	1	0	5
Top-down staff	2	2	1	0	3
Multidisciplinary task force	5	3	4	3	9
Mixed	4	1	0	3	4
Unclassified/other	1	0	0	0	1
Total	21	21	6	7	38
CAC (9 issues)					
Direct bottom-up	3	30	1	3	31
Indirect bottom-up	4	6	1	3	6
Staff-initiated	5	5	0	2	7
Direct delegation	11	5	7	1	16
Top-down staff	6	3	2	0	8
Multidisciplinary task force	5	3	4	5	7
Mixed	1	2	2	1	3
Unclassified/other	1	4	1	3	5
Total	36	58	18	18	83
Total (all organizations)	86	92	40	30	162

NOTE: Data for unclassified/other configurations are not included in the analysis of Figure 3.3 but are used in the overall comparison of the three organizations in Figure 3.4.

PART II

STUDIES OF GROUPS
IN ORGANIZATIONS

Social science folklore has it that studies of small groups in relatively isolated or socially bounded locales offer the most suitable opportunities for qualitative researchers to ply their trade. Groups in such situations can be intimately studied, their individual members known, and their activities carefully attended to and denoted. Such groups can then be dissected like fetal pigs and displays mounted of the group's division of labor, task norms, functional roles, and output, variously defined. All are well-known categories that many feel are best given description and measure by the use of qualitative research methods. Such a view is unduly limiting, however, because the qualitative study of groups in organizations takes on far more substantive and theoretical concerns than those tied simply to the internal functioning of well-defined groups. The three selections that follow, indeed, take the study of groups in organizations into far broader intellectual domains and, as such, put forth some of the most general theoretical claims to be made on the basis of qualitative work.

The first selection, "The Macropolitics of Organizational Change," examines and documents the shifting fortunes of small-group activities and ideologies in three countries between 1960 and 1980. Robert Cole's 1985 analysis of small-group activities in the workplaces of Japan, Sweden, and the United States rests on many years of following research literatures, interviewing key informants and recognized country experts, conducting organizational surveys, and observing and participating in group-based workplace changes in the three societies. The chapter is something of a study of studies disciplined by considerable scholarly attention and personal experience. The published result is a comparative analysis of what Cole labels the participative group movement. The grand story that emerges from the wealth of empirical material Cole has in mind and hand, however, is a cautionary and localized one wherein the ups and downs of the movement are explained in the main not by general social science concepts but by institutional and historical contingencies peculiar to each of the countries studied.

The second selection is a quite traditional group study in terms of focus, method, and representational mode, but not message. "Tightening the Iron Cage" is a closely detailed, ethnographic account of self-managed work teams in a single organization in the United States. This 1993 article by James Barker turns on the description of a value-based, managerially inculcated, and managerially sanctioned code of conduct—called concertive control—apparently governing individual and team behavior in the organization. So powerful is the code that it appears not unlike a quasi-Maoist device of the kind that terrified the Chinese communists during the Cultural Revolution. Barker's story is an edgy one, informed by critical theory and written as a disturbing realist tale of an organization in which resistance to the group is alienating and submission is comforting, perhaps even liberating.

The third and last chapter in this section plunges into a kind of underwater world of linguistic phenomena occurring in group settings. The Jacques Cousteau of this world is a conversational analyst with an ethnomethodological stripe. This is not the world of glossed, highly edited discourse and taken-for-granted normative features, but a deep-water microworld comprising forms of talk that manufacture for group members an emergent, rather fragile social structure. "Status Degradation and Organizational Succession" is an utterance-by-utterance study of the author's own dismissal as chairman of a small graduate student committee charged with opening a coffee lounge on the campus of a western Canadian university. Robert Gephart's 1978 study displays in almost painful detail just how conversational gambits, turns of talk, background knowledge, and interpretational schemes join together to produce for members of the committee a sense of the group as an organization with particular matters to attend to and important things to do. From the ethnomethodological perspective outlined in the study, the group creates an organization through linguistic practices and uses the resulting but usefully vague concept as a resource when confronting problems of an immediate, here-and-now sort. Getting rid of Gephart is one of these pressing problems. It is also a very practical problem, and the way members of the group recognize and subsequently attend to it is put forth in great detail and justified by a general and theoretically greedy set of principles.

The three studies that follow cover a good deal of ground. Cole looks to the macroworld of states and institutions for hints of the fate of the participatory work groups. Gephart looks to the microworld of talk to understand his own fate. Barker's story falls somewhere between these poles as he gives evidence of just how those stuck in an organization shaped by self-managed work teams make out. Personal experience underpins all three studies, albeit in quite different ways. But personal experience is also a reader's resource, since the degree to which each story rings true to our own lived experience becomes a test of verisimilitude and truth. There is perhaps no better test.

4

THE MACROPOLITICS OF
ORGANIZATIONAL CHANGE

A Comparative Analysis of
the Spread of Small-Group Activities

Robert E. Cole

Beginning in the early 1960s, a number of movements emerged in a wide variety of national settings for various kinds of worker "participation" in shopfloor activities. These movements seemed to promise to go beyond

AUTHOR'S NOTE: The data for the Japan portion of this article were collected during my tenure as Fulbright Research Scholar 1977–78. I am indebted to the Fulbright Commission for their support and to the Japan Institute of Labour for providing research facilities. I also express my appreciation to the German Marshall Fund, which provided a research grant for collection of the Swedish data. Research facilities in Sweden were provided by the Department of Applied Psychology at Gothenberg University. Data collection for the U.S. portion was made possible by a grant from the Henry Luce Foundation, Inc. I am especially indebted to the countless number of business organizations and associations in all three countries that gave freely of their time in an attempt to educate me in the intricacies of organizational change. While I am grateful to the institutional benefactors, they are not responsible for my findings.

My greatest intellectual debt is to Andrew Walder. Our joint working paper, "Structural Diffusion: The Politics of Participative Work Structures in China, Japan, Sweden, and the United States" (Cole and Walder, 1981), provided much of the framework and language that led to this article. Finally, *ASQ* reviewers and editors were most generous with high-quality advice. Reprinted from *Administrative Science Quarterly*, 30 (Dec. 1985): 560-585.

simply human relations and to reverse the historic process of deskilling that had characterized developments in the first half of the twentieth century (Bendix, 1974; Braverman, 1974; Nelson, 1975; Stone, 1975; Montgomery, 1976; Edwards, 1979). Usually initiated by management groups, these post-World War II movements involve efforts to change patterns of shopfloor organization from the specialization and compartmentalization that have characterized modern factory life. Often tagged as a form of "participative management" by their proponents, these new work structures tend to afford workers more participation in the execution of decisions than in their formulation. They usually include a stress on small-group activity, stimulating worker involvement in more facets of shopfloor operations and problem solving, and a more active mobilization of worker involvement and commitment than is common in most industrial regimes. To focus the research effort, I concentrated on small-group activities, rather than on those that expand the range of tasks a worker performs or those that involve indirect forms of participation such as membership on boards of directors.

Comparative analysts of participative organizational forms typically compare the structural characteristics and the value rationality underlying these altered forms of organization (e.g., Dachler and Wilpert, 1978; Rothschild-Whitt, 1979). Their agenda for research is to specify those matters over which employees are to exercise some control, compare the mechanisms through which workers are to participate in these decisions, measure the amounts of control these forms delegate to employees, compare the different value systems underlying different programs of participation, and evaluate the relative effectiveness of various strategies in terms of productivity and job satisfaction (see Tannenbaum et al., 1974; Katzell, Yankelovich, et al., 1975; Bernstein, 1976; Cummings and Molloy, 1977).

The comparative agenda here is different. The purpose of this analysis is to explain why movements to popularize these new work structures have been sustained in some countries and not in others and why when they spread, they are maintained to the degree they are. This involves exploring the processes through which diffusion occurs and the issue of whether these movements represent faddish episodes or have the capacity for more long-lasting impact. Most generally, the questions being asked are, why and how do organizations change? The answers to these questions are important in their own right, because the phenomenon of work-reform movements has generated considerable interest across several social science disciplines and through much of the world. Moreover, many of the considerations grow out of the issues raised in the human relations school, traditionally constituting one of the largest if not the largest body of empirical literature in organizational analysis (Perrow, 1979: 109).

An explanation of the differing outcomes of these national work-reform efforts is of theoretical import as well. Because the level of analysis in this study is cross-national and because the units of analysis are industries and national environments, the findings are directly relevant to two concerns that have drawn a great deal of attention in recent literature. The first is the impact of power and politics on organizational form. Much recent theorizing has stressed these phenomena as explanations for the course of change in organizations (i.e., Harvey and Mills, 1970; Perrow, 1970; Zald, 1970; Pfeffer, 1978; Burawoy, 1983). The bulk of theory and research, however, has focused at the level of the organization as a setting for politics—the "micropolitics" of organization. The cross-national analysis presented here, by contrast, points to the importance of politics and loci of power at the level of industries or nations, as well — the "macropolitics" of organizational change. Here, I also join those recent efforts to delineate more specifically the nature and effects of organizational environments on organizational change. These objectives parallel recent efforts by Burawoy (1983), though our research strategy and conclusions are often strikingly different.

By focusing on macropolitics, one can distinguish the forest from the trees in a way that much contemporary theorizing and empirical research fail to do. Thus, in the case of research on small-group activities, researchers will often report factors within the organization that inhibit or enhance the probability of success, with success being measured in terms of survival of the innovation or contributions to improved quality, productivity, or increased participation, or job satisfaction. These critical factors may include the mode of innovation, the amount of authority given to group sponsors and leaders, the make-up of the group, its leadership, the group's procedures and objectives, the nature of technology, how the small-group activities fit with wider organizational practices, the extent to which they threaten managerial prerogatives, and so forth. A pattern seen in other domains of organizational research is beginning to emerge in which we are left with a variety of often contradictory studies showing how under different conditions one or another variable contributes marginally to affecting outcomes. Perrow (1979: 96–112) documented just such a pattern in his scathing critique of the human relations literature. He showed how the accumulated literature failed to demonstrate a clear link between leadership and morale, on the one hand, and productivity, on the other. The application of increasingly complex research methodologies and causal models only resulted in a loss of applicability and theoretical power. The variables became so numerous that we could hardly generalize to organizations or even to types of organizations.

By shifting from the microanalysis of a phenomenon to an examination of the macropolitics, we create the opportunity to get a grip on the broader environmental factors driving innovation. As Perrow (1979: 110) put it, "it may be, hopefully, that any theory that has the power to explain a good deal of organizational behavior will have to deal with more general variables than leadership and small-group behavior." Perrow further suggests that in treating these macrovariables, we may assume that the specific *micro*variables associated with small-group behavior are randomly distributed and thus have little effect when a large number of organizations are being studied.

In keeping with this vision, I will show in this study of small-group activities the importance of understanding the position of the national business leadership toward such innovations and how this interacts with national labor-market conditions and the positions of national union leaders. The overall hypothesis is that this will produce a far better and more generalizable predictor of success, as measured in the spread of small-group activities across and within firms, than an analysis of the micropolitics of small-group activities would allow.

THE STUDY

The analysis is limited to three countries: Japan, Sweden, and the United States, and focuses on the period 1960–1980. These are countries in which the author has linguistic competence and has carried out field and archival research based on primary source materials and interviews. In the case of Sweden, in addition to the voluminous scholarly literature in Swedish on the subject of small-group activities (semi-autonomous work groups), the newspaper coverage was also extensive, and this allowed a different vantage point on developments. These data sources were supplemented with interviews of key informants and recognized experts in the unions, companies, universities, the employer federation, and research institutes. Volvo and Saab personnel were particularly receptive to discussions; as key innovators their cooperation was especially useful.

For the U.S., in addition to the scholarly literature on direct participation on the shop- and office-floor level, the author has been an active observer of the diffusion process of quality circles. My survey of some 176 early adopters of quality circles in the U.S. also yielded important background information (Cole and Tachiki, 1983).

In the case of Japan, a significant scholarly and management literature exists in Japanese on the subject of quality circles. Selected company visits and interviews supplemented this literature, as did interviews with employer federation officials and union leaders. The Japanese Union of Scientists and Engineers (JUSE), a key actor in the diffusion process, was particularly forthcoming in its cooperation and specifically in arranging for a variety of meetings with key informants. In addition, my U.S. counterpart survey of 302 early adopters of quality circles yielded important background data.

These three nations span a range of variation favorable to the comparative task. The United States is an example of limited change relative to the other two. Despite considerable advocacy of work reforms in academic and government circles, actual changes in the U.S. were rather limited through the 1970s. Of the other two nations, both of which have experienced significant although varying degrees of institutionalization of small-group activities, Sweden may be characterized as social democratic and Japan as liberal capitalist. These different political systems encapsulate considerable variation in the dimensions: group interest, labor-market conditions, managerial problems, political organization, and institutional mobilization.

INTRODUCTION OF SMALL-GROUP ACTIVITIES:
THREE NATIONAL EXPERIENCES

The United States

In the early 1970s there were extensive discussions in the United States in academic, government, and foundation circles about the need to "humanize work" and raise the quality of worklife for employees. The proposed programs for change carried various labels, such as job enrichment, job enlargement, job redesign, and job humanization. By increasing employee participation in workplace decisions, increasing job variety, and making more effective use of worker potential, it was argued, not only would the quality of worklife be enhanced, but organizational efficiency and worker productivity would be improved. The central argument made by advocates was that new work structures should be designed to allow employees to control aspects of their work that most directly affected their everyday lives. Small-group activities were central to that vision.

Efforts in the 1960s and 1970s to institutionalize these new work structures met with limited success. Generally speaking, most job redesign in the 1970s took place in new plants—often nonunion—with very little being accomplished in established ones (Davis and Cherns, 1975). Even in reputedly successful experiments, the innovation did not diffuse widely to other plants within the company (Walton, 1978). Widely publicized programs were often discontinued or scaled down a few years after their initiation, with little fanfare (e.g., quality control circles at Lockheed Air Missile). With few exceptions, American union leaders have been distinctly cool to proposed innovations affecting the boundaries and content of established jobs (e.g., Industrial Union Department, 1978). The movement received consistent support only from a scattered group of concerned academics.

Major institutional actors — management, unions, government—displayed little interest in introducing new work structures. The result through the 1970s was isolated, piecemeal experimentation. To be sure, not all such activities are widely reported nor easily counted. Some companies, particularly in newer industries such as electronics (e.g., Hewlett-Packard, DEC), prided themselves on developing a more participative management style than in the old-line manufacturing industries, without the adoption of specific programs. It must also be recognized that one's assessment of the degree of diffusion in the U.S. may reflect more one's initial value premises and expectations than it does any empirical evidence. Notwithstanding, as a general statement, it seems reasonable to conclude that *relative* to the changes taking place in the two other countries under consideration, movement toward adoption of small-group activities was slow in the United States.

The growing internationalization of the U.S. economy, and particularly the powerful competitive threat posed by the Japanese in recent years, has forced U.S. management and labor to reexamine small-group activities. While data from a 1981 national survey of firms show high rates of adoption and trial on the part of individual companies, there is far less evidence of institutionalization (New York Stock Exchange, 1982). The same survey shows that quality circles had the highest rate of growth of human-resource innovations and had become synonymous for American managers with the quality of worklife movement. Yet, at the same time, there is ample evidence of strong management resistance to accepting quality circles at all levels of management (Cole and Tachiki, 1983).

Japan

The Japanese movement began in the early 1960s and accelerated after the middle of that decade. To be sure, there were prewar cultural models as manifested in the use of small work groups for solving productivity problems. But overall, strong authoritarianism and hierarchy were the central prewar legacies.

The key organizing principle for the postwar innovations is known as "small group-ism" (*shōshūdanshugi*). Management focused on decentralization of decision making. Employees were to assume increasing responsibilities for a variety of everyday functions—most notably maintenance, safety, and quality control—that previously had been the province of management representatives. The vehicle for this increased responsibility was small-group organization. By the late 1970s, various Japanese surveys estimate that some 50 percent of Japanese firms with more than 30 employees were practicing some form of decentralized decision making based on small-group activities (Cole, 1979: 135). Quality circles were among the most popular forms, with 1.7 million registered members accounted for by 200,000 registered circles; the number of unregistered circles is conservatively estimated to be four times that number.

Quality circles typically meet on the average of one hour a week and are relatively autonomous units composed of a small group of production or clerical workers from each workplace. The workers are taught elementary statistical techniques and modes of problem solving and are guided by their leaders in selecting and solving job-related quality problems and improving methods of production. While workers participate in decision making through these kinds of small-group activities, it is clear that this approach does not threaten the hierarchical structure of management authority. Foremen have not been significantly threatened by the reforms, in part because they typically serve as circle leaders.

Sweden

Swedish efforts to develop new work structures began in the late 1960s, with an emphasis on autonomous self-steering work groups (*självstyrande grupper*) as the basic unit of production organization. These ideas spread rapidly, accompanied by a long and intensive public debate on the need for democratized industrial organization in Swedish society. While the diffusion of such practices has clearly been more limited than in Japan, the actual extent to which these practices have been institutionalized is difficult to specify. This is, in part, because there has not been an extensive system of formal registration and surveys as in Japan. The ideal of the autonomous work group, with workers making all their own decisions regarding work allocation, recruitment, planning, budgeting, and purchasing (Agervold, 1975: 46–65) is rare in actual practice. Yet, modified versions of this decentralized system of work organization appear in most large Swedish firms. One contrast with the Japanese case is that early Swedish efforts—in part because of the political setting of social democracy—explicitly challenged the hierarchy of managerial authority, particularly that of foremen. Consequently, middle managerial opposition was more common than in Japan, leading to a less complete diffusion of small-group activities.

General Observations on the Cases

The contrast of the U.S. with the experiences of Japan and Sweden is striking. In each of the latter countries over the past two decades, small-group activities in one form or another have been adopted and sustained to a considerable degree. Despite wide differences in culture, economy, and politics, the Japanese and Swedish initiatives all have emphasized the small group as the core unit of workshop organization and participation in these small groups as a source of work motivation. In comparing the Swedish and Japanese experiences, one could say that the Swedes tried more and accomplished less while the Japanese tried less and accomplished more. By contrast, the Americans tried still less and accomplished very little.

In thinking about the dependent variable — the spread and institutionalization of small-group activities in the three nations — it is clear that reporting on the three national experiences is like comparing apples and oranges. In practice, availability of data and the nature of the three national experiences led us to compare the evolution of quality circles in the U.S. and Japan and semiautonomous work groups in Sweden. Quality circles are "off-line" activities, that is, workers engaged in these problem-solving teams separate from their "normal work" activities. Semiautonomous groups, however, are designed to give teams of workers more control over the work process itself.

In Japan, the language used to describe the key innovations was decentralization of responsibility, and the term participation seldom appeared. In the U.S., the debate was dominated by the terms participation in management, QWL (Quality of Worklife), and EI (Employee Involvement). In Sweden, the notions of joint influence and democratization of the workplace punctuated the early debate.

This different language is not a random phenomenon. It tells us a great deal about objectives and who were the central actors controlling the debate in each country. In the case of Japan, focusing the debate on decentralization of responsibility tells us that management was in charge; they could impose their own categories and labels on developments. In Sweden, the focus on industrial democracy tells us, first, that management did not have full control of the agenda of solutions and definition of problems. Moreover, the Swedes had a highly centralized labor-management decision-making system. This meant that advocates of small-group activities within labor, management, and academic circles could argue forcefully and believably that there was something missing at the shop- and office-floor level in terms of democratic decision making and that semiautonomous work groups could fill this vacuum. In the U.S., unlike many Western European countries, the labor movement had an active shopfloor presence. This preempted to a large extent the industrial democracy theme at the shop-floor level and, instead, there is a rather more modest focus on participation, leadership, and employee involvement.

It would be an artificial and sterile exercise to try to winnow down these different approaches to small-group activities to the lowest common denominator so as to assure an identical dependent variable across countries. Rather, the tack taken here is to acknowledge these differences and take them into account in explaining the extent to which small-group activities diffused in the three countries and how and why they took the different forms they did.

Although management has been the primary initiator of these new work structures, there is another driving force. Underlying the initiative in Sweden, and to a far lesser extent in the U.S., is a focus on industrial democracy. Fuller participation in the decisions of the firm and over one's daily activities is seen as contributing to the democratization of the firm. Burawoy (1983: 602–603) ignored this theme, though many unions, most notably in Sweden, stressed industrial democracy as a basis for cooperating in the initiation and shaping of these new activities. Even in the United States, union supporters have heavily stressed the theme of industrial democracy (Bluestone, 1978: 21–24). How this additional driving force interacts, complements, or opposes management initiatives is a matter for empirical examination in each nation, industry, and firm.

Managerial Interests and the Incentives to Innovate

Improving the quality of working life and reducing worker alienation and self-actualization are the benefits of small-group activities most often stressed by academic proponents. Industrial administrators, however, are less motivated by these sorts of concerns, and it is they who must introduce and institutionalize these innovations. Management is concerned more with performance and economic payoff. To understand the diffusion of small-group activities, we must look more closely at the forces driving management to change existing practices; we must look for something other than a liberal reforming impulse.

Sweden and Japan

Extensive interviews with Japanese and Swedish managers and an examination of the relevant literature in these countries make clear that the driving force for innovation was quite similar in both cases. Both countries have faced severe labor-shortage problems over the last two decades.

In Japan, industrial employers confronted an increasingly tight labor market in the late 1960s and early 1970s. It became more difficult for the major manufacturing firms to recruit and retain those select employees they desired (Minami, 1973). Compared with the United States, labor turnover in Japanese industry was still quite low, but it occurred in the context of a serious shortage of recent male graduates entering the labor force, especially middle-school graduates. Replacing existing workers was thus both difficult and costly because there was no pool of workers willing to take the most disagreeable jobs in the manufacturing sector. Political and economic leaders considered and later rejected Southeast Asian immigration as a desirable option.

Rapidly rising educational levels in Japan, further, led to an increasing proportion of new labor-force entrants who were unwilling to accept the least demanding jobs. The educational system was producing an increasing number of high school graduates who had come to expect white-collar jobs commensurate with their educational levels. Instead, an increasing number were being assigned to blue-collar jobs.

By the late 1960s and early 1970s the labor shortage was most serious for those manufacturing sectors that had the most standardized and routinized jobs and were characterized by hard physical labor under difficult conditions.

Surveys reported extremely high turnover among new recruits to these industries (Ministry of Labour, 1974: 72). These circumstances constituted an important motivational force for Japanese managements to search for solutions to minimize their problems. Small-group activities appeared to be one possible strategy to make firms more attractive to well-educated potential recruits, thereby reducing turnover and labor unrest and contributing to productivity and quality goals. There was, however, little assurance of the outcome, and innovators operated under great ambiguity and uncertainty. Furthermore, other strategies were pursued simultaneously, such as locating labor-intensive production facilities off-shore, in Southeast Asia. Firms in industries that suffered most from recruitment and retention problems— notably automobiles and steel—were some of the most active in early efforts at innovation. All this occurred in a context of growth in internationalization of the economy and resultant concerns that managers must make better use of their human resources if they were to survive in world competition.

The labor situation facing Swedish managers was similar but even more serious than in Japan. In Sweden a severe labor shortage had developed by the mid-1960s, educational levels had also risen rapidly, and labor-force entrants were increasingly unwilling to accept routine or arduous jobs. Swedish employers sought initially to alleviate these problems by acting to expand the labor force. They began more actively and quite successfully to recruit economically inactive women. A second strategy was to increase the employment of migrant aliens. The number of aliens taking jobs in Sweden increased steadily to 20 percent of total employment in the mining and manufacturing sectors (Statistiska Centralbyrån, 1978: 195).

By the late 1960s, Swedish manufacturers became increasingly disenchanted with the above strategies. It was still difficult for them to find enough workers to fill the least desirable jobs. Moreover, they were having to rely on what they considered to be labor of the lowest quality, and the large influx into Sweden of foreigners, concentrated in the least desirable jobs, came to be seen as a threatening social problem. Absenteeism and turnover, further, swelled to unprecedented proportions. Annual employee turnover reached 50 percent during 1970 in a number of metropolitan industries—notably auto manufacturing. Sweden's legislated unemployment and sick-pay benefits had made turnover and absenteeism relatively costless to employees.

All of these factors spurred management to consider strategies for restructuring work to bring native male Swedish workers back into the factories and cut turnover and absenteeism to manageable proportions. As in Japan, major innovations in work structures took place in precisely those industries suffering the most severe recruitment, turnover, and absenteeism problems.[1] Volvo Corporation, the largest Swedish private firm, experienced some of the most severe problems and later achieved fame as an innovator in creating new work structures. Multiskill training and teaching employees a fuller range of job tasks were part of the approach to small-group activities in Sweden. These practices facilitated a work-floor adjustment to high rates of absenteeism and turnover.

The United States

It is instructive to contrast the United States with Japan and Sweden. A large pool of unemployed labor exists in the United States to fill the most disagreeable jobs. Despite high rates, by world standards, of labor turnover, replacements have been readily available through this pool. This constituted a major barrier to the diffusion of small-group activities in the United States in the 1970s —there were no obvious economic incentives to interest managers in innovation. Until Japanese competition became impossible to ignore in the late 1970s, no pressing managerial problems triggered searches for new methods (Wool, 1973: 38–44).

The differences between the U.S. and Sweden and Japan are most striking in the auto industries during the early 1970s. Swedish auto officials found that some U.S. auto plants had turnover figures similar to Swedish auto firms —around 50 percent per year. Surprised that most American managers did not perceive this as a serious problem, they concluded that U.S. managers were accustomed to greater job mobility of workers and reasoned that they could train people for simple jobs so quickly that the turnover figures did not matter (Gyllenhammar, 1977: 7–9). Indeed, the assumption that large quantities of unskilled labor would circulate annually through the firm reinforced the strategy of using industrial engineers to increasingly simplify job content.

Although the original GM-UAW agreement on Quality of Worklife (QWL) was signed in 1973, little occurred until the late 1970s, despite selected "showcase" plants. Innovation that did occur was often piecemeal, rather than through the more systemic approach developed in Sweden (Tichy and Nisberg, 1976). Although Kanter (1983: 221–347) documented high-level management concerns with participative management as a solution to problems with turnover and absenteeism within GM in the early 1970s, it is striking how long such discussions were confined to the corporate level.

It was not until the Japanese threat of the late 1970s and early 1980s that U.S. auto manufacturers began broadly to operationalize solutions addressing the costs of high rates of absenteeism and turnover. They came to conclude that they were suffering a competitive disadvantage from failing to mobilize their human resources through a participative strategy. Data from our 1981 survey of the universe of early adopters of quality circles reveal that the greatest number of adopters were in automotive parts and manufacturing and the electronics industries (Cole and Tachiki, 1983). Early adopters tended to be in manufacturing sectors characterized by highly labor-intensive industries, industries in which quality has been a high priority in the past, and those in which quality and costs have received new emphasis as a result of Japanese competition. Auto and electronics both partially fit this characterization, although they differ in degrees of unionization, rate of growth, etc.

IDEOLOGY AND ORGANIZATION: MOBILIZING FOR STRUCTURAL CHANGE

If our preceding descriptions are accurate, we would expect the relative interests of major institutional actors to be reflected in the emergent national infrastructures for diffusing small-group activities. Specifically, one would predict that when at least one of the major parties to the labor market—especially management, given its leadership position in market economies—becomes strongly committed to small-group activities as a solution, a well-organized national infrastructure will be created. Through definition and publicizing of "best practices" and providing legitimacy, such organizations provide the national leadership critical to the emergent movement as it develops at the plant level.

In the cases of Japan and Sweden, the major incentive for management to develop this commitment to innovate was an evolving set of managerial problems relating to labor shortage that made earlier strategies ineffective. Motivation, however, is a necessary but insufficient condition for change. Managerial groups have to mobilize to implement these innovations. This has involved, in each case, the articulation of an ideology that justifies these changes and serves to persuade other members of the industrial community either to support or not to resist them.[2] It also involves the creation of an organized infrastructure of communication and organization with which the resources of the innovating groups can be mobilized and changes introduced and institutionalized in firms. The emergence of a national infrastructure reflects the consensus of top management that they have identified the direction in which they would like to move; its leaders articulate the ideology that legitimates the new movement. It is this interplay of ideology and organization that is at the core of the rapid spread of new organizational practices. Without such an interplay, the emergent practices are more likely to assume the status of fad.

The United States: Late and Weak Managerial Mobilization

American managers had little incentive to reform existing work structures in the 1960s and 1970s. As a result, organization and mobilization for the diffusion of participative work structures involved "mavericks" trying to convince managements that such innovations were in their interest. These advocates were primarily from loose networks of academics, management experts, and occasional businessmen and union leaders. On this basis we would expect that the organized efforts to spread small-group activities would vary markedly from the same processes in Japan and Sweden.

Failing strong interest by the national business leadership, "outside" organizations like the Ford Foundation sought to stimulate institution building in the 1970s. However, achievements have been quite modest relative to what occurred in Sweden and Japan. Government-encouraged initiatives proved to be of modest value because of sharp fluctuations in the level of government support and because the government was not in a position or prepared to provide management the long-term incentives that were necessary.

With the upsurge of experimentation in the U.S. in the 1980s, there has been a notable increase in the activities of various research and training organizations focusing on small-group activities, in particular, the American Society for Training and Development, the American Management Association, and the OD Network. These kinds of organizations are not likely to create a national infrastructure, but they do supply much of the raw material for supporting its emergence.

Although there were a number of possible contenders for leadership of the small-group activity movement in the U.S., none individually or collectively have come to play the same extensive role as key organizations did in Sweden and Japan. Existing national organizations reflecting top-management interests, like the National Association of Manufacturers, the Chamber of Commerce, and the Business Roundtable, saw the locus of their activities as Washington, with lobbying as the chosen method to achieve their ends.

Other organizations interested in the participation movement, such as the Work in America Institute, focused on improving labor-management relationships in the unionized sector, primarily through labor-management committees. This calls attention to a major problem in building an integrated national infrastructure in the United States. Those who focus on working with the unionized sector ignore 80 percent of the labor force. Those who include the nonunionized sector invite the suspicions of the unions that the real agenda is union busting. The failure of big business to accept unions as a legitimate force in the U.S. has worked against building a national infrastructure for small-group activities and has led, rather, to a splintering of efforts.

The American Society of Quality Control (ASQC) was a different kind of contender. It is a voluntary professional association composed primarily of middle-management specialists in quality. ASQC members did not, however, have a great deal of status in their firms. Just as importantly, ASQC proved to be so tied up in knots by their bureaucratic structure of rules regulating organizational innovation and limited by their reliance on volunteer labor that they failed to provide leadership for the small-group activity movement.

The American Productivity Center, established in 1977 with top-management support from key business organizations, was a clear candidate for providing nationally recognized leadership for the small-group activity movement. For the most part, especially in its early years, however, its high-level corporate sponsors and board members saw the path to productivity improvement in terms of traditional approaches, like enhancing availability of capital at favorable terms, technology investment, and taxation policy. Again, these individuals were more at home negotiating and lobbying for solutions in Washington than in the factories and offices of America. Union leaders on the board were just as comfortable focusing on the "big issues" associated with traditional labor-management concerns. Yet, support for small-group activities in terms of their productivity and quality payoffs requires the acceptance of a view that many small changes, in the aggregate, yield big changes.

The closest thing to a national organization designed to promote small-group activities is the International Association of Quality Circles (IAQC), begun in 1977 by two consultants; it served at least indirectly to promote their own business. That in itself is typically American. The organization officially reported some 7,000 members by the mid-1980s, and 90 chapters. It conducts a great deal of introductory training in circle activity and promotes national conferences.

While these are not insignificant achievements for a volunteer organization, IAQC continues to experience severe problems in carrying out its mission, moving from one crisis to another. The problems they have had illustrate well the differences between the U.S. experience and the Swedish and Japanese experiences. IAQC difficulties stem, above all, from an elected Board of Directors, composed now primarily of middle- and lower-ranking management officials (including quality-circle facilitators), most of whom have no experience running a complex national organization. Lacking national recognition, they were unable to bestow the mantle of legitimacy on the organization as the leader of the national small-group activity movement. Operationally, they have great difficulty tapping the coffers of major businesses and foundations, and financial instability has been a continuing problem. They have also had to rely heavily on volunteers, with all the problems of follow-through that this entails. Finally, consultant influence, while no longer dominant, has continued to create problems with consultants pushing to keep the organization out of activities where IAQC would be in competition with "their own members"—as the consultants like to phrase it. This has limited organizational initiatives. IAQC has yet to show that it will be able to legitimate and provide resources for the growth of the small-group activity movement in a way that occurred in Sweden and Japan.

Organized efforts in the United States to effect the implementation of small-group activities have emphasized careful research, measurement, and prior scientific demonstration of their effectiveness. By contrast, experience in Sweden and Japan shows that when management has a motivation to innovate, funding is forthcoming, organized infrastructures develop quickly, and efforts to institutionalize new work structures move ahead full speed with relative inattention, sometimes even active disinterest, in effectiveness research.

Japan: Early and Effective Managerial Mobilization

Japanese managers are far more likely than their American counterparts to think of solutions to managerial problems as coming from the area of human relations rather than technical relations. There are a number of historical and cultural precedents for this (Cole, 1979: 108–111). This view has been reinforced by the rapid translation and absorption of the American human relations literature in Japan. For these reasons, Japanese managers, when faced with the labor-supply problems of the late 1960s, readily turned to restructuring work arrangements and organizing workers in small-group activities designed to arouse in workers a sense of loyalty to the firm and an internalization of company goals. These activities have been carefully controlled, and involvement is not always voluntary for workers. These arrangements are premised on considerable sharing of information with workers on production schedules and plant objectives and performance (Cole, 1979: 224–250).

Not surprisingly, high-level management groups provided crucial leadership for the implementation of small-group activities. The Japan Federation of Employers' Associations (Nikkeiren) was especially important. Nikkeiren, while analogous in function to the National Association of Manufacturers in the United States, is more specialized in labor and personnel matters and more prestigious and powerful than its American counterpart. Many of Nikkeiren's early small-group activities can be dated from 1966. By 1970 the chairman of Nikkeiren, believing he perceived a trend toward "all-employee management," advocated support for this trend at a top-management seminar. Since that time Nikkeiren has engaged in a wide range of publicizing activities designed to explain and spread such approaches (Nakayama, 1972).

Specialized organizations such as the Japan Union of Scientists and Engineers (JUSE) also developed departments designed exclusively to propagate specific kinds of small-group activities. JUSE is a national nonprofit organization dedicated to providing services to participating Japanese companies in the areas of quality and reliability. It is composed of university professors in engineering and science, as well as engineers from leading firms, but is closely tied to business circles. Since 1948, shortly after its founding, the chairman of JUSE has either been the chairman of Keidanren (Japanese Federation of Economic Organizations), the most powerful business association in Japan, or a former chairman. Furthermore, the intellectual leadership of JUSE has been provided to a great extent by Ishikawa Kaoru, the secretary general. His father was the first chairman of Keidanren to sit simultaneously as chairman of JUSE. These linkages provided legitimation for JUSE initiatives; JUSE assumed the major leadership role in developing and diffusing the concept and practice of quality-control circles. With corporate sponsors, JUSE could employ professional staff and not rely on volunteers for its core administrative functions. Central to its mission was gathering company experiences, defining "best practices" and feeding the information back to the field in its conferences and publications. Specific mechanisms included publishing a low-priced magazine for foremen and circle members, a plethora of training programs and publications, and a quality-control-circle registration system. JUSE also created quality-control-circle conventions for companies to share circle experiences.

In summary, we see a firm linkage between the emergence of a national infrastructure designed to spread the innovation and top-management leadership and support in the private sector. It is this linkage that makes less likely the outcome of short-term faddish commitments and increases the probability that institutionalized firm-level structures will develop.

Sweden: Early Joint Management-Union
Initiatives Followed by Weakened Commitment

In Sweden, management was attracted by ideas that originated at the Tavistock Institute in England (Emery and Trist, 1969) and were propagated in Sweden by the Norwegian scholar Einar Thorsrud (Thorsrud and Emery, 1969). Tavistock ideas emphasized the development of the organization as a sociotechnical system, the interaction of social and technical factors in the organization of the workplace, and prescribed the development of small, cohesive work groups, which would maintain a high level of independence and autonomy. Jobs would be enriched, individual responsibility increased, learning possibilities enhanced, and, most importantly, from the standpoint of Swedish management, jobs would be more attractive to desirable recruits and labor turnover and absenteeism could be reduced.

The Swedish Employers' Confederation (Svenska Arbetsgivareföreningen — SAF) made a high-level decision in the mid-1960s to support small-group activities on the shopfloor. The Tavistock ideas provided a coherent ideological framework and a practical direction for reform efforts. SAF, committed to Thorsrud's ideas, entrusted their program for research and popularization to its technical department, which began a large-scale training and publications program. Another organizational offshoot of SAF, the Personnel Administration Council (Personaladministrativa Rådet), guided several important projects and played a key liaison role between academic research and the world of business (e.g., Björk, Hanson, and Hellberg, 1973).

In Sweden, unlike Japan and the United States, the strength and the orientation of organized labor was such that these management initiatives for changes in the workplace had to be taken in cooperation with labor unions. In 1966, SAF, together with the white-collar (TCO) and blue-collar (LO) union federations, established the Development Council for Cooperative Questions (Utvecklingsrådet for Samarbetsfrågor) to facilitate labor- management cooperation.

The Development Council set up a special group for research, called URAF. Its general task was to make clear which factors stimulated workplace democratization and which factors hindered it. Its specific purpose was to initiate and supervise projects and conduct research. These efforts were anchored in development groups at the company level in which both management and labor were represented. URAF sponsored ten key pilot projects during 1969–1970. These pilot projects were well reported, usually in a favorable light, by both labor and management groups (e.g., Landsorganisation, 1976), and the reports served to stimulate further initiatives.

However important URAF was in the crucial early periods of the reform movement, this kind of cooperative union-management activity fell off markedly by the early 1970s, for two reasons. First, the unions began to articulate a competing ideology of worker control. LO wanted not only sociotechnical participation in an atmosphere of cooperation, but more power for workers and the unions in the firm. Second, the employers' confederation, SAF, felt shackled by cooperative activity, especially with the increased militance of the unions, and preferred to proceed on its own with a freer hand (as its counterparts in Japan were able to do).

As LO turned increasingly toward legislation to further its aim of enhancing industrial democracy, SAF shifted its main initiatives to its own technical department and away from cooperative activity with the unions. URAF was finally abolished in 1978. Similarly, SAF's interest in small-group activities weakened with the passage of the Co-Determination Law and the threat of the "wage earners fund";[3] this shift in focus came to be reflected in the spinning off of the technical department as a separate enterprise in the early 1980s. These developments, in effect, resulted in a weakening of the national infrastructure and thereby contributed to a loss of momentum in the movement itself.

INTERESTS AND ORIENTATION OF ORGANIZED LABOR

The development of widespread managerial interest in innovation and the creation and use of organized infrastructures for national communication and mobilization do not uniformly assure successful diffusion. Other loci of interests, organization, and power must be entered into the political calculus. In this case, the strength, interests, and orientation of labor are crucial in determining the shape and outcome of the diffusion process. In each of the three nations, labor has exhibited a different orientation toward shopfloor reforms, and this has served to shape the outcomes of the diffusion process in different ways.

The United States: Union Suspicion

With the notable exception of the United Auto Workers and later the Communications Workers of America, advocates of new work structures in the United States generally have failed to gain strong union-wide support for their programs. The major spur to across-the-board activity came in the early 1980s from the internationalization of the economy. In the auto industry, there were some impressive achievements in the early 1980s with widespread establishment of employee-involvement groups and employee-participation groups, as the circles were known respectively at Ford and GM. Notwithstanding, in the eyes of many union officials and workers, many of these initiatives became negatively associated with concessions in bargaining. General UAW support for the Quality of Worklife programs showed signs of evaporating by the mid-1980s (cf. Thomas, 1984). Deep division within the top leadership of the union as to the proper position toward QWL made forward movement difficult.

The leaders of most other major unions have generally been even more suspicious of management motives, seeing small group activities as a management scheme to get more productivity from workers without sharing the increased economic rewards (Industrial Union Department, 1978). Another concern is that these approaches often break down established job boundaries, thereby resulting in "speedups" and reducing manpower requirements. They are also seen as a threat to existing collective bargaining structures (Sorge, 1984). Finally, many union leaders, not incorrectly, see small-group activities as a device to avoid or weaken unionization by building loyalty to management. The result has been active union distrust of such reforms.

This union orientation arises from specific features of American industrialization and of the tradition of unionism that arose during the period, as a subsequent comparison with Japan will highlight. One of the most notable features of American unionism historically has been its orientation toward control of job opportunities (Perlman, 1968), which took place often under conditions of labor shortage, with a failure of workers to assert themselves collectively as an organized force in national politics. It was decisively shaped, further, by the struggle between craft unions and management over control of the production process and the forms of remuneration involved, as management moved to reorganize the production process around the turn of the twentieth century (Stone, 1975; Montgomery, 1976). Behind the movement to reorganize production known as Taylorism (Braverman, 1974; Nelson, 1975) was a managerial strategy prompted by comparatively high wages in American industry, by contemporary world standards—wage levels that were the product of a labor shortage in industrializing America and relatively strong craft unions in older industries. To compete in international markets, U.S. managers adopted a high-wage, low-cost strategy. Since labor was relatively expensive, there were strong incentives for American managers to economize on its use and cut unit costs—thus the aggressive strategy of substituting machinery for labor and subdividing, analyzing, and reorganizing the labor process.

In the face of these managerial initiatives, unions were faced with two options. First, they could continue to struggle for the maintenance of craft control over the production process. Second, they could accept the shifting overall trend of power in industry and push for quantitative improvements in worker rewards within the emerging new patterns of labor relations—in effect, a rearguard action against scientific management and Taylorism. The first option was rejected in the face of management and government power arrayed against the unions. Instead, the unions generally adopted the more limited second strategy, where collective bargaining came to legitimate an increasingly extreme division of labor (Fox, 1974: 201, 204–205). In order for unions to control job opportunities, standardized rules of wage determination and job allocation had to be developed where none existed before. To negotiate and conclude labor contracts on this basis assumes the determination of pay rates on the basis of explicitly defined jobs. In pursuing this strategy, it became in the union's interest to set clear, precise job boundaries and negotiate pay rates for each job. These practices became institutionalized in American work structures as industrialization proceeded, the scale of enterprises grew, and internal labor markets assumed increasing importance. There evolved a complex set of industrial relations rules in which the equity principle— predicated on the ability to identify and compare sets of clearly defined jobs— became a central basis for wage determination. In this context, contemporary American unions are suspicious of small-group activities because they often threaten vested union interests in existing job structures, pay scales, and collective bargaining arrangements.

Japan: Union Indifference and Uninvolvement

Japan's industrialization process gave rise to different forms of unionism and to markedly different union strategies than those that arose in the United States. First, Japan experienced labor surplus rather than labor shortage throughout much of its past industrialization, and wages were quite low by international standards. Second, union organizations were suppressed or severely restricted in their activities in the pre-World War II period and again in the 1950s (Ayusawa, 1966: 302–304; Cook, 1966: 97–98). Japan's history of industrial development was such that the Japanese skipped the craft stage of union organization (Dore, 1973), precisely the stage at which the model of precise job specification was most carefully worked out in the American experience. Under these conditions, Japanese industries could compete in foreign markets, because labor was cheap. Unions, relatively weak and facing a large pool of potential replacement workers, found job security a more viable goal than control of job opportunities. Given these conditions, when scientific management principles were adopted in Japan, time-and-motion studies were used not for job determination but simply to determine "correct" job procedures. Managers were interested in developing a disciplined workforce motivated to take on cost reduction and other management goals as a personal challenge. This desire, in interaction with union interests in job security, led to the institutionalization of "paternalism"—the emphasis on principles of permanent employment and promotion and pay according to a seniority system.

Japanese management's control of worker training under the seniority wage system, combined with the lack of a national labor movement in the course of industrialization, led to an acceptance of management's prerogative to decide unilaterally on work assignments, job demarcation, and the restructuring of job boundaries, along with changes in technology. Even today, management generally has a discretionary right to move its workforce about without union interference (Okamoto, 1975). In this context, neither management nor labor saw great benefit in tying wage determination to specific job performance. The interplay of union and management interests that led to sharp job demarcation and union commitment to these work structures in the United States led to the opposite outcome in Japan.

This different historical pattern led to Japanese labor's relative indifference to the introduction of small-group activities. Its agenda for participation focused instead on cooperation with management to set up an elaborate system of labor-management consultation committees at all levels of the firm. Because small-group activities are within the historically agreed-upon realm of managerial prerogatives and because they are consistent with union goals of creating greater economic prosperity, Japanese unions have maintained their relative uninvolvement in these changes.

Sweden: From Cooperation to Contention

Swedish trade unions, unlike those of Japan and the United States, took an active role in organized efforts to establish small-group activities in industry. The nature and effect of this involvement, however, has been quite complex and has had a mixed impact on the diffusion process. As an organized national force, Swedish unions are extremely potent, with organization rates of around 80 percent of the entire workforce (with almost similar rates of organization in blue- and white-collar sectors). These levels are far higher than the

American and Japanese rate. Nationally, moreover, the organization of the Swedish trade-union movement is highly centralized, and through a 44-year Social Democratic government that ended only in the 1976 elections, organized labor has been a much stronger force in national politics than its counterparts in the United States and Japan (Korpi, 1978: 74–75). The Social Democrats returned to power in 1982.

Historically the Swedish union movement has been hostile to the idea of direct workshop participation, not unlike most American unions. This orientation was not due to a vested union interest in existing job definitions, but rather to the unions' commitment to centralized national bargaining. The unions feared that increasing the decision rights of small groups in the shop would undermine this.

The union strategy for expanding workplace power in the mid-1960s focused on company-level works councils. A series of threats to the organizational integrity and discipline of the unions, beginning around 1970, changed the union leadership's orientations and moved them to support small-group activities as part of a strategy to democratize Swedish firms. In late 1969 a wildcat strike took place at the state-owned LKAB iron mine. The participants were well-paid miners who were protesting inept and unresponsive union and state officials as much as poor working conditions and lack of wage equity (Korpi, 1970; Dahlström et al., 1971; Hammarström, 1975). The LKAB strike, followed by a wave of wildcat strikes throughout Sweden during 1970 and 1971 (Berglind and Rundblad, 1975), set in motion a national debate on the meaning of work, the proper trade-union role, what employees had a right to expect from their work, and the possibility of restructuring work and authority relationships in the workplace. Media coverage of these issues was intense (Karlsson, 1969).

It was during this period that Thorsrud's ideas about autonomous work groups were being propagated among management circles. Direct workplace participation by workers through small-group activities appealed to top union officials as one way to accommodate the disaffected and rebellious rank and file while moving toward democratization of the firm.

This crucial early period of cooperation, however, was short-lived. The momentum of political events required changes that were beyond the scope of the initial experiments with small-group activities. LO in its 1971 convention endorsed a historic reversal of policies. Where previously the union had been indifferent or hostile to worker participation, it now committed itself fully to the worker-participation movement, demanding power for workers at all levels of the company. It demanded that this be guaranteed not merely through cooperation or bargaining with management to support small-group activities, but through national legislation. The LO policy, endorsed also by the white-collar federation, TCO, led to the passage of the Co-Determination Law.

This represents a crucial shift in Swedish union strategy. Traditionally, Swedish trade unions were notable for their ability to agree with management on certain areas in which mutual interests could be served through cooperative action. Initially, this was the case for worker participation, as unions cooperated with management in the setting up of works councils and later through participation in URAF with experiments stressing small-group activities. They expected this activity to lead to greater worker and union input at all levels of decision making within the firm. When they found that management resisted efforts to extend worker participation beyond small-group activities at the shop and office floor, pressure grew for the shift in union policy that eventually took place in 1971. In this watershed year, the previously cooperative policy gave way to a new strategy of having the Social Democratic government enact legislation that would facilitate the democratization of the firm through union negotiation on the basis of these laws. The unions saw the Co-Determination Law as a collective bargaining model for controlling participatory activities rather than bringing about direct participation of workers. This vision worked against the development of small-group activities, and the shift from cooperation to contention served to slow the initially rapid progress of their diffusion, since there now was a basic tension over the direction and scope of reform.

Implicitly, this shift in union position had another consequence that slowed the progress of shopfloor innovations. Small-group activities now became just one of several levels on which worker participation and union power were being pursued. In 1971 the LO congress also endorsed various representation schemes, including board of director membership for employees (passed into law in 1972), and expanded works councils, but there has been considerable union infighting over the priorities assigned these various forms of participation.

It remains to be seen whether the norms to be worked out to operationalize the Co-Determination Law will revitalize the small-group activity movement. The lack of a clear idea on how to concretize the legislation, combined with the shift to a non-Social Democratic government in 1976, led to a paralysis of the small-group activity movement. With the return of the Social Democratic government in 1982, new life seems to have been breathed into small-group activities (Mellbourn, 1984: 16). Slogans of the new movement are worker participation in "development" and "change" and "local solutions for local problems." In the private sector, this translates into a more flexible approach on the part of the unions. In early 1986, Volvo, Sweden's largest private employer, announced plans for rebuilding its largest plant as well as for a new plant. Both plans contained a strong emphasis on small-group activities.

THE MACROPOLITICAL DIMENSIONS OF WORK REFORM

From the case-by-case comparison, summarized in Figure 4.1, we can extract and highlight the macropolitical dimensions of work reform. To the extent that there is contention over the implementation of small-group practices—when groups have different interests with regard to change, articulate competing ideologies, and act on their respective interests—implementation becomes politicized. To the extent that different groups have congruent interests and cooperate in such efforts or to the extent that one group is indifferent to the change, the process is, in our terms, nonpoliticized. Whether the process of change becomes politicized or not has an important impact on the outcome, but this impact is not a simple one. A comparison of the three cases shows that the effect of degree of politicization is contingent on other variables at work in each national situation.

Nonpoliticized Patterns: The United States and Japan. In the United States, neither unions, management, nor politicians exhibited strong interest in small-group activities: unions because they would challenge vested interests in existing job structures and disturb long-standing strategies for the pursuit of their interests through collective bargaining, management because there were no acute problems with existing practices, and politicians because there was no manifest constituency. Unlike Sweden, there was no impact of the issue upon public opinion or national political discourse. With such a lack of commitment on the part of all major institutional actors, a strong national infrastructure failed to develop. The result was that no one contender or group of contenders effectively promoted the small-group activity movement in the United States.

In Japan, also, the process of change has been nonpoliticized. Unlike the United States, however, there has been a very widespread application of small-group activities. In Japan, management became interested in such reforms because of difficult labor-market problems they faced in the mid-1960s and concern about utilizing an increasing educated labor force. With the development of such a commitment, employers used existing organizations to create a national infrastructure for the diffusion of solutions such as small-group activities. Japanese unions, unlike their American counterparts, had no interest in opposing these changes in the workplace. Similarly, the ruling Conservative government had little incentive to take positions or action on this matter.[4] Therefore, in the absence of involvement by government, unions, and political parties, the implementation of these new work structures proceeded as a well-coordinated case of managerial innovation. There were

	Timing and Scope of Innovation	Management Incentives to Innovate	Characteristics of Mobilization	Political Dimensions
United States	Piecemeal experimentation in 1960s and 1970s. Limited primarily to blue-collar workers at the shopfloor level.	Few incentives perceived.	Many piecemeal efforts, absence of well-funded and centralized infrastructure for diffusion.	Neither government, union, nor management leadership committed to innovation. Unions often hostile.
Japan	Began early 1960s. Now widely diffused. Limited initially to blue-collar workers at the shopfloor level.	Significant labor shortage and rapidly accelerated education levels with raised expectations.	Management organizations provide well-funded and organized infrastructure for diffusion.	Top management develops commitment to innovation. Unions in private sector passively accept.
Sweden	Began late 1960s. Now widely diffused. Spread rapidly to white-collar and public sector. Operative from shopfloor level to board of directors membership.	Severe labor shortage and rapidly accelerated education levels with raised expectations.	In early years, joint union-management efforts develop effective infrastructure for diffusion. Later management organizations provide focus for shop- and office-floor efforts.	Top management, union leaders, and government all develop commitment to innovation. Union committed but sets its own agenda.

Figure 4.1 Summary of national experiences

NOTE: I am indebted to Linda Kaboolian for suggesting this summary format.

no conflicts over reforms, as in Sweden, that threatened to push them in directions feared by managers, and there was no entrenched union opposition to such changes in traditional work structures, as in the United States. As a result, small-group activities diffused rapidly and thoroughly, management being able to control carefully the direction, scope, and content of reform in a way that Swedish management found impossible.

Politicized Pattern: Sweden. In Sweden, as in Japan, strong management interest in small-group activities resulted from serious turnover and recruitment problems due to changes in the domestic labor market. Union orientation toward such reforms, however, shifted from disinterest to cooperation and then to contention in a relatively short period of time. This rapid shift in union orientation coincided with the quick politicization of the issue. The issue of democratization of industrial life came to the center of public attention, with high media coverage, and spurred the Social Democratic government into action. More important, it resulted in a rapid shift in union orientation and strategy, as the centralized union hierarchy was threatened with challenges from below. Initially hostile to shopfloor participation and preferring centralized control, the Swedish union confederations quickly moved toward support of shopfloor reforms and eventually came to contend with management over the direction of reform by pursuing legislation to enforce changes. This meant that Swedish managers, unlike their Japanese counterparts, were unable to control carefully the direction, scope, and content of reform after the initial period of management-union cooperation. Later moves by the unions to extend democratization to worker involvement in decisions relating to capital investment and the like threatened traditional management prerogatives and authority. As a result of this basic tension, the initially rapid diffusion of small-group activities slowed as management became wary of changes that it could not completely control. The less complete diffusion of small-group activities in Sweden, despite the consensus of all major institutional actors that such reforms were desirable, is due to this basic management-labor contention over the direction of reform. This contention was heightened by the subsequent loss of power of the Social Democrats to the conservatives in the 1976 election.

THE MACROPOLITICS OF ORGANIZATIONAL CHANGE

The explanation of why change took place in some countries and not in others has two essential components. The first is the motivation of management to introduce small-group activities, rooted in perceived managerial problems. In two of the cases examined in the period 1960–1980, such motivation was present (Japan and Sweden) and arose from the characteristics of a changing national labor market; such motivation, however, also derives from more generalized concerns as well. The interaction of these generalized concerns with specific motivators poses enormous problems for social science as we ask what kinds of data will provide meaningful explanations of management behavior. We are dealing with an environment composed of numerous problems and solutions with various degrees of saliency at different times, acting and reacting upon each other in a variety of ways over time. While I have identified labor-market factors as critical to precipitating out small-group activities, these factors are part of a broad constellation of factors in the total social system. How do managements' conceptions of problems and solutions actually crystallize in relation to competitive ideas? Certainly, longitudinal analysis is necessary. Questionnaire surveys alone are inadequate to the task. A variety of research tools prove useful, including participant observation, nondirective interviews that allow interviewees to explore the full social framework in which decisions are made, and surveys of management journals to see what managers are saying to each other. This suggests that a good social science answer is likely to be a work of art, as one sews together disparate pieces of information from various data sources. That is a disturbing answer from a positivistic perspective, but it has the potential to be a far better one, at least for the kinds of questions being asked here. This article, still exploratory in many ways, is an attempt to do some of the initial stitching.

The second and determining factor in the spread of small-group activities is the political process that surrounded the change: the efforts of organized managerial or labor groups to enforce their preferences with regard to the change and their ability to call resources into play to do so. Crucial in this regard is the congruence or divergence of management and labor interests with regard to change; especially the orientation of labor unions, given their traditional strategies and their respective abilities to enforce their preferences. These fluid political processes are summarized in Figure 4.2.

This explanation of cross-national differences in the diffusion and survival rates of small-group activities does not rely on organizational level or group-level variables as much as it does on macropolitical processes. We can predict with some confidence that if a national business leadership is committed to small-group activities as a solution to perceived problems, and this is uncontested by labor, a national infrastructure to legitimate and promote small-group activities will come into place. This is independent of any small-group effects or organizational variables that might affect the process in a given company. It is this kind of analysis that allows us to see the forest for the trees. Similarly, if we take as our dependent variable cross-national differences in some of the most often-studied organizational variables—degree of task specialization and degree of differentiation of roles in the shopfloor—we find a similar situation. That is, our analysis suggests the importance of macropoli-

	Traditional Union Orientation	Union Perception of Small-Group Activities	Union Action	Union Means to Enforce Preferences	Degree of Conflict Consensus with Management	Outcome
United States	Control of job opportunities; vested interest in existing job definitions and related pay scales.	Suspicion; threatens structure of bargaining at industry level; disinterest.	Little union action.	Industry-level agreements; factory-level negotiation.	Did not become an issue.	Very limited spread of new structures.
Sweden	Centralized national collective bargaining and political action through Social Democratic Party.	Initially suspicious, later saw as a means to satisfy rebellious rank and file, still later as one prong of strategy for work control.	Began own efforts, initially in cooperation with employers, later on own.	National-led labor agreements and passing of legislation through SDP.	Initial active cooperation, later contention of direction and extent of changes.	Initial rapid change, later halted due to conflict over course.
Japan	Stress job security; allow management prerogative of organizing workplace.	Neutral; did not threaten vested interests.	Uninvolved, although consulted at plant level.	Industry-led agreements; factory-led negotiation.	Consensual process of change.	Thorough, rapid process of change.

Figure 4.2 Macropolitical dimensions of the process of change

121

tical variables in explaining these outcomes; such explanations are rarely seen in the literature.

These observations clearly go well beyond the study of small-group activities and provide support for Perrow's (1979) observations about moving away from microanalysis of many questions to broader explanatory factors in order to expand the generalizability and applicability of our theories.

It may indeed be that the most profitable route to studying the impact of macropolitical factors is to see these factors as a subset of a still broader set of environmental factors (cf. Freeman, 1978; Meyer, 1978). The differential survival and success rates of organizations and the creation of organizations are currently much studied from a population ecology perspective (Aldrich, 1979). It is apparent from this analysis of the variation in the type and form of national infrastructures for the diffusion of small-group activities that the explanations of such outcomes could benefit substantially from the introduction of macropolitical variables. Conditions affecting the ability of organizations to extract resources from the environment (as exemplified by the resource dependence model) have long been a concern of those stressing the impact of environments on organizations. The analysis here suggests, however, that the role of macropolitical factors in resource acquisition has been underplayed in much previous research. Conversely, integrating the study of macropolitical factors into environmental research frees the study of macropolitical factors from the constraints of its primarily Marxist framework, which simply cannot do justice to the varied empirical outcomes.

The macropolitical perspective can also be useful in the study of innovation. Studies of factors affecting the adoption and diffusion of organizational innovation typically stress organization-level variables (Kimberly, as cited in Aldrich, 1979: 98), with at best some attention given to selected economic variables. Yet, it is apparent from this analysis that the adoption and diffusion of managerial innovations, e.g., small-group activities, depend in large part on the macropolitical factors outside the organization.

It might be asserted in response to this study that the changes described are not "normal" instances of organizational change, that they constitute special cases of well-defined national movements, and therefore the key explanations are necessarily macropolitical. The movements analyzed here, however, are the direct counterparts of previous movements that transformed industrial organization early in this century—the movements for the open shop, for scientific management, Taylorism, and Fordism. All these movements involved the same kind of interplay between management and labor, the same kind of managerial response to perceived problems, and the same kind of organization and mobilization for change through organized infrastructures. These are not abnormal instances of change. Social change usually takes place through these broader, macropolitical processes, and their effects on the micro-organization of factories can be quite profound.

Of course, macropolitics does not explain everything, or even most things, about the way factories and other enterprises are organized. We already have a rich literature telling us what these other variables at lower levels of social organization are. A great deal depends on the questions being asked. For the questions raised in this article, why small-group activities developed differently in the three countries, organization-level variables are not the most important ones. Comparative sociology makes a contribution here by highlighting factors that are always at work in any national setting and historical context. Because they exert relatively constant effects across a range of smaller units of organization, such factors are not clearly perceived without being studied in a comparative framework.

NOTES

1. Burawoy (1983) did not include labor shortage as a motivating factor for workplace innovations. While he referred to market forces and the labor process as factors in the emergence of "hegemonic despotism," a reputedly new stage of capitalism, he did not allow for differences in labor supply that affected the form of new work structures in the four nations he examined (U.S., England, Japan, and Sweden). His analysis, which compared one workshop in England with another in the U.S., was designed to hold labor process and market factors constant. This method highlights the macropolitical factors but entirely excludes the labor-market characteristics that are an important empirical link between the macropolitical factors and the organization of work.

2. This important concept cannot be treated adequately in the space available. Central to the analysis is Bendix's (1974) notion of "managerial ideology"; my use of the concept focuses on organized management efforts to promote change.

3. The Democracy of Work (or Co-Determination) Law (Medbestämmandelagen) passed in 1976 provides Swedish workers and their unions with legal authority to bargain collectively over a wide range of management decisions that previously had been strictly managerial prerogatives.

4. There seems to be little basis, other than that it fits the Marxist perspective, for Burawoy's contention that state involvement in the Japanese industrial relations system is quite low. Similarly, his description of Japan as closely approximating "the despotic order of early capitalism in which the state offers little or no social insurance and abstains from the regulation of factory apparatuses" (Burawoy, 1983: 599) is innocent of all facts (see Shirai, 1983; Gould, 1984).

REFERENCES

Agervold, Mogens. 1975. "Swedish experiments in industrial democracy." In Louis Davis and Albert Cherns (eds.), *The Quality of Working Life*, 2: 46–65. New York: Free Press.

Aldrich, Howard. 1979. *Organizations and Environments*. Englewood Cliffs, NJ: Prentice Hall.

Ayusawa, Iwao. 1966. *A History of Labor in Modern Japan*. Honolulu: East-West Center Press.

Bendix, Reinhard. 1974. *Work and Authority in Industry*. Berkeley, CA: University of California Press.

Berglind, Hans, and Bengt Rundblad. 1975. "The Swedish labor market in transition." Unpublished paper, University of Gothenberg.

Bernstein, Paul. 1976. *Workplace Democratization: Its Internal Dynamics.* Kent, OH: Kent University Press.

Björk, Lars, Reine Hanson, and Peter Hellberg. 1973. *Ökat Inflytande i Jobbet* (Increased Influence on the Job). Stockholm: Personaladministrativa Rådet.

Bluestone, Irving. 1978. "Human dignity is what it's all about." *Viewpoint,* 8(3): 21–24.

Braverman, Harry. 1974. *Labor and Monopoly Capital: The Degradation of Work in the Twentieth Century.* New York: Monthly Review.

Burawoy, Michael. 1983. "Between the labor process and the state: The changing face of factory regimes under advanced capitalism." *American Sociological Review,* 48: 587–605.

Cole, Robert E. 1979. *Work, Mobility, and Participation: A Comparative Study of American and Japanese Industry.* Berkeley, CA: University of California Press.

Cole, Robert E., and Dennis Tachiki. 1983. "A look at U.S. and Japanese quality circles: Preliminary comparisons." *Quality Circles Journal,* 6(2): 10–16.

Cole, Robert E., and Andrew Walder. 1981. "Structural diffusion: The politics of participative work structures in China, Japan, Sweden, and the United States." Working Paper Series #226, Center for Research on Social Organization, University of Michigan.

Cook, Alice. 1966. *An Introduction to Japanese Trade Unionism.* Ithaca: Cornell University Press.

Cummings, Thomas, and Edmond Molloy. 1977. *Improving Productivity and the Quality of Work Life.* New York: Praeger.

Dachler, H. Peter, and Bernhard Wilpert. 1978. "Conceptual dimensions and boundaries of participation in organizations: A critical evaluation." *Administrative Science Quarterly,* 23: 1–39.

Dahlström, Edmund, et al. 1971. *LKAB och Demokrati.* Stockholm: Waldström and Wedstrand.

Davis, Louis, and Albert Cherns (ed.). 1975. *The Quality of Working Life,* 1. New York: Free Press.

Dore, Ronald. 1973. *British Factory—Japanese Factory.* Berkeley, CA: University of California Press.

Edwards, Richard. 1979. *Contested Terrain.* New York: Basic Books.

Emery, Fred, and Eric Trist. 1969. "Sociotechnical systems." In Fred Emery (ed.), *Systems Thinking:* 281–296. London: Penguin.

Fox, Alan. 1974. *Beyond Contract: Work, Power and Trust Relations.* London: Faber and Faber.

Freeman, John. 1978. "The unit of analysis in organizational research." In Marshall Meyer and Associates (eds.), *Environments and Organizations: Theoretical and Empirical Perspectives:* 335–351. San Francisco: Jossey-Bass.

Gould, William. 1984. *Japan's Reshaping of American Labor Law.* Cambridge, MA: MIT Press.

Gyllenhammar, Pehr. 1977. *People at Work.* Reading, MA: Addison-Wesley.

Hammarström, Olle. 1975. "Joint worker-management consultation, the case of LKAB, Sweden." In Louis Davis and Albert Cherns (eds.), *The Quality of Working Life,* 2: 66–82. New York: Free Press.

Harvey, Edward, and Russell Mills. 1970. "Patterns of organizational adaptation: A political perspective." In Mayer N. Zald (ed.), *Power in Organizations:* 181–213. Nashville, TN: Vanderbilt University Press.

Industrial Union Department, AFL-CIO. 1978. "The quality of working life." *Viewpoint,* 8(3): 1–29.

Kanter, Rosabeth. 1983. *The Change Masters.* New York: Simon & Schuster.

Karlsson, Lars Erik. 1969. *Demokrati på Arbetsplatsen* (Democracy at the Workplace). Stockholm: Prisma.

Katzell, Raymond, Daniel Yankelovich, et al. 1975. *Work, Productivity, and Job Satisfaction.* New York: Psychological Corporation.

Korpi, Walter. 1970. *Varför Strejkar Arbetarna?* (Why Do Workers Strike?). Stockholm: Tidens Förlag.

———. 1978. *The Working Class in Welfare Capitalism.* London: Routledge & Kegan Paul.

Landsorganisation. 1976. *Arbetsorganisation* (Work Organization). Stockholm: Tidens Förlag.

Meyer, John. 1978. "Strategies for further research: Varieties of environmental variation." In Marshall Meyer and Associates (eds.), *Environments and Organizations: Theoretical and Empirical Perspectives:* 352–368. San Francisco: Jossey-Bass.

Mellbourn, Anders. 1984. "MBL inte så dårlig som sitt rykte" ("The Co-Determination Law is not as bad as it's rumored to be"). *Dagens Nyheter,* April 29: 16.

Minami, Ryoshin. 1973. *The Turning Point in Economic Development: Japan's Experience.* Tokyo: Kinokuniya Bookstore.

Ministry of Labour. 1974. *Koyōknari shindan shiyō* (Indicators of the Conditions of Employment Administration). Tokyo: Employment Security Office.

Montgomery, David. 1976. "Workers' control of machine production in the nineteenth century." *Labor History,* 17: 485–509.

Nakayama, Saburo. 1972. *Zen'in sanka keiei no kangaekata to jissai* (All-Employee Management Participation: Viewpoints and Practices). Tokyo: Japan Federation of Employers' Associations.

Nelson, Daniel. 1975. *Managers and Workers.* Madison, WI: University of Wisconsin Press.

New York Stock Exchange. 1982. *People and Productivity.* New York: New York Stock Exchange.

Okamoto, Hideaki. 1975. "Jizen kyōgisei no ronri" ("The logic of the prior consultation system"). In Nihon Rōdō Kyōkai (ed.), *Haichi Tenkan o Meguru Rōshi Kankei:* 43–93. Tokyo: Japan Institute of Labour.

Perlman, Selig. 1968. *A Theory of the Labor Movement.* Originally published in 1928. New York: Augustus Kelly.

Perrow, Charles. 1970. "Departmental power and perspectives in industrial firms." In Mayer Zald (ed.), *Power in Organizations:* 59–79. Nashville, TN: Vanderbilt University Press.

———. 1979. *Complex Organizations: A Critical Essay,* 2d ed. New York: Random House.

Pfeffer, Jeffrey. 1978. "The micropolitics of organizations." In Marshall Meyer and Associates (eds.), *Environments and Organizations: Theoretical and Empirical Perspectives:* 29–50. San Francisco: Jossey-Bass.

Rothschild-Whitt, Joyce. 1979. "The collectivist organization: An alternative to rational-bureaucratic models." *American Sociological Review,* 44: 509–527.

Shirai, Taishiro (ed.). 1983. *Contemporary Industrial Relations in Japan.* Madison, WI: University of Wisconsin Press.

Sorge, Marjorie. 1984. "UAW lists top priorities for talks in Canada." *Automotive News* (Detroit, Crain Automotive Group), April 23: 4, 8.

Statistiska Centralbyrån. 1978. *Arbetsmarknads-statistisk Årsbok 1977* (Yearbook of Labor Statistics 1977). Örebro: National Central Bureau of Statistics.

Stone, Katherine. 1975. "The origins of job structures in the steel industry." In Richard Edwards, Michael Reich, and David Gordon (eds.), *Labor Market Segmentation:* 27–84. Lexington, MA: Lexington Books.

Tannenbaum, Arnold S., Bogdan Kravčič, Manachem Rosner, Mino Vianello, and Georg Wieser. 1974. *Hierarchy in Organizations.* San Francisco: Jossey-Bass.

Thomas, Robert. 1984. "Participation and control: New trends in labor relations in the auto industry." CRSO Working Paper #315. Ann Arbor, MI: University of Michigan, Center for Research on Social Organizations.

Thorsrud, Einar, and Fred Emery. 1969. *Medinflytande och Engagemang i Arbetet* (Participation and Engagement in Work). Stockholm: Utvecklingsrådet for Samarbetsfrågor.

Tichy, Noel, and Jay N. Nisberg. 1976. "When does work restructuring work? Organizational innovations at Volvo and GM." *Organizational Dynamics,* 5: 1 (Summer): 63–80.

Walton, Richard. 1978. "Teaching an old dog food new tricks." *Wharton Magazine,* Winter: 38–47.

Wool, Harold. 1973. "What's wrong with work in America?" *Monthly Labor Review,* 96 (3): 38–44.

Zald, Mayer. 1970. *Power in Organizations.* Nashville, TN: Vanderbilt University Press.

5

TIGHTENING THE IRON CAGE
Concertive Control in Self-Managing Teams

James R. Barker

> I don't have to sit there and look for the boss to be around, and if the boss is not around, I can sit there and talk to my neighbor or do what I want. Now the whole team is around me and the whole team is observing what I'm doing.

"Ronald," a technical worker in a small manufacturing company, gave me this account one day while I was observing his work team. Ronald works in what contemporary writers call a postbureaucratic organization, which is not structured as a rule-based hierarchy. He works with a team of peers who are all equally responsible for managing their own work behaviors. But Ronald described an unexpected consequence of this team-based design. With his voice concealed by work noise, Ronald told me that he felt more closely watched now than when he worked under the company's old bureaucratic system. He said that while his old supervisor might tolerate someone coming in a few minutes late, for example, his team had adopted a "no tolerance" policy on tardiness and that members monitored their own behaviors carefully.

AUTHOR'S NOTE: I wish to thank Patricia A. Adler, Phillip K. Tompkins, George Cheney, Brenda J. Allen, Lars Thøgar Christensen, and Michael Pacanowsky for their advice and criticisms during the writing of this essay. In addition, John H. Puckett provided the necessary support and coordination that enabled me to complete the research project. Reprinted from *Administrative Science Quarterly*, 38 (Sept. 1993): 408–437.

Ronald's comments typify life under a new form of organizational control that has prospered in the last decade as a means of avoiding the pitfalls of bureaucracy. This form, called "concertive control," grows out of a substantial consensus about values, high-level coordination, and a degree of self-management by members or workers in an organization. This article describes and analyzes the development of concertive control after Ronald's company, "ISE Communications," converted to self-managing (or self-directing) teams, a concertive structure that resulted in a form of control more powerful, less apparent, and more difficult to resist than that of the former bureaucracy. The irony of the change in this postbureaucratic organization is that, instead of loosening, the iron cage of rule-based, rational control, as Max Weber called it, actually became tighter.

THE PROBLEM OF CONTROL

Control has been a central concept in organizational theory since the time of Weber and remains perhaps the key issue that shapes and permeates our experiences of organizational life. Barnard (1968: 17) best stated the importance of control when he wrote that a key defining element of any organization was the necessity of individuals to subordinate, to an extent, their own desires to the collective will of the organization. For individuals to achieve larger goals they must actually surrender some autonomy in organizational participation. Because of this basic tension, control is always problematic in any organization.

To work through this problem, an organization's members—managers and workers alike—must engage in ongoing formal and informal "processes of negotiation in which various strategies are developed . . . [that] produce particular outcomes" for the organization (Coombs, Knights, and Willmott, 1992: 58). Herein lies the essence of control as it becomes manifest in organizational activity. For any organization to move toward its goals and purposes, its "particular outcomes," its members must interactively negotiate and implement some type of strategy that effectively controls members' activities in a manner functional for the organization.

Edwards's Three Strategies of Control

Edwards (1981) has identified three broad strategies that have evolved from the modern organization's struggle with controlling members' activities. First is "simple control," the direct, authoritarian, and personal control of work and workers by the company's owner or hired bosses, best seen in nineteenth-century factories and in small family-owned companies today.

Second is "technological control," in which control emerges from the physical technology of an organization, such as in the assembly line found in traditional manufacturing. And third and most familiar is bureaucratic control, in which control derives from the hierarchically based social relations of the organization and its concomitant sets of systemic rational-legal rules that reward compliance and punish noncompliance.

A pivotal aspect of Edwards's model is that the second and third strategies, technological and bureaucratic control, represent adaptations to the forms of control that preceded them, each intended to counter the disadvantages of the previous form. Technological control resulted not only from technological advances in factories but also from worker alienation and dissatisfaction with the despotism too often possible in simple control. But technological control proved subject to such factors as worker protests, slow-downs, and assembly-line sabotage. The stultifying effects of the assembly line, with workers as just cogs in the machine, still produced worker alienation from the company. The bureaucratic form of control, with its emphasis on methodical, rational-legal rules for direction, hierarchical monitoring, and rewards for compliance such as job security, already existed in the nineteenth century and was further developed to counter the problems inherent in technological control. The bureaucracy and bureaucratic control, which become manifest in a variety of forms (Riggs, 1979; Perrow, 1986), have matured into the primary strategy available to managers to control work effectively in the modern organization. But, as with its predecessors, this strategy of control, too, is problematic.

Bureaucratic Control and the Iron Cage

Weber articulated the bureaucracy as the dominant form of modern control, in both positive and negative senses. While the bureaucracy offers the fairest and most efficient method of control, its system of rational rules may become troublesome, as seen in the infamous "red tape" that constrains and slows the bureaucracy and makes it unresponsive to environmental changes. Also, as Weber warned us, we, in our desire for organizational order and predictability, tend to focus too much on the rationality of the rules in and of themselves, overintellectualizing the moral and ethical values critical to our organizational lives and making decisions according to the rules, without regard to the people involved (Kalberg, 1980: 1158). We become so enmeshed in creating and following a legalistic, rule-based hierarchy that the bureaucracy becomes a subtle but powerful form of domination.

This notion of the inevitable, highly rational, but powerfully oppressive bureaucracy refers to what Weber (1958: 180–181) called the "iron cage." Weber saw the bureaucracy and bureaucratic control as an irresistible force of high rationality that would commandeer and consume all other forms of control. For Weber (1978), we would, out of our desire for order, continually rationalize our bureaucratic relationships, making them less negotiated and more structured. These structures ultimately become immovable objects of control: "Once fully established, bureaucracy is among those social structures which are the hardest to destroy. Bureaucracy is *the* means of transforming social action into rationally organized action (Weber, 1978: 987). As organizational activity increasingly becomes saturated by bureaucratic rationalization processes, it is increasingly constrained by them. A rule requiring a customer service representative to have all refund decisions approved by someone two hierarchical levels above may impede the representative's ability to meet a customer's demands for a quick response. Thus a rule that apparently benefits an organization's effectiveness (getting managerial approval and oversight of refunds) also constrains its effectiveness (slows down response). In Weber's (1978: 987–988) words, the individual organizational actor in a modern bureaucracy "cannot squirm out of the apparatus into which he has been harnessed."

Weber's image of how we become trapped in an iron cage of bureaucratic control suggests that control, as it becomes manifest as organizational activity through Edwards's three strategies, has become less apparent, or not as readily personal, as it has become more imbedded in the social relations of organizational members (Tompkins and Cheney, 1985; Barker and Cheney, 1994). Control in the bureaucratic organization becomes impersonal because its authority rests ultimately with the system, leaving organization members, in many cases, with what Weber (1958: 182) called "specialists without spirit, sensualists without heart." Whereas the nineteenth-century mill owner overtly controlled workers, ordering, directing, and firing them at will, the bureaucracy's rules are more indirect: They control workers by shaping their knowledge about the "right" ways to act and interact in the organization. A worker seeks supervisory approval for a decision because that is what the worker is supposed to do. The "apparency" of control becomes hidden in the bureaucracy's seemingly natural rules and hierarchy. Thus, bureaucratic control leaves us in a paradoxical situation. The same rational activities that enable collective organizational interaction eventually come to constrain that activity in ways often difficult for us to perceive, much less comprehend, the consequences and ramifications. Our bureaucratic rules ultimately confine us as solidly as if we were in a cage bound by iron bars.

Concertive Control as a Fourth Strategy

Almost since the beginning of modern organizational study, influential theorists have argued that decentralized, participative, and more democratic systems of control offer the most viable alternatives to the bureaucracy's confining routines and rules (e.g., Follett, 1941; Lewin, 1948). This continual push toward participation and a flat organizational structure has become something of an obsession in managerial literature in the last decade or so

(Eccles and Nohria, 1992). Contemporary writers have unleashed a flood of literature announcing the "coming demise of bureaucracy and hierarchy" (Kanter, 1989: 351) and detailing the dawn of a postbureaucratic age in which control emerges not from rational rules and hierarchy but from the concertive, value-based actions of the organization's members (Soeters, 1986; Ogilvy, 1990; Parker, 1992). Characteristic of this movement are influential business consultants such as Tom Peters (1988) and Peter Drucker (1988) who have urged corporate executives to de-bureaucratize their firms and adopt more ideologically based designs drawn around unimpeded, agile authority structures that grow out of a company's consensual, normative ideology, not from its system of formal rules. By cutting out bureaucratic offices and rules, organizations can flatten hierarchies, cut costs, boost productivity, and increase the speed with which they respond to the changing business world.

Tompkins and Cheney (1985) argued that the numerous variations these authors have offered on the postbureaucratic organization represent a new type of control, "concertive" control, built on Edwards's three traditional control strategies. This form represents a key shift in the locus of control from management to the workers themselves, who collaborate to develop the means of their own control. Workers achieve concertive control by reaching a negotiated consensus on how to shape their behavior according to a set of core values, such as the values found in a corporate vision statement. In a sense, concertive control reflects the adoption of a new substantive rationality, a new set of consensual values, by the organization and its members.

This negotiated consensus creates and recreates a value-based discourse that workers use to infer "proper" behavioral premises: ideas, norms, or rules that enable them to act in ways functional for the organization. For example, a newly concertive company may have a vision statement that states, "We are a principled organization that values teamwork." This value may lead one of its members to create a discourse that calls out the premise that "To be principled and value teamwork, we all must come to work on time." The actors can then infer a method of acting (coming to work promptly at 7:00 A.M. not at 7:30), without the traditional supervisor's direction, that is functional for the organization. Thus concertive control becomes manifest as the team members act within the parameters of these value systems and the discourses they themselves create. These new collaboratively created, value-laden premises (manifest as ideas, norms, and rules) become the supervisory force that guides activity in the concertive control system. In concertive control, then, the necessary social rules that constitute meaning and sanction modes of social conduct become manifest through the collaborative interactions of the organization's members. Workers in a concertive organization create the meanings that, in turn, structure the system of their own control. Rule generation moves from the traditional supervisor-subordinate relationship to the actors' negotiated consensus about values.

A second and more important difference between the concertive control model and its bureaucratic predecessor lies in the locus of authority. In the concertive organization, the locus of authority, what actors see as the legitimate source of control to which they are willing to submit (Whitley, 1977), transfers from the bureaucratic system and its rational-legal constitutive rules to the value consensus of the members and its socially created generative rules system. Under bureaucratic control, employees might ensure that they came to work on time because the employee handbook prescribed it and the supervisor had the legal right to demand it, but in the concertive system, employees might come to work on time because their peers now have the authority to demand the workers' willing compliance.

The key question is whether or not the concertive system offers a form of control that conceptually and practically transcends traditional bureaucratic control. I address this question by examining the process through which actors in a concertive organization collaborate to form the rules that structure their day-to-day work and how they give this process legitimate authority. I report on the processes of control that became manifest as a manufacturing organization changed and adapted to a concertive-based structure, in the form of a self-managing, or self-directed team design.

Self-Managing Teams:
An Exemplar of Concertive Control

Currently, the most popular planned organizational change to a postbureaucratic structure is the transformation of a traditional, hierarchically based organization to a flat confederation of concertively controlled self-managing teams. Xerox, General Motors, and Coors Brewing have all initiated this kind of change over the last few years. Although self-managing teams have gained much of their popularity in recent years, they are not a new phenomenon. Research and writing on the subject originally dates from Trist's study of self-regulating English coal miners in the 1950s (Trist et al., 1963; Trist, 1981) and includes the Scandinavian experience with semiautonomous teams (Bolweg, 1976; Katz and Kahn, 1978) and early U.S. team experiences, most notably the Gaines Dog Food plant in Kansas (Walton, 1982; Ketchum, 1984). The contemporary version of the self-managing team concept draws on both the past experiences with teams in Europe and the U.S. and the more recent influence of Japanese-inspired quality circles in Western organizations (Sundstrom, De Meuse, and Futrell, 1990; Sewell and Wilkinson, 1992).

Proponents of self-managing teams have described it as a radical change in the traditional managerial and authority structure of an organization (e.g., Orsburn et al., 1990; Wellins, Byham, and Wilson, 1991). In line with the impulse toward postbureaucratic, concertive-based organizations, they assert that traditional management structures entail inflexible hierarchical and bureaucratic constraints that stifle creativity and innovation. These rigid organizations are top-heavy with managers and unresponsive to changing, dynamic markets, ultimately reducing their competitive viability. From the proponents' viewpoint, U.S. organizations must radically change their managerial structure by converting to worker-run teams and eliminating unneeded supervisors and other bureaucratic staff (traditional management structures). Proponents argue that self-managing teams make companies more productive and competitive by letting workers manage themselves in small, responsive, highly committed, and highly productive groups. Thus, the self-management perspective proposes a "radical" shift from hierarchical supervision to hands-off, collaborative worker management.

This change from supervisory to participatory structures means that workers in a self-managing team will experience day-to-day work life in vastly different ways than workers in a traditional management system. Instead of being told what to do by a supervisor, self-managing workers must gather and synthesize information, act on it, and take collective responsibility for those actions. Self-managing team workers generally are organized into teams of 10 to 15 people who take on the responsibilities of their former supervisors. Top management often provides a value-based corporate vision that team members use to infer parameters and premises (norms and rules) that guide their day-to-day actions. Guided by the company's vision, the self-managing team members direct their own work and coordinate with other areas of the company.

Usually, a self-managing team is responsible for completing a specific, well-defined job function, whether in production or service industries. The team's members are cross-trained to perform any task the work requires and also have the authority and responsibility to make the essential decisions necessary to complete the function. Self-managing teams may build major appliances, process insurance claims, assemble component parts for computers, or handle food service for a large hospital. Along with performing their work functions, members of a self-managing team set their own work schedules, order the materials they need, and do the necessary coordination with other groups. Besides freeing itself from some of the shackles of bureaucracy and saving the cost of low-level managers, the self-managing company also gains increased employee motivation, productivity, and commitment. The employees, in turn, become committed to the organization and its success (Orsburn et al., 1990; Mumby and Stohl, 1991; Wellins, Byham, and Wilson, 1991).

Most current research on self-managing teams concentrates on the functional or economic outcomes of the change to teams. Another body of practitioner-oriented writing recounts how self-managing teams increase organizational productivity, profitability, and employee satisfaction, as well as how corporations deal with problems encountered during the transition to teams (Dumaine, 1990; Lewis, 1990). Other research on self-managing teams tends toward organizational design issues that concern implementing the change (Andrasik and Heimberg, 1982; Carnall, 1982), attitudinal attributes of teamwork (Cordery, Mueller, and Smith, 1991), and leadership requirements within and outside the team (Manz and Sims, 1987). As Sundstrom, De Meuse, and Futrell (1990) and Hackman (1986) have pointed out, however, we still have very little empirical knowledge of how self-managing teams construct new and functional forms of control and how these forms compare with how we have conceptualized control in the past. ISE Communications offered me a useful case for examining this aspect of organizational control longitudinally.

METHODS

ISE Communications

ISE Communications, a small manufacturing company located in a mountain-state metropolitan area, converted from a traditional manufacturing structure to self-managing teams in 1988. ISE manufactures voice and data transmission circuit boards for the telecommunications industry and employs about 150 people, with approximately 90 in manufacturing. ISE was originally a division of a large telecommunications firm, and the ISE management team bought it outright in 1984, although the large firm still remains ISE's largest customer. ISE has the traditional manufacturing, engineering, sales/marketing, human resources, and executive staffs found in most production companies. ISE pays its manufacturing employees by the hour, while the support staff members are on salary.

As expected of a manufacturing company in a large metropolitan area, ISE's production workers represent a cross-section of the local working-class community. Out of 90 manufacturing workers (the worker population when I ended my research in Fall 1992), the ratio of females to males fluctuates but tends to stay around two-thirds female to one-third male. Latino/as, African-Americans, and Asian-Americans are ISE's main ethnic groups, making up about 60 percent of the workforce. At any given time, ISE's manufacturing department employs around 15 percent temporary workers that the company trains in-house. In fact, only one job on the teams, an electronic technician, requires training not provided by ISE.

Manufacturing circuit boards involves requesting board parts (resistors, potentiometers, transistors, etc.) from the supply room, assembling these parts onto a circuit board, and soldering the parts to the boards. The workers must then test the boards for electronic problems, trouble-shoot any problems they find, and make any necessary repairs. This becomes a time-consuming and labor-intensive process. After a board passes the final tests, the workers must package it and process the necessary shipping paperwork. Building and testing boards requires repetitive tasks that easily become monotonous. Unfortunately, the errors that arise from monotony mean costly and lengthy retesting delays or repairs. The work requires close attention to detail and tightly coordinated effort.

Early in my research (Spring 1990), ISE was struggling to survive in a highly competitive and innovative marketplace that demanded flexibility, an emphasis on customer service, and increasing productivity. By the time I wrote this essay two and a half years later, ISE had increased both productivity and profitability. ISE's executives believed that the change to teams was a major reason for their company's success.

"Jack Tackett," the manufacturing vice president and one of ISE's founding members, developed and instigated the company's change to self-managing teams. After reading the works of Crosby, Peters, Drucker, and other consultants, studying manufacturing philosophies like "Just In Time" (JIT)—a company-specific manufacturing method that emphasizes low inventories, first-line decision making, and fast, effective employee action—and taking the pulse of ISE's competition, Jack decided that his company's very survival depended on converting to self-management. As he told me:

> I thought that if we did things the same way all the time, we were headed for disaster. We could not meet customer demands anymore. Hierarchy insulates people from the customer. The traditional organization cannot know the customer, they are in the dark about what goes on around them with the manager making all the decisions. You can't succeed with that anymore. The demands of the market are too dynamic for a company to be controlled by a handful of managers. The whole company needs to be focused on customer needs and I needed to marshal the resources of the whole organization, not just a few. . . . You have to look forward and say what will it take to survive. You can't look inwardly all the time. You can't look back and say, "Well, we survived this way." I say that we aren't going to survive if we always consider what we're doing now to be successful for the future.

In 1986, Jack proposed a plan for implementing self-managing teams at ISE to his management staff. Jack actually convinced many of them that the change to teams was absolutely necessary for ISE to survive—which, for some of them, meant giving up their management jobs, although Jack did arrange lateral moves for them within ISE—and recruited them to help him institute the change. Some thought that the change was a "stupid idea." But Jack was adamant that self-management was *the* way to revitalize the company:

> I had it firmly set in my mind that this was the way we had to go and these guys [the reluctant supervisors] were going to come up to speed or I was gonna get rid of them. And this team process was the natural opportunity to give people the chance to either get on board on their own or to fall by the wayside.

TABLE 5.1 Structure of ISE Before and After the Change to Teams

Before the Change	After the Change
1. Three levels of managerial hierarchy between the vice president and the manufacturing workers.	1. Managerial hierarchy extends directly from the manufacturing teams to the vice president.
2. Manufacturing assembly line organizes the plant. Workers manufacture boards according to their individual place on the line.	2. Team work areas organize the plant. Teams are responsible for complete fabrication, testing, and packaging of their assigned circuit boards.
3. Line and shift supervisors form the first managerial link.	3. Teams manage their own affairs, elect one person to coordinate information for them.
4. Workers have little input into work-related decisions. Managers make all decisions and give all directions.	4. Team members make their own decisions within guidelines set by management and the company vision statement. Teams have shared responsibility for their own productivity.
5. Management disciplines workers.	5. Team members discipline themselves.
6. Management interviews and hires all new workers.	6. Team members interview, hire, and fire their own members.

And the change proceeded with surprisingly little managerial turnover.

After more than a year of planning and training in teamwork skills, which included drafting and distributing ISE's vision statement, Jack and his advisory group started one self-managing team on a trial run in early 1988. He planned slowly to convert the entire production department to teams over the course of a year.

After working through some difficulties, the new team soon began to work better than Jack or anyone else had expected, so Jack and his group decided to expedite the complete conversion. First, they increased the pace of employee training in teamwork, self-supervision, and JIT manufacturing. Then, over a weekend in August of that year, Jack had the manufacturing area completely remodeled and set up for three self-managing teams, originally called red, white, and blue teams. His group rearranged machines, worktables, and other equipment to form three distinct and self-sufficient work areas that gave each team all the necessary equipment needed to produce the types of circuit boards that the new teams would build. The work areas had separate sections for circuit board assembly, testing, repair and touch-up, troubleshooting, and packaging/shipping, all the key tasks required in making a complete circuit board. On Monday, Jack divided the workers into three teams and assigned each team to manufacture or configure two or three particular types of boards (the teams did not make the same types of boards). Table 5.1 summarizes the differences between ISE's operations before and after the change.

Jack, the former managers, and the workers now began the difficult process of adjusting to their new work environment. The workers struggled with establishing concertive control, which meant they had to negotiate such supervisory issues as accepting responsibility, making decisions, and setting their own ground rules for doing good work, such as deciding who was going to perform which tasks, whether or not the team needed to work overtime or on weekends, and whether to hire or fire team members. For his part, Jack tried to build a supportive climate for the teams. He put three of the former supervisors into a nonsupervisory support group focused on helping the teams solve technical problems. He also provided new team-building and inter-personal-skill training programs. If a team came to him with a problem, Jack would only offer suggestions, requiring the team to make the decision. Then he would support the decisions that the teams made, right or wrong, as long as the teams learned from their mistakes. I began my research at ISE during this initial phase of adjustment to self-management, as the new teams were creating the collaborative process that characterizes the dynamics of concertive control.

My interest in self-managing teams came from my own experience with them. Prior to returning to graduate school, I worked as the "leader" of a self-managing team for a large trucking company, which gave me a well-informed perspective on ISE's experience. I first met Jack at a social event in January 1990, where, after finding out about our mutual interest in teams, he invited me to come study what was happening at ISE.

Data Collection

When I first arrived at ISE, Jack introduced me as a researcher from the university interested in writing about self-managing teams and told me to roam around the plant as I wanted. I initially set about meeting people and getting to know the workplace. I spent my first six months there talking with members of each team and various management and support personnel. I watched workers at different stages of production and asked questions about how and why they were doing various tasks. During this period, I cultivated key informants on each team and developed plans and guides for in-depth worker interviews.

During my initial learning phase, I established a schedule of weekly, half-day (four-hour) visits to ISE. I normally alternated between morning and afternoon visits, and I also included some early evening observations of the second shift. I decided on a weekly schedule, mainly because ISE was a 90-minute drive from my residence. Occasional schedule variations occurred, when key events were happening at ISE and I would visit more than once a week, and when I had academic constraints, which would limit my visits to once every two weeks or so for brief periods.

After my first six months, I began an extended process of gathering data, primarily from in-depth interviews, observations, and conversations with key informants, but also from such sources as company memos, flyers, newsletters, and in-house surveys. Then I would withdraw from the setting to analyze the data, write, and develop revised research questions. I would repeat this process by returning to the setting, collecting more data, and then analyzing, writing, and revising again. I also observed and recorded team and company meetings, collected examples of naturally occurring team interactions, and closely followed one team's experiences for four months. In addition, I interviewed nonmanufacturing workers and former ISE employees. When my data collection ended, I had accumulated 275 research hours and conducted 37 in-depth interviews that ranged from as short as 45 minutes to as long as two hours.

In conducting the interviews, I tried as much as possible, given the constraints of voluntary participation, to stratify the interviews roughly across teams, including full-time and temporary employees and crossing ethnic and gender lines. I also interviewed Jack, the team coaches, and a few other members of the management and support staffs. I asked open-ended questions about how the teams made decisions, solved problems, and did day-to-day work. Finally, I probed into their responses for key examples.

During all phases of my data collection, my observer role at ISE did not change. The team members knew that I was studying and writing about their work processes. They were very cooperative and generally accommodated my needs for observation space and interview time. While I would, on occasion, discuss my observations with Jack, I have never filled a formal consulting role, nor has Jack ever asked me to disclose what I considered to be sensitive information about my informants.

Data Analysis

I began my analysis by working from the basic question, "How are the control practices in ISE's new team environment different from the control practices in place prior to the change to teams?" This basic question allowed particular themes about control to emerge from my data that I could compare, revise, and refine as I collected more data and grew more familiar with the case. The particular themes and data analyses I present here emerged from my application to the database of sensitizing concepts (Jorgensen, 1989) primarily drawn from Tompkins and Cheney's (1985), Giddens's (1984), and Weber's (1978) theories of value-based control and constitutive rules. For example, I would examine my data by asking such general questions as, "How has a value-consensus occurred in the team's interactions?" or "Have any teams developed new decision premises or rules?" As significant themes emerged from my data, I would ask about them in subsequent interviews, which allowed their interrelated patterns and subthemes to take shape.

From this analysis I developed an analytical description of the general character of concertive control as it became manifest during ISE's experience with teams, which I present below. To help ensure the validity of this analytical conceptualization and its attendant claims, I cross-checked my interview data with my field notes and observations, interviews with management or support staff, and relevant hard data (team performance results, consultant surveys, human resource data, previous team-training programs). Finally, I reviewed my analysis, claims, and conceptualizations with colleagues not familiar with or participating in the setting (Adler and Adler, 1987).

The result of my analysis is a three-part narrative about the three phases of the evolution of concertive control at ISE. The first phase covers the period of consolidation following the turbulence of the change to teams (late-1988–late-1990). In this phase, the teams began to develop and apply concertive consensus about values that allowed them to infer functional decision premises and interact effectively with each other. The second phase (late-1990–late-1991) saw the teams develop strong norms from their value consensus and begin to enforce these norms on each other as a set of rules. The third phase (late-1991 to mid-1992) saw the stabilization and formalization of these new systems of rules. The rules became rationalized and codified and served as a strong controlling force of team actions.[1]

THE DEVELOPMENT OF CONCERTIVE CONTROL

Phase 1: Consolidation and Value Consensus

Phase 1 began with the chaos of Jack's abrupt changing of the manufacturing area to teams over that weekend in August 1988. While the workers knew that the change was coming, they still walked into a whole new experience on Monday morning. Bonnie, an original ISE employee, described the scene for me:

> Well, it was mass confusion. Nobody knew where they were sitting, what team they were on. They had an idea of what was going on at that point and what the team aspect was all about. As far as details, no idea! So, basically, everybody was just kind of like *wow*, this is kinda fun! Because everything was different, it was wonderful in a way, the atmosphere had changed. It was fun to see who you were going to be sitting with, what team you were going to be on, what you were going to be doing. For me it was like, what board am I going to be working on? 'Cause before, I had a certain board that I had worked on from the beginning [of her tenure at ISE] and I still wanted to be working on it.

Jack assigned workers to the three new teams by drawing names out of a hat. He also assigned a former manager to coach each of the teams for six to nine months until they got used to managing themselves. Jack directed these

coaches, who had themselves been key players (and believers) in the transition
to teams, not to direct the teams overly but to let them learn how to manage
themselves. The coaches saw their role primarily as preventing disasters and
helping the teams to keep the production flowing.

The challenge for the teams during this first phase was learning how to
work together and supervise themselves functionally: They had to learn how
to get a customer's order manufactured and out the door. To do this, they had
to merge, or consolidate, a variety of differing perspectives on how to do good
work. For example, the new team members knew the separate activities
involved in circuit board production, but they did not know how to control
their individual efforts so that they could complete the whole process themselves. They knew how their former supervisors valued good work, but they
lacked a means of articulating this value for themselves. To meet this need,
the teams began developing their own value consensus as to what constituted,
both collectively and individually, good work for the teams and patterns of
behavior that put this consensus into action. Jack had already provided the
foundation of this consensus in the vision statement that he had written for
his new teams.

When ISE began converting to self-managing teams, Jack, along with ISE's
president, crafted a vision statement that articulated a set of core values and
goals, which all employees were to use to guide their daily actions. ISE's
seven-paragraph vision statement functioned in the consolidation phase as a
socially integrating myth that merged basic human values and "day-to-day
[employee] behavior with long-run [organizational] meaning and purpose"
(Peters and Waterman, 1982: 282). Within this context, ISE's vision statement
gave Jack a formula for creating his new concertive organization that centered
on all the new team members working together in concert under the guidance
of shared values rather than the old ISE managerial hierarchy.

The vision's fourth paragraph detailed the essential values that the teams
would draw from during the consolidation phase:

> We will be an organization where each of us is a self-manager who will:
>
> — initiate action, commit to, and act responsibly in achieving objectives
> — be responsible for ISE's performance
> — be responsible for the quality of individual and team output
> — invite team members to contribute based on experience, knowledge and ability.

The values expressed here, such as personal initiative, responsibility, commitment to the team, quality of individual and team contributions, along with
Jack's directive for all to be self-managers, provided the necessary and
legitimated preconditions for the teams to draw their value consensus, essential for concertive control.

Early in my research I saw a framed copy of the vision statement near Jack's
desk and asked him what he saw as its purpose. He replied, "The vision

provides the company the guiding light for driving day-to-day operations for each of the teams." The goals and values in ISE's vision statement served as the nexus for consolidating the teams' material reality (how work gets done) with their ideational reality (their values) (Jermier et al., 1991: 172). When ISE converted to self-management, Jack distributed copies of the vision statement to all team members, and framed copies appeared in each team's area and in central locations like the break room. This led the new team members to talk with each other separately and at team meetings about the vision, particularly its fourth paragraph, and how it related to their work. Out of this talk came the functional patterns that allowed the teams to work together.

When I first began my research (early 1990), I readily noticed the results of this process. The team members talked openly about initiating action, taking ownership for their team's success, taking responsibility for satisfying ISE's customers' needs, emphasizing team quality, and expecting member contributions. The teams had learned to direct their work through planned and ad-hoc team meetings run by a peer-elected coordinator who did just that—coordinated information, such as production schedules, parts supplies, and companywide memos. All the teams met formally for about 15 minutes at the start of the workday to plan the day and solve any known problems. When serious problems arose during the workday, such as an unknown parts shortage holding up production, the teams would meet briefly and decide how to deal with the problem.

During team meetings workers would spend some time talking in administrative terms about the work they had to do and in abstract terms about values expressed in the vision: responsibility, quality, member contribution, commitment to their team and the company. The most prevalent example of these discussions occurred when team members had to decide whether or not to work overtime to meet their production schedules. My illustration comes from my field notes of one of many such situations the blue-team members found themselves in while I was tracking their decision making during the fall of 1990.

Early Friday afternoon, Lee Ann, the coordinator, was anxiously awaiting word from the stockroom that a shipment of circuit potentiometers had arrived. The vendor, about 800 miles away, had promised the shipment would arrive that morning, and the blue team had to get a customer's board order out that evening. Jim, from the stockroom, came running down to the blue team's area about 12:30 to tell Lee Ann that the potentiometers had just arrived, and she called the other eleven members of the team together for a short meeting.

> She looked at the team, "We've got the 'pots' in but it's gonna take us two extra hours to get this done. What do you want to do?"
> Larry groaned, "Damn, I've got plans for five-thirty!"

Suna spoke up, "My daughter's school play's tonight!"

Johnny countered, "But we told Howard Bell [their customer] that we would have these boards out today. It's our responsibility."

Tommy followed, "We're gonna have to stay. We have to do this right."

What followed was a process in which the team negotiated which values and needs (individual or team) would take precedence here and how the team would work out this problem. The team decided to work late; members valued their commitment to a quality product delivered on time to their customer more than their individual time. Lee Ann volunteered to coordinate for the late shipment and to tell Jack Tackett that they would be working overtime (they could do this without his approval). Another team member went to arrange for the building to stay open for them. Larry said that he could put off his plans for two hours. The team agreed to let Suna leave, but she promised to work late the next time they were in a bind.

This vignette depicts how the teams concertively reached a value consensus that, in turn, controlled their individual and collective work. They brought the abstract values of the vision statement into concrete terms. The team members agreed on the priority of their commitment to the team's goals and responsibility for customer needs, and they acted based on this value consensus. These points of agreement also set strong precedents for future action. The blue team's agreement to work overtime to meet customer needs was not a one-time quick fix; it became a pattern that team members would follow as similar situations arose. In a conversation some time after the above meeting, Diego described for me the continuing power of the blue team's value consensus about personal responsibility: "I work my best at trying to help our team to get stuff out the door. If it requires overtime, coming in at five o'clock and spending your weekend here, that's what I do."

Although there were slight differences, this value consensus and these decision premises emerged powerfully and with remarkable consistency across the new teams. Early in 1991, I was sitting with Wendy watching her work with the blue team. I asked her how she reacted to missing a customer requirement:

I feel bad, believe it or not. Last Friday we missed a shipment. I feel like *I* missed the shipment since I'm the last person that sees what goes to ship. But Friday we missed the shipment by two boards and it shouldn't have been missed. But it was and I felt bad because it's me, it's a reflection on me, too, for not getting the boards out the door.

Over time, the teams faced many situations that called for members to reach some sort of value consensus. Other values, not explicitly stated in the vision but influenced by its general thrust, began to appear in the team members' talk and actions. These values helped them unite, learn how to work together, and navigate the turbulence of the change and the possible failure of the company. Team members like Wendy talked about taking ownership of their work, being committed to the success of their team, and viewing ISE as a family and their teammates as family members. Debbie, another original team member, told me about this new feeling of ownership: "Under the old system, who gave a hoot if the boards shipped today or not? We just did our jobs. Now, we have more buy-in by the team members. We feel more personal responsibility for the product." Other values included the need for everyone to contribute fully. The team members called this "saying your piece" at team meetings so that the team's decision would be better (and their consensus stronger). Another part of this value was the need for all team members to learn all the jobs required by the team so that they could fill in and cover for each other.

This was also a time when ISE was struggling desperately and almost went under. In mid-1990, layoffs reduced the teams from three to two. The power of their values helped the teams navigate this difficult period. One of my most vivid memories of this time comes from Liz, who became one of my primary key informants. In August 1990, when the workers did not know if ISE would survive the quarter, she told me how she thought of ISE as a family and how she "spends more time with these people than my real family." She told me that if ISE closed down, "I'm gonna turn the lights out. I love this place and these people so much, I've got to be the last one out. I've gotta see the lights go out to believe it."

The teams' value-based talk and action during the consolidation phase created, in Weber's terms, a new substantive rationality. The team members had committed themselves "first and foremost to substantive goals, to an ethic" that overrode all other commitments (Rothschild and Whitt, 1986: 22). Substantive rationality, in this context, extends from what Weber called "a unified configuration of values" (Kalberg, 1980: 1164) held by a collectivity of people, in this case ISE's team members. This value configuration, or consensus, is intellectually analyzable by the members; they use it to make sense of and guide their everyday interactions. In an organizational situation, a consensus about values informs and influences members' outlooks on and processes of work activity, such as decision making. In doing this, the members place a psychological premium on themselves to act in ethical ways in terms of their values (Weber, 1978: 36; Kalberg, 1980: 1165). These values, then, are morally binding on the team members because they represent the will of the teams and were arrived at through the democratic participation of the team members (Homans, 1950: 125–127; Rothschild and Whitt, 1986: 50). The old rationality and ethic of obeying the supervisor had given way to a new substantive rationality, the teams' value consensus, and a new form of ethical rational action, working in ways that supported the teams' values: Wendy's taking personal responsibility for her team's failure, Debbie's buying in to the team's success, Johnny's reminding the team of its customer commitment, and Diego's willingness to come in at 5 A.M. all illustrate this point.

These examples also point out another significant aspect of substantive rationality. The ethical rational action spawned by a value consensus will take on a methodical character (Kalberg, 1980: 1164): The teams will develop behavioral norms that put their values into action in consistent patterns applicable to a variety of situations, just as team members applied their norm of working overtime to meet customer demands to a variety of situations requiring extra work. Thus, the teams could turn their value consensus into social norms or rules. The teams had manifested the essential element of concertive control: Their value-based interactions became a social force that controlled their actions, as seen in Larry's willingness to forgo his plans in order to work overtime for the team. Authority had transferred from ISE's old supervisory system to the team's value consensus. These norms of ethical action, based in consensual values, penetrate and subjugate other forms of action by the team members. As this occurs, these norms take on a "heightened intensity" (Kalberg, 1980: 1167); they become powerful social rules among the team (Hackman and Walton, 1986; Hackman, 1992). This process played a pivotal role in the next phase of ISE's experience with teams.

There were four key points in the consolidation phase: (1) The teams received ISE's vision statement, which framed a value system for them; (2) the teams began to negotiate value consensus on how to act in accordance with the vision's values; (3) a new substantive rationality emerged among the teams that filled the void left by the former supervisors and the formal rationality associated with following their directives (the teams' values now had authority); and (4) the teams began to form normative rules that brought this rationality into social action.[2] The consolidation phase left ISE with a core group of long-time ISE team workers, committed to the company and to teamwork. The employees had developed a consensus about what values were important to them, what allowed them to do their work, and what gave them pride. And they would guard this consensus closely.

Phase 2: Emergence of Normative Rules

ISE did survive through 1990. In early 1991, the company began to prosper, and a large number of new workers had to be integrated into the teams. These workers were unfamiliar with the teams' value consensus and they posed an immediate challenge to the power relationships the older employees had formed. Further, when ISE began to hire new workers, they hired them on a temporary basis and let the teams decide who to hire on as full-time workers. ISE also added four new teams to the two remaining original teams, for a total of six—red, blue, a new white, and green, silver, and aqua. Jack had to place some of the older, experienced workers on these new teams to help them get organized, and the teams had to integrate their new teammates into their value-based social order. As the team's value consensus and particular work ethic began to penetrate and subjugate the new members' individual work ethics, this process took on a heightened intensity. The substantive rationality of the teams' values gave them authority, which they would exercise at will.

Members of the old teams responded to these changing conditions by discursively turning their value consensus into normative rules that the new workers could readily understand and to which they could subject themselves. By rationalizing their value-based work ethic, the new team members could understand the intent and purpose of their team's values and norms (e.g., why it was important to work overtime to meet a customer need), use the norms to make sense of their daily work experience, and develop methodical patterns of behavior in accordance with the team's values (Miller and O'Leary, 1987; Hackman, 1992).

The longer-tenured team members expected the new workers to identify with (they called it "buy into") the teams' values and act according to their norms. By doing this, ISE's teams were asserting concertive control over the new workers: The new members began to take part in controlling themselves. Slowly, the value-based norms that everyone on the team once "knew" became objective, rationalized rules that the new members could easily understand and follow.

Around March–April 1991, I began to notice that the way the team members talked, both informally and at team meetings, had changed. They did not talk so much about the importance of their teamwork values as they did about the need to "obey" the team's work norms. Team meetings began to have a confrontational tone, and the new workers' attitudes and performance became open topics for team discussion. When the longer-tenured team members saw someone not acting in accordance with their norms, such as not being willing to do whatever it took for the team to be successful, they said something about it. Liz, an original team member, told me of the old team workers' feelings: "We've had occasions where we've had a person say, 'I refuse to sit on the [assembly] line.' And we had to remind him, 'Hey, you are a part of the team and you go where you're needed and you do it.' " Team meetings became a forum for discussing norms and creating new rules. Team members could bring up anybody's behavior for discussion. Again, Liz clarified their feelings: "If you notice that somebody's not getting anything done, then we can bring it up at a meeting, you know, and ask them what the problem is, what's causing them not to be able to get their work done."

The new team members began to feel the heat, and the ones who wanted to be full-time members began to obey the norms. The teams' value-based concertive control began to penetrate and inform the new workers' attitudes and actions. Stephi, who was a temporary employee at the time, told me how she personally tried to conform to the values and norms of her team:

> When I first started I really didn't start off on the right foot, so I've been having to re-prove myself as far as a team player. My attitude gets in the way, I let it get in the way too many times and now I've been watching it and hoping they [her team] will see the change in me and I can prove to them that I will make a good ISE employee.

Stephi's words indicate that concertive control at ISE now revolved around human dignity. The team members rewarded their teammates who readily conformed to their team's norms by making them feel a part of the team and a participant in the team's success. In turn, they punished teammates who had bad attitudes, like Stephi, with guilt and peer pressure to conform (Hackman and Walton, 1986; Mumby and Stohl, 1991; Hackman, 1992). The power of the team's concertive work ethic had taken on its predicted heightened intensity.

A pivotal occurrence during this phase was the teams' value-based norms changing from a loose system that the workers "knew" to a tighter system of objective rules. This transformation most often occurred when new members were not acting according to the team's work norms, such as coming to work on time. Danny told me how easily this change came about:

> Well we had some disciplinary thing, you know. We had a few certain people who didn't show up on time and made a habit of coming in late. So the team got together and kinda set some guidelines and we told them, you know, "If you come in late the third time and you don't wanna do anything to correct it, you're gone." That was a team decision that this was a guideline that we were gonna follow.

The teams experienced the need to make their normative work ethic easily understandable (and rewardable and punishable), and they responded by making objective guidelines.

The team members' talk turned toward the need to follow their rules, to work effectively in concert with each other. In mid-1991, I found Ronald, a technician and my key informant on the green team, angrily cleaning up a mistake made by a new technician who had not followed the rules: "All this should have been caught three months ago, and I'm just now catching it. And upon looking into it, it was because the tech wasn't taking his responsibility for raising the flag or turning on the red light when he had a problem." Later that day, I was sitting with the silver team when I saw Ryan confront a newer team member who was working on four boards at a time instead of one, which the team had discovered increased the chance for error. Ryan stood above the offender and pointed at him, "Hey quit doing that. You're not allowed to do that. It's against the rules."

By turning their norms into rational rules, the teams could integrate new members and still be functional, getting products out the door on time. The "supervisor" was now not so much the teams' value consensus as it was their rules. You either obeyed the rules and the team welcomed you as a member, or you broke them and risked punishment. This element of concertive control worked well. As Danny, a temporary worker at this time told me, "If you're a new person here, you're going to be watched."

Even the coordinator's role and responsibilities became more objectified during this phase. Some teams agreed on five specific tasks for the coordinator to do, other teams had seven. The teams now elected coordinators for six-month periods rather than one month. The coordinator role began to take on the aura of a supervisor. People began to look to coordinators for leadership and direction. Lee Ann, a coordinator at this time, told me one day, "Damn, I feel like a supervisor, I just don't get paid for it."

The second pivotal occurrence during this phase involved how authority worked among the teams. After the consolidation phase, authority had moved from the former supervisory system to the new value consensus of the teams, but during the second phase, the old team members, all full-time employees, were the keepers of this new system. They identified strongly with it and expected new members to demonstrate their worthiness to participate with them in the concertive process. They began to use rewards and punishments to encourage compliance among the team members. Temporary workers either obeyed the rules and became integrated into this system, or they found the door. The teams' interactions left little room for resistance. This placed strong pressure on the temporary workers to conform to their team's rules. Tommy, a temporary worker then, explained the pressure:

> Being temporary, you could come in any day and find out you don't have a job no more. So, that's kind of scary for a lot of people who have, you know, kids and a lot of bills to take care of. So they tend to hold it in, what they want to say, to the point where they can't do it anymore and they just blow up, which causes them to lose their job anyway.

Before the change to teams, the line supervisors would generally tolerate some degree of slackness among the workers and allow someone many chances to screw-up before taking drastic action. But now the team members exercised their new-found authority with much less patience. In mid-1991, I walked into the blue team's area one morning and found the temporary workers very agitated and the full-time workers nowhere around. I asked Katie what was happening. She said that the full-time workers had gone off to fire Joey. Joey was a temporary who worked hard but had a tendency to wander off across the shop and socialize. While he did not do this often, he had the knack of doing it when Martha, the coordinator, or another full-time worker happened to notice his absence. The previous day, Joey had been caught again. That morning, after the team meeting, the full-time workers said that they were going to go to the conference room to talk about Joey's problem. Right before I came to the team's area, they had called him back to the conference room. Katie looked back over her shoulder toward the conference room and sighed, "He's a good worker, but they [the full-time workers] don't see that. They don't know him. Now they're back there, judge, jury, and executioners."

While peer pressure may be essential to the effective work of any team (Walton and Hackman, 1986: 186; Larson and Lafasto, 1989: 96), the dynamics of ISE's teams during this phase go much deeper. The above episode was not a simple case of the full-timers beating up on the temporaries. What seemed to be peer pressure and power games on the surface was in fact a manifestation of concertive control. Authority here rests in the team's values, norms, and now rules. Team members rewarded themselves for compliance and punished themselves for noncompliance. They had invested their human dignity in the system of their own control (Parker and Slaughter, 1988; Mumby and Stohl, 1991). As participants in concertive control, the team members had begun a process of functionally constructing both their work activity and their own identities (Cheney, 1991).

The second phase represents a natural progression of the value-based substantive rationality the teams had created in phase 1. The teams demystified their value consensus for new members by making it intellectually analyzable. The norms of phase 1 now became guidelines or rules, increasingly objectified and clarified for the team members, which allowed for effective interaction. The values forming the teams' substantive rationality provided the boundaries of action and interest within and among the teams (Kalberg, 1980: 1170), but the control of actions and interests in the teams is not stable; it has to be fixed at particular points in time. The emergence of rational rules during the second phase served this function. These rules made concertive control concrete, almost as tangible as their old supervisor's book of job descriptions. It was the locus of authority resting with the teams themselves, however, that gave the rules their power. It empowered the teams to enable certain activity and constrain others. The locus of authority made concertive control work for ISE's teams.

Four key points characterize the development of concertive control at ISE during the second phase: (1) The teams had to bring new members into the particular value-based social systems they had created during phase 1; (2) to meet this need, the teams began to form normative rules for doing good work on the teams, creating what Hackman and Walton (1986: 83) called a team's "core norms." Longer-tenured team members expected the new members to identify and comply with these rules and their underlying values; (3) the rules naturally began to take on a more rationalized character; and (4) concertive control functioned through the team members themselves sanctioning their own actions. While the influx of new members may have served as a catalyst for the emergence of normative rules on the teams, the rules came about through the natural progression of the team's value consensus into what Weber called a "methodical way of life" on the organizational/team level (Kalberg, 1980: 1164). This was how the new members could learn their teams' value consensus and participate in their new form of control. Further, these particular tensions between full-time and temporary workers were not enduring. What did last was the impact of rationalizing the rules and the fact that authority rested with the peer pressure of the teams.

Phase 3: Stabilization and Formalization of the Rules

During this time (late-1991 to mid-1992), the company began to stabilize and turn a profit. A large number of temporary workers had been integrated into the full-time pool during phase 2, which resulted in the number of temporary workers falling from a high of almost 50 percent at times in phase 2 to as few as 10 percent during phase 3. But the stabilization phase also saw the teams' normative rules become more and more rationalized: Their value-based substantive rationality was giving way to rationalization (Cooper and Burrell, 1988: 93). What were simple norms in phase 1 (we all need to be at work on time) now became highly objective rules similar to ISE's old bureaucratic structure (if you are more than five minutes late, you're docked a day's pay). On the surface, day-to-day control still looked much different than when ISE had traditional supervisors, but, on a deeper level, this control seemed hauntingly familiar and much more powerful.

The most noticeable change occurred in the coordinator's role. From my first days at ISE, I had tracked a continual pressure to make the coordinator's duties clearer and more specified. Thus, the coordinators' work gradually had become more formalized. If the team members needed something from the human resources department, they would ask the coordinator to get it. If Jack needed information about a team's work, he would ask the coordinator for it. The coordinators began to take on more and more specific tasks: scheduling, tracking production errors, holding regular meetings with each other, and so forth. In early 1992, the role became formalized as a permanent position, now called facilitator. The teams nominated workers for the six positions, and a committee of workers and managers (including Jack) interviewed the nominees and selected the new facilitators. These six workers received a 10 percent boost in their hourly wage to signify their new importance. They also drew up a list of duties for the role, which really just formalized what the old coordinators had already been doing. Lee Ann, who became the blue team's facilitator saw this process, too, as she told me about a month after assuming the new role: "It's more formalized acceptance that somebody is gonna be the one to answer the questions, and you might as well have someone answering the questions of the team and of management. And, I get paid for it, too." The most interesting aspect of the change in the coordinator role for me was that the workers wanted it, not so much to reinvent hierarchy on the teams but because formalizing their work life seemed so natural to them.

Formalizing the aspects of their work appeared to give the teams a sense of stability that would insulate them from the turmoil of the past year, and so rules proliferated in all aspects of the teams' activity. As Brown (1978: 368) suggested, the rules were taking on their own rationality and legitimacy. What was once an abstract value, such as "a team member should be able to do all the work roles on the team," had now become a set of specific guidelines for how long new members had to train for a specific function (assembling, testing, repairing, etc.) and how long a team member would have to work in assembly before rotating to a new team job, such as repair.

During phase 3, I saw the teams' social rules become more and more rigid. The teams seemed to be trying to permanently fix their social rules. Two examples stand out for me. In mid-1992, I was talking with Liz, who had also become a facilitator, about how members directed each other's actions now, as opposed to three years before. Liz told me that her team had been talking about drafting a "code of conduct" for team members that spelled out the behaviors needed to be a good team member. She began to get very excited about the possibilities of making these actions clear and concrete. She said, "If we can just get this *written down* [emphasis hers]. If we can just get our code of conduct in writing, then everyone will know what to do. We won't have so many problems. If we can just get it written down." I found the second telling example when I visited ISE again two weeks later. I had been following how the teams were dealing with attendance and how their rules for coming into work on time were becoming more specific. A team member who came in five minutes or more late would be charged with an "occurrence" and considered to be absent for the whole day. If a worker accumulated four occurrences in a month, the team facilitator would place a written warning in that person's company file. A worker who came in less than five minutes late received a "tardy," and seven tardies equaled one occurrence. While I knew that all the teams had some kind of attendance policy, what I found this day truly surprised me. When I walked into the red team's area, I saw a new chart on its wall. The chart listed each team member's name down the left-hand side and had across the top a series of columns representing days of the week. Beside each name were color-coded dots that indicated "on time," "tardy," or "occurrence." The team had posted this board in plain sight for all team members to see, and the team updated its board every day. I found a similar chart in use by the other teams.

Three thoughts went through my mind. The first was the powerful insight of Ronald's comment, which opened this article: "Now the whole team is around me and the whole team is observing what I'm doing." The second was that this policy seemed uncannily similar to something I would have expected to find in the old supervisory system. The third was that the teams had now created, in effect, a nearly perfect form of control. Their attendance behavior (and in a way their human dignity) was on constant display for everyone else on the team to monitor: an essentially total system of control almost impossible to resist (Foucault, 1976). The transformation from values to norms to rules had gained even more heightened intensity.

The fact that the teams were creating their own rational rule systems was not lost on all the team members, but they expressed the feeling that these rules were good for them and their work. As Lee Ann told me at this time:

> We are making a lot of new rules, but most of them come from, "Well see, because so and so person did such and such, well we're not gonna allow that anymore" [concertive control at work]. But the majority of the rules that we are putting in are coming from what the old rules were [before the change to teams]. They had a purpose. They did stop people from making, like expensive mistakes. . . . With more people on the teams, we have to be more formal. We have seventeen people on my team. That large amount of people moving is what's causing the bureaucracy to come back in.

Lee Ann's use of "bureaucracy" perplexed me. Had ISE's teams reinvented a bureaucratic system of control? Certainly the substantive rationality and its focus on value consensus that characterized phase 1 now had become blurred with a new formal rationality that focused on making rules, which appeared to fit with Weber's prediction that "a *multiplicity* of rationalization processes . . . variously conflict and coalesce with one another at all societal and civilizational levels" (Kalberg, 1980: 1147), including among ISE's teams. And certainly much of the pressure toward formalization came from the team's need to be productive and efficient in order for ISE to survive in its competitive market (Kalberg, 1980: 1163). But as I later reflected on Lee Ann's comment and my experience at ISE, the nature of this blurring of substantive and formal rationality became clearer.

The progression of the teams' value-based work ethic from norms to rational rules indicated that the workers had created micro-level disciplines that rationalized their work behaviors so as to make them purposeful, functional, and controlled (Foucault, 1980; Barker and Cheney, 1994). Discipline, here, refers to a willingly accepted social force that rationalizes organizational work to ensure normalized and controlled individual and collective action. During phase 3, the teams developed formalized rule systems out of the normative ethics of their original value consensus. These disciplinary systems enabled the teams to work effectively, integrate new members easily, and meet their production demands. The team members willingly accepted these disciplines because they themselves had created them. And these disciplines appeared to work. During phase 3, ISE became profitable again. ISE's top management believed that the change to teams was one of the key reasons (along with other key changes in engineering and marketing) for the company's success. Jack credited the change to teams with cutting his factory costs 25 percent since 1988.

But the teams' formalization of their value system and norms did not mean that they had recreated a bureaucracy. Authority in ISE's concertive system rested with the teams and their interactions with each other. The character of ISE's concertive control was still much different than when it operated under bureaucratic control. As they integrated more temporary workers into the ranks of full-time members, the team members still held authority over each other. They still expected each other to follow the rules and, as evidenced by their attendance charts, still monitored each other's behavior carefully. The team members themselves still rewarded or punished each other's behavior. They did not give this function to the new facilitators: they kept it for themselves.

Close to the end of my data collection, Liz told me of an incident that had occurred a few days before, involving Sharon, a single mother who had some difficulty getting to work at 7 A.M. The team had been sensitive to her needs and had even given her a week off when one of her children was sick. The day before the incident, enough time had passed for Sharon to drop one of her many occurrences. She even announced this to the team by making a joke of it, "I just dropped one occurrence, so that means I can have another." The next morning one of her children was sick again and she was late. And the team remembered her "joke" of the night before.

When Sharon showed up, the team reacted in the same way a shift supervisor in ISE's old system might have. The team confronted Sharon immediately and directly. They told her that they were very upset that she was late. They bluntly told her how much they had suffered from having to work short-handed. Stung by the criticism of her peers, Sharon began to cry. The team's tack shifted to healing the wounds they had caused. They told her that they had not meant to hurt her feelings but that they wanted her to understand how her actions had affected them. They asked her to be certain to contact them immediately when she had a problem. The episode closed with the team telling her, "we really count on you to be here and we really need you here." When I checked a month later, Sharon had not recorded another occurrence.

In phase 3, the team members still kept the authority to control each other's behaviors: concertive control still occurred within the teams. In many ways, the formalization of the team's normative rules made this process easier, as seen in the incident with Sharon. The teams had created an omnipresent "tutelary eye of the norm,"[3] with the team members themselves as the eye, that continually observed their actions, ready either to reward or, more important, punish. Being under the constant eye of the norm appeared to me to have an effect on the workers. To a person, the older team workers told me that they felt much more stress in the team environment than they had under the old ISE system. The newer members also complained of the constant strain of self-management. This sense of heightened stress that ISE's workers expressed to me was similar to that found in other team-based organizations (e.g., Grenier, 1988; Mumby and Stohl, 1991). Parker and Slaughter (1988) even called the self-management concept management by stress.

My key informants also appeared more strained and burdened than in times past. I had watched Liz change from the totally committed team member in 1990, who saw her team as a family and wanted to be the last one to turn out the lights, to a distant, distracted facilitator in 1992, too harried and pressured to take any enjoyment in her team or to think of it as a family. Lee Ann, in a conversation with me in August 1992, expressed the same feelings:

> After you've been here awhile, you're gonna get super-involved, then you're gonna get burned out. I see this with person after person. You get really involved, you take it home with you, you eat with it, you sleep with it. You work 12-, 16-hour days and you just burn out. You may step out just a bit, let someone else get super-involved for awhile, then you'll pick it up again. But you won't have that enthusiasm anymore.

The tutelary eye of the norm demanded its observants become super-involved or risk its wrath, and critical to this phase, the eye also demanded that its observants demonstrate this involvement by following its rules, its rational routine. That was work life in the eye of the norm, in ISE's brand of concertive control.

In phase 3, the teams' activity appeared to stabilize around sets of formalized rules that provided a rational and effective routine for their day-to-day actions. As in the previous phases, this formalization did not change the locus of authority in the teams but rather strengthened it. The team members directed and monitored each other's actions. Concertive control still occurred within the teams themselves. Four key points characterize phase 3: (1) The normative rules of phase 2 became more and more objective, creating a new formal rationality among the teams; (2) the teams appeared to "settle in" to the rational routine these formal rules brought to their work; the rules made it easier for them to deal objectively with difficult situations (such as Sharon's coming in late) by establishing a system of work regulation and worker self-control; (3) the team members felt stress from the concertive system, but they accepted this as a natural part of their work—they did not want to give up their feeling of being self-managers, however, no matter how intense the system of control became; and (4) the work life at ISE stabilized into a concertive system that revolved around sets of rational rules, as in the old bureaucracy, but in which the authority to command obedience rested with the team members themselves, in contrast to the old ISE. The team members had become their own masters *and* their own slaves.

CONSEQUENCES OF CONCERTIVE CONTROL AT ISE

Table 5.2 summarizes and juxtaposes the manifest and latent consequences emerging from the system of concertive control that evolved at ISE between 1988 and 1992. This table depicts how concertive control, in a process akin

TABLE 5.2 Manifest and Latent Consequences of ISE's Experience with Concertive Control

Manifest	*Latent*
1. Teams developed value consensus by drawing from ISE's vision statement.	1. Teams began to form a value-based substantive rationality, which led them to develop a mutually shared sense of ethical rational action at work.
2. Team members identified with their particular value consensus and developed emotional attachments to their shared values.	2. Authority transferred from ISE's old bureaucratic control system to the team's value system. The team members' human dignity became invested in submitting to this authority.
3. Teams formed behavioral norms from the values that enabled them to work effectively, thus putting their vaues into action.	3. The teams became methodical about putting their values into action. Their values began a natural progression toward rationalization, which allowed the values and norms to be intellectually analyzable by all members.
4. Older team members expected new members to identify with the norms and values and act in accordance with these value-based norms.	4. Concertive control became nested in the team. Members themselves took on both superior and subordinate roles, monitoring and directing.
5. The teams' normative rules grew more rationalized. Team members enforced their rules with each other through peer pressure and behavioral sanctions.	5. ISE's concertive system became a powerful force of control. Since they had created it themselves, this control was seemingly natural and unapparent to the team members.
6. Teams further objectified and formalized the rules and shared these rules with each other. The work environment appeared to stabilize.	6. The teams had developed their own disciplines that merged their substantive values with a rule-based formal rationality. These disciplines enabled the teams to work efficiently and effectively. The teams controlled their work through a system of rational rules and the self-monitoring of their own individual and collective actions.

to Lewin's (1946) model of "unfreezing-moving-refreezing," matured from a loosely held consensus about abstract values to a tightly bound system of rational rules and powerful self-control. ISE's experience with teams and the analysis I have reported here are consistent with other research reports of self-management systems at the level of the worker (e.g., Grenier, 1988), which suggests that concertive control has a particular character: Concertive control, as it becomes manifest in organizational interaction, is more powerful and has a greater ability to control than the bureaucratic system it replaces.

Writers on concertive control have warned that this new system could become a stronger force than bureaucratic control. Tompkins and Cheney (1985: 184) asserted that concertive control would increase the strength of control in its system, and Tannenbaum (1968) proposed that if management will give up some of its authority to the workers, it will, in turn, increase the effectiveness of control in the firm. Tannenbaum (1968: 23) wrote that participative (self-managing in this case) organizations could not be productive "unless they have an effective system of control through which the potentially diverse interests and actions of members are integrated in concerted, that is, organized behavior. The relative success of participative approaches, therefore, hinges not on reducing control but on achieving a system of control that is more effective than that of other systems." This "more effective system of control," in terms of self-managing teams, comes from the authority and power teammates exercise on each other as peer managers.

Peer management increases the total amount of control in a concertive system through two important dynamics. The first is that concertive workers have created this system through their own shared value consensus, which they enforce on each other. But in doing so, as seen in ISE's experience, the teams necessarily create a system of value-based rational rules, such as their strict attendance policy. They have put themselves under their own eye of the norm, resulting in a powerful system of control.

The second reason for the increased power of concertive control is that the way it becomes manifest is less apparent than bureaucratic control. Team members are relatively unaware of how the system they created actually controls their actions (Tompkins and Cheney, 1985). Concertive control is much more subtle than a supervisor telling a group of workers what to do. In a concertive system, as with ISE, the workers create a value-based system of control and then invest themselves in it through their strong identification with the system (Barker and Cheney, 1994). Because of this identification, the team members are socially constructed by the system they have created (Mumby and Stohl, 1991). When this happens, the team members readily accept that they are controlling their own actions. It seems natural, and they willingly submit to their own control system. ISE's team members felt that developing a very strict and objective attendance policy was a natural occurrence. Likewise, their challenging Sharon's personal dignity when she violated the policy was another natural occurrence. And ISE's teams work effectively without Jack's constant (i.e., more apparent) monitoring. Thus, ISE's team workers are both under the eye of the norm and *in* the eye of the norm, but from where they are, in the eye, all seems natural and as it should be. Their system of rational rules winds tighter and tighter about them as the power of their value consensus compels their willful obedience.

ISE's experience with concertive control, then, is consistent with two theoretical predictions about the future of organizational activity. The first, which extends from Weber (1978) to Foucault (1976, 1980), asserts that organizational life will become increasingly rationalized and controlled. The second, which emerges primarily from Tompkins and Cheney (1985), Tannenbaum (1968), and Edwards (1981), posits that organizational control will become less apparent and more powerful.

The development of concertive control at ISE also complements the traditional literature on work-group norms and team development (e.g., Sundstrom, De Meuse, and Futrell, 1990; Hackman, 1992). ISE's experience with concertive control illuminates the linkages between the emergence of group norms and the broader organizational issues of authority, rationality, power, and control.

ISE's teams developed a concertive system of control that grew from value-laden premises to strong norms, to rational rules for good work in the teams. ISE's system became deeply embedded in the social relations of the members, which served to conceal the character of concertive control. Because of this, the concertive, value-based rules increased the overall force of control in the system, making it more powerful than bureaucratic control had been. Unlike the bureaucratic hierarchy, authority and the possibility of appeal first and finally resided in the peer pressure of the teams.

ISE's experience with concertive control still begs the question: Does the concertive system offer a form of control that conceptually and *practically* transcends traditional bureaucratic control? My analysis of ISE's experience with teams indicates that, on the one hand, a concertive system creates its own powerful set of rational rules, which resembles the traditional bureaucracy. But, on the other hand, the locus of authority has transferred from the hierarchical system to the teams' values, norms, and rules, which does not resemble the bureaucracy. Concertive control works by blurring substantive and formal rationality into a "communal-rational" system (Barker and Tompkins, 1993). Concertive workers create a communal value system that eventually controls their actions through rational rules.

More important, however, my analysis suggests that concertive control does not free workers from Weber's iron cage of rational rules, as the culturalist and practitioner-oriented writers on contemporary organizations often argue. Instead, an ironic paradox occurs: The iron cage becomes stronger. The powerful combination of peer pressure and rational rules in the concertive system creates a new iron cage whose bars are almost invisible to the workers it incarcerates. ISE's team workers, as Weber (1978: 988) warned, have harnessed themselves into a rational apparatus out of which they truly cannot squirm. As ISE's experience demonstrates, uncommitted workers do not last in the concertive system. Concertive workers must invest a part of themselves in the team: they must identify strongly with their team's values and goals, its norms and rules. If they want to resist their team's control, they must be willing to risk their human dignity, being made to feel unworthy as a "teammate." Entrapment in the iron cage is the cost of concertive control.

NOTES

1. Although the line that divides the point at which an idea in a worker's mind becomes a behavioral norm and then a rule is very indistinct, the concepts of concertively generated and collaboratively held value consensus, norms, and rules are important heuristics for explaining the processual nature of concertive control. Simon (1976: 223) distinguished between value-based and factual-based decision premises. No longer guided by the old factual premises of the traditional supervisor, ISE's workers found themselves in a process of creating value premises and turning them into factual premises. Adopting these heuristic concepts and expressing their relationship as a transition from value consensus to norms to rules enables me to discuss this elusive process analytically.

2. ISE's teams developed in ways consistent with traditional studies of small groups and teams, most notably Tuckman's (1965), Homans' (1950), and Lewin's (1946) models of group formation and Walton and Hackman's (1986) model of work-group value and norm development. While cognizant of the parallels ISE's teams have to these fundamental models, I have sought to situate the story of how the teams developed a new form of control within the broader framework of the social forces (rationality, authority, social rule generation, etc.) that shaped the teams' organizational context.

3. I am indebted to Professor Lars Thøgar Christensen of Odense University in Denmark for coining this phrase.

REFERENCES

Adler, Patricia A., and Peter Adler. 1987. *Membership Roles in Field Research*. Beverly Hills, CA: Sage.

Andrasik, Frank, and Judy Stanley Heimberg. 1982. "Self-management procedures." In Lee W. Frederiksen (ed.), *Handbook of Organizational Behavior Management*: 219–247. New York: Wiley.

Barker, James R., and George Cheney. 1994. "The concept and the practices of discipline in contemporary organizational life." *Communication Monographs*, 61(1):19–43.

Barker, James R., and Phillip K. Tompkins. 1993. "Organizations, teams, control, and identification." Unpublished manuscript, Department of Communication, University of Colorado, Boulder.

Barnard, Chester. 1968. *The Functions of the Executive*. (Originally published in 1938.) Cambridge, MA: Harvard University Press.

Bolweg, Joep F. 1976. *Job Design and Industrial Democracy*. Leiden: Martinus Nijhoff.

Brown, Richard Harvey. 1978. "Bureaucracy as praxis: Toward a political phenomenology of formal organizations." *Administrative Science Quarterly*, 23: 365–382.

Carnall, C. A. 1982. "Semi-autonomous work groups and the social structure of the organization." *Journal of Management Studies*, 19: 277–294.

Cheney, George. 1991. *Rhetoric in an Organizational Society: Managing Multiple Identities*. Columbia, SC: University of South Carolina Press.

Coombs, Rod, David Knights, and Hugh C. Willmott. 1992. "Culture, control, and competition: Towards a conceptual framework for the study of information technology in organizations." *Organization Studies*, 13: 51–72.

Cooper, Robert, and Gibson Burrell. 1988. "Modernism, postmodernism, and organizational analysis: An introduction." *Organization Studies*, 9: 91–112.

Cordery, John L., Walter S. Mueller, and Leigh M. Smith. 1991. "Attitudinal and behavioral effects of autonomous group working: A longitudinal field study." *Academy of Management Journal*, 34: 464–476.

Drucker, Peter E. 1988. "The coming of the new organizations." *Harvard Business Review*, Jan.–Feb.: 45–53.

Dumaine, Brian. 1990. "Who needs a boss?" *Fortune*, May: 52–60.

Eccles, Robert G., and Nitin Nohria. 1992. *Beyond the Hype: Rediscovering the Essence of Management*. Cambridge, MA: Harvard Business School Press.

Edwards, Richard C. 1981. "The social relations of production at the point of production." In Mary Zey-Ferrell and Michael Aiken (eds.), *Complex Organizations: Critical Perspectives*: 156–182. Glenview, IL: Scott, Foresman.

Follett, Mary Parker. 1941. *Dynamic Administration: The Collected Papers of Mary Parker Follett*, Henry C. Metcalf and L. Urwick, eds. London: Pitman.

Foucault, Michel. 1976. *Discipline and Punish*. New York: Vintage.

———. 1980. *Power/Knowledge*. New York: Pantheon.

Giddens, Anthony. 1984. *The Constitution of Society: Outline of the Theory of Structuration*. Berkeley: University of California Press.

Grenier, Guillermo J. 1988. *Inhuman Relations*. Philadelphia: Temple University Press.

Hackman, J. Richard. 1986. "The psychology of self-management in organizations." In Michael S. Pallak and Robert O. Perloff (eds.), *Psychology and Work: Productivity, Change, and Employment*: 89–136. Washington, DC: American Psychological Association.

———. 1992. "Group influences on individuals in organizations." In Marvin D. Dunnette and Leaetta M. Hough (eds.), *Handbook of Industrial and Organizational Psychology*, 2d ed., 3: 199–267. Palo Alto, CA: Consulting Psychologists Press.

Hackman, J. Richard, and Richard E. Walton. 1986. "Leading groups in organizations." In Paul S. Goodman and Associates (eds.), *Designing Effective Work Groups*: 72–119. San Francisco: Jossey-Bass.

Homans, George C. 1950. *The Human Group*. New York: Harcourt, Brace & World.

Jermier, John M., John W. Slocum, Jr., Louis W. Fry, and Jeannie Gaines. 1991. "Resistance behind the myth and facade of an official culture." *Organization Science*, 2: 170–194.

Jorgensen, Danny L. 1989. *Participant Observation: A Methodology for Human Studies*. Newbury Park, CA: Sage.

Kalberg, Stephen. 1980. "Max Weber's types of rationality: Cornerstones for the analysis of rationalization processes in history." *American Journal of Sociology*, 85: 1145–1179.

Kanter, Rosabeth Moss. 1989. *When Giants Learn to Dance*. New York: Simon & Schuster.

Katz, Daniel, and Robert L. Kahn. 1978. *The Social Psychology of Organizations*. New York: Wiley.

Ketchum, L. D. 1984. "How redesigned plants really work." *National Productivity Review*, 3: 246–254.

Larson, Carl E., and Frank M. J. Lafasto. 1989. *Teamwork: What Must Go Right/What Can Go Wrong*. Newbury Park, CA: Sage.

Lewin, Kurt. 1946. "Research on minority problems." *Technology Review*, 3: 48.

———. 1948. *Resolving Social Conflicts: Selected Papers on Group Dynamics*. New York: Harper & Row.

Lewis, Betty. 1990. "Team-directed workforce from a worker's view." *Target*, Winter: 23–29.

Manz, Charles C., and Henry P. Sims. 1987. "Leading workers to lead themselves: The external leadership of self-managing work teams." *Administrative Science Quarterly*, 32: 106–128.

Miller, P., and T. O'Leary. 1987. "Accounting and the construction of the governable person." *Accounting, Organizations and Society*, 12: 235–265.

Mumby, Dennis K., and Cynthia Stohl. 1991. "Power and discourse in organizational studies: Absence and the dialectic of control." *Discourse and Society*, 2: 313–332.

Ogilvy, Jack. 1990. "This postmodern business." *Marketing and Research Today*, Feb.: 4–20.

Orsburn, Jack D., Linda Moran, Ed Musselwhite, and John H. Zenger. 1990. *Self-Directed Work Teams: The New American Challenge*. Homewood, IL: Irwin.

Parker, Martin. 1992. "Post-modern organizations or postmodern organizational theory?" *Organization Studies,* 13: 1–17

Parker, Mike, and Jane Slaughter. 1988. *Choosing Sides: Unions and the Team Concept.* Boston: South End Press.

Perrow, Charles. 1986. *Complex Organizations: A Critical Essay.* New York: Random House.

Peters, Thomas J. 1988. *Thriving on Chaos.* New York: Knopf.

Peters, Thomas J., and Richard Waterman, Jr. 1982. *In Search of Excellence: Lessons from America's Best-Run Companies.* New York: Harper & Row.

Riggs, Fred. 1979. "Introduction: Shifting meanings of the term 'bureaucracy.' " *International Science Journal,* 31: 563–584.

Rothschild, Joyce, and J. Allen Whitt. 1986. *The Cooperative Workplace.* Cambridge: Cambridge University Press.

Sewell, Graham, and Bary Wilkinson. 1992. " 'Someone to watch over me': Surveillance, discipline and the just-in-time labour process." *Sociology,* 26: 271–289.

Simon, Herbert A. 1976. *Administrative Behavior: A Study of Decision-Making Processes in Administrative Organizations,* 3rd ed. New York: Free Press.

Soeters, Joseph L. 1986. "Excellent companies as social movements." *Journal of Management Studies,* 23: 299–312.

Sundstrom, Eric, Kenneth P. De Meuse, and David Futrell. 1990. "Work teams: Applications and effectiveness." *American Psychologist,* 45: 120–133.

Tannenbaum, Arnold S. 1968. *Control in Organizations.* New York: McGraw-Hill.

Tompkins, Phillip K., and George Cheney. 1985. "Communication and unobtrusive control in contemporary organizations." In Robert D. McPhee and Phillip K. Tompkins (eds.), *Organizational Communication: Traditional Themes and New Directions:* 179–210. Newbury Park, CA: Sage.

Trist, Eric L. 1981. "The evolution of socio-technical systems." Occasional Paper No. 2. Toronto: Quality of Working Life Centre.

Trist, Eric L., G. Higgin, H. Murray, and A. B. Pollock. 1963. *Organizational Choice.* London: Tavistock.

Tuckman, Bruce W. 1965. "Development sequences in small groups." *Psychological Bulletin,* 63: 384–399.

Walton, Richard E. 1982. "The Topeka work system: Optimistic visions, pessimistic hypothesis, and reality." In Robert Zager and Michael P. Roscow (eds.), *The Innovative Organization:* 260–287. New York: Pergamon.

Walton, Richard E., and J. Richard Hackman. 1986. "Groups under contrasting management strategies." In Paul S. Goodman and Associates (eds.), *Designing Effective Work Groups:* 168–201. San Francisco: Jossey-Bass.

Weber, Max. 1958. *The Protestant Ethic and the Spirit of Capitalism.* New York: Scribner's.

———. 1978. *Economy and Society.* Guenther Roth and Klaus Wittich, eds. Berkeley: University of California Press.

Wellins, Richard S., William C. Byham, and Jeanne M. Wilson. 1991. *Empowered Teams: Creating Self-Directed Work Groups That Improve Quality, Productivity, and Participation.* San Francisco: Jossey-Bass.

Whitley, Richard. 1977. "Organizational control and the problem of order." *Social Science Information,* 16: 169–189.

6

STATUS DEGRADATION AND ORGANIZATIONAL SUCCESSION
An Ethnomethodological Approach

Robert P. Gephart, Jr.

Developing innovative theories and methods for enriching our understanding of social organization has become the subject of growing concern. While there are innumerable potential means of accomplishing this goal, four possibilities discussed in the current literature seem particularly useful.

First, several social scientists have suggested that increased attention be given to the study of everyday life activities in naturally occurring settings (Garfinkel, 1967; Douglas, 1970; Turner, 1974). Weick (1974), in particular, has related this suggestion to potential innovations in organizational theory. Second, there is concern for encouraging generation of hypotheses (Lundberg,

AUTHOR'S NOTE: This article was written with the support of doctoral fellowships awarded by Xerox of Canada, Ltd. and the University of British Columbia. The author wishes to thank Thad Barnowe, Peter Frost, Bill Johnston, Vance Mitchell, Bill Reeves, Ron Taylor, Bev Zubot, Bill Zwermann, and anonymous *ASQ* reviewers for helpful comments at various stages of this project. Conversations with Roy Turner were basic to the author's grasp of ethnomethodology; the present article is a partial response to a question originally posed by Professor Turner during the author's Ph.D. preliminary examination. However, none of the above organizations or persons should be held responsible for the points of view ultimately taken in this article. Reprinted from *Administrative Science Quarterly*, 23 (Dec. 1978): 553–581.

1976) and the "discovery of grounded theory" (Glaser and Strauss, 1967). Third, an interest in human cognition and sense-making practices has been rekindled and linked to the social construction of organizational realities (Berger and Luckmann, 1966; Weick, 1969, 1977; Jehenson, 1973; Pondy and Mitroff, 1978). Finally, methodologists have advocated a renewed interest in qualitative case analysis. Thus Campbell (1975) asserts that case studies are particularly useful because they allow examination of multiple theoretical implications in a single study.

This article enacts these suggestions by approaching the study of organizational succession using qualitative data obtained in a participant observation study of an emerging organization. I undertake an ethnomethodological analysis of the members' sense-making practices whereby they socially construct an enforceable organizational reality and implement it by accomplishing organizational succession. My concern is, therefore, to develop a grounded theory of organizational succession. Before discussing the present investigation, it is useful to outline previous succession research in order to provide points of contrasts and departure for an alternative approach to understanding succession phenomena.

A REVIEW OF ORGANIZATIONAL SUCCESSION LITERATURE

Members of organizations commonly are assigned, acquire, or achieve some formal status denoted by a term invoked to locate them as occupants of a position in a formalized (written) hierarchy termed "the formal structure" of the organization.[1] Succession in organizations may be defined as the process whereby the particular incumbent of such a position changes. Succession therefore involves changes in the status of two or more persons, the predecessor and the successor.

Organizational succession can be studied using a variety of theoretical perspectives and research methodologies. Such perspectives are often complementary, with each theory and/or method shedding light on specific aspects of succession. These studies can be typified in terms of two rather distinct approaches.

The more common approach involves searching for, and testing hypotheses relating to, concomitants or correlates of organizational succession. Such an approach relies heavily on quantitative data and quantitative analytical techniques for comparative case analyses. This approach has matured considerably in recent years, moving from examination of simple relationships among two or three variables using the chi-square test (e.g., Grusky, 1961) to complex multivariate designs (e.g., Pfeffer and Salancik, 1977). Most of this research uses published organizational data in the form of *Fortune 500, Moody's Industrial Manual,* and *Standard and Poor's Register of Corporations, Directors, and Executives* (Grusky, 1961; Helmich and Brown, 1972; Pfeffer and Leblebici, 1973; Helmich, 1974) or baseball records (Grusky, 1963; Gamson and Scotch, 1964; Gordon and Becker, 1964). Other studies have used questionnaires (Kriesberg, 1962; Pfeffer and Salancik, 1977).

This approach has generated numerous insights. However, as is the case with any perspective, it has certain limitations or tradeoffs. These studies use aggregated statistical data suitable to answering macro questions regarding aggregates of organizations. They do not, and perhaps cannot, explore the micro-sociological processes which occur in situated, face-to-face interactions involved in organizational succession within a specific organization. Studies of this type thus do not examine concrete activities in everyday settings.

A related limitation is the exclusive concern with the formal organization generally found in these studies. Only the formal organization constituted by formal positions as defined by organization charts is examined. This practice ignores the manner in which positions and statuses are negotiated and change, the meanings created and utilized by organizational members, and the entire range of informal organizational phenomena to be found in the organizational setting. The primary limitation of this approach to the study of organizational succession is thus exclusion from consideration of a large range of important phenomena, due to failure to examine the actual behavior and meanings of organizational members, particularly those who produce succession.

A second approach to the study of succession involves analysis of specific cases, focusing on the effects of succession on the organization. Studies included in this approach are those by Christensen (1953), Gouldner (1954), Guest (1962a, 1962b), Zald (1965), and Kotin and Sharaf (1967). These studies use participant observation, interviews, and documentary analysis to provide accounts of members' activities, meanings, and concerns.

These qualitative case analyses are empirically rich descriptions of succession but are limited in their concerns. First, they obscure important events by reporting general summaries of events rather than transcripts of the conversations which constituted the events. For example, Zald's section on the process of election (1965: 56–57) does not report any segments of the conversation involved in, or concommitant with, the selection process. Second, the theoretical and conceptual schemes which emerge in the studies are insightful but are underdeveloped and fail to organize the vast array of reported and reportable events into a coherent framework. Thus Zald (1965) is one of the few qualitative researchers to develop an explicit propositional set. Third, most studies focus on successor selection and give little attention to the stages involving successor departure. Finally, many concepts such as "the organization" are not clarified or linked to a theory of participants' meanings and sense making.

Olsen's (1976a, 1976b) excellent study of decision making in the selection of a dean at a major American university is related to this case-analytic approach. This study applies a range of methodologies to test the adequacy of various decision models and cognitive balance theories. Despite the relevance of the study to understanding organizational succession, it is primarily concerned with analyzing decision making in successor selection, not with testing or generating a substantive theory of succession. Further, while it hints at the process of the social construction of organizational realities, it does not undertake explicit analysis of the process nor does it report or analyze dialogue from conversations as constitutive of the social construction process. This study is important and insightful but leaves several interesting aspects of organizational succession unexamined.

This selective review of succession literature indicates that the suggestions for enriching organizational theory discussed in the first section of this article are applicable to succession research. Following this reasoning, the limitations of current research and theory can be overcome in several specific ways. First, we could examine micro-sociological processes, including verbal dialogue embedded in naturally occurring face-to-face interactions which produce succession. Second, research could move beyond the formal conception of the organization by examining informal phenomena and developing a more heuristic conception of "organization" which reflects the members' meanings and sense-making practices. Finally, a theory or theories of organizational succession could be developed by inductive construction of grounded theory based on qualitative analyses of specific cases of organizational succession. The remainder of this article seeks to accomplish these tasks.

A PRELIMINARY ETHNOMETHODOLOGICAL MODEL FOR ORGANIZATIONAL ANALYSIS

Ethnomethodology is concerned with the methods by which social actors or "members" construct "everyday life" social realities.[2] Such actors are viewed as engaged in constructing and reconstructing social realities through generating and using meanings to make events sensible.

A dramaturgical metaphor is often employed; actors must manage appearances and constantly ad lib essentially vague social roles in an emergent stream of existential being and awareness. A basic assumption is that social reality is not merely a stable entity passively entered and apprehended, but one which requires actors (members) to work at accomplishing this "reality for all practical purposes."

Ethnomethodologists seek first to understand common activities of organizational participants in the language these participants use, that is, the concepts of actors in their daily lives (Schutz, 1962). But these first-order terms and meanings are built into second-order theoretical constructs—the social scientific concepts of the constructs of actors in their daily lives (Schutz, 1962). Grounding the theoretical constructs in everyday life constructs is necessary to ensure the adequacy of the theory for explaining the everyday activities, meanings, and settings of social actors.

Given the desire for understanding natural settings as they happen, ethnomethodology favors observational strategies such as participant observation. Research results commonly include presenting conversational dialogue and analyzing its features. Theoretical analysis is thus concerned with explaining specific cases, but this does not mean it relinquishes trans-situational interests. As Zimmerman and Pollner point out (1970: 95):

> The practices through which a feature is displayed and detected, however, are assumed to display invariant properties across settings whose substantive features they make observable. It is to the discovery of these practices and their invariant properties that inquiry is to be addressed.

The Concept of Organization

Ethnomethodology has a particular interest in "the procedures and considerations actors invoke in relating terms of rational common-sense construction to things in the world" (Bittner, 1974: 75). One such common-sense term, also employed in social science dialogue, is the concept of organization. I noted earlier that social scientists often refer to the organization as an entity literally constituted by the formal organization, including organization charts. But as Bittner (1974) notes, bureaucrats themselves do not take the formal scheme literally; they take for granted a background stock of knowledge which fills in the rational scheme, makes it sensible, and is basic to the mode in which it is used in actual activities. From the ethnomethodological perspective, the meaning of concepts such as organization "must be discovered by studying their use in real scenes of action" (1974: 75)—that is, by studying how participants involved in those scenes use their everyday constructs to make a variety of everyday events, objects, and activities meaningful.

The organizational scheme "emerges as a generalized formula to which all sorts of problems can be brought for solution" (Bittner, 1974: 76). Thus the formal organizational chart and rules are not mere static representations of the ideal structure of the organization. They are schemes "for interpretation that competent and entitled users can invoke in yet unknown ways whenever it suits their purposes" (pp. 76–77). The schemes are invoked in new situations in a creative manner to explain behavior, to prescribe and justify sanctions for deviance, and generally to give an organizationally relevant meaning to phenomena which otherwise would not have such meaning. Thus the organization is constituted by linguistic devices and interpretational schemes which members use to make sensible certain conduct, events, and states of affairs and to methodically locate them as falling within the purview of "the organization."

Bittner (1974) has identified three typical forms or ways in which members construct the organization verbally, and these forms can be elaborated as follows. The *gambit of compliance* (move of compliance) refers to utterances in which members display a conception of the organization as an entity demanding compliance by actors. They may construct the organization by mentioning rules, using them to define behavior, and indicating such rules which "belong to the organization" require, demand, and warrant conformity. Thus a factory foreman may construct the organization by means of the following gambit of compliance confronting a tardy employee with: "Around here we start work at 7:30 sharp. Be here on time."

In the *model of stylistic unity*, members' utterances display a concern for, and the nature of, the proper style of organizational behavior. Models of stylistic unity are a background against which members identify the odd, improper, and uncouth activities (behavior in bad taste) of their fellow participants. The issue here is one of taste and style, not of consistency with legal or formal policy specifications. Thus, in constructing the organization as a model of style, members verbalize an image of obviously proper form for certain events and activities they locate within the organization. For example, a secretary may do this by making the following comment about a coworker: "How can she wear a dress like *that* to work? Maybe on a date but *not* to work!"

In the *model of functional integrity*, members work at demonstrating how some, perhaps seemingly irrelevant or unrelated, activities or events affect the functioning of the organization. They thus use, and display verbally, theories of the organization which portray it as having certain needs and requirements for continued existence. The following utterance shows such a construction: "If the contract doesn't go through, the whole place will fall apart. The shop will close."

From the ethnomethodological perspective, the organization must be regarded as a linguistic device and resource constructed during human sense-making activities. We cannot, therefore, assume that conceptions and constructions of the organization are stable or that all participants share them. Rather, these conceptions are problematic and essentially vague. Members must work to define activities as falling within the organizational scheme. As members confront practical problems, they invoke the organization as a scheme furnishing solutions, but this scheme is reconstructed, modified, and negotiated continuously to fit the practical problems at hand. Also, each member has a different biography and background knowledge which is used to fill in essentially vague aspects of the member's conception (Schutz, 1962). Finally, there is a social distribution of knowledge about the organization (Berger and Luckmann, 1966).

Thus, while members may assume that they share aspects of the organizational scheme, situations arise where these assumptions are demonstrably incorrect. Various competing schemes may emerge, each with its proponents and adherents. Negotiation of a common scheme then becomes the problem at hand, as each member or group seeks to negotiate and enforce agreement on its scheme as proper, correct, real, moral, and so on. Members' conceptions of the rules demanding compliance, their models of stylistic unity, and their schemes of the organization as a functional integrity may evolve in a dialectical or multilectical process as common-sense theories of reality are confronted by, and imposed on, concrete situations, activities, and meanings.

Social Rules

The concept of social rules is a second-order theoretical construct which may be useful in understanding members' conceptions of an organization. Social rules may be defined as verbal or written specifications of activity in relation to objects, modes of communication, temporal states and boundaries, and the position of actors in the social structure. The concept of social rules subsumes those first-order or common-sense constructions which are referred to in natural language as rules, laws, policy, proposals, and so on. For example, members may refer to a company's written policy regarding overtime. Such a policy (first-order term) invariably specifies who (structural position) may, must, or may not work overtime and when (temporal state), thereby implying some work activity related to objects in the work environment and to overtime pay rates. The policy also generally specifies the appropriate means of notifying workers that they are requested to work overtime (modes of communication). The social science construct of social rules thus subsumes overtime policy.

Social rules may be grouped into three categories: incipient rules, conventional rules, and formal rules. Incipient rules are proposals for action which have not yet been formally instituted or become common practice. A motion at a council meeting is an incipient rule until passed by majority vote. Conventional rules are generally accepted rules of the social order, including common social practices. Leaving one's work station a few minutes before the work day ends is a conventional rule for numerous factory workers, although it is perhaps resisted by management. Conventional rules are therefore not necessarily consistent with formal rules, which are the written policy statements or laws outlined in the official communication media of the organization. Overtime policy is an example of a formal rule.

Social rules may be regarded as resources involved in the social construction of the organization. Verbal moves, such as a gambit of compliance, propose and utilize social rules as interpretive schemes constitutive of aspects of the organization.

Organizational Succession as
Status Degradation

Organizational succession involves the negotiation of status of two or more members, retrospectively termed the predecessor and the successor. While status is always a negotiated phenomenon (Cicourel, 1972), its negotiation is clearest in situations and events such as succession, where it is an explicit concern of members. Thus, succession is a good arena in which to examine status transformation processes and the social construction of organizational reality. Conversely, examination of such processes will enrich our understanding of succession.

Review of past research and various accounts of succession indicate that one manner in which members differentiate types of succession is with reference to the cause of predecessor departure. Thus, succession can be described as caused by a predecessor's (1) death, (2) retirement, (3) forced removal (demotion, firing), (4) voluntary resignation, or (5) promotion, transfer, or advancement. Each type of succession has its unique aspects, meanings, activities, and effects. One direction for research is to fill these categories in with empirical examples describing how each type of succession gets done and what it means to members.

The present study focuses on a case of succession involving the forced removal of a predecessor. Forced removal is one element in the general theoretical category of status degradation. A status degradation ceremony is a situated event in the degradation process constituted by "any communicative work between persons, whereby the public identity of an actor is transformed into something lower in the scheme of social types" (Garfinkel, 1956: 420).

As an ideal-type process, status degradation requires that (1) a deviant (rule-violating) activity and a perpetrator be identified, (2) violated rules be shown to derive from values the group considers to be ultimate in nature, (3) a denouncer emerges and becomes a public figure supporting these ultimate values on behalf of the group, and (4) the perpetrator is defined as a deviant motivational type preferring not just one deviant act but deviant acts in general.

While Garfinkel's model is concerned with jury trials, the total identity of an actor, and hence global status redefinition, a more limited form of status degradation occurs in organizations and may be termed organizational status degradation. The success of this degradation is defined as the degree of status transformation of the rule violator where this is related to his or her ability to perform roles incumbent on a social position. The successful degradation ceremony involves relocating an actor in a lower formal social position with lessened status, formal authority, and power to control certain resources. Even where the degradation is not successful in removing him from a social position, the ceremony may serve to put the actor on probation. His performance of duties associated with his position will not be immediately affected.

However, future violations will cause him to be labeled a repeat violator, and the past violation may influence the course and outcome of future degradation attempts.

Status degradation ceremonies are important situated activities and events in organizational life because they require the members to display and use their background conceptions of the organization as well as agree on the entity termed "the organization." That is, a status degradation would seem to require (1) agreeing on who the incumbent is, (2) what his position and status are, and (3) that some social order constituting the organization is breached. Therefore, I propose that negotiating status in organizational status degradation ceremonies involves negotiating and constructing the organization as a reality independent of its particular members but with determining power over their activities, that is, it involves the social construction of enforceable organizational reality.

The primary purpose of the present study is to investigate how the organization, as an interpretive scheme, is negotiated, constructed, and used as a resource in accomplishing degradation. By focusing on one type of succession and studying members' sense-making practices, the usefulness of an ethnomethodological approach may be illustrated and our understanding of succession enriched.

METHOD

Collection and Preparation of Data

Data reported in this study were collected by observing the events reported and examining various documents produced by the organization under study. Field notes were produced as follows. A researcher, while present in observational settings, noted (in shorthand) the conversational utterances of members, their activities, and characteristics of the settings. As soon as possible after leaving the setting (generally immediately thereafter), the researcher reviewed the notes and used them to construct a description of the events which had transpired.

Settings. Formal meetings of a Graduate Students' Centre[3] Operation's Committee (GSCOC) and a Grad Representative Council (GRC) were observed, as were informal gatherings of members and various graduate students. Formal meetings were regularly scheduled and announced, open to all members of the graduate student community, and held in the Graduate Centre. Observations were collected by taking notes because this activity was consistent with the "meeting" nature of the setting; commonly, committee members and others in attendance took notes at various points during the meeting. Visible use of a tape recorder would have disrupted the setting, and use of a hidden tape recorder would have been unethical. Informal gatherings were observed during regular Centre hours. Note taking was also consistent with this situation as many Centre patrons carried notebooks and used them to study at the Centre.

Researchers. The author of the present study was one researcher, and he prepared the field notes which refer to informal gatherings and GRC meetings. However, as he was a central participant at GSCOC meetings, where note taking interfered with full participation, a second researcher was asked to attend those meetings, which occurred after September 19, 1974, and to prepare a record of conversational dialogue occurring at each meeting.

The second researcher attended GSCOC meetings in the role of observer, watching and listening without entering the discussion. The observer was a graduate student in sociology with field research experience and was somewhat knowledgeable about the Centre but did not hold any formal positions in the organizations under study. It seems safe to assume the observer did not disrupt GSCOC meetings, as several other noncommittee members attended the meetings, generally with the expressed purpose of "just seeing what's going on." The record of the critical November 1974 degradation ceremony presented below was prepared by the observer.

Relations Among Participants

The author was a primary participant in the activities described here. He was the original leader of the organization (chairman of GSCOC), and functioned in that position from the beginning of the study until he was removed from office (degraded) some thirteen months later. (His utterances are indicated by the initials RG.)

GSCOC had a fluctuating membership prior to September 1974. The bulk of data reported here occurred after that date, and during this time membership was quite stable. There were eight GSCOC members in September 1974, after GSCOC was restructured. Two of these resigned before November, and the six remaining members were all present at the critical degradation ceremony.

All six were graduate students at the start of the study and patronized the Centre on one or more occasions prior to December 1973. All were known to one another prior to that date, having met at graduate association meetings. RG, IS, IM, and BS were "regulars" throughout the course of the study, as they were present during most of the bar service functions (two or three per week). IS was, perhaps, the closest friend of RG (among the committee members), but all four were well acquainted and generally friendly toward one another. DA and LB were students in the same department and interacted frequently in courses. While acquaintances of RG, they were not regarded by him as friends, though they exchanged pleasantries whenever they met on campus. DA and LB seldom patronized the Centre, and when they did so, it was at official GRC functions or at Friday afternoon happy hours in the company of departmental colleagues. DA and LB seldom interacted with RG, IS, IM, or BS other than during GRC or GSCOC meetings.

The second researcher had met all GSCOC members prior to attending the GSCOC meetings but was little more than an acquaintance to members other than RG. These members knew the researcher only as a graduate student in sociology.

Construction of the Present Account

The following account is based on conversational activity at formal GSCOC meetings. While informal discussions held outside the formal meetings were relevant to the degradation process, they are generally not reported or analyzed here for several reasons. First, the social production of formal status degradation was of major interest, and the formal degradation itself occurred at an official meeting. Second, formal meetings were settings where various viewpoints were explicated and negotiated. Researchers had access mainly to informal gatherings of persons resisting degradation, not to meetings of those supporting it. Thus, examining talk at formal meetings minimizes the possibly one-sided nature of descriptive accounts which would have been constructed using field notes of informal gatherings. At the same time, the dialogue of the formal meetings is assumed to represent much of the range of topics, interests, and views held by members and expressed in informal gatherings. Third, only a limited amount of data could be presented in a paper such as this, and focusing on the formal degradation ceremony limited the range of data to be included. Finally, a good record of talk at the formal degradation ceremony was available and could be included in its entirety. While the researcher exercised selectivity in choosing to report degradation talk in formal rather than informal gatherings, presenting the entire discussion eliminates selectivity in reporting particular utterances within the discussion. The reader may thus examine the rather complete data base from which the theory was constructed and decide more readily on the relevance and adequacy of the theoretical analysis vis-à-vis the basic data.

The data presented in this study were collected as part of another project (Gephart, 1975) some two years before this article was written. Field notes recording conversations were not analyzed or examined from the time of their production until the present article was begun, and the events were not conceived as "succession" during the earlier project. In May 1977, the author became interested in organizational succession and realized the as yet unanalyzed field notes might contain data concerning succession. Armed with the theoretical concepts of social rules, organization, and status degradation, the field notes and formal documents were analyzed in the hope of generating a low-order theory of one form of succession. The remainder of this article reports the results of this endeavor.

THE EMERGENCE OF THE POSITION
OF GRADUATE CENTRE CHAIRMAN

The events described in this paper concern the chairmanship of the Graduate Students' Centre Operations Committee (GSCOC) at a western Canadian university between October 1, 1973 and November 30, 1974. The Centre Committee is a standing committee of the Graduate Representatives Council (GRC); GRC is a primary policy-making body of the Grad Students' Association and was the primary source of Centre funding.

The position of chairman was created in October 1973. GRC had acquired a room on campus and proposed to make it a graduate center, although the nature and functions of the center were unclear. At the first GRC meeting of the year, the GRC chairman asked for volunteers to open the Centre, plan its activities, and run it. RG volunteered and was formally appointed "chairman of opening" (GRC minutes, 10/23/73).[4] Discussion resulted in a $5,000 budget and the hope of opening the Centre as a coffee lounge during weekdays and a bar on weekends. The GSCOC was created by formal motion a few weeks later with RG as its chairman. At the time RG stated, "I think we need to formalize the committee so people will listen to us."

Despite its formal underpinnings, the committee functioned informally. No formal meetings were held and members consisted of regular patrons who ran the Centre, under RG's guidance, on a day-to-day basis. Policy was a matter of convention and the chairman was the task leader. He phoned people to organize events, obtained liquor permits for special functions, requested people to serve as staff members, and generally ran Centre affairs as he saw fit.

Although the Centre grew in patronage and sales, receipts for purchases were accumulated in a drawer, cash from liquor sales was kept in a can, and no formal bookkeeping system was instituted. By June 1974, GSCOC members decided that their present space was inadequate; following negotiations with the university administration, a more desirable location was obtained, to be effective September 1.

The Centre's original funds were largely consumed by operational expenses and initial capital outlays. In mid-June 1974, a summer budget was requested and received, under the provision "all monies to be accurately accounted for before more monies allocated to the Centre" (GRC minutes, 6/13/74). By September, the Centre had moved to the new space and had developed a shortage of funds. On behalf of the GSCOC, RG requested further operating funds in the form of a proposed $17,000 budget. One GRC member argued at the meeting debating the budget request, "Our old motion requires a funds accounting before more funds are released." The GSCOC request was then ruled out of order and GSCOC was instructed "to present a full account of expenditures to date" (GSCOC minutes, 9/9/74).

Preliminary Degradation Attempts

The next GRC meeting was scheduled for September 19 with the GSCOC financial report the only item on the agenda. RG attempted to present the report on behalf of GSCOC but was repeatedly heckled and interrupted by dissidents. GSCOC had maintained a checking account throughout the summer. One dissident GRC member stated it was "unconstitutional for someone other than the treasurer to have access to a checking account" (GRC minutes, 9/19/74). The GSCOC report was deemed inconsistent with proper accounting procedures, as illustrated by the following statement by a dissident member: "What is this mess? There's no way in hell an accountant would accept it. It's just not proper. We passed a motion at the time we gave you the funds saying you had to account for all the funds in a proper manner. There's no way this is acceptable. The Centre committee should be disbanded. . . . We've been ripped off." GRC finally passed a motion that "the Centre committee be disbanded and that a new one be struck and that RG be commended for his labors" (GRC minutes, 9/19/1974: 2). GRC sentiment was expressed in one member's statement: "In the future, proper bookkeeping and accountability are absolutely essential. No more of this shit." In the reconstruction of the GSCOC, RG was narrowly reelected chairman, defeating his primary denouncer (DA) by a 10-to-7 vote. Two dissident GRC members were appointed to GSCOC, including DA. Concern for ensuring proper financial accountability led GRC to move that "a manager be hired to be responsible for the operations of the Centre. . . . " (GRC minutes, 9/19/1974). The rationale was expressed by the GRC treasurer: "Look, let's hire a manager. Make him file proper financial reports regularly. If he screws up, we can fire him. And he can be bonded so we don't lose any money if he takes off on us." Thus while RG maintained his position as chairman, GRC funding of the Centre was cut off until a manager was hired. An initial attempt to separate operational roles from policy formulation was begun by this proposal to hire a manager.

The restructured committee began to have formal meetings regularly, differentiated into subcommittees, and selected a secretary to keep minutes. All of these were tasks which were not previously undertaken. The first internal rules which emerged included a formal rule that the bar service be temporarily closed due to lack of financing and an incipient rule that the chairman act only as directed by the committee. This incipient rule was constituted by members' talk, such as one member's statement: "Look, if we're going to work as a proper committee, then the chairman has to do what we want. He can't go out and do things on his own without our authorization."

The bar was closed for one evening following the committee's policy but was reopened on the decision of the chairman when a group of patrons supplied funds for bar service. At the next committee meeting an attempted degradation occurred when certain members sought to legislate an indefinite closing of the Centre, disband the committee, and remove the chairman due to his discretionary action. The attempt occurred as follows:

> LB: Mr. Chairman, I understand the bar service was in operation on Saturday night. Is this correct?
>
> RG: Yes, but I had the permission of the members I could contact, and the funding. . . .
>
> DA: (to RG) You had no right to do that. We specifically passed a motion that there was to be no bar service. And policy is policy. Until GRC allows funds and a manager is hired to keep proper accounting records, there is to be no bar service. . . . You violated our policy. . . . You never pay any attention to what this committee decides. You don't act on behalf of us —you do whatever you want.

A motion to disband the committee was subsequently defeated, with the chairman casting the deciding vote. However, the committee passed this motion: "The committee censures action of the chairman and the committee points out to the chairman he has no authority to operate outside the direction of this committee" (GSCOC minutes, 9/30/1974).

A Successful Status Degradation Ceremony

The chairman functioned as unpaid manager and coordinator of the Centre while GRC withheld funding. The search for a manager was unsuccessful, due to the vicissitudes of obtaining a firm financial commitment from the GRC.

The chairman became dissatisfied with committee policy which repeatedly failed to request operating funds in formal reports to the GRC and prohibited the chairman from requesting funds directly. In November 1974, RG attended a GRC meeting and requested and obtained funding for payment of a manager's salary. At the next GSCOC meeting, this behavior became a matter of discussion and the basis of a successful status degradation ceremony. The following lines contain the entire discussion of degradation.

> 1. RG: The next item on the agenda—Mr. A.—the chairman's resignation.
> 2. LB: I'll take the chair for this discussion, Mr. Chairman. Mr. A.?
> 3. RG: Maybe DA wants to resign.

4. **DA:** I don't prepare to resign. Mr. RG gave an impromptu speech at GRC last night. It would have been appropriate to say no report. It was an extraordinary meeting—there was no reason to have our report. We had no opportunity to prepare a report. The only thing which bothers me is that his speech was done under committee reports, as if he represented the committee.

5. **RG:** I was only trying to get us terms of reference. . . .

6. **LB:** We went through this before. We passed motions saying you could only give formal reports.

7. **DA:** Your talk was out of place. If you're not prepared to abide by our rules, resign.

8. **IM:** RG's speech was out of place but his review of our meeting in lieu of a report was OK. Would we have had a report?

9. **DA:** We don't circulate reports. All our rules were thrown out last night.

10. **IS:** We were going along, doing well. But last night people got the idea our committee was in conflict. Our public image is shattered.

11. **RG:** Let me summarize what I did. I asked to give an informal report — not a formal committee report, just a personal one. I asked for other opinions. You said we needed terms of reference regarding exclusive use of space before setting up admission policy. I was leading up to that and. . . .

12. **LB:** You're not in a position to do that, RG. At the last state [incomprehensible] we decided the Centre committee discusses bar reports.

13. **DA:** You had every way to avert problems. I asked for your resignation as you're not serving the interests of the committee. We've warned you before.

14. **LB:** Our minutes say that if it came up again you'd resign.

15. **DA:** The whole business is odious.

16. **BS:** RG felt that it was a good time to educate GRC. He didn't have the authority — but it wasn't a deliberate attempt to flout authority.

17. **DA:** Didn't this committee decide to give only formal reports? At the time I pointed out that this was not official. RG made the motion—I didn't want to stop him when he put it on the agenda and make it look like a conflict. I hoped he'd avoid it.

18. **IM:** The business of the manager's salary—whose job—ours or theirs?

19. **LB:** If we'd known last night was GRC meeting, a report would have been there. I can't attend meetings Tuesday or Thursday as I have classes. The issue is one of procedure.

20. **RG:** I said it was not a committee report. We needed to determine a salary for the manager to keep running. And we could discuss, although not vote on, the exclusive space issue.

21. **LB:** You had no call to comment at all. You can't bring up the manager's salary—the executive hadn't made a decision. We have no authority until the executive decision.

22. **BS:** I thought a manager was hired at $200.00. Who hired him?

23. **RG:** I did—as an executive member.

24. **LB:** This is irrelevant. Mr. DA requests the resignation by the chairman on grounds of misconduct. Constrict your comments to that issue.

25. **IM:** If the chairman resigns, who will be the chairman? We have to consider that.

26. **DA:** It's up to GRC—the president—can we appoint one?

27. **RG:** So if you vote me out, the Centre is in limbo until the next GRC meeting.

28. **LB:** You're suggesting no one wants it?

29. **DA:** We would all want to be chairman. It requires no work—or very little, only doing what the Centre committee specifies. Is RG acting as chairman or acting on his own? Either he or the rest of us must go.

30. **LB:** Anyone comment? If we pass the motion then he resigns.

31. **RG:** I thought I was in the chair.

32. **LB:** No, you can't be. We're talking about you.

33. **RG:** The chairman does have duties. It takes up to 40 hours a week to run this place. We need a dynamic person. . . .

34. **LB:** The hours are irrelevant. Excess time is an exercise in futility.

35. **BS:** I hoped this was buried 6 weeks back—the committee must be reconstituted. The committee will disband if the chairman resigns.

36. **RG:** Does the committee intend I get off the committee?

37. **IM:** If RG resigns, we need a temporary chairman.

38. **LB:** GRC can reaffirm you or reappoint you. Will you resign or do we have to move you resign?

39. **RG:** I'm not resigning.

40. **DA:** I'd hoped you'd resign and avoid this distasteful procedure. I move the chairman be removed.

41. **RG:** You can't vote me out. You can only recommend it to GRC.

42. **LB:** I'll turn the chair over to IM and call the question.

43. **IM:** All in favor? (Members in favor raise their hands—three of five members vote in favor, thereby passing the motion in accord with majority rule.) I guess the motion is carried.

44. **RG:** Can I be on the committee? I interpret the situation that the chairman is elected independently of committee members. Therefore, I'm off the committee.

45. **DA:** I nominate IS as chairman.

46. **IS:** I nominate DA as chairman.

47. **BS:** This is like table tennis.

48. **IS:** May the nominees speak? I can't see myself as the chairman type. I just really don't know what I want to say. My immediate reaction is negative.

49. **LB:** Are you withdrawing?

50. **IS:** May I?

51. **DA:** My initial reaction is I don't want the job.

52. **RG:** How about a rotating chairman?

53. **DA:** I don't think a chairman has to do all RG has.

54. **LB:** The chairman just does committee work.

55. **DA:** The only thing is that I don't want this to be regarded as a political power move.

56. **RG:** Madame chairman may I be allowed to speak? (LB nods assent.) How can we have a chairman who doesn't show up to keep the Centre open?

57. **LB:** I'll say this about you—you're the world's greatest cheap shot artist.

58. **DA:** If this is Mr. RG's behavior or attitude, we may not ask Mr. RG to be on the committee.

59. **IS:** As far as I can see, it only means assuming the chair, calling meetings, and taking the initiative on certain occasions where a few tasks are required. What about cochairmen?

60. **IM:** It would be hard to do.

61. **LB:** OK.

62. **BS:** Is there any necessity beyond procedural reasons to have a chairman? I can't see any, so I'll abstain.

63. **LB:** We've outlined these but haven't done any. For example a formal balance sheet was set up, but no one has collected them. And we need a positive report to GRC regarding finances and so on.

64. **IM:** I haven't handed these things in — we give them to the GRC treasurer.

65. **LB:** If BS abstains, only one votes.

66. **RG:** Nominees? Can't they vote?

67. **LB:** Certainly.

68. **DA:** I'll flip you—call (to IS) (LB flips a coin. IM calls heads).

69. **LB:** DA won the toss — he's got the job.

70. **DA:** Is RG on the committee?

71. **IS:** I move RG be invited to remain a committee member.

72. **DA:** Anyone opposed? RG stays on the committee.

At this point, conversation shifted away from the degradation to other policy issues. Following the conclusion of the meeting, RG turned the keys to the Centre over to DA, thereby signifying that DA was now in charge.

Post-Ceremony Transmission
of News of Degradation

The status transformations were not fully enacted at the meeting but required talk outside it. A number of people had to be informed of the change in leadership, particularly people with whom the GSCOC chairman necessarily interacted in accomplishing his duties.

Examples of announcements of the change in chairman include the following. The day after the degradation RG informed an assistant vice president of the university with whom he worked closely, "I'm no longer Centre chairman. I've been replaced." The administrator responded, "So, they threw you out, huh? Who's in charge now? . . . Will he call me or should I contact him?" The president of the students' union greeted RG by stating [before RG had an opportunity to speak] "Well Gephart, they finally ousted ya! Did they throw ya out completely, or are ya still on the committee?" Finally, at the next GSCOC meeting a graduate student approached RG with a request to use the Centre for a departmental social event. LB overheard this and interrupted the conversation, stating "There's no use talking to him. He's only a member of the committee. Talk to DA, he's the chairman now, and the only one who has the authority to officially discuss it with you."

ACCOMPLISHING STATUS DEGRADATION: AN ETHNOMETHODOLOGICAL ANALYSIS

The material presented in this case covers the emergence of the focal organization, formalization of a leadership position, emergence of the first leader, and finally the leader's degradation and replacement. Hence the case is a fairly complete longitudinal study of the initial occurrence of succession in one organization. Having described this succession using first-order linguistic constructions—that is, members' concepts—I shall now begin the task of making scientific sense of members' common-sense constructions.

Specifying the components of the degradation process is an initial step in the analysis. The dramaturgical metaphor suggests a means of identifying and presenting these. One finds a set of actors (characters) including the actor to be succeeded, chairpersons at various meetings, and other participants. Some of these actors seek to facilitate degradation, others resist it, and finally successor candidates are proposed. The process unfolds in particular situations which recur across the various acts or phases in the production. Actors' conversations identify certain precipitating events which become central to the plot. The script is largely composed of moves or gambits which interpret the events and construct the divergent organizational schemes. Table 6.1 summarizes these components in case-specific and general terms. It may be used as a guide or program for reading the analysis, as well as a framework for studying other cases of degradation.

Background and Emergence
of the Formal Organization

Perhaps the most striking feature of the emergence of the organization is the process whereby incipient and conventional rules emerge and then are formalized. The first formal rules to emerge when the Graduate Centre was organized released slack resources for center use and thereby created both the Centre and a leadership position. Conventional rules created by the leader were formalized at his request to establish organizational legitimacy. That is, the rules specified a formal structure which could be referred to as "the reason" for certain requests and activities.

The next phase of formalization was precipitated by requests for increased funding. Rules were created and explicated to outline the resource allocation procedure. Attempts to obtain funding prior to complying with rule demands

TABLE 6.1 Components of an Organizational Status Degradation

General Categories	Specific Elements
Set of actors:	
Actor to be succeeded	RG
Chairperson	RG, LB, IM, DA (in order)
Witnesses giving testimony:	
1. Facilitators	Denouncers: DA, LB, IS
2. Resisters	Defenders: IM, BS, (RG)
Successor candidates	DA, IS
Succession occasions as situated events	GSCOC meeting; GRC meetings
Phases in succession	Emergence of the formal organization.
	Preliminary degradation attempts.
	A successful degradation ceremony.
	Post-ceremony events.
Set of events defined as precipitating (anecdotes, examples, evidence, etc.)	RG's behavior at GRC meeting; RG's past offenses; GSCOC accounting practices
Organizational schemes	See Table 6.3.

for proper accounting were denied by a gambit of compliance and a reiteration of the rules.

Events in the emergence phase are outlined in Table 6.2 which also specifies important points of later phases of degradation. Schemes of the organization were first constructed in the emergence phase and elaborated in later phases. Table 6.3 summarizes these schemes.

Preliminary Degradation Attempts

The Centre's attempt to present an accounting was interpreted as inadequate; several rules and conventions, such as generally accepted accounting principles, were invoked, and dissenters proposed schemes which displayed the leader as a deviant. The organization's members apparently held an image of the Centre which led them to consider their accounting practices legitimate, but alternative schemes were forced on them. The outcome of negotiation resulted in the formal dissolution of the Centre committee, an act which seems to symbolically display the ascendancy of the dissenter organizational scheme over the previous scheme (Table 6.3).

Despite the rise of critics, the initial leader was able to retain the formal chairmanship. The committee was reconstituted, but several changes in the formal rule scheme were made to constrain the leader's behavior and prevent future rule infractions. Rules suspending funding then became a resource for the dissenters' subsequent attempts to degrade the leader.

The unsuccessful attempt by committee members to remove the leader involved explicit reference to violation of incipient and formal rules as the

TABLE 6.2 A Schematic Outline of the Status Degradation Process

---

Background and emergence of the formal organization
  Preorganizational phase: slack resources arise

  Emergence of the organization: formal rules are created which (a) release slack resources for creation of the new organization and (b) specify a leadership position and initial incumbent

  Formal organizational structure elaborated: most aspects of organization remain in conventional or incipient form

  Leader's request for further funding causes funding agency to elaborate formal rules for funding

Preliminary degradation attempts
  Increasing requests for funding met by demands for display of adherence to funding rules

  Subsequent meeting held to discuss rule compliance
    Organizational scheme, developed by dissidents, is used to display the impropriety of past behavior

    Organization formally disbanded; leader is degraded

    Organization formally reconstituted; degraded leader succeeds himself and dissident members appointed to organization

    Formal rules created that (1) modify leadership position and (2) cut off funds until compliance with funding rules is demonstrated

  Dissident members attempt to degrade leader at organization meeting
    Leader's behavior is interpreted as violating recently developed incipient and formal rules

    Dissenters' organizational scheme is explicated, degradation attempt fails
    Incipient rules limiting leader's behavior are formalized.

A successful degradation ceremony: see Table 6.4

Post-ceremony transmission of news of the degradation
  Important others are informed of degradation and successor
  Various actors "talk through" the event, retrospectively make sense of it

---

"reason" for the degradation attempt. Thus again we find the degradation attempt constituted by the dissenters' gambit of compliance. Although they were unable to remove the chairman, the dissenters were able to explicate their organizational scheme by formalizing an incipient rule limiting the chairman's discretion. This rule became a critical resource for the successful degradation.

A Successful Status Degradation Ceremony

The successful degradation ceremony climaxed the events reported in the study. It occurred in a specific situation (GSCOC meeting: see Table 6.1) within a rather brief time, yet it included several distinct stages which unfolded over time with clearly demarcated verbal boundaries. The following analy-

TABLE 6.3 Members' Models of Organizational Reality

	Component denouncers' (facilitators') image
Compliance	All formal rules demand compliance, which is the first and primary task of the chairman; failure to comply will lead to removal of the chairman. The most important formal rules are the financial report rule, the closed bar rule, the "formal reports only" rule, and rules outlining the chairman's duties and authority.
Functional Integrity	Compliance is imperative or the Centre will ultimately be closed by external agencies; short-term "self-closure" is a measure preventing long-term problems.
	The chairman represents the organization; hence all his activities are relevant to its functional integrity. However, the identity of the particular chairman is irrelevant.
Style	Behavior has a proper form. Appearances must be managed to avoid giving the organization a bad image.

	Defenders' (resisters') image
Compliance	Rules are incomplete guides to action and should be interpreted, disregarded, and elaborated as operational contingencies warrant.
Functional Integrity	The most important task is to keep the Centre open: it will die or suffer otherwise. Having a chairman is essential to keeping the Centre functioning.
Style	Proper style derives from and is interpretable as acting to keep the Centre open.

sis is an elaboration of the process of degradation which is abstracted in Table 6.4.

Stage I. Establishing succession as a problem at hand. (Utterances 1–7 in the conversation reproduced on p. 565.) RG announces the start of discussion and the topic (U1) in accordance with the rules of procedure. DA then begins to outline the facts of the case. The activity, "RG's utterances at a recent GRC meeting," is given (U4) as the offending act and its offensiveness is asserted. However, it requires some background to understand why in DA's conception of the organization RG's utterances were improper. This "why" emerges later: to DA it is "obvious," yet RG denies this obviousness and proposes a seemingly vague account (U5) of his behavior. DA and LB emerge as denouncers; LB asserts that RG is a deviant motivational type, a repeat violator (U6), and establishes that compliance to a rule is demanded, that the rule was previously enacted, and that it may now be used to define RG's behavior as improper. Finally, DA reiterates the nature of the deviant act and explicates the consequences he sees as implied by interpreting the behavior as such.

The first stage thus includes initially denouncing RG as an offender, indicating the offense, and a proposal for rectifying the problem: the chairman's resignation. The denouncers' gambit of compliance is countered by

TABLE 6.4 A Schematic Outline of a Successful Status Degradation Ceremony

---

Stage I: Establishing succession as a problem at hand (U1-U7).[a]
  Presentation of precipitating events by facilitators.

  Gambit of compliance as preliminary statement of facilitators' organizational scheme.

  Interpretation of events as relevant to succession.

  Initial defense of the actor to be succeeded.

Stage II: Interpreting the facts or events (U8-U24).
  Agreement on a set of activities or events as central to discussion.

  Actor to be succeeded and/or resisters elaborate their organizational scheme seeking to discount immediate necessity or relevance of succession.

  Explication of facilitators' organizational scheme.

  Moves and countermoves by facilitators and resisters whereby each group seeks to establish the primacy of its own scheme and to discredit or undermine the other's.

  Facilitators accomplish succession as a topic at hand and establish and enforce a limited range of talk as relevant to topic at hand.

Stage III: What next if? (U25-U37).
  Collective search and proposal of solutions to various succession-related problems: competing organizational schemes displayed as resources for solution of the problems.

  Facilitators seek closure on issues by further specifying and enforcing a rule of "talk to the topic."

Stage IV: Accomplishing the status change of the actor to be succeeded (U38-U43).
  Alternative means of accomplishing the change are proposed and eliminated.

  The status change is formally accomplished: the actor to be succeeded becomes the succeeded actor.

Stage V: Selecting a successor (U44-end).
  The new status of the succeeded member is discussed.

  Successors are proposed and dismissed.

  Ground rules for choosing a successor are negotiated and made explicit.

  The successor is chosen and formalized.

  The succeeded member's new status is formalized.

---

a. Refers to the numbered utterances in the discussion reproduced on pp. 172-175.

RG's seemingly vague defense indicating he had other reasons which may or may not be justified but which are not discussed at this point. As we shall see, these "other purposes" involve an alternative conception of "the organization." RG is claiming proper compliance himself — but compliance to a different organizational scheme than the scheme(s) invoked by DA and LB (Table 6.3). Nonetheless, status degradation is established as the topic of discussion.

Stage II. Interpreting the facts (U8-24). All participants have agreed that RG did produce utterances at the GRC meeting but the meaning of these utterances for purposes at hand needs to be established. Members therefore explicate their conceptions of the organization and seek to impose these schemes on the facts.

RG's defense is predicated primarily on an attempt to show that his speech was personal and informal. That is, he was not acting as chairman but as an individual and therefore his behavior cannot be interpreted by Centre rules (U11 and U20). He further accounts for his behavior by invoking an image of functional integrity (U20) and claims earlier that the image is consistent with GSCOC desires (U5) to obtain terms of reference. RG's background corroboratively integrates the seemingly disparate issues: the impromptu speech, keeping the Centre running, getting terms of reference, and hiring a manager. He proposes that all these issues are integrally related to the continued functioning of the organization, and he interprets his behavior as conforming to organizational demands (see Table 6.3).

RG is not his only defender. IM (U8) leads off the defense by appealing to RG's proposed image (which emerges later in U11 and U20) of functional integrity. However, this meaning is clear only retrospectively after RG has explicated the scheme. Thus IM suggests that some type of report was necessary and, although an impromptu speech was not stylistically proper, RG had complied with DA, IS, and LB's generally acceptable conceptions of the organization.

Further, BS enters the discussion on RG's behalf (U16) by proposing that while RG's behavior may violate various demands, it is not behavior which should be regarded as indexing RG's motivational type; that is, "it wasn't a deliberate attempt." BS therefore displays the idea that intentionality is a critical aspect of motivational typifications and seeks to undermine attempts to define RG's behavior as "intentionally malicious."

The prosecution/denouncement involves similar explication of conceptions of the organization. DA suggests RG's behavior is not merely a simple breach, but a complex, total, and hence serious one: "*all* our rules were thrown out." IS agrees (U10) and explicitly proposes a proper style for the chairman's presentation of the committee image: the chairman should publicly refrain from displaying internal committee conflict. It seems members hold a theory which regards maintaining proper appearances as a means of ensuring personal and/or organizational integrity and functionality. This theory is then used to recognize and account for improper appearances and is linked with formal specifications of the organization (see Table 6.3).

RG's defense (U11) is denied and countered by LB's gambit of compliance (U12), which implies "we've agreed earlier on who discusses bar reports, and it's not you, RG." The previous agreement thus represents another background expectancy breached in what appears to LB an obvious manner. Thus, while RG has asserted (U11) his adherence to compliance demands, LB disputes this. DA and LB then continue to define RG as a deviant motivational type, as indicated by RG's "obvious intentionality" (implied by DA in U13 "had every way to avert problems") and repeated violations (U13). They propose that the organization clearly specifies a solution (U14 and see also Table 6.4: RG should resign) and further emphasize the issue of improper style (U15).

DA also contrasts his own behavior with RG's to establish that his own was stylistically proper as an attempt to preserve the Centre's image. He closes by reiterating the obvious intention of RG's behavior (U17) in an implicit manner. His "I'd hoped he'd avoid it" indicates that "it" was potentially avoidable and in light of earlier documented claims RG indeed could have avoided it.

DA explicitly specified one of the rules RG allegedly violated and interpreted it to suit his purposes at hand: making a successful denouncement. The formal rule he invoked appears in earlier GSCOC minutes with a discussion of a broad and general policy report the committee was preparing:

> Moved LB/OP that the committee report be circulated to committee members for approval prior to submission to GRC approved. No opposition. (GSCOC minutes, 9/30/74)

The formal rule does not (to me) obviously state that the committee decided to give only formal reports, that RG could speak to GRC only in the role of GSCOC chairman, or even that all future reports were to be approved by GSCOC prior to presentation to GRC. Rather, it seems to have limited reference to one particular report being prepared. Thus the denouncer's primary task is to establish that the rule can "obviously" be generalized to all reports. By establishing this, RG can be held responsible for violating the rule. And we have seen that much of RG's defense relies upon interpreting the formal rule alternatively; for example (U11), "I asked to give an informal report" indicates that the rule allows for informal reports. The conflict thus involves what constitutes a committee report and what may be interpreted as an improper report. The formal-reports-only rule proposed by denouncers is linked to a formal alleged-to-exist rule that future violations require resignation (U14). Hence the present situation that "the facts are interpretable by the rules and demand RG's resignation" presents readily solved problems.

Interestingly, the "future-violations-resignation" rule which LB claims to exist in the minutes does not appear explicitly, and indeed no such explicit sanctions are contained in any of the rules. LB's appeal is to a shared background she views as sufficiently concrete to be invoked as a formal shared agreement. Agreement occurs by fiat, as no one disputes LB's claims of the existence of this rule.

IM begins an approach (U18) which can be shown to be an attempt to undermine the denouncement of RG. While not explicitly stated here, RG's utterances at the GRC meeting involved proposing motions to establish a manager's salary. Thus, if IM can establish that the salary is not GSCOC business, then discussion of it cannot be interpreted as a committee report and RG cannot be degraded for making an unauthorized report. LB's response (U19) indicates that she takes for granted that the salary is GSCOC business, hence "the issue is one of procedure" and committee rules *are* relevant.

RG's defense (U20) is again countered by LB's gambit of compliance (U21), but here compliance is demanded vis-à-vis rules linked to the activity of another organizational entity, the executive. LB proposes a rule of sequential authority whereby RG should have no say in the issue of a manager until the executive decides. BS (U22) indicates that the sequence has been followed (manager was hired). If this is so, then following LB's claims either RG (or GSCOC) should have discussed the salary or some "new rules" BS is not aware of were invoked ("who hired the manager?"). BS thus demands grounds for the hiring. RG uses the occasion to clear himself of a potential breach of rules by asserting (U23) that he hired the manager in compliance with "executive" rules; that is, his activity is interpretable by another organizational form.

LB's statement (U24) is an important step in doing an agreement on the degradation. It explicates the issue and agrees on its constitution — talk is about the chairman's resignation not about managerial hiring. And it clarifies the grounds for the proposed sanctioning. IM, BS, and RG have tried to link two events, RG's resignation and the hiring of a manager, by indicating that hiring a manager is essential to keeping the center functioning, and RG's impromptu speech was necessary toward hiring a manager (gambit of functional integrity). By ruling discussion of the manager's salary out of order, LB enforces a rule of correspondence that denies the basic defense of meeting organizational needs (continue functioning: see Table 6.3) as well as that the speech was personal and therefore not negatively sanctionable. RG invokes the executive as a potential interpretational scheme, but LB rules any talk about other roles and/or organizational schemes out of order. By definition, then, RG's behavior has no legitimate interpretational scheme (according to LB and the procedural rules she enforces) other than that proposed in the denouncement of RG.

The practical accomplishment of the degradation, then, consists in the production of "facts" and agreement on an interpretational scheme which informs the facts and constitutes them as a warrant for degradation. The search is not for facts pro and con which allow a decision, but rather the prospective determination of facts which retrospectively warrant the conclusion or outcome, that is, degradation.

Stage III. What next if? (U25–U37). LB's (U24) statements seem to be a boundary bringing closure to the second stage of degradation talk. The third stage is initiated by IM (U25) with a statement which inquires what the organization consists of for dealing with replacement and may possibly be a defensive move for RG, where "having a chairman" is considered functionally necessary.

DA (U26) admits the committee scheme as it exists cannot provide a solution but suggests that the GRC can. RG uses DA's statement to make explicit the functional integrity image (U27) and the denouncers agree with the need for some type of chairman while asserting that RG's resignation does not pose a problem for functional integrity (see Table 6.3). At this point a critical concern and basic distinction between the two organizational realities emerges. In suggesting that RG's appeal to functional integrity is groundless, DA (U29) proposes specifying the chairman's duties by limiting the chairman to "what the Centre committee specifies." The job "requires no work" and it is therefore not difficult to find a replacement for RG. Indeed, DA emphasizes the desirability of the position (U29): "We would all want to be chairman." Thus, DA specifies an image of the chairman position which is vastly different from RG's (U33). Having seemingly demonstrated the imminent replaceability of RG, DA demands that the members choose an interpretational scheme (U29) and presumably replace RG.

LB seeks closure on the issue (U30) and again enforces a rule of correspondence as a means of limiting RG's defense and arriving at the facts which fit a guilty interpretation of RG. This move involves reiterating the issue and casting it in the form of a motion—a program calling for action and agreement. LB uses the motion as a resource by implying that it is and has been the issue of discussion, although no such motion has as yet been explicitly presented. RG attempts to thwart LB's closure move by questioning the proper form of her behavior and is shown that obviously the form is proper. That is, she implicitly invokes a rule that the chairman leave the chair during a discussion of his activities. This rule is apparently acceptable to RG and is part of his background stock of knowledge, as evidenced by his failure to challenge it.

At this stage in the ceremony, talk suggests that RG's degradation is both imminent and obvious to all, including RG. Both he and his defenders pose the problem "after RG resigns, what next?" and discuss possible outcomes (for example U25 and U36). One significant problem is deciding what to do with RG after his degradation (U36), a matter solved or at least postponed by appealing to an external solution (U38). Another problem is ensuring the Centre's functional integrity (U35, U37), although appeals to this problem are a concern largely of RG, IS, and BS.

Stage IV. Accomplishing the status change of the actor to be succeeded (U38–U43). The next task is, then, the actual degradation of RG. LB (U38) dismisses other unresolved issues and changes the topic to concluding the ceremony. The concluding decision option was specified earlier (U29). LB thus sets up the final sequence by directing the issue at RG (U38), who refuses to accede to the denouncers' demands (U39) that he resign. DA uses this refusal to show that RG once again is displaying improper style and thus forcing "this distasteful procedure" (U40).

DA makes the closing gambit by formalizing the motion. When RG resists by a gambit of compliance to GRC rules (U41), LB makes the closing move. Based on generally accepted rules of procedure, she relinquishes the chair to IM (thereby removing one RG supporter from the voting procedure, as the acting chairman cannot vote on an issue except in case of tie) and demands closure by calling the question (U42). The only proper response is a vote on the issue.

IM utters the final ritual statements common to all such "votings." The denouncers' organizational scheme triumphs as the motion passes and RG is degraded. Thus, negotiated agreement is achieved by majority rule, consistent with rules of procedure which members regard as the acceptable means of "doing a formal agreement." And the negotiated organizational reality of denouncers (Table 6.3) becomes enforceable by the successful passage of the degradation motion.

Stage V. Selecting a successor (U44–U71). Following the status degradation ceremony, DA was selected to replace RG, and RG's new status as regular committee member was decided. The primary denouncer successfully displayed himself as the embodiment of the organization generally acceptable to a majority of members, which provided "obvious" warrant for selecting him as RG's successor. The actual device used to produce a successor (the coin flip) seems to demonstrate that either IS or DA were acceptable to others; both were denouncers of RG. And the lack of formal rules specifying how a successor was to be chosen allowed for innovation in the form of the coin flip decision method.

Post-Ceremony Transmission
of News of the Degradation

The formal degradation ceremony was only one phase in the ongoing negotiation and transformation of the members' status, although it was perhaps the major one. After the formal ceremony, the degradation had to be announced to relevant persons. During these talks, members attempted to interpret the meaning of the ceremony and the probable activities of the new chairman.

It was during these announcements that significant others came to interpret the ceremony as degradation, or a lowering of RG's status. This is evidenced by utterances which display the chairman of the committee as in charge of the Centre, whereas ordinary members are not. Thus members and others viewed the position of chairman as linked to differential authority and duties and as the highest status position on the committee. Also, a variety of utterances which display RG as having been "thrown out" as chairman emphasize the degradation. Therefore it seems correct to speak of the events as degradation and to assert that the members themselves assigned such a meaning to the events.

A PRELIMINARY GROUNDED THEORY OF STATUS DEGRADATION AS A TYPE OF ORGANIZATIONAL SUCCESSION

The findings from the analysis of the status degradation process and ceremony are summarized by the following propositions, testable in other cases. These propositions specify a dynamic process which underlies the structural components outlined in the tables.

Assumption: Attempts to implement organizational schemes involve negotiation of them through conversational activity.

Proposition 1: During the negotiation process, members employ a gambit whereby compliance with organizational rules is indicated as a condition for the continued existence of "the organization" as members conceive it. This is accomplished by linking the rules to a scheme of the organization as a functional integrity — that is, demonstrating that compliance is a constitutive condition of the functional integrity of the scheme as reality.

Proposition 2: During the negotiation process, members employ a gambit whereby a behavioral style which is and remains outside the explicit governance of specific formal rules is nonetheless linked to and used as further evidence of the motivational state of some person currently under discussion for breaching compliance demands associated with rules of the organization.

Proposition 3: Resistance to or violation of important conventional or incipient aspects of an organizational scheme lead to attempts to formalize solutions to problematic aspects of the scheme.

> *Corollary 1:* A shared agreement is more problematic while the scheme is "pre-formal": formalization generally involves making the scheme more explicit, hence facilitating increased agreement on its consistency and referents.

> *Corollary 2:* Members are more willing to accept a formal than a nonformal scheme as an interpretive possibility when dealing with important matters.

> *Corollary 3:* Formal rules, once invoked, must be oriented to even if the orientation involves merely demonstrating that the formal rules are not applicable. That is, even if members agree a scheme is irrelevant, attempts to

impose it require others "do work" to demonstrate or account for this irrelevance.

Proposition 4: Members regard formal agreement violations as obviously sanctionable, whereas enforcement of nonformal schemes and rules is more problematic because the alleged violator can appeal to (1) the vagueness of the scheme and (2) his lack of knowledge of the existence of it as a shared and enforceable scheme. Such appeals are offered as excuses and accounts for the alleged violation and may be accepted where the violator's account is deemed reasonable, given situational contingencies mitigating strict adherence to the rule(s).

Proposition 5: Succession in the form of status degradation occurs where:

(a) an (enforceable) organizational reality is constructed and displayed as a relevant interpretational scheme for members' behavior,

(b) the organizational scheme displays the behavior as problematic because (1) it violates important organizational rules, (2) it evidences improper style, poor taste, and/or deviant motivation, (3) it is harmful to or disruptive of the functional integrity of "the organization," and

(c) the "solution" to the behavioral problem is specified by the denouncers' organizational scheme as removal of the member from office.

Proposition 6: Where succession occurs due to status degradation, the successor will be an actor whose words and deeds are "the embodiment of" (explicitly consistent with) the organizational scheme enforced in the accomplishment of the degradation.

The term "enforceable" refers to criteria sufficient for implementation, as established by background rules of procedure of the organization. For example, in the case of the GSCOC, a motion is considered passed or enforceable where a majority support it.

FUTURE RESEARCH AND PRACTICAL IMPLICATIONS

In this article I have developed a grounded, substantive theory of organizational succession in the form of status degradation. The theory has been formalized in propositions and tables in an effort to facilitate elaboration of it into a general theory of succession. Glaser and Strauss (1967) suggest that this may be accomplished best by comparing several case-specific, low-order substantive models in a process they term "the constant comparative method." There are several ways the present study could be used in future attempts to accomplish this, and indeed such future endeavors constitute tests of its heuristic utility.

First, other in-depth case analyses of the social accomplishment of status degradation in the form of succession should be conducted to test, modify, and elaborate the present model. The general utility of the present theoretical conceptions of organization and social rules could be examined, gaps in the propositional framework could be closed, and a more elaborate model constructed.

Second, case analyses of various types of succession, including (1) retirement, (2) voluntary resignation, (3) status degradation, (4) promotion, transfer, and advancement, and (5) death could be undertaken; low-order models developed for each; and then a general theory could be constructed which subsumes each of the lower-order models. The present model could serve as a basic conceptual and propositional scheme to be tested, modified, and elaborated on a case-by-case basis so that the higher-order theory would be consistent with major points of each case and thus responsive to them.

Such an endeavor would clarify the similarities and differences among each type of succession. For example, Table 1 presents the components of status degradation. They are specified in general form so that they may be applied, and explicated by application to, other cases and types of succession. Similarly, Tables 6.2 and 6.4 outline the status degradation process. Examining a case of succession due to death may yield another outline of phases and stages which could be compared to the stages of degradation to clarify similarities and differences between the two types of succession. Propositions regarding the social accomplishment of succession based in death could be generated and similarly compared to degradation propositions, with the comparative endeavor producing integrating propositions. Theory testing and elaboration would proceed in dialectical fashion, as new cases are run through the previous models to produce more adequate and more general theory. Indeed, construction of a cross-cultural theory of succession could proceed by building on the political-anthropological cases of succession provided in Goody (1966) and Burling (1974).

Finally, the methodology, concepts, and general framework advocated here could be applied to phenomena other than succession. One could use the present theoretical conception of an organization to examine phenomena such as organizational socialization, where old members help formulate the organization for the new member. One could examine aspects of such formulations and expect to uncover the three methodical uses discussed here as well as perhaps others. Similarly, social scientists may choose to qualitatively examine phenomena in their own life worlds and experiences by collecting field notes and using such data to produce theories of significant aspects of their everyday life activities. Conversations are particularly amenable to such analyses and are basic to accomplishing most activities within organizational settings. For example, talking about one's department head is potential data for theorizing about how members attribute causation to leaders' behavior, a topic for research suggested by Pfeffer (1977). The point is that developing concepts for analyzing everyday life activities by examining one's own experiences seems a useful and inexpensive way of enriching organizational theory.

This final point relates to the primary practical implications of an ethnomethodological approach. Practicing managers have everyday life experiences with concrete organizational problems as a major source of data about their organizational worlds. They often make records of conversations and other aspects of situations by taking notes or by having a subordinate do so. As organization theorists develop concepts and theories which make scientific sense of such common-sense, qualitative data, managers can be trained to use these theories. Such theories will have immediate practical importance because they are fundamentally constructed from and directed toward the analysis of concrete behavior and problems in everyday life organizational settings. And, of course, attempts by organizational participants to apply such theories to practical problems will provide opportunities for examining how useful the theories are, therefore further enriching contemporary theories of organization.

CONCLUSION

This article has attempted to enrich succession research by studying actual activities, including conversational practices, of members. I have inductively constructed a substantive theory of status degradation as a form of organizational succession which focuses on the process whereby organizational schemes are constructed, modified, and invoked as interpretational frameworks used by members to make sense of scenic events and to accomplish succession as a practical outcome of organizational behavior.

The model which emerged is based on phenomenological concerns of members' sense making and the social construction of reality. It is not a completed product in the sense that it is "final for once and for all" but, rather, it is a pause in the researcher's multilectical attempts at making social scientific sense of the ongoing social world in which he finds himself inextricably immersed, for all practical purposes. The theory is thus a low-order substantive theory which invites elaboration and explication through systematic observations and reflections on the sensuous stream of experience which constitutes living. The theory could be elaborated through comparison with other substantive theories constructed from similar events and formalized into a more general theory of organizational succession. I suggest, then, that the science and theory of organizational behavior will be greatly enriched by inductive construction of grounded theories based on qualitative observations of concrete activities in everyday life situations.

NOTES

1. While this section contains a general overview of succession research, no attempt is made to provide a comprehensive review of the literature. Helmich (1977) offers a recent attempt at such a review.

2. A general statement of ethnomethodology is beyond the scope of this article. Overviews may be found in Garfinkel (1967), Douglas (1970), Cicourel (1973), Turner (1974), and Mehan and Wood (1975). Sudnow (1967) contains a classic application of ethnomethodology to the study of social organization.

3. "Centre" is spelled using a "tre" ending in deference to the Middle English spelling preferred by Centre committee members.

4. In the following sections, material taken from committee minutes is explicitly noted by referencing the source, whereas material from field notes is quoted without an explicit source reference. Copies of the GRC and GSCOC minutes and field notes may be obtained from the author.

REFERENCES

Berger, Peter L., and Thomas J. Luckmann. 1966. *The Social Construction of Reality*. New York: Doubleday.

Bittner, Egon. 1974. "The concept of organization." In Roy Turner (ed.), *Ethnomethodology: 69–81*. Markham, ON: Penguin.

Burling, Robbins. 1974. *The Passage of Power*. New York: Academic Press.

Campbell, Don T. 1975. "Degrees of freedom and the case study." *Comparative Political Studies*, 8: 178–193.

Christensen, C. Roland. 1953. *Management Succession in Small and Growing Enterprises*. Andover, MA: Andover Press.

Cicourel, Aaron V. 1972. "Basic and normative rules in the negotiation of status and role." In David Sudnow (ed.), *Studies in Social Interaction: 229–259*. New York: Free Press.

———. 1973. *Cognitive Sociology*. London: Macmillan.

Douglas, Jack. 1970. *Understanding Everyday Life*. Chicago: Aldine.

Gamson, William A., and Norman A. Scotch. 1964. "Scapegoating in baseball." *American Journal of Sociology*, 70: 69–72.

Garfinkel, Harold. 1956. "Conditions of successful degradation ceremonies." *American Journal of Sociology*, 61: 420–424.

———. 1967. *Studies in Ethnomethodology*. Englewood Cliffs, NJ: Prentice Hall.

Gephart, Robert. 1975. "The development of a graduate students' centre." MA thesis, University of Calgary.

Glaser, Barney, and Anselm L. Strauss. 1967. *The Discovery of Grounded Theory: Strategies for Qualitative Research*. Chicago: Aldine.

Goody, Jack. 1966. *Succession to High Office*. Cambridge, England: Cambridge University Press.

Gordon, Gerald, and Selwyn Becker. 1964. "Organizational size and managerial succession: A reexamination." *American Journal of Sociology*, 70: 215–222.

Gouldner, Alvin. 1954. *Patterns of Industrial Bureaucracy*. Glencoe, IL: Free Press.

Grusky, Oscar. 1961. "Corporate size, bureaucratization, and managerial succession." *American Journal of Sociology*, 67: 261–269.

———. 1963. "Managerial succession and organizational effectiveness." *American Journal of Sociology*, 69: 21–31.

Guest, Robert H. 1962a. "Managerial succession in complex organizations." *American Journal of Sociology*, 68: 47–54.

———. 1962b. *Organizational Change: The Effect of Successful Leadership.* Homewood, IL: Dorsey.

Helmich, Donald L. 1974. "Organizational growth and succession patterns." *Academy of Management Journal,* 17: 771–775.

———. 1977. "Executive succession in the corporate organization: A current integration." *Academy of Management Review,* 2: 252–266.

Helmich, Donald, and Warren Brown. 1972. "Successor type and organizational change in the corporate enterprise." *Administrative Science Quarterly,* 17: 371–381.

Jehenson, R. 1973. "A phenomenological approach to the study of the formal organization." In G. Psathas (ed.), *Phenomenological Sociology: Issues and Applications:* 219–247. New York: Wiley.

Kotin, Joel, and Myron R. Sharaf. 1967. "Management succession and administrative style." *Psychiatry,* 30: 237–248.

Kriesberg, Louis. 1962. "Careers, organization size, and succession." *American Journal of Sociology,* 68: 355–359.

Lundberg, Craig C. 1976. "Hypothesis creation in organizational behavior research." *Academy of Management Review,* 1: 5–12.

Mehan, Hugh, and Houston Wood. 1975. *The Reality of Ethnomethodology.* New York: Wiley.

Olsen, Johan P. 1976a. "Choice in an organized anarchy." In James G. March and Johan P. Olsen (eds.), *Ambiguity and Choice in Organizations:* 82–139. Oslo: Universitetsforlaget.

———. 1976b. "The process of interpreting organizational history." In James G. March and Johan P. Olsen (eds.), *Ambiguity and Choice in Organizations:* 338–350. Oslo: Universitetsforlaget.

Pfeffer, Jeffrey. 1977. "The ambiguity of leadership." *Academy of Management Review,* 2: 104–112.

Pfeffer, Jeffrey, and Huseyin Leblebici. 1973. "Executive recruitment and the development of interfirm organizations." *Administrative Science Quarterly,* 18: 449–461.

Pfeffer, Jeffrey, and Gerald R. Salancik. 1977. "Organizational context and the characteristics and tenure of hospital administrators." *Academy of Management Journal,* 20: 74–88.

Pondy, Louis, and Ian I. Mitroff. 1978. "Beyond open system models of organization." In B. M. Staw and L. L. Cummings (eds.), *Research in Organizational Behavior, 1:* 1–36. Greenwich, CT: JAI Press.

Schutz, Alfred. 1962. *Collected Papers I: The Problem of Social Reality.* The Hague: Martinus Nijhoff.

Sudnow, David. 1967. *Passing On: The Social Organization of Dying.* Englewood Cliffs, NJ: Prentice Hall.

Turner, Roy. 1974. *Ethnomethodology.* Markham, ON: Penguin.

Weick, Karl E. 1969. *The Social Psychology of Organizing.* Reading, MA: Addison Wesley.

———. 1974. "Amendments to organizational theorizing." *Academy of Management Journal,* 17: 487–502.

———. 1977. "Enactment processes in organizations." In Barry M. Staw and Gerald R. Salancik (eds.), *New Directions in Organizational Behavior:* 267–300. Chicago: St. Clair.

Zald, Mayer. 1965. "Who shall rule? A political analysis of succession in a large welfare organization." *Pacific Sociological Review,* 8: 52–60.

Zimmerman, Don, and Melvin Pollner. 1970. "The everyday world as phenomenon." In Jack Douglas (ed.), *Understanding Everyday Life:* 80–103. Chicago: Aldine.

PART III

STUDIES OF ORGANIZATIONAL IDENTITY AND CHANGE

The roaring success of the American comic strip Dilbert reminds us of the mocking contempt many employees have for their bosses and the popular management theories they import willy-nilly to the workplace. Such management theories often seem to come christened with silly acronyms, tarted-up in fancy scientific language and, so fast do they rise and fall, written in disappearing ink. Much mass-marketed management theory is thin gruel indeed. Full of vapid rationalization and superficial fad, more than a few best-selling management books offer little more than an intellectual, if not ideological, justification for the foolhardy, flavor-of-the-month notions top executives rain down on lower- and mid-level employees. Airport bookstores are today stuffed with organizational salvation texts preaching the latest gospel of BPR, learning organizations, ABC accounting, 360-degree evaluation, rightsizing, or (fading fast) TQM. One can hardly keep up with such theories, let alone skewer them properly.

Nowhere is the penchant for fad and folderol more prominent than in the managerial discourse surrounding organizational identity and change. In the United States, at least, the popularity of advice tracts and change manifestos may reflect an acute, widespread, and apparently pressing need among managers for guidance as the venerable cultural patterns associated with organizational life unravel with the internationalization of business, shifts in markets, innovations in technology, and alterations in governance structures. Stability, it seems, has given way to variability, and it should be no surprise that top executives trapped in unsettled times are on the lookout for ways to swiftly redirect and alter the character of organizations over which they assume responsibility and are increasingly held accountable. Yet where chief executive officers (or their consultants) get their Masters-of-the-Universe ideas probably matters less than the consequences of putting such ideas into play. The problematic nature of organization change is a topic over which many serious organizational researchers and theoreticians have spilled much ink.

Scholarly studies of organizational identity and change are often—perhaps most often—qualitative. Symbolic meaning and unfolding history are necessarily central features of any account of collective identity or social change. And although there is certainly a variety of theories floating about to explain such matters, few if any can claim much predictive success. Most are broadly descriptive, basing their claims on the interpretation of a carefully constructed case or set of cases. Because narrative is the name of this game, students in the area must often draw on methods and styles that originate in the humanities and arts as well as the social sciences. Over the years, the writing about organizational identity and change seems to have avoided much (but not all) of the mischief engendered by runaway variable analysis and hypothesis testing. At any rate, when done well, studies of organizational identity and change provide a tasty mix of representation and interpretation, as authors balance the interaction of events, ideas, and institutions with the intentions and feelings of human actors and do so in historically sensitive fashion. Four such studies are presented in this section.

The first is probably the most widely read and cited article in this collection. Burton Clark's "The Organizational Saga in Higher Education" was published in 1972 and has since served as an inspiration to many students trying to understand how a sense of unity and devotion, uniqueness and purpose comes to members of formally established organizations. Sagas are anything but corporate mission statements neatly printed on business cards. Rather, an organizational saga is a memorable and credible account of past events and achievements built up by many people over a lengthy period of time. Clark illustrates the creation and operation of sagas in the groves of academe— Antioch, Reed, and Swarthmore—where collective beliefs about the distinctiveness and worth of a given college run deep. The text itself is written as an essay, provides no methodological discussion, and offers up little evidentiary support beyond the anecdotal for either the concept of an organizational saga or the particular form it takes in any one of the three colleges. Yet the article has had enormous influence. In the context of its time and place of publication, Clark's writing is a classic of experimental, evocative, almost musical prose.

The second selection, by John Maniha and Charles Perrow, tells a much-overlooked story of an organization whose altogether pedestrian saga, if it can be said to have one at all, comes from the outside and would hardly fill its members with a sense of honor. "The Reluctant Organization and the Aggressive Environment" is a fascinating story of a sleepy, low-profile municipal youth commission, with apparently little reason to exist, that is suddenly transformed—by no fault of its own—into a visible and viable public agency with important goals to meet. This is a ground-up case study, fashioning what few concepts it needs on the wing as the case unfolds. In many ways, this 1965 work foreshadows the new institutionalization theories of the 1980s focusing on an organizational field as the shaper of organizational goals, strategies, and practices. The field in this case are actors and organizations external to the youth commission who successfully (and relatively swiftly) jolt the nine-member body out of its slumber. From what the authors call "a modest analysis of a modest organization," a number of immodest conclusions are drawn. They are sharp ones, designed perhaps to jolt the organizational research community out of its slumber. But as Maniha and Perrow no doubt discovered, the research community slept on for some time. It is now awake.

The third chapter represents a well-known example of cross-breeding social science and cultural history to produce a brief, highly focused, yet altogether elegant analysis of organizational change. "From Evangelism to General Service" looks at the rather steady growth of the YMCA in the United States as an example of successful organizational transformation. Sitting silently behind this somewhat ironic claim by Mayer Zald and Patricia Wallace are other public welfare organizations that, over time, do not change and, therefore, do not grow. Most, it seems, go into sharp decline, and some vanish entirely. The authors' interest, however, is solely on the YMCA, whose success is attributed to a small set of structural, mostly internal characteristics, such as the federated structure of the organization and the low level of ideological commitment exhibited by those attracted to and employed by the organization. The 1963 narrative rests largely on secondary sources, although a reader wishing to learn of the methods employed in the study must look to extratextual notes for clues, and few confessional tidbits as to methods are provided. Grand analytic schemes are absent in this historical case study, but the authors borrow from the writings of others, as needed, several serviceable and hearty sensitizing concepts such as the "enrollment economy" and the "ideological organization," on a concept-by-concept basis. The textual tone is wise, reliable, rather genial, and reassuring, despite the omniscient third-person that characterizes most of the narrative. Few studies have lived longer lives in organization studies, and although Zald and Wallace are remembered for the story they told, not for the way they told it, the two are surely connected.

The fourth and final selection is Nicole Woolsey Biggart's fine-grained case study of the 1970-71 reorganization of the U.S. Post Office Department (renamed, not insignificantly, the U.S. Postal Service). This is a top-down, precisely focused case study in which the subject is deliberately chosen to illustrate a quite general set of theoretical ideas accepted from the outset. "The Creative-Destructive Process of Organizational Change" uses the Post Office as an unusually demonstrative model of what must be done if a new, sweeping form of organization—encompassing its formal structure, ideology, power alliances, leadership styles, decision-making models, and technology—is to be built on and over an existing old form. This 1977 tale of an unlikely phoenix rising is told by making selective use of public records from which documented events are sorted into the analytic categories used to frame and explain the creation of the new organization. Destruction of the old is at the core of this story. As the details of the story accumulate, annihilation becomes the center-piece of a rather grand social change theory Biggart embraced, which, viewed now from our fin de siècle perspective, appears remarkably clairvoyant.

The four chapters that follow attend to the section theme in rather similar ways. All are strong narratives focusing on dramatic shifts in organizational states of affairs. Studies of identity and change are ready-made for narrative. All four chapters also blend analytic methods drawn from the humanities and social sciences. This interdisciplinary combination may account for the prominent constitutive role history, culture, and language are given in the human thought, action, and organization textualized in these studies. All are, at heart, action-driven studies of particular people doing particular things in particular organizations at particular times. A most concrete and pragmatic spirit thus animates these studies. The theories that accompany and no doubt shape these writings are more evoked than described or codified. This, in the end, may well account for their attractiveness.

7

THE ORGANIZATIONAL
SAGA IN HIGHER EDUCATION

Burton R. Clark

S aga, originally referring to a medieval Icelandic or Norse account of achievements and events in the history of a person or group, has come to mean a narrative of heroic exploits, of a unique development that has deeply stirred the emotions of participants and descendants. Thus a saga is not simply a story but a story that at some time has had a particular base of believers. The term often refers also to the actual history itself, thereby including a stream of events, the participants, and the written or spoken interpretation. The element of belief is crucial, for without the credible story, the events and persons become history; with the development of belief, a particular bit of history becomes a definition full of pride and identity for the group.

INTRODUCTION

An *organizational saga* is a collective understanding of unique accomplishment in a formally established group. The group's definition of the accom-

AUTHOR'S NOTE: Revised version of paper presented at the 65th Annual Meeting of the American Sociological Association, September 1970, Washington, D.C. I wish to thank Wendell Bell, Maren L. Carden, Kai Erikson, and Stanley Udy for discussion and comment. Parts of an early draft of this article have been used to connect organizational belief to problems of governance in colleges and universities (Clark, 1971). Reprinted from *Administrative Science Quarterly*, 17 (June 1972): 178–184.

plishment, intrinsically historical but embellished through retelling and re-writing, links stages of organizational development. The participants have added affect, an emotional loading, which places their conception between the coolness of rational purpose and the warmth of sentiment found in religion and magic. An organizational saga presents some rational explanation of how certain means led to certain ends, but it also includes affect that turns a formal place into a beloved institution, to which participants may be passionately devoted. Encountering such devotion, the observer may become unsure of his own analytical detachment as he tests the overtones of the institutional spirit or spirit of place.

The study of organizational sagas highlights nonstructural and nonrational dimensions of organizational life and achievement. Macro-organizational theory has concentrated on the role of structure and technology in organizational effectiveness (Gross, 1964; Litterer, 1965; March, 1965; Thompson, 1967; Price, 1968; Perrow, 1970). A needed corrective is more research on the cultural and expressive aspects of organizations, particularly on the role of belief and sentiment at broad levels of organization. The human-relations approach in organizational analysis, centered largely on group interaction, showed some awareness of the role of organization symbols (Whyte, 1948: chap. 23), but this conceptual lead has not been taken as a serious basis for research. Also, in the literature on organizations and purposive communities, "ideology" refers to unified and shared belief (Selznick, 1949; Bendix, 1956; Price, 1968: 104-110; Carden, 1969), but the concept of ideology has lost denotative power, having been stretched by varying uses. For the phenomenon discussed in this article, "saga" seems to provide the appropriate denotation. With a general emphasis on normative bonds, organizational saga refers to a unified set of publicly expressed beliefs about the formal group that (a) is rooted in history, (b) claims unique accomplishment, and (c) is held with sentiment by the group.

To develop the concept in this article, extreme cases and exaggerations of the ideal type are used; but the concept will be close to reality and widely applicable when the phenomenon is examined in weak as well as strong expression. In many organizations, even some highly utilitarian ones, some segment of their personnel probably develop in time at least a weak saga. Those who have persisted together for some years in one place will have had, at minimum, a thin stream of shared experience, which they elaborate into a plausible account of group uniqueness. Whether developed primarily by management or by employees, the story helps rationalize for the individual his commitment of time and energy for years, perhaps for a lifetime, to a particular enterprise. Even when weak, the belief can compensate in part for the loss of meaning in much modern work, giving some drama and some cultural identity to one's otherwise entirely instrumental efforts. At the other end of the continuum, a saga engages one so intensely as to make his immediate place overwhelmingly valuable. It can even produce a striking distortion, with the organization becoming the only reality, the outside world becoming illusion. Generally the almost complete capture of affect and perception is associated with only a few utopian communities, fanatical political factions, and religious sects. But some formal rationalized organizations, as for example business and education, can also become utopian, fanatical, or sectarian.

Organizational sagas vary in durability. They can arise quickly in relatively unstructured social settings, as in professional sports organizations that operate in the volatile context of contact with large spectator audiences through the mass media. A professional baseball or football team may create a rags-to-riches legend in a few months' time that excites millions of people. But such a saga is also very fragile as an ongoing definition of the organization. The story can be removed quickly from the collective understanding of the present and future, for successful performance is often unstable, and the events that set the direction of belief can be readily reversed, with the great winners quickly becoming habitual losers. In such cases, there seems to be an unstable structural connection between the organization and the base of believers. The base of belief is not anchored within the organization nor in personal ties between insiders and outsiders, but is mediated by mass media, away from the control of the organization. Such sagas continue only as the organization keeps repeating its earlier success and also keeps the detached followers from straying to other sources of excitement and identification.

In contrast, organizational sagas show high durability when built slowly in structured social contexts; for example, the educational system, specifically for the purposes of this article, three liberal arts colleges in the United States. In the many small private colleges, the story of special performance emerges not in a few months but over a decade or two. When the saga is firmly developed, it is embodied in many components of the organization, affecting the definition and performance of the organization and finding protection in the webbing of the institutional parts. It is not volatile and can be relegated to the past only by years of attenuation or organizational decline.

Since the concept of organizational saga was developed from research on Reed, Antioch, and Swarthmore, three distinctive and highly regarded colleges (Clark, 1970), material and categories from their developmental histories are used to illustrate the development of a saga, and its positive effects on organizational participation and effectiveness are then considered.[1]

DEVELOPMENT OF SAGA

Two stages can be distinguished in the development of an organizational saga, initiation and fulfillment. Initiation takes place under varying conditions and occurs within a relatively short period of time; fulfillment is related to features of the organization that are enduring and more predictable.

Initiation

Strong sagas do not develop in passive organizations tuned to adaptive servicing of demand or to the fulfilling of roles dictated by higher authorities (Clark, 1956, 1960). The saga is initially a strong purpose, conceived and enunciated by a single man or a small cadre (Selznick, 1957) whose first task is to find a setting that is open, or can be opened, to a special effort. The most obvious setting is the autonomous new organization, where there is no established structure, no rigid custom, especially if a deliberate effort has been made to establish initial autonomy and bordering outsiders are preoccupied. There a leader may also have the advantage of building from the top down, appointing lieutenants and picking up recruits in accord with his ideas.

Reed College is strongly characterized by a saga, and its story of hard-won excellence and nonconformity began as strong purpose in a new organization. Its first president, William T. Foster, a thirty-year-old, high-minded reformer from the sophisticated East of Harvard and Bowdoin, went to the untutored Northwest, to an unbuilt campus in suburban Portland in 1910, precisely because he did not want to be limited by established institutions, all of which were, to his mind, corrupt in practice. The projected college in Oregon was clear ground, intellectually as well as physically, and he could there assemble the people and devise the practices that would finally give the United States an academically pure college, a Balliol for America.

The second setting for initiation is the established organization in a crisis of decay. Those in charge, after years of attempting incremental adjustments (Lindblom, 1959), realize finally that they must either give up established ways or have the organization fail. Preferring that it survive, they may relinquish the leadership to one proposing a plan that promises revival and later strength, or they may even accept a man of utopian intent. Deep crisis in the established organization thus creates some of the conditions of a new organization. It suspends past practice, forces some bordering groups to stand back or even to turn their backs on failure of the organization, and it tends to catch the attention of the reformer looking for an opportunity.

Antioch College is a dramatic example of such a setting. Started in the 1860s, its first sixty years were characterized by little money, weak staff, few students, and obscurity. Conditions worsened in the 1910s under the inflation and other strains of World War I. In 1919 a charismatic utopian reformer, Arthur E. Morgan, decided it was more advantageous to take over an old college with buildings and a charter than to start a new one. First as trustee and then as president, he began in the early 1920s an institutional renovation that overturned everything. As president he found it easy to push aside old, weak organizational structures and usages. He elaborated a plan of general education involving an unusual combination of work, study, and community participation, and he set about to devise the implementing tool. Crisis and charisma made possible a radical transformation out of which came a second Antioch, a college soon characterized by a sense of exciting history, unique practice, and exceptional performance.

The third context for initiation is the established organization that is not in crisis, not collapsing from long decline, yet ready for evolutionary change. This is the most difficult situation to predict, having to do with degree of rigidity. In both ideology and structure, institutionalized colleges vary in openness to change. In those under church control, for example, the colleges of the more liberal Protestant denominations have been more hospitable than Catholic colleges, at least until recently, to educational experimentation. A college with a tradition of presidential power is more open to change than one where the trustees and the professors exert control over the president. Particularly promising is the college with a self-defined need for educational leadership. This is the opening for which some reformers watch, the sound place that has some ambition to increase its academic stature, as for example, Swarthmore College.

Swarthmore began in the 1860s and had become by 1920 a secure and stable college, prudently managed by Quaker trustees and administrators and solidly based on traditional support from nearby Quaker families in Pennsylvania, New Jersey, and Maryland. Such an organization would not usually be thought promising for reform, but Frank Aydelotte, who became its president in 1920, judged it ready for change. Magnetic in personality, highly placed within the élite circle of former Rhodes scholars, personally liked by important foundation officials, and recommended as a scholarly leader, he was offered other college presidencies, but he chose Swarthmore as a place open to change through a combination of financial health, liberal Quaker ethos, and some institutional ambition. His judgment proved correct, although the tolerance for his changes in the 1920s and 1930s was narrow at times. He began the gradual introduction of a modified Oxford honors program and related changes, which resulted in noteworthy achievements that supporters were to identify later as "the Swarthmore saga" (Swarthmore College Faculty, 1941).

Fulfillment

Although the conditions of initiation of a saga vary, the means of fulfillment are more predictable. There are many ways in which a unified sense of a special history is expressed; for example, even a patch of sidewalk or a coffee room may evoke emotion among the believers, but one can delimit the components at the center of the development of a saga. These may center, in colleges, on the personnel, the program, the external social base, the student subculture, and the imagery of the saga.

Personnel. In a college, the key group of believers is the senior faculty. When they are hostile to a new idea, its attenuation is likely; when they are passive, its success is weak; and when they are devoted to it, a saga is probable. A single leader, a college president, can initiate the change, but the organizational idea will not be expanded over the years and expressed in performance unless ranking and powerful members of the faculty become committed to it and remain committed even after the initiator is gone. In committing themselves deeply, taking some credit for the change and seeking to ensure its perpetuation, they routinize the charisma of the leader in collegial authority. The faculty cadre of believers helps to effect the legend, then to protect it against later leaders and other new participants who, less pure in belief, might turn the organization in some other direction.

Such faculty cadres were well developed at Reed by 1925, after the time of its first two presidents; at Antioch, by the early 1930s, after Morgan, disappointed with his followers, left for the board of directors of the new TVA; and at Swarthmore, by the 1930s, and particularly by 1940, after Aydelotte's twenty years of persistent effort. In all three colleges, after the departure of the change agent(s), the senior faculty with the succeeding president, a man appropriate for consolidation, undertook the full working out of the experiment. The faculty believers also replaced themselves through socialization and selective recruitment and retention in the 1940s and 1950s. Meanwhile, new potential innovators had sometimes to be stopped. In such instances, the faculty was able to exert influence to shield the distinctive effort from erosion or deflection. At Reed, for example, major clashes between president and faculty in the late 1930s and the early 1950s were precipitated by a new change-oriented president coming in from the outside, disagreeing with a faculty proud of what had been done, attached deeply to what the college had become, and determined to maintain what was for them the distinctive Reed style. From the standpoint of constructing a regional and national model of purity and severity in undergraduate education, the Reed faculty did on those occasions act to create while acting to conserve.

Program. For a college to transform purpose into a credible story of unique accomplishment, there must be visible practices with which claims of distinctiveness can be supported; that is, unusual courses, noteworthy requirements, or special methods of teaching. On the basis of seemingly unique practices, the program becomes a set of communal symbols and rituals, invested with meaning. Not reporting grades to the students becomes a symbol, as at Reed, that the college cares about learning for learning's sake; thus mere technique becomes part of a saga.

In all the three colleges, the program was seen as distinctive by both insiders and outsiders. At Swarthmore it was the special seminars and other practices of the honors program, capped by written and oral examination by teams of visiting outsiders in the last days of the senior year. At Antioch it was the work-study cycle, the special set of general education requirements, community government, and community involvement. At Reed it was the required freshman lecture-and-seminar courses, the junior qualifying examination, and the thesis in the senior year. Such practices became central to a belief that things had been done so differently, and so much against the mainstream, and often against imposing odds, that the group had generated a saga.

Social Base. The saga also becomes fixed in the minds of outside believers devoted to the organization, usually the alumni. The alumni are the best located to hold beliefs enduringly pure, since they can be as strongly identified with a special organizational history as the older faculty and administrators and yet do not have to face directly the new problems generated by a changing environment or students. Their thoughts can remain centered on the past, rooted in the days when, as students, they participated intimately in the unique ways and accomplishments of the campus.

Liberal alumni, as those of Reed, Antioch, and Swarthmore here, seek to conserve what they believe to be a unique liberal institution and to protect it from the conservative forces of society that might change it—that is, to make it like other colleges. At Reed, for example, dropouts as well as graduates were struck by the intellectual excellence of their small college, convinced that college life there had been unlike college life anywhere else, and they were ready to conserve the practices that seemed to sustain that excellence. Here too, conserving acts can be seen for a time as contributing to an innovation, protecting the full working out of a distinctive effort.

Student Subculture. The student body is the third group of believers, not overwhelmingly important but still a necessary support for the saga. To become and remain a saga, a change must be supported by the student subculture over decades, and the ideology of the subculture must integrate with the central ideas of the believing administrators and faculty. When the students define themselves as personally responsible for upholding the image of the college, then a design or plan has become an organizational saga.

At Antioch, Reed, and Swarthmore, the student subcultures were powerful mechanisms for carrying a developing saga from one generation to another. Reed students, almost from the beginning and extending at least to the early 1960s, were great believers in the uniqueness of their college, constantly on the alert for any action that would alter it, ever fearful that administration or faculty might succumb to pressures that would make Reed just like other colleges. Students at Antioch and Swarthmore also offered unstinting support

for the ideology of their institution. All three student bodies steadily and
dependably transferred the ideology from one generation to another. Often
socializing deeply, they helped produce the graduate who never quite rid
himself of the wish to go back to the campus.

Imagery of Saga. Upheld by faculty, alumni, and students, expressed in
teaching practices, the saga is even more widely expressed as a generalized
tradition in statues and ceremonies, written histories and current catalogues,
even in an "air about the place" felt by participants and some outsiders. The
more unique the history and the more forceful the claim to a place in history,
the more intensely cultivated the ways of sharing memory and symbolizing
the institution. The saga is a strong self-fulfilling belief; working through
institutional self-image and public image, it is indeed a switchman (Weber,
1946), helping to determine the tracks along which action is pushed by men's
self-defined interests. The early belief of one stage brings about the actions
that warrant a stronger version of the same belief in a later period.

As the account develops, believers come to sense its many constituent
symbols as inextricably bound together, and the part takes its meaning from
the whole. For example, at Antioch a deep attachment developed in the 1930s
and 1940s to Morgan's philosophy of the whole man and to its expression in
a unique combination of work, study, community participation, and many
practices thought to embody freedom and nonconformity. Some of the faculty
of those years who remained in the 1940s and 1950s had many memories and
impressions that seemed to form a symbolic whole: personnel counselors, folk
dancing in Red Square, Morgan's towering physique, the battles of community government, the pacifism of the late 1930s, the frequent dash of students
to off-campus jobs, the dedicated deans who personified central values. Public
image also grew strong and sharp, directing liberals and radicals to the college
and conservatives to other places. The symbolic expressions themselves were
a strong perpetuating force.

CONCLUSION

An organizational saga is a powerful means of unity in the formal place. It
makes links across internal divisions and organizational boundaries as internal
and external groups share their common belief. With deep emotional commitment, believers define themselves by their organizational affiliation, and
in their bond to other believers they share an intense sense of the unique. In
an organization defined by a strong saga, there is a feeling that there is the
small world of the lucky few and the large routine one of the rest of the world.
Such an emotional bond turns the membership into a community, even a cult.

An organizational saga is thus a valuable resource, created over a number of years out of the social components of the formal enterprise. As participants become ideologues, their common definition becomes a foundation for trust and for extreme loyalty. Such bonds give the organization a competitive edge in recruiting and maintaining personnel and helps it to avoid the vicious circle in which some actual or anticipated erosion of organizational strength leads to the loss of some personnel, which leads to further decline and loss. Loyalty causes individuals to stay with a system, to save and improve it rather than to leave to serve their self-interest elsewhere (Hirschman, 1970). The genesis and persistence of loyalty is a key organizational and analytical problem. Enduring loyalty follows from a collective belief of participants that their organization is distinctive. Such a belief comes from a credible story of uncommon effort, achievement, and form.

Pride in the organized group and pride in one's identity as taken from the group are personal returns that are uncommon in modern social involvement. The development of sagas is one way in which men in organizations increase such returns, reducing their sense of isolation and increasing their personal pride and pleasure in organizational life. Studying the evocative narratives and devotional ties of formal systems leads to a better understanding of the fundamental capacities of organizations to enhance or diminish the lives of participants. The organization possessing a saga is a place in which participants for a time at least happily accept their bond.

NOTE

1. For some discussion of the risks and tensions associated with organizational sagas, particularly that of success in one period leading to later rigidity and stagnation, see Clark (1970: 258-261). Hale (1970) gives an illuminating discussion of various effects of a persistent saga in a theological seminary.

REFERENCES

Bendix, R. 1956. *Work and Authority in Industry*. New York: Wiley.

Carden, M. L. 1969. *Oneida: Utopian Community to Modern Corporation*. Baltimore: Johns Hopkins University Press.

Clark, B. R. 1956. *Adult Education in Transition: A Study of Institutional Insecurity*. Berkeley: University of California Press.

———. 1960. *The Open Door College. A Case Study*. New York: McGraw-Hill.

———. 1970. *The Distinctive College: Antioch, Reed, and Swarthmore*. Chicago: Aldine.

———. 1971. "Belief and loyalty in college organization." *Journal of Higher Education*, 42: 499–515.

Gross, B. M. 1964. *The Managing of Organization,* 2 vols. New York: Free Press.

Hale, J. R. 1970. "The making and testing of an organizational saga: A case-study of the Lutheran Theological Seminary at Gettysburg, Pennsylvania, with special reference to the problem of merger, 1959–1969." Unpublished Ed.D. dissertation, Columbia University.

Hirschman, A. O. 1970. *Exit, Voice, and Loyalty.* Cambridge, MA: Harvard University Press.

Lindblom, C. E. 1959. "The science of 'muddling through.' " *Public Administration Review,* 19: 79–88.

Litterer, J. A. 1965. *The Analysis of Organizations.* New York: Wiley.

March, J. G. (ed.). 1965. *Handbook of Organizations.* Chicago: Rand McNally.

Perrow, C. 1970. *Organizational Analysis.* Belmont, CA: Wadsworth.

Price, J. L. 1968. *Organizational Effectiveness: An Inventory of Propositions.* Homewood, IL: Irwin.

Selznick, P. 1949. *TVA and the Grass Roots.* Berkeley: University of California Press.

———. 1957. *Leadership in Administration.* New York: Harper & Row.

Swarthmore College Faculty. 1941. *An Adventure in Education: Swarthmore College Under Frank Aydelotte.* New York: Macmillan.

Thompson, J. D. 1967. *Organizations in Action.* New York: McGraw-Hill.

Weber, M. 1946. *From Max Weber: Essays in Sociology.* Translated and edited by H. H. Gerth and C. Wright Mills. New York: Oxford.

Whyte, W. F. 1948. *Human Relations in the Restaurant Industry.* New York: McGraw-Hill.

8

THE RELUCTANT ORGANIZATION AND THE AGGRESSIVE ENVIRONMENT

John Maniha
Charles Perrow

O rganizations are usually defined as rational systems for coordinating the efforts of individuals toward a goal or goals. Increasingly, attention has been focused upon such topics as informal goals, the succession of goals, adaptation to the environment, intended rationality, and so on.[1] The nonrational, informal, and adaptive aspects generally appear with growing institutionalization, as Selznick persuasively argues.[2] But implicit in this view is the assumption that organizations start out as rationally designed instruments with a charter directed toward a clear set of goals designed to fulfill some social need. The distinctively sociological analysis is relevant when the compromises and affective networks of history have accumulated and fleshed out the structure and processes of the organization. We would like to present one case history where an organization had every reason not to be born and had no goals to guide it. It was used by other organizations for their own ends, but in this very process it became an organization with a mission of its own, in spite of itself, and even while its members denied it was becoming an action group.

AUTHORS' NOTE: Reprinted from *Administrative Science Quarterly*, 10 (Sept. 1965): 238–257.

The organization under study is the Youth Commission made up of nine private citizens appointed by the mayor of a city of some 70,000 persons. The origins and first year of the Commission were reconstructed from structured interviews with most of the principals concerned, within and without the organization, the minutes of the Commission, documents and letters in their file, and newspaper accounts. In the second year, the meetings of the Commission were observed, and interviews were held with the heads of other agencies, public officials, and private citizens involved in or concerned with the affairs of the Commission. All Commission members, except one who had moved away, were interviewed at length at least once.[3] The account is basically historical, starting with the community environment, the specific origins of the Commission, its search for a role, its utilization by other groups and, finally, its emergence as an organization with an action role.

SETTING

"Collegetown" considers itself a progressive community with few major problems. As the mayor once put it, when speaking of youth problems, "We've always known about the '5 percent' of the kids who go bad, but we've always felt that Collegetown had only 2 percent." Much of this image comes from the view that not only does the city have a large percentage of well-educated professional citizens—university professors, scientists, and engineers—but that it draws these citizens into government through the use of semiofficial commissions. The commissions are made up of a cross section of the community elite—wealthy landowners, the business elite, representatives of the leading Protestant churches, university people, and sometimes representatives of the new electronics and aerospace industries. Commissions informally share responsibility for legislation passed by the City Council and serve as sounding boards of elite public opinion on some of the issues upon which the Council should act.

Some commissions are noncontroversial as, for example, the group of seven citizens formed to advise the Council on how Collegetown could, according to the mayor, retain its "character . . . by trying to strike a balance between progress, as defined by growth, and the traditional character of our community." The Citizens Recreation Commission at the time of the study was somewhat more powerful, since it influenced the allocation of recreation resources. The Human Relations Commission, dealing with more explosive issues, such as civil rights, minority housing, and zoning, had been forced into a controversial role by the pressure of liberal organizations. The Youth Commission started out innocuously enough, but by the end of its second year was making headlines and was even accused by members of the Human

Relations Commission of invading their strife-ridden domain. In view of its origins, the change was significant.

ORIGINS

The formation of the Youth Commission was not prompted by any dramatic evidence of need in the area, nor by demands of agencies dealing with youth, citizen groups, or political groups. Several cities in the region were reported to be forming youth commissions, but generally in response to dramatic evidence of problems. During the preceding administration a small group had looked into the problems of youth and made at least one report to the City Council, but it received no publicity and little could be learned of its activities.

The idea of forming the Youth Commission came from a councilman who was a candidate for reelection. He initially explored the idea with his friends, some of whom were prominent in youth affairs, and while they agreed there might be some value in it, reportedly they expressed concern that the service might be a duplication of existing facilities. The Director of the YMCA had a more explicit caution. He recalled that he told the councilman that he "thought it was a good idea but expressed the hope that the Commission would not be an action group." The councilman used the proposal as a campaign plank during the election. Surprise was expressed by workers in both parties when, following his reelection, he continued to pursue the idea. He presented it to the Council as an ordinance, which then required two readings and a vote. One member of the Council characterized the atmosphere at the first reading as apathetic. The ordinance passed and came up again one month later for final action. At this point another councilman, a retired businessman and past chairman of the United Fund and Community Chest, proposed that the word "commission" be changed to "committee" —a term connoting less stature and influence. His proposal was defeated, and with the second councilman registering the only nay, the ordinance was officially passed, again apathetically.

The official goals of the charter were sufficiently straightforward to confer upon it the broad responsibility of appraising conditions and influences affecting youth, evaluating existing services, and recommending to the Council measures which it could take "to promote the best interests of children and youth in the city." It was to report to the Council every four months, advising the Council of current developments relating to youth. Just how the Commission was to go about its tasks was not spelled out. It was noted in the charter that it "shall not undertake or carry out youth projects," but this was followed by the ambiguous qualification "though after specific request therefrom may render such assistance as it deems appropriate to other agencies supporting youth projects or actions." What "appropriate assistance" might be, or the scope of support, was apparently left to the Commission to decide. They decided quite early; indeed, by the time the members were selected, other agencies had, in effect, decided for them.

FORMING A RELUCTANT ORGANIZATION

As soon as the ordinance was passed, the town newspaper informed the public of the "appraising, evaluating, and recommending" goals of the Commission. The mayor immediately received queries from the heads of agencies concerned with youth. They wished to know what was to be appraised, who was to be evaluated, and whether this was not a duplication of existing services. It appeared that the autonomy and integrity of some 29 existing agencies were threatened. The Commission was not the mayor's idea, and he attempted to assuage their fears. His nine appointments to the Commission can be interpreted in this light:

1. *High School Principal*—The group's first chairman. He was head of the city's only public high school, which served about 2,000 students and held a very visible position in the community. He was highly respected by all the Commission members for his knowledge of youth problems and his candid and forthright approach. The high school had been a focal point for some disturbances in the past and thus had a more than usual interest in youth problems.

2. *YMCA Director*—Representative of one of the organizations most conscious of public relations. He was a friend or acquaintance of the mayor and several councilmen, as well as most of the other heads of agencies serving youth in Collegetown. The YMCA had also had problems with juvenile disturbances on its premises and had been criticized for this in the past.

3. *Catholic*—Athletic coach at a Catholic high school. He rarely came to meetings and took almost no part in them. He was interested in pursuing his sports activities with youth and working with them on a face-to-face basis and felt the Commission should be talking with the youth of the community. In an interview, he said, "I was asked to be on the Commission because they needed a Catholic. There aren't a lot of us here, but enough to be represented."

4. *Negro Woman*—She also recognized why she was appointed and was frank about it. She belonged to a great many other organizations, including the Human Relations Commission, and was a friend of the mayor and several powerful families in Collegetown. White leaders depended upon her to be prudent about the race issue, and she was in great demand for organizations

requiring a Negro representative. Vocal elements in the Negro civil rights movement did not feel she spoke for her race, and she in turn did not strongly identify with the Negro community in Collegetown.

5. *Junior High School Teacher*—A son of the mayor. His access to City Hall was utilized by the Commission in technical matters, and he may also have informed his father about developments in the group. He did not appear to find the connection between his relationship to the mayor and his Commission membership awkward.

6. *Protestant Minister*—Four of the eight other members of the Commission belonged to his church. The minister clearly represented organized religion and Christian morality, reminding members, for example, that even so-called unenforceable laws must be observed. He can be seen as the link between the Commission and the powerful Collegetown Ministerial Association.

7. *Physician*—Professor of public health at the University. He was elected chairman at the close of the Commission's first year. He was interested in the welfare of youth and was also acting chairman of a state-wide health organization dealing with children. The presence of a physician would ordinarily be a requisite of such an organization.

8. *University Faculty Member*—In physical education. He belonged to a great many service groups and was active in many phases of community work. He was very interested in the affairs of the Commission and probably the most vocal member of the group. But his role was mainly that of a public-spirited citizen and a concerned father of an adolescent. He was also at the same time the Chairman of the Citizens Recreation Commission.

9. *Nurse*—She replaced another woman who moved away and who had been president of the Women's Auxiliary of the Junior Chamber of Commerce and, as secretary of the group, was said to have played almost no role in deliberations. Her replacement, the nurse, was also promptly made the group's secretary. She said she was appointed to the Commission because "they needed a housewife." Her role was subordinate; she rarely spoke at meetings, and she admitted to being awed by the other "strong members who are authorities on youth."

The appointments, then, covered two of the powerful agencies most involved with youth—the high school and the YMCA—and added representatives from four other obvious fields: religion, recreation, medicine, and housewifery. Two minority groups were included: a Negro and a Catholic. The ruling political party was represented at least by the mayor's son, and initially also by the representative from the Junior Chamber of Commerce. It can be assumed that most of the members were in sympathy with the political party in office. None of the many authorities in delinquency from the university, such as social workers, sociologists, or psychologists, were included, nor was a representative of the major Negro youth organization, which had programs similar to the YMCA. Any of these might have urged a more active role for the Commission.

At the organization meeting of the group, the mayor discussed the implications of the creation of a group to study youth problems in a city which prided itself on the lack of such problems. He said he was "not sure" Collegetown had any youth problems, but if it did he "certainly wanted to know about them." He would also cooperate in any way he could with the group, and if the Commission needed anything to let him know. One member recalls that he mentioned stamps and envelopes. He then explicitly advised them to move very slowly and cautiously in order to allay the suspicions of several agencies. He concluded by expressing his admiration for the fine group of public-spirited citizens he had chosen, and appointed the high school principal as chairman.

THE FIRST YEAR: PROTECTING THE MINIMAL ROLE

"Goals appear to grow out of interaction both within the organization and between the organization and its environment."[4] In the case of the Commission, much of the salient environment was built into the organization—representation of the two largest youth organizations in the city and of the city administration. The high school principal and the director of the YMCA immediately became the key personnel in the Commission. They were instrumental in defining a no-action study-group role for the Commission at its first meeting. The goals of the Commission had been clearly set forth in the charter—appraise, evaluate and recommend—but appraisal, or more accurately, "listening," became the only operative goal.[5]

During its first year, and for some months after, the agency invited the heads of the major youth agencies in the city to describe the program and problems of their agencies. Each presentation was followed by a polite question-and-answer period. The presentations of the agencies appear to have been optimistic and self-satisfied, and the questions of the members were innocuous. Even so, some of the members felt that the agencies minimized their problems. For example, the head of the county health agency announced that there were almost no health problems among the youth in the city and that this could be attributed to the fine cooperation between private physicians and his department. Several Commission members, not particularly prone to gloomy views, privately debunked the statement. They had enough contact with juveniles to know that many poor children suffered from inadequate health facilities, and even the mayor was reportedly surprised when informed of the presentation. But the head of the agency was not questioned about this in the discussion session.

It was a Commission member, the minister, who tested the reluctance of the Commission to become active. Assigned to report on what the churches were doing with youth, with a panel discussion of his report by a group of ministers to follow at a later session, the minister stated that, in fact, the churches were doing virtually nothing and deplored the fact. The report was quickly tabled and the panel discussion cancelled. One Commission member, a member of the minister's congregation, said, "We decided the panel should be postponed until further study could be made of the report. Of course, it never was. The report would have set up barriers." The minister subsequently played a minor role at the meetings.

More informal means were used to allay the suspicion of groups. The YMCA director, a self-proclaimed listening post in the town, informed the chairman that the head of the Juvenile Division of the Police Department was suspicious of the role of the Commission. This led to an informal meeting, and in the Commission's first annual report, the Commission supported the Police Department's request for more personnel.

Sensitivity to public criticism characterized the two dominant men in the Commission in its first year, the principal and the YMCA director, and concern with the image of the town became a preoccupation of the group. The high school principal set the tone of cautious procedure for the Commission. The high school was occasionally the scene of vandalism and delinquency, and he was sensitive to potential criticisms. In the second year, he was involved in a direct controversy with the local newspaper, which, he claimed, was placing the school in an unfavorable light by publishing accounts of delinquency by high school students—he argued that they could just as well have been identified as Collegetown youths or the children of certain families. He felt the school was being made to look like "a training school for punks." The YMCA director also had similar experiences in which his organization was criticized for lack of supervision during its functions. He took on the role of seeing that no one was misquoted, misinterpreted, or otherwise compromised in dealing with the press. Another member was quite concerned that College town had a reputation among other cities as being a "hoody town." All agreed with the statement of one member that "throwing these accusations and sensational terms around indiscreetly can give our town a bad reputation that will stick for years."

During the first year several formal and informal attempts by relatively weak groups were made to enlist the help of the Commission in meeting problems related to youth. The Commission resisted these attempts on the grounds of the no-action policy made explicit by the two dominant members and shared by others. For example, a local Protestant minister tried to get the Commission interested in doing something about all-night parties after the senior prom at the high school. The minister was referred to the PTA, since his proposal was "beyond the role of the Commission, because we are not an

action group." A more constructive role for the Commission was sought by
the head of the City Recreation Board, who attempted to enlist the Commission's
aid in keeping city recreation facilities open on school nights. Although
the Commission did not refuse to consider the proposal, it ignored it, and no
formal action was taken on it, even though a member of the Citizens
Recreation Commission was on the Youth Commission.

At the end of the year the Youth Commission was required to submit an
annual report to the City Council. Perhaps in keeping with the Commission's
minimal role, it had only had a few carbon copies made. To the surprise of
the members, there were a number of requests for copies from agencies and
citizens following the announcement of the report in the newspaper. The
report was then mimeographed and distributed to those who requested it. The
interest probably reflected both a concern with problems of youth by the
citizens and a concern with the role and recommendations of the Commission.
The report, however, did much to allay the suspicions of the agencies. It was
noncontroversial and minimized youth problems. It contained a few minor
recommendations and was full of praise for the work the community youth
agencies were doing, given the limitations that were beyond agency control.
The report reaffirmed that the Commission was "fully cognizant of its legal
limitation to require action on its recommendations by any agency, civil or
legal body. The Commission's prime responsibility is to bring to the attention
of the community and the several responsible agencies, through its report to
the city council, the results of its findings and its recommendations for the
alleviation or resolution of problems and issues of the youth of Collegetown."
The report ended with a section on proposed plans for the coming year, one
of which reads, "Make a more detailed analysis of the role of the Youth
Commission."

The distribution of mimeographed copies of the annual report marked the
end of the first phase of the Commission's development—the study-group
role—and the beginning of its second phase, involving an action role. The
annual report was more than a symbolic calendaring of a new year; it stirred
interest in the group by others in the community, allayed suspicions, and
prompted criticism. At the same time, the term of the high school principal
as chairman expired, and he did not wish to serve as chairman for another
year. A new chairman was elected, the public health physician. This, it turned
out, was a fateful decision. The physician differed from the other members in
not having a local constituency—he did not represent the schools, the YMCA,
the recreation department, Catholics, Negroes, or housewives. He might be
seen as representing physicians or the university, but neither of these was
involved, as an organization, in community youth affairs. Without a constituency,
the physician could act as a free agent. He alone seems to have played
the role of member of a Commission rather than a representative of some
interest group. In fact, at the end of the second year, he remarked that he was

not so sure that the YMCA director and the high school principal really ought to be on the Commission: "They have difficulty separating their roles as director and principal from their roles as Commission members. They often speak and act in terms of their own organizations and not the Commission." As a corollary of the physician's role, he did not have great public visibility and was able to move inconspicuously in informal negotiations with groups.

THE EMERGING ACTION ROLE

There was nothing to indicate that the Youth Commission would do more than continue its role as a study group in its second year. Because it existed, however, it was there for others to utilize. As the head of the Juvenile Division of the Police Department put it, "The Commission can do a lot to help all agencies. We all need support. People listen to them because their opinions carry weight and prestige."

There were some who urged the Commission to take a more active, constructive role. In the early part of the second year, they asked an expert in juvenile delinquency and related community problems from the university to address them. He exhorted them to make an aggressive and sincere effort to attack the city's many youth problems. Members replied that this was "not the Commission's role," but the faculty member then read them the official goals as stated in their charter and reminded them that their role was to appraise, evaluate, and recommend programs. Furthermore, he reminded them that other organizations in the city, like the Human Relations Commission, had not let their official charter goals stand in the way of the development of an aggressive approach to community problems. The Commission appeared unmoved.

Shortly after this, the Commission invited an official of the State Youth Commission, which had no affiliation with the local one, to address them on youth problems. He praised their annual report, but then told them that they should seize the opportunity created by good feeling and the interest in the Commission to forge ahead with some kind of constructive program. Again, the members listened but did not discuss these exhortations or apparently take them seriously at the time.

The Commission continued its study role but was pressed into a more active role by the City Council itself. A well-publicized brawl broke out between a group of high school youths and students from the university. Publicity in the newspaper, letters to the editor, letters to the mayor and City Council, and direct pressure upon the Council from some of the citizens, who protested the lack of control by the police, demanded some kind of response. The response was an ordinance drafted by the city attorney, which would give the police power to arrest those whom they suspected of being about to cause a disturbance. The mayor and the Council were reluctant to handle the ordinance from the start. Casting about for a device to suggest action while delaying any, the Council seized upon the Commission. As one councilman said, when he was asked why the Commission had been brought into the matter, "We didn't know what to do with the ordinance and needed more time to think about it and test out more opinions." A joint meeting between the Council and the Commission was called.

The meeting illustrated both the ambiguous role of the Commission and the apprehensions which some Council members had about its goals. The high school principal began the discussion by stating frankly that he did not know what the Council expected of the group and was waiting for positive leadership from the Council. All evening the Council and mayor solicited opinions from Commission members about various aspects of the youth problem: Could we use a dragstrip? What sort of problems do the schools have? Are youth at the YMCA hard to control? Do you think the police juvenile division needs more men? The Commission members gave their opinions and attempted, in some cases, to speak for the community at large, but several times they sought from the Council a definite statement of purpose for their organization. None was forthcoming. Indeed, the councilman who had voted against the Commission felt that he should warn the Commission to proceed slowly and be very careful about recommendations. He feared that "half-baked schemes" might be proposed by the Commission. "Just because something worked in another city, doesn't mean it will work in Collegetown," he added. Finally, the mayor asked the Commission to make a recommendation on the proposed ordinance and submit it to the Council.

The Commission met, but there was little consensus at first. The YMCA director was immediately concerned about public opinion and, in effect, admitted that a no-action role was no longer feasible. "We have to recommend the ordinance. If we don't and it's not passed, the first time something happens we'll be blamed for it. Anyway, the ordinance won't do any good, but if they think they need it then give it to them." But some other members felt the ordinance was potentially threatening to civil rights. The principal was not present but sent a letter stating that he was against the ordinance because it was unconstitutional. Finally, the new chairman reluctantly formulated a compromise agreeable to the YMCA director. It met its obligation to the city administration by recommending passage but qualified its support by adding that it should be passed only if some means could be found to protect civil rights and that other so-called "unenforceable" laws were attended to.

Opposition to the ordinance from groups concerned with civil liberties eventually caused the mayor to postpone action indefinitely. Although the newspapers gave prominence to the recommendations of the Commission, its members did not feel that they had been compromised by the administration's decision to postpone action. Most of them, when interviewed, said that their actions as an organization were not especially noticed by the community.

The next group to seize upon the potentialities of the Youth Commission was the United Fund. This organization had originally been suspicious of the Youth Commission. Following the issuance of the Commission's annual report, the planning committee of the United Fund asked the principal of the high school to discuss the Commission and its role with them. This meeting apparently allayed many suspicions since, shortly afterwards, the head of the United Fund wrote to the Commission regarding the meeting saying, "You have focused for this committee what the committee already knew and was concerned about; and you have done it with a realistic appreciation of the limitations we have in the face of so exacting and imperative a task and, finally, you have pointed the way to our working together." The planning committee of the United Fund decided that it would be beneficial to have a discussion comparable to that held with the high school principal on a community-wide basis. A seminar was proposed which would be cosponsored by the United Fund and the Youth Commission. This proposal was made to the YMCA director, suggesting that the new chairman of the Commission was still not visible or believed to be a powerful member. The YMCA director and the principal decided that the Commission should not cosponsor the seminar because they were "not an action group" and so informed the United Fund. They rather casually informed the other members of the request and the group agreed with their action. All agreed, however, that the Commission should at least go on record as actively supporting the project, though it could not cosponsor it.

Less than three months later, at least partly through the leadership of the new chairman of the Youth Commission, the Commission found itself cosponsoring the seminar. The proposal received favorable publicity in the press, which commended the Commission and the United Fund for this constructive and positive step.

The City Council and the United Fund were both influential agencies in the community. So was the Probate Court, and the third and even more significant line of action that engaged the Commission stemmed from this source. A judge from the court, who was an officer in a state-wide group promoting a project concerned with protective services for juveniles, met with the chairman of the Youth Commission and urged him to look into the project, which involved setting up protective services for children, which fell outside the jurisdiction or responsibility of existing youth agencies. For example, a community agency could be established to assume responsibility for the prosecution of parents of abused children. The initial step would be a survey of the community resources to see if a protective-service agency was needed. At the urging of the judge, the Commission met with a representative of the state-wide project. During the meeting, the judge stated frankly that he saw a real need for the program and would like to see the Commission sponsor it. Whatever their individual feelings, the Commission members must have found it difficult to turn down a request from this influential source.

The Commission was now pressed to explore the role of recommending to other agencies a study by an outside group, which would assess the effectiveness of agencies in the community and might propose yet another agency to fill in the gaps. The implications of perhaps finding such a need were not lost upon agency heads. There would be implied criticism of existing facilities. A new organization might be created which would upset the balance of power and the accommodative division of labor existing among some 29 community agencies and affect the distribution of United Fund resources. At a joint meeting of the agency heads, some sought to avoid the responsibilities and the burdens that such an organization might exact from them, and others attempted to place themselves in a position where they could have a share in its control. At the conclusion of our field work, agency heads had only agreed to confer with their respective organizations to see if approval would be given for a study in which they would have to cooperate, and even this agreement was reluctant in many cases.

By this time—the end of the Commission's second year—meetings were lively and participation was more enthusiastic. This change had begun when the antibrawling ordinance had been discussed and quickened further during the planning of the seminar. A good deal of excitement was now generated in connection with the protective-service project. As one member put it with enthusiasm, "We are about to commit ourselves." The YMCA director characteristically saw the project as "a major test for the Commission since it involves an expenditure of a lot of money and other responsibilities." While it certainly seemed as if they had compromised their hard-earned nonintervention reputation, the action implications of the project appeared to have been lost upon most of the Commission members. In final interviews, all members (except the chairman, who recognized the action role implicit in current developments) affirmed that the Commission should not be an action group, nor should it be granted any more formal powers than it had. They affirmed that the group had no authority to go to any agency with plans and that they had merely to keep themselves informed and await requests from others for their advice and information. The mayor's son summed it up well:

> Working with a lot of different groups as we are, groups like the churches, the city agencies, and private agencies, all of which are separate and autonomous, the city really can't give us any more power than we already have. All must work cooperatively and without force with these separate groups. We can only study the situation and wait for others to ask our opinion.

The study-group role was even pressed anew by some members in the final interviews. One said, somewhat wistfully, "We haven't talked to all the agencies yet." Another complained, "We haven't talked to the kids yet."

A postscript to our study was provided just one year after the end of the field work. A newspaper story reported that a survey initiated by the Youth Commission and the Probate Court had found that "at least 1,350 children in the county are known to suffer from neglect by their parents or guardians." The mayor, in summoning the Commission, councilmen, judges, and police department to a meeting, stated again his belief that only about two per cent of the youthful population were in trouble with authorities, but he stressed that, "The Community must take constructive action; it must stop dividing itself."

The chairman of the Youth Commission, who had been unanimously encouraged by members to continue in office another year, was reported to be contacting those in charge of welfare matters in the state "to seek possibilities for state support for a protective service here." Even more significantly, the Commission was also "considering the addition of a staff person to coordinate the work of all involved groups." The role of action and controversy, which had been so predictably rejected by the carefully selected members of the Commission, had been embraced.

DISCUSSION

There are many conclusions on organizational analysis to be drawn from this modest analysis of a modest organization. For one thing, not all organizations start out as rationally designed instruments directed toward a predetermined goal specified in their charter. As obvious as this may seem, there has been little attempt to explore the origins of organizations in these terms. Such an exploration immediately confronts one with the influence of the environment upon organizational behavior—a point analyzed systematically by Selznick from the beginning of his work[6] but still receiving only scattered attention in its own right.[7]

Other organizations constituted the most significant part of the environment in this case. The vicious rivalry and conflict that can occur between agencies has been described by Miller in his "Interinstitutional Conflict as a Major Impediment to Delinquency Prevention," and there are echoes of his distressing analysis here.[8] Agencies everywhere seem to fear the loss of their autonomy and invasions of their domain. In a rare admission of problems on this score, the mayor of Collegetown noted that the community "must stop dividing itself." But the surprising thing is that the Youth Commission survived at all, threatening, as it did, the domain of other agencies. The formal powers of the second chairman, as a free agent without a local constituency, may have proved decisive here, though we are unable to document this point. Perhaps even more important was the fact that while most active members had constituencies they sought to serve, the organization itself, as an organization, had none beyond that of youth in general. Were it given a specific task in its charter, for example to study or promote racial integration, or recreational facilities, or health services, it would not have been as available for supporting ordinances, seminars, or protective services.[9]

But the significant generalization is related to the power that inheres in the very fact of an organization's existence. An organization can be a tool or weapon[10] to those outside of it as well as those who direct it. The uses to which some community organizations are put may be minor, as when they merely indicate "something is being done" about a problem even if they are expressly designed to do little beyond providing that indication. But a greater potential exists. A formal organization is visible and has an address to which communications can be sent; it has a legitimate, official area of relevant interest;[11] and it can speak with one voice, amplified by the size and prestige of its members and allies. It is equipped to be used for organized action even if its members wish to avoid action, as was the case with the Youth Commission. Reluctant as it may have been, the Commission had no choice but to exist for some time, and within a short time organizations turned to it as a source of support for their activities, exploiting the potential derived from its presence and broad purview, despite its self-imposed operative goals of merely existing and "listening."

All organizations can be used for purposes that go beyond their normal goals. In the process of meeting their goals and surviving, they generate power which can be put to uses that are independent of the achievement of normal goals. The potential power of a business firm is being utilized when it is a source of testimonials, sponsorship, or support for political, social, or economic activities that are unrelated to its basic task of providing goods or services. When the American Medical Association supports the farm organizations in their relentless war on daylight-saving time or takes a stand on the treaty-making powers of the presidency, its power as a medical group is being used by other groups. When organized labor is drawn into a political camp, or liberal groups used by "front" organizations,[12] or when a PTA is used to spearhead political reform, or when an organization seeks to have its prestige claims validated by appropriate groups in an effort to control their dependency upon the environment,[13] existing tools are being activated and used by others.

Although such use of an organization often has no significant impact upon the organization, it can shape the organization and even constitute an unacknowledged or unwitting goal for the organization. Elsewhere, this has been labeled as a "derived goal"—derived from the normal activity of the organization and not essential to that activity.[14] Initially, the Youth Commission wished merely to exist and to provide a polite and sympathetic hearing to all agencies. But this was a weak and vulnerable mission in the face of demands from powerful groups, and the uses derived from its existence became the open and acknowledged goals of the Commission. This, at least, appears to be the significance of the newspaper report at the end of the third year. The organization was raising funds and hiring a staff and thus would grow in the face of a presumably hostile environment, and it would pursue such services as overseeing the activities of other organizations and conducting and coordinating protective services. The width of its province—matters affecting youth—and the existence and legitimacy of its machinery for investigating, validating, and organizing made it an available organizational weapon and transformed it.

Though its goals were changed by others, it need not be a captive of others. Presumably, among the possible options open to the once reluctant organization, after its third year of existence, is the one of becoming a reasonably viable and powerful central agency in the community concerned with youth problems, free to utilize other agencies in the environment aggressively, even including the Probate Court.

NOTES

1. For a representative sampling see Philip Selznick, "Foundations of the Theory of Organization," *American Sociological Review*, 13 (1948), pp. 25–35; David Sills, *The Volunteers* (Glencoe, Ill.: Free Press, 1957); Herbert Simon, *Administrative Behavior* (2nd ed.; New York: Macmillan, 1957), especially the introduction; and James D. Thompson et al., *Comparative Studies in Administration* (Pittsburgh: University of Pittsburgh, 1959).

2. Philip Selznick, *Leadership and Administration* (New York: Row, Peterson, 1957).

3. The Commission agreed to serve as a research site for a seminar paper in organizational analysis, with the chairman hoping thereby that the role of the Commission in the community might be clarified. J. Maniha conducted the field work, while C. Perrow had primary, though not exclusive, responsibility for the framework of the analysis and much of the writing.

4. James D. Thompson and William J. McEwen, "Organizational Goals and Environment: Goal Setting as an Interaction Process," *American Sociological Review*, 23 (1958), 28–29.

5. On the concept of "operative goals," see Charles Perrow, "The Analysis of Goals in Complex Organization," *American Sociological Review*, 26 (1961), 854–866.

6. Philip Selznick, *op. cit.*; also *TVA and the Grass Roots* (Berkeley: University of California, 1949).

7. See, for example, Sol Levine and Paul E. White, "Exchange as a Conceptual Framework for the Study of Interorganizational Relationships," *Administrative Science Quarterly*, 5 (1961), 583–601; Eugene Litwak and Lydia Hylton, "Interorganizational Analysis," *Administrative Science Quarterly*, 6 (1962), 395–421; and Thompson and McEwen, *op. cit.*

8. Walter B. Miller, "Interinstitutional Conflict as a Major Impediment to Delinquency Prevention," *Human Organization*, 17 (1958), 20–23.

9. We are not inclined to attribute the survival of the Commission to crises such as the brawl or a growing awareness of real problems. Mounting concern is always present, particularly in retrospect. Every few years an opportunity such as the protective-service project presents itself, but unless it falls within the province of a group that already exists, the opportunity may not even be perceived by most observers.

10. This word is borrowed from Selznick, who uses it in a much more dramatic sense in *The Organizational Weapon* (New York: McGraw-Hill, 1952). It has more general utility than has been recognized.

11. An organization powerful in its own right becomes, moreover, like the physician, a generalized wise man wielding influence over a variety of areas. See the example of the American Medical Association mentioned in the next paragraph.

12. Philip Selznick, *The Organizational Weapon, op. cit.*

13. Charles Perrow, "Organizational Prestige, Some Functions and Dysfunctions," *American Journal of Sociology,* 66 (1961), 335–341.

14. Charles Perrow, "Organizational Goals," in David Sills (ed.), *International Encyclopedia of the Social Sciences* (rev. ed.; New York: Crowell-Collier, 1968). *Derived goals* are distinguished from *system goals,* which relate to system characteristics of the organization, such as its emphasis upon growth, stability, risk, etc., and from *product goals,* which relate to the type and characteristics of the goods or services produced, such as the emphasis upon quality, quantity, variety, etc. Derived goals may, in time, become system or product goals.

9

FROM EVANGELISM TO GENERAL SERVICE

The Transformation of the YMCA

Mayer N. Zald
Patricia Denton Wallace

A s the environments of organizations change, as the needs or demands of clientele change, organizations must, if they are to persist, be able to adapt goals, structure, and services. Even if they manage to persist despite environmental changes, organizations differ in their direction of change. In the process of organizational operation, some seem to displace original goals, becoming more rigid in operation and detached from their potential membership base, as for example, in the Townsend movement and the Women's Christian Temperance Union.[1] On the other hand, other organizations are able to transform goals without narrowing them, to maintain a high degree of organizational flexibility, and to develop an enlarged membership base, as in the case of the Young Men's Christian Association (YMCA), one of the most pervasive service organizations in the United

AUTHORS' NOTE: Revised version of a paper delivered at the meetings of the American Sociological Association, Washington, D.C., September 1962. Financial support for the larger study from which this article is drawn has been provided by a research grant from the National Institutes of Health, USPHS (M-6319). Reprinted from *Administrative Science Quarterly*, 8 (Sept. 1963): 214–234.

States. Starting as an evangelical association for young men, the YMCA has become a general leisure-time and character-development organization found in almost every city (96 percent of cities with more than 50,000 population[2]).

The YMCA has shown a remarkable ability to adapt itself to differing community needs and to expand its membership base to groups previously outside of its purview. Where originally it served only young men, it now serves both sexes and all age groups. And its rate of growth, from about one million members in 1930 to over two and one-half million in 1957, has been faster than the population at large.[3] At the same time that it has been growing, it has discontinued programs that either did not seem to meet membership needs or that were taken over by other agencies. As an organization, then, the YMCA has been growing and adapting; it is a successful organization. Like all organizations, however, the YMCA fills a particular niche in the organizational life of communities. It has tended to have a stronger base in lower-middle-class and middle-class areas than in working-class areas, and it has tended to recruit board members from Protestant elites rather than from other elites. Furthermore, unlike many service organizations that focus on control of deviants or on rehabilitation, the YMCA is largely concerned with developing the skills and character of its members. Here we are interested in examining the features that account for the YMCA's particular niche in American society, as well as the components of organization that contribute to organizational flexibility and growth. This article is essentially a study of the transformation and molding of organizational character; it attempts to delineate those characteristics that give the YMCA its distinctive features and shape its mode of response to environmental pressures and change.

After the discussion of the transformation of the YMCA from an evangelistic social movement to a general service organization, our analysis of organizational operation will be primarily cross-sectional and structural, focusing on four central factors: (1) the dependence of the YMCA on a paying clientele, (2) its federated structure, (3) the YMCA secretary's lack of a highly developed ideology and his dependence on the local board or director, and (4) the legitimation of a wide range of programs and services by broad character-development goals.

HISTORY

The key to the successful transformation of the YMCA is the shift from its emphasis on religious proselytization to its emphasis on goals of character development—physical, intellectual, and social, as well as spiritual. Once this change occurred, new programs could be instituted within the framework of these goals and legitimated by them to meet the shifting demands of clientele.

Early History and Expansion

The YMCA was founded in London in 1844 as an evangelical lay organization to convert single young men, who, during the burgeoning period of industrialization and urbanization, were migrating to the city in large numbers.[4] The movement grew rapidly. Within several years, YMCAs were started in Boston and other American cities. Initially, only those converted to evangelical churches could become members. Soon, however, young men were allowed to join even if not converted, although the management of the association was reserved to members of evangelical churches.

A few months after it started, many of its lasting characteristics were already in practice: members paid dues; wealthy businessmen contributed to its support; it was interdenominational; and, at least in England and America, control was reserved to the laity, although ministers might be included on the boards of directors.

Although the causes of the association's expansion are not clear, certain factors stand out. First, the definite Christian orientation of the movement tied it into the religious revivals of the time. The YMCA participated in organizing tent revivals as well as sponsoring prayer meetings, Bible readings, and lecture series. Thus the YMCA movement had definite goals and programs that focused its members' energies.

Second, the movement spread by a diffusion process based on local enthusiasm rather than by a process of centralized direction and allocation of personnel. Visitors to the London YMCA or to the early YMCA in Boston became enthusiastic about the idea and took it back to their own communities. This method of expansion depended on strong local support, ensuring a continuing base in each community.

Finally, each local YMCA usually had a reading room, a list of job openings, a coffee shop, and a list of wholesome boarding homes. These gave the association a material base in the community and also allowed it to minister to some of the basic needs of the young, single male.

Transformation of the Organization

The question of the transformation of the organization, however, is distinct from that of initial growth and success. The factors facilitating growth may be precisely those that hinder later change. Specifically, the narrowly evangelistic goals of the YMCA that were important to its early success might have, in the increasingly secularized society of the late nineteenth and early twentieth centuries, led to an organizational impasse, cutting the organization off from the main stream of American life.

Three interrelated trends characterize the successful adaptation of the YMCA to a changing society and consequent new demands by clientele. As we have noted, the basic goal of the organization changed from evangelism to the broader and more secularized one of developing the "whole man";[5] membership criteria were successively broadened to include all religions, ages, and both sexes; and control was extended to followers of any religion.

Within the framework of the new goal, program emphasis shifted away from the overtly religious to the development of the mental, physical, and social capacities of members. The inclusion of activities for physical training created more conflict than did programs for mental or intellectual development, because it challenged conservative religious views of the proper forms of recreation.[6] Their addition, however, is an important indicator of the ability of the YMCA to identify changing clientele needs correctly and to meet them. With increasing leisure time and the decline of physical work in the late nineteenth century, Americans rapidly developed an interest in sports and physical exercise.[7]

From 1860 to about 1900 the emphases on physical development and on general evangelism were both debated issues in many YMCAs, and emphasis on overt or formal religious programs was declining. By the early 1900s, local YMCAs—in America, at least[8] —had begun to reduce their religious services because of the low public response to these programs.[9] In the depression of the 1930s, staffing of religious programs was largely eliminated in order to reduce expenses.

The other great transformation of the YMCA, the greater inclusiveness of membership and the extension of participation in control to those who were not members of evangelical churches, also broadened the base of the organization. Inclusion of women in the program dates from the beginning of public lectures, although formal membership was not granted until 1934. In general, the YMCA experienced less difficulty in extending services to other age groups and to women (although competition with the Young Women's Christian Association, a completely separate organization, was a subject for negotiation) than in extending control to others than members of evangelical churches. YMCAs in predominantly Roman Catholic countries began to define evangelical churches as including the Roman Catholic Church; however, in the United States it was not until the 1930s that active membership (that is, voting membership) was extended to Catholics and Jews. Under current interpretations, anyone who believes in the general purpose of the YMCA may participate in policy making, and a limited number of Jews as well as Catholics serve on the boards of directors of various YMCAs.[10]

How can we account for this general broadening of goals and greater inclusiveness of membership and control groups? The transformation of membership criteria is easily understood. Originally restricted to young men in order to meet the common interests of the large number of single men living in the cities at the time of its inception, the YMCA, unlike some other men's social groups, was not created as a refuge from women; nor were its evangelistic activities limited to men. Extension of service to women and to other age groups allowed the organization to broaden its scope of operation. Greater inclusiveness of membership was clearly in the interest of the controlling groups of the YMCA who wished to see its growth. Less clear, however, are those elements of organizational structure that permitted and fostered change in control and, most important, in the scope of programs.

The basic organization conditions that allowed the organization to transform its evangelical goals seems to have been its inter-denominational character and its control by laymen rather than clergy. Neither church organization nor clerical ideology constrained the direction of organizational change. If the YMCA had been dominated by a single denomination, it probably would have been absorbed into it.[11] Also since both its staff and directors were not members of the clergy, considerations of church policy and theology were less important than if the organization had been controlled by clergymen. Laymen committed to the organization and to its general Christian goals were free to assess the societal changes and concomitant practical needs that could be met by the organization.

Constant Elements in Organizational Operation

Although the YMCA has experienced radical transformation during its 100-year history, there are several constant elements in its operation: it has avoided political embroilments, and its services have been preventive rather than rehabilitative. Ever since controversy arose over the appearance of pro-abolition speakers on the YMCA podium, the YMCA, especially at the local level, has supported a policy of avoiding controversial problems not directly defined as relevant to its character-building goals. Where the YWCA has always defined its mission as more contingent on social reform, actively pursuing the solution of such problems as race relations, the YMCA has generally implemented its goals by serving clientele rather than by attempting to change the environment. In part, this approach is historically based on its origin as a membership association rather than as a charitable institution. Hopkins asserts that both in its inception and continuing practice, the YMCA has been guided by people of the white-collar classes to help members of their own class.[12] Although this is partly true, many members of the YMCA subscribed to social gospel and *noblesse oblige* notions of reform. The YMCA actively contributed to relief for the needy, through the distribution of food and clothing, and to the incorporation of immigrant masses through its Americanization and language classes. Ideas of social gospel and social reform springing from the organization's basic Christian identification are ever-present, but subordinated, forces for charitable and rehabilitative work.

The policy of political noninvolvement and of a preventive program is related, as will be shown, to elements of organizational structure, specifically to the federated relationship among associations, to control of the organization by a lay elite, and to an "enrollment economy." The discussion of organizational structure and operation that follows draws heavily on elements suggested in our historical review.

ORGANIZATIONAL STRUCTURE AND OPERATION

Effect of Transformation on Program and Clientele

The transformation of organization goals and criteria for membership has had important consequences for the program and the clientele of the organization. The YMCA's explicit purpose of character development limits the organization in only two ways—it must attempt to help people develop, rather than merely to sell them services, and it must help them develop along socially approved lines. Broadly stated goals permit wide diversification and are conducive to organizational flexibility. These goals encourage the use of varied means. Any program is encouraged that "helps people to develop." Programs have ranged from athletic activities to bridge and dancing classes, club programs for adolescents, and residence rooms for single men and women. To support typical programs, the YMCA must provide only supervisory staff and such rather general facilities as meeting rooms or gymnasiums, which can be used for other programs.

The breadth of YMCA programs can be further understood in the light of the organization's dependence on a paying clientele. Because of its enrollment economy,[13] programs are instituted and discontinued according to membership demands. In meeting clientele needs the YMCA has included, in its definition of character development, courses that help people advance in their jobs, such as courses in typing, supervision, and human relations. The statement of goals in Christian terms, however, has lent continuity to the organization as it changed programs and justified to staffs and boards an expenditure of time and energy even when such expenditure was financially unrewarding. Moreover, Christian purposes give the organization a basic legitimacy, which purely secular organizations often cannot claim.

The transformation of membership criteria is another factor in the YMCA's flexibility. The broad goals of character development do not specify a market with respect to age or sex, permitting the organization to adapt its programs to the composition of the population and the competing services of the local community. For example, if other agencies serve youth, or if there are few youths in the community, the YMCA can serve older people. Since 1940, the number of women in the organization has quintupled (see Table 9.1). Moreover, the number of young men between eighteen and thirty years of age who are members has been decreasing, both relatively and absolutely, for over three

TABLE 9.1 Membership of Men and Women in the YMCA, 1930–1960, by Age (in percentages)

Year	Total Membership	Under 12 Yrs.	12–17 Yrs.	18–29 Yrs.	30 Yrs. and Up
Men					
1930	1,034,109	8.0	22.4	46.3	23.3
1940	1,224,410	12.7	28.4	34.5	24.4
1950	1,840,273	19.1	26.0	28.0	26.9
1957	1,939,977	25.8	23.8	16.6	33.7
1960[a]	2,069,327	30.0	22.8	14.5	32.7
Women					
1941[b]	98,666	13.5	32.7	29.7	24.1
1950	248,088	18.0	43.9	19.1	18.9
1957	487,833	22.1	40.9	15.8	21.2
1960[a]	590,583	23.5	39.7	14.6	22.2

SOURCE: Clifford M. Carey, "Perspectives for YMCA Growth in the 1960's," in *1959 YMCA Year Book* (New York, 1959).
a. Estimates.
b. No previous official records.

decades. Much soul-searching among YMCA staffs has accompanied this decline, which signifies the loss of a goal-defining target population. The decline may be attributed to the fact that young men are no longer as isolated in large cities, or to a decrease in their interest in religion. Whatever the explanation, the important point is that the YMCA has been able to expand its membership without this group.

We have already noted that its goals and enrollment economy tend to make the YMCA a general service organization for the middle class, or at least the more integrated members of the society. This tendency is reinforced by an organizational structure that ties the local YMCA closely to the wishes of the local governing body and the local clientele. Both the flexibility and limitations of YMCA organizations are based on its federated structure, the relationship of local elites to professional staff, and its financial base. When these factors, contributing to strong control from the local community, are related to the problem of managing membership sentiment, we can see the constraints tying the organization to an essentially middle-class and preventive orientation.

Federated Structure

Spreading from community to community by a diffusion process, local YMCAs have been outgrowths of community action rather than imposed or created from outside. Structurally, the stress has been on local autonomy.

Five levels of organization exist: the local association, the metropolitan association, the area council, the National Council, and the World Council. In smaller communities the YMCA is locally controlled and operated. In a metropolitan area, even though buildings are likely to be owned by the metropolitan association rather than by the local department or branch, strong emphasis is placed on the autonomy of the individual branch (department) and staff. Furthermore, the National Association and its staff are supported by dues paid by the local associations, and members of the National Council are elected, not appointed. Executive staff members of the local YMCA are appointed by the local board of directors. Thus, though uniform professional standards have been established (a national records system is operated, personnel files are circulated, and national aims are formulated), the local community sharply constrains organizational policy.

The federated system with its emphasis on local autonomy has ideological support. Around the turn of the century, there was intense conflict between the local associations and the International Committee (the then dominant national organization).[14] In a series of meetings, the faction pressing for local autonomy and control prevailed. Related to its Protestant origins, the YMCA ideology stresses the importance of maintaining a self-governing association.

Elite Control and the Professional Secretary

If a federated structure were coupled with local, professional control, the constraints of the local community might be lessened. However, the YMCA is unusual among private service organizations in its commitment to lay control, and board members are largely drawn from local elites. The pressures in most large-scale organizations toward increased managerial and professional control, although present, are strenuously resisted in the YMCA. For instance, at least two-thirds of the delegates to national conventions must be lay members; board participation and involvement is sought; a committee structure that ensures a broad base of consultation and involvement on program as well as financial decisions is maintained.

Lay control of the local YMCA is important because of the attitudes and values of the controlling boards and because of the relationship of the YMCA professional to his board members. Although originally composed of young men, today the controlling boards of the YMCA are primarily recruited, as are most boards of private agencies, from the upper ranks of local business circles. A small number of lawyers and doctors is included. YMCA board members are also often active churchmen.

The secretary contributes to maintaining lay dominance and broad character-development goals for the YMCA in two ways. First, his own social background and attitudes predispose him to accept the dominant modes of YMCA operation. Second, his relationship to the board and his own professional image lead him to accept and even encourage board dominance; he does not assert a professional ideology or skill pose.

Although many different types of people are recruited to the secretaryship, a dominant type can be constructed. The "ideal-type" secretary is a Protestant from a medium-size town, of a lower-middle-class background. He has attended a small, often denominational, college and may have considered becoming a teacher or minister. It is likely that he was a member of the YMCA during his adolescence, and he may have gone either to a YMCA or to some other religiously oriented camp, an experience of meaning for him. He is a good churchman, but not especially articulate in theological discussion. He prefers physically active programs to more passive and verbal programs and, both by personal preference and professional necessity, he is likely to be a Rotarian or a Kiwanis member.[15] Although he is more liberal in social outlook than his board, he accepts their authority and respects their point of view.

He does this for several reasons. Inasmuch as the executive secretary of the YMCA in a small town is employed by the lay board, he is more dependent on them than many professionals. Even in a metropolitan association, getting along with the board is a prerequisite of successful operation. Although he is recommended for the position by staff higher up in the hierarchy of the Association, his success or failure depends greatly on his ability to work with the local board and satisfy it. While this is true of any executive of a welfare agency, the dependence of the local YMCA secretary is intensified by his lack of ideological insulation from the board.[16]

A branch may have only a few professionals on its staff and, more important, the secretary does not possess either a set of skills or a specialized knowledge base that could legitimate his claim to greater wisdom in association affairs, as doctors, engineers, lawyers, or even social case workers have. To be certified as a secretary, an applicant needs a bachelor's degree, with a few courses relevant to YMCA history and religious philosophy, and YMCA work experience; no specific academic discipline is required or preferred. Since he does not have a sharply defined professional ideology, the secretary is not likely to initiate radical changes in program or to uphold professional standards that cannot be met by his board. Although, like other professionals, the YMCA secretary manipulates the composition of the board to achieve his ends, his own attitudes and values are not likely to lead him into sharp conflict with them. YMCA secretaries are rarely fired because of theological or ideological conflicts with the board.

The control that the secretary does have, based on full-time involvement and his greater knowledge of alternatives and program, is offset by his having grown up in a movement whose organizational ideology specifies lay dominance and emphasizes that the secretary's job is not to define goals, but rather to help others to implement theirs.[17] The secretary is therefore not likely to define his own role as that of leader; he sees himself as an educator.

Lay control and the absence of professionals with a strongly developed ideology and professional code support the YMCA's broad goals. The lack of ideological attachment to programs helps account for the flexibility of means,[18] while lay, interdenominational control minimizes ideological attachments to goals. These factors, however, do not explain the middle-class orientation of the YMCA. Although the recruitment base of the staff and their ideology do not immediately lend themselves to working with social deviants or less-integrated members of the society,[19] the financial bases of the local YMCA and the problem of managing membership sentiments make possible a better understanding of this orientation of the organization.

Financial Base and the Problem of
Managing Membership Sentiments

Like voluntary health and welfare organizations, such as the American Cancer Society, Family Service Agency, and settlement houses, the YMCA is dependent on the Community Chest or direct contributions to meet its needs. Unlike these, however, membership fees and returns for business services, such as cafeterias and hotel rooms, are a major source of funds.[20] Almost all programs are expected to "pull part of their own weight."

This dependence on membership fees and business features limits its clientele base and, at the same time, fosters organizational flexibility. Since its conception of organizational goals is diffuse, the YMCA has the flexibility to initiate and abandon programs in accordance with clientele demand. Although dependent on membership fees for financial solvency, the YMCA has continued to support programs that do not pay their own way. Both its club and youth programs, as well as its international work, require considerable financial support. Even though a local YMCA strives for financial solvency, its programs are not all equally self-sufficient. It would be possible for it to support social-service programs while having fee-supported programs in other areas. That it does not is largely a function of the problem of managing membership sentiment.[21]

Concisely stated, it is easier to do missionary work at a distance than at home. Since the lay membership that controls and participates in the YMCA often uses the facilities that they support financially, the use of these same facilities by social deviants, such as delinquents, or other social "undesirables" as Negroes, constitutes an organizational risk. Unless both boards and membership are especially prepared and educated, moves to incorporate the socially unintegrated are likely to have adverse effects on commitment, participation, and financial support.

There are three types of relationship that the YMCA can have with groups that are not incorporated into the middle class. First, they may provide charitable services. For example, the YMCA has participated in the distribution of clothes for the needy, the epitome of missionary work at a distance. Second, as the unincorporated groups become more socially acceptable, as they take on attributes and behavior patterns of the middle class, the YMCA may assimilate them. As working-class affluence has increased, and as the leisure patterns of sports and recreation typifying the middle classes have spread, there have been no barriers other than economic ones to working-class participation in the YMCA. Third, the YMCA can develop out-reaching programs specifically aimed at incorporating and involving the "undesir-ables." Such programs would involve the YMCA in attempts to solve social problems, and if the undesirables were brought into contact with other members, might lead to the alienation of members.

On the other hand, initiation of these "social-problem" programs would reaffirm the Christian identity of the organization for both professionals and lay leaders. To the extent that such programs are financed by foundation or Community Chests rather than by members, financial dependency on an uncommitted clientele would be eliminated, and professional reference groups would become salient. Programs to incorporate the socially deviant have been rare, however.

Missionary work at a distance helps to maintain a sense of Christian commitment while it avoids involvement in controversial domestic social problems. Since the YMCA is not ideologically committed to solving social problems, it typically avoids local social-service work, and the secretary avoids alienating both board and membership. Although his Christian commitment might lead him to confront his board on race-relations problems, the secretary finds it easiest to maintain support in the local community if he avoids controversy and social reform. Officers and staff of the national and area organization, on the other hand, are in a position to suggest programs that are not closely dependent on conservative elements in the community. Lay as well as staff leadership on the national level are also bound to be more committed to the abstract purposes of the organization than those using the YMCA on the local level and are likely to see it as an international fellowship of Christians rather than as a general-service organization. Moreover, profes-sional staffs at the national or metropolitan level are less dependent on lay personnel and interact more with other professionals. Their ideological position is therefore freer.

Factors like the low level of professionalization, the dependence on local elites, and the role of membership participation may impose limits on the ability of the organization to pursue its basic goals. The consequent limitations of organizational pursuits can be seen as a set of organizational dilemmas. The very factors that have contributed to growth may create problems of effec-tiveness.

ORGANIZATIONAL DILEMMAS AND ROLE PROBLEMS

Two major role problems may arise from the character of YMCA goals and operation, the dilemma of membership dependency and the dilemma of program formulation. The two are interrelated and contribute to the role problems of the YMCA secretary.

Dilemma of Dependence on Membership. Any organization must meet the needs of clientele if it is to succeed. Many organizations, however, and especially "people-changing" organizations, assume that the goals and special knowledge of staff give them a clearer picture of client needs than the clients themselves have. Social workers, doctors, and clergymen share the belief that the professional has tools and knowledge that make his wisdom and knowledge of client needs superior to that of the client. The YMCA secretary, too, believes that he best knows how to promote the greater personal development of members.

Since client payment for services is essential to the maintenance of the YMCA, however, the staff are constrained by an enrollment economy; they find that they must sell such products as recreation facilities, hotel rooms, swimming classes, bridge and dancing classes, which may only tangentially relate to their goal of character building, to leading members away from egocentrism, and to building membership involvement. In fact, in the past, programs that personnel felt were directly related to their goals, e.g., Bible classes and discussion of current affairs, were discontinued for want of support. In recent years, the club program for adolescents has also shrunk.[22]

The flexibility of means in relation to goals permits the organization to meet its needs by offering programs of interest to clientele, but its dependence on clientele willingness to pay limits its program and impact to items that clients recognize as useful to themselves. Given low professional identity and the emphasis on fiscal solvency, it is easy for the staff to replace poorly paying programs with financially rewarding ones. And since clients may not be committed to the Christian aspects of YMCA goals, the secretary finds himself working for a clientele with limited commitments to basic goals.[23]

Dilemma of Program Formulation. The dilemma of dependence on clientele is related to the dilemma of program formulation. We refer to more than just the limitation to clientele-financed programs; we refer to the general structure of character building and preventive approaches. Both the middle-class and Christian bases of the organization lead it to a conception of organization programs that restrict its clientele to those who seem to be adapting successfully to the society. The problem for organization staff members is twofold: how do you know you are being effective, and how do you maintain your belief in the importance of your work? The first problem is solved by recourse to counts of program participation: how many people used the swimming pool or attended classes? The second is solved by the secretary's largely unquestioning belief that the actions he engages in are of value. This belief is supported by the people who surround the secretary, especially his board—a salient and authoritative reference group. However, both staff members and relevant publics sometimes question the ultimate value of the purely recreational facilities.

The dilemmas of client dependence and program formulation may contribute to role problems for the secretary. Can he see the results of his efforts—the development of character? Does he have an ideology that permits him to justify his own self-conception and role? Does he have a set of professional relationships that develop and encourage his active pursuit of his aims?

To some extent we are posing a set of false problems. For many secretaries, the YMCA is a totally satisfying experience. The kinds of activities offered are consonant with his personal values. Since he does not have either high intellectual or financial aspirations, and since he likes physical activity and working with people, but is not especially introspective, the YMCA provides a good fit for his personality.[24] What follows probably applies to a minority of the YMCA secretaries, more to the program and youth club secretaries than to those who direct physical education activities, and more to the service-oriented secretary than the activity-oriented secretary.

The problems of the service-oriented secretary tend to make him disenchanted. In private conversation, the secretary refers to the fact that "many people think they can buy the Y," or "they think they are getting a commodity; they don't have a sense of the Y as a movement—a movement of Christians working for a better world." The secretary can see the Christian element of the organization most in work that he himself does not do, in the YMCA's international work, for instance. Disenchantment stems from the clientele-based nature of the program. The immediacy of the satisfactions of an adoption worker or a volunteer working for the Infantile Paralysis Foundation is frequently absent. The YMCA secretary often has to be satisfied with activities rather than perceived changes in people as measures of achievement.

Not only is the secretary involved with programs that often lack immediacy, but he is also in direct and continuous contact with clients and boards and in minimum contact with fellow professionals. Since his own professional identity is not clearly related to a set of skills or ideology, he is unable to impose his definitions of goals or activities on either the board or clientele. Both the problem of disenchantment and the problem of professional identity are rooted in the very structure of the organization.

CONCLUSIONS

The historical transformation of the YMCA led it to become a general, all-purpose, service organization. In analyzing its basic elements, we have stressed the breadth of the YMCA's goals and means, the wide range of clientele served, the dependency on elite control, the low professionalization of staff, and the preventive and character-developing nature of its programs. We have also pointed to the relation of the YMCA's financial dependency to its success. For any individual YMCA, the factors discussed are variables, not constants.

Our analysis has stressed that the organization has been largely tied to a relatively well-integrated base, but there are pressures for change within the organization. The mere fact that older buildings are located in rapidly changing neighborhoods creates pressures for new programs and financial arrangements. Furthermore, the shifting currents of the educational system lead to different staff perspectives. These changes, if and when they come, may require changes in the financial structure of the organization and in the recruitment of staff. As the community becomes unable to support the YMCA, external funds may have to be tapped, causing problems for local autonomy and providing a new set of standards for goal definitions. These changes may require that the staff learn a new argot and techniques in order to deal with deviant groups. They may also affect the basic identity of at least part of the organization and are likely to be resisted by staff and boards alike.

Our analysis has purposely focused on the YMCA alone, but the aspects of organizational structure discussed should be useful in analyzing the process of change in other organizations. We offer four propositions about organizational change implied by our discussion.

1. *Federated structure:* To the extent that organizations have decentralized and relatively autonomous decision centers, they can adapt to environmental changes quickly, in accordance with local needs and pressures. Parts of the organization may experiment with new programs even before other parts recognize the need for change. On the other hand, with centralized organizations, once they do recognize that environmental pressures require changes, the rate of change may be much faster.

2. *Broadly defined organizational goals and rules:* To the extent that organizational goals commit the actor to narrowly defined objects or to only one program, we would expect organizations to have difficulty in adapting to environmental changes that seriously affected the appeal of those programs. On the other hand, broadly defined goals and means permit an organization to encompass many types of programs and thus permit flexibility.[25]

3. *Low development of professional ideology:* Our analysis suggests that low professionalization facilitates change. The more ideologically committed the professional is to the means he uses, the more difficult it will be to change the organization in which he operates.

4. *Enrollment economy:* An enrollment economy is immediately sensitive to the changed demands of the market place. Organizations that are dependent on some form of enrollment economy (a form of competitive market place) are forced to recognize quickly the environmental changes affecting the

demand for services. On the other hand, organizations protected from the market place, such as religious organizations, welfare organizations, or social movements, may soon find themselves poorly adapted to the changing order.

NOTES

1. Sheldon Messinger, "Organizational Transformation: A Case Study of a Declining Social Movement," *American Sociological Review,* 20 (1955), 3–10. Also Joseph Gusfield, "Social Structure and Moral Reform: A Study of the Women's Christian Temperance Union," *American Journal of Sociology,* 61 (1955), 221–232, and "The Problems of Generations in an Organizational Structure," *Social Forces,* 35 (1957), 323–330.

2. Clifford M. Carey, "Perspectives for YMCA Growth in the 1960's," in *1959 YMCA Year Book* (New York, 1959).

3. *Ibid.*

4. Historical detail can be found in Luther L. Dodgett, *The Founding of the Association, 1844–1855 (History of the Young Men's Christian Association,* Vol. I; New York, 1896); and in C. Howard Hopkins, *History of the YMCA in North America* (New York, 1950).

5. We do not mean to imply that the change from evangelistic to broad, character-development goals occurred all at once or before any changes in program. Quite the opposite, YMCAs in local communities slowly added programs which met with public response; in this process, original goals were transformed.

6. For a discussion of this conflict in the Chicago YMCA, see Emmett Dedmon, *Great Enterprises: 100 Years of the YMCA of Metropolitan Chicago* (New York, 1957), p. 100.

7. For a discussion of the spread of sports and the church's reaction to them, see Foster Rhea Dulles, *America Learns to Play: A History of Popular Recreation 1607–1940* (New York, 1940), esp. chap. xii, "The New Order," pp. 201–210.

8. YMCAs in Europe, especially in Germany, have always been more religiously zealous and pietistic than those in England and the United States, and those in England retained a closer connection to religion than those in America. Dodgett (*op. cit.,* pp. 171–172) asserts this for 1855, and YMCA staff today still claim that the differences exist. But these national differences are beyond the scope of this chapter.

9. The YMCA had provided more than just Bible classes; it acted as a coordinating agency for interdenominational interests. Some YMCA leaders thought of it as the new Universal Church, and the YMCA has always worked for church cooperation. As the churches developed their own coordinating mechanisms, such as local and federal councils of churches, and as they developed their own Sunday schools and auxiliaries, the demand for YMCA services in these areas diminished. On the other hand, the YMCA's relationships with the denominations, especially the more conservative ones, had always been somewhat strained, for the clergy of various denominations were bound to find the YMCA's religious teaching at variance with their own doctrine. For a discussion of these relationships, see S. Wirt Wiley, *History of YMCA-Church Relations in the United States* (New York, 1944). In a sense, the YMCA was "pulled" into general services by the transformation of society and "pushed" by the increasing capabilities of the institutions of the churches.

10. See Clifford M. Carey, *YMCA Boards and Committee of Management* (New York, n.d.), p. 11. Where some 27 percent of the YMCA's membership are Catholic, only about 5 percent of the members of the YMCA's boards of directors are Catholic.

11. Some sects are begun by lay evangelists who begin spreading word of the Lord, hoping to get members to join already established denominations. On the history of the Elim Four Square Gospel, see B. Wilson, *Sects and Society* (Berkeley, Calif., 1961). What would have happened to the YMCA if George Williams had become a full-time evangelist, requiring financial support, rather than a merchant prince of London? This may have been a crucial organization choice

point. Dwight Moody, the famous American evangelist, was the secretary of the Chicago YMCA. He left the organization to become a full-time evangelist in the 1860s; the organization's character was already established.

12. Hopkins, *op. cit.*, p. 6.

13. An "enrollment economy" exists when the meeting of financial needs is dependent on the enrollment of members in activities or classes. The term is Burton Clark's in his "Organizational Adaptation and Precarious Values: A Case Study," *American Sociological Review,* 21 (June 1956), 332.

14. Dedmon, *op. cit.*, pp. 147–156.

15. A recent study by Roy Grinker, with the collaboration of Roy Grinker, Jr., and John Timberlake, suggests that at least one of the major sources of professional YMCA personnel, George Williams College, has a student body which largely conforms to this picture. The students have average intelligence (110 median), very little psychopathology, and low mobility aspirations. They are active churchmen, relatively unintrospective, and accept authority and tradition. See "Mentally Healthy Young Males (Homoclites)," *Archives of General Psychiatry,* 6 (June 1962), 405–453. See also Emil F. Faubert, "Mr. YMCA Secretary" (mimeo., 1961).

16. On the necessity of insulation for the maintenance of ideological organization, see James D. Thompson, "Organizational Management of Conflict," *Administrative Science Quarterly,* 4 (1960), 389–409.

17. In "Politics as an Ecology of Games," *American Journal of Sociology,* 26 (1960), Norton Long argues that professionals in welfare and service agencies must build and maintain a community elite if they are to be successful. This is especially true of the YMCA secretary. Since the program he is running does not have the immediacy of appeal of such an agency as the cancer foundation, the secretary must build a continuing relationship between his organization and local elites if he is to be successful.

18. The lack of a specific professional skill requirement also contributes to organizational flexibility in the use of personnel. The number of accredited YMCA secretaries in the United States has remained around 4,000 since 1930, although membership has tripled. Since the organization does not assert that only professionals are competent to deal with clients, the YMCA has greatly increased its use of part-time and volunteer personnel. As Clark points out, the very nature of the enrollment economy also leads to using a large number of part-time employees, since specialists are required to staff varied activities (Clark, *op. cit.*, p. 334).

19. There is no reason why the YMCA *should* work with the socially deviant and less integrated, but historically there have been both internal and external pressures for the YMCA to work with socially deviant groups. The question at stake here is why the YMCA *has not generally* responded to this pressure. Some programs of the YMCA of Chicago have aimed at the socially deviant. The special conditions necessary for maintaining this type of program will be analyzed in a later paper.

20. On the average, 32 percent of YMCA income came from dues and program fees in 1961, 34 percent from business features such as residences, 25 percent from contributions and endowments, and 8 percent from miscellaneous sources. Cf. Clifford M. Carey and Sanford M. Reece, eds., *1962 YMCA Year Book and Official Roster* (New York, 1962), p. 34.

21. Hans W. Mattick suggested the phrase "managing membership sentiments." See also Arthur Vidich and Joseph Bensman's discussion of the lack of mission work among the unchurched by the ministers of Springdale, in *Small Town and Mass Society: Class Power and Religion in a Rural Community* (New York, 1960), p. 257.

22. Clark, *op. cit.*, argues that the worker in adult education is buffeted by pressures of a paying clientele to lower his professional standards. He is put in conflict by his allegiance to the strong external peer group of educators to uphold his standards. This source of cross pressure with clientele or board demands is largely lacking in the YMCA. The peer professional group of the YMCA secretary (Association of Organization Secretaries) exists largely within the organization. Some secretaries identify strongly with welfare-service groups, which give them an independent basis for standards; others identify strongly with the churches. But for many YMCA secretaries, professional standards are largely based on organizational practices.

23. A management consultant firm which did a survey of the membership of one YMCA in 1940 concluded: "It is evident from the findings of this investigation that, in the minds of the majority of the members and former members, and, to a slightly smaller extent among

non-members, the Department of the YMCA is primarily a place in which to swim, to play handball, to play billiards and pool, to lift weights, and to make acquaintances among congenial young men of like tastes. In other words, the Department appears to be coordinate, in the thinking of most of the men interviewed, with the gymnasiums and swimming pools provided by the parks, schools and other public and semi-public institutions. A membership in the YMCA seems to them to represent the purchase of the privilege of using the Department's pool, gymnasium and recreational facilities. There is very little evidence that the majority of the men interviewed have any real conception of the function of the YMCA other than a place for athletic activities, recreation and an opportunity to meet other young men.

"Certainly, there is little evidence that the men take a real or sincere interest in the Department as an institution. Their attitudes toward it and toward the acceptance of responsibility through work on committees and councils is extremely superficial."

24. Personal conversation with Roy Grinker, M.D.

25. Of course, broadly defined goals with little specificity may permit *too much* flexibility, in that they may result in a weak commitment.

10

THE CREATIVE-DESTRUCTIVE PROCESS OF ORGANIZATIONAL CHANGE
The Case of the Post Office

Nicole Woolsey Biggart

S tudies of organizational change have most often been concerned with the reasons for change and have taken the process for granted. Researchers have attempted to identify the stimuli that trigger adaptive behaviors and have seen change as a product of such influences as organizational structure (Hummon, Doreian, and Teuter, 1975), growth and ageing (Labovitz and Miller, 1974), technological innovation (Bell, 1973), environmental changes (Sherwood, 1976), constituency changes (Mazmanian and Lee, 1975), leadership style (Meyer, 1975), and the dissatisfaction of the deprived (Benson, 1973). Such studies emphasize the initiating cause and the evolutionary nature of the process rather than seeing change as inherently problematic. Even those that do identify change as problematic treat it as a problem of the creation of territories and structures (Downs, 1967) or of managerial "teams" and conducive climates (Golembiewski and Kiepper, 1976).

It is not generally recognized that change is an act of destruction as much as of creation. Because most organizations do change slowly, experimenting

AUTHOR'S NOTE: I would like to thank Gary G. Hamilton, University of California, Davis, for his help and encouragement. Reprinted from *Administrative Science Quarterly*, 22 (Sept. 1977):410–426.

with and selectively incorporating new forms, the destruction of old forms and methods is relatively obscured. But the destructive process must either precede or exist simultaneously with the creative. This act of undoing and dismantling is important theoretically: reorganization presumes the rejection or supercession of old methods in favor of the new and the organization must systematically destroy former, competing structures before it can successfully implant the new.

Generally, destruction is an extreme concept but in an organization it rarely finds expression in any dramatic way, principally because few organizational changes are of revolutionary dimension and are often never completed before opposing interests can mute the effects. The concept of destruction as part of organizational change is useful because it properly describes the treatment of organizational accouterments that have lost their use or are in disfavor.

Destruction, as used in this article, includes any action that abolishes, discredits, suppresses, or otherwise renders useless an organizational structure. Among the features a new regime often destroys in the course of conversion are the former formal structure, leadership, ideology, power alliances, decision-making model, and technology. This process can in some ways be thought of as the resocialization of the organization: an organization cannot be isolated from its former self (although symbolic attempts such as moving the corporate headquarters and changing the name are common), but punishments can be meted out for reestablishing old patterns and rewards granted those adopting new ways. Empirically, this process is important because it explains many of the actions prior to and during government and corporate reorganizations, actions which may otherwise be incomprehensible or attributed to other causes.

THE MODEL

The 1971 reorganization of the U.S. Post Office Department (POD) into the U.S. Postal Service (USPS) is an unusually demonstrative model of the creative-destructive process for several reasons. First, it is an extraordinarily large organization. At the passage of Public Law 91-375, the Postal Reorganization Act, the POD had over 700,000 workers, almost 1 percent of the U.S. workforce (Annual Report of the Postmaster General, FY 1971). In the federal government, only the military was a larger employer, and among private organizations only AT&T was comparable. Such dimensions tend to magnify organizational processes.

Second, the reorganization was close to revolutionary in scope. In one momentous action the President and Congress transformed the POD's formal structure and legal relationships, forms that had existed virtually unchanged for 100 years.

Third, the reorganization was not evolutionary, that is, the culmination of internally felt needs or power struggles. Rather, it was a transformation imposed by a coalition of external interests onto a bureaucracy that neither sought nor welcomed the change. The majority of the employees had taken pride in or at least were comfortable with the forms that were repudiated by the external interest groups.

Finally, the Post Office is a public organization whose activities are more available to public scrutiny than most private organizations.

The structure of the Post Office has features of both industry and government and is, therefore, both similar and unlike other organizations. While the Post Office is not a typical organization structurally, the processes of change in this extreme model demonstrate what can be found generally throughout organizations. This study distinguishes broad analytic categories that appear to have had importance in this case. In some instances the assignment of events to a particular category has been arbitrary because few organizational activities perform a single function or act in any unitary way.

Formal Structure

Article I, Section 8 of the United States Constitution grants Congress the right to "regulate commerce . . . to establish post offices and post roads," but it was not until 1792 that the Post Office had consolidated its position as a permanent agency (Cullinan, 1968: 27). Congress retained the exclusive right to establish and regulate post offices, a right of considerable power in a growing nation that depended heavily on the mails for the conduct of business and the maintenance of communications. The Post Office Department was located under the Executive Branch and the President appointed the Postmaster General who in turn appointed his top aides. The Congress assumed the role of a board of directors and involved itself in the daily decisions of the POD. The Senate reserved the right to confirm postmaster appointments made by the President. Thus Congress and the Executive branch shared the single largest source of patronage in government (Cullinan, 1968: 79).

This pool of favors was traditionally managed by the Postmaster General who was typically the President's campaign manager or close political adviser; his postal management chores were usually secondary to his political duties (Fowler, 1967). This posed no problem as long as Congress continued to appropriate funds for maintaining a deficit operation; but expensive capital expenditures needed for modernizing the growing concern were always passed over in favor of more popular and visible public programs, and, during the 1960s, the Vietnam War. Emergency appropriations usually paid for the hiring of additional workers to process and deliver the mail. The Post Office thus became heavily labor intensive with net assets per employee only 1/25th as great as those of AT&T (Kappel Commission, Annex I, 1968: 17).

Eighty-one percent of the POD budget went for salaries (Annual Report of the Postmaster General, FY 1969: 166).

These political conditions strongly influenced the internal structure of the Post Office Department. The Postmaster General presided over a headquarters staff of six Assistant Postmasters General, each with a separate bureau (Finance and Administration, Personnel, Transportation and International Services, Operations, Facilities, Research and Engineering) plus the Chief Postal Inspector and the General Counsel. Because Congress retained the important powers of budget allocation, capital expenditures, wage determination and price control, and made planning impossible by refusing to grant long-term appropriations, the only activity of any consequence left to postal administrators was the daily operation of the mail network. The Bureau of Operations, in charge of mail processing, dominated all the other bureaus, controlled over 80 percent of the budget (Kappel Commission, Annex I, 1968: 44), and reviewed and approved all significant decisions by any other office. Structurally, each person in Headquarters had his functional counterpart in each of the 15 Regional Offices, and he in turn had his counterpart in each post office. The strong vertical hierarchy discouraged activities between peers at any level and coordination was pushed to the very top, where it was controlled by the Bureau of Operations.

Control was exercised primarily through detailed and numerous directives such as the weekly *Postal Bulletin* and, especially, the *Postal Manual*. The *Manual* was a continuously revised nine-pound compendium of postal regulations, rates, and operating procedures that prescribed actions and behaviors for every possible contingency. Innovation and local discretion were not rewarded, only administration "by the book." The tenure system tended to preclude innovative persons from access to positions of authority. A worker was not eligible for promotional consideration for five years (*Postal Bulletin,* November 10, 1990: 2), and, realistically, selection took several years longer until a worker became the most senior candidate. The policy was not designed to attract ambitious or creative people to the supervisory ranks. The seniority system tended to discourage innovation while the *Manual* kept the system from breaking apart by making innovation unnecessary and impossible.

The result was a very rigid, authoritarian system unable to cope with change but well suited to maintaining a standard level of performance. The highly decentralized physical operation (44,000 facilities), strong vertical hierarchy, and rule-governed behavior combined to place what power there was in the hands of a few top administrators in Washington who ruled through voluminous directives and maintained adherence to the system through two primary sources, the Postal Inspection Service and Postal Service Officers (PSOs). The Postal Inspection Service, the POD's internal police force, conducted surprise inspections of post offices about once a year. Ostensibly to see that postal employees did not embezzle taxpayers' funds, they conducted detailed reviews

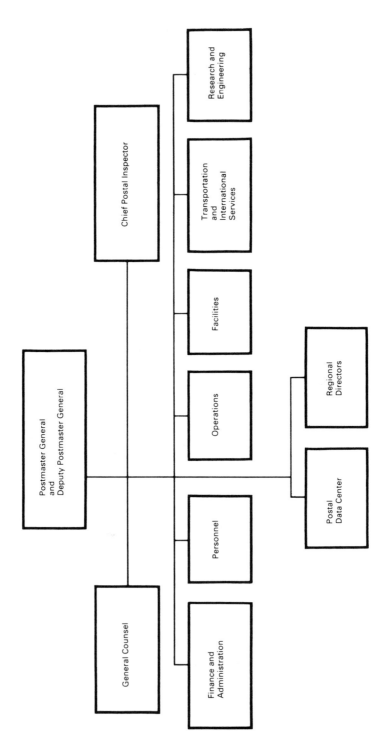

Figure 10.1 Post Office Department, 1968

of postal procedures and reported "irregularities" of *Manual* policies to the Regional Directors. In addition, they made unannounced visits to inspection galleries, enclosed catwalks suspended from the ceiling of every post office with more than 20 or 30 employees. Inspection galleries give one-way views of the floor below and have entrances at the buildings' exteriors so that even the postmaster sometimes did not know when surveillances were being conducted. Thus rule-governed behavior was maintained mostly by fear.

Another, though transient, control was the use of Postal Service Officers as trouble shooters in the 1960s. They mediated between the regions and the thousands of postmasters that reported directly to them. Such measures were fairly effective in maintaining the system in an orderly manner with emphasis on uniformity and speed of service. Monitoring and policing activities largely substituted for management.

Laurence O'Brien, President Johnson's campaign manager and Postmaster General, carried on his duties in much the same manner as his predecessors, but during the 1960s the mounting mail volume, outdated equipment, and unresponsive management system led to a crisis that could not be ignored. In the autumn of 1966, the Chicago Post Office, the largest mail processing facility in the world, ceased to function. O'Brien testified before a House Subcommittee, "ten million pieces of mail were logjammed. . . . Outbound mail sacks formed small grey mountain ranges while waiting to be shipped out" (House Subcommittee on Departments of the Treasury and Post Office and Executive Office of the President, February 27, 1965: 5), and for three weeks the mail was almost stationary. This situation forced O'Brien to take emergency hiring measures to start processing again.

The Chicago breakdown led him to push for an overhaul of the system; he favored a corporate structure that would give important powers to the Postmaster General. Reform was an acceptable idea to many, but the concept of a corporate structure was revolutionary and had few supporters. Publishers were afraid of losing millions of dollars in rate subsidies, the unions had nurtured a comfortable relationship with Congress for decades that they were reluctant to dismiss, and rural constituents, knowing how expensive rural post offices were to maintain, had nothing to gain by a more efficient service. Congress held hearings on the matter, however, and O'Brien made an effective spokesman for reform. Congressman Thomas Steed (Democrat, Oklahoma) summarized O'Brien's testimony:

> Mr. Steed: General . . . would this be a fair summary; that at the present time, as the manager of the Post Office Department, you have no control over your workload, you have no control over the pay rates of the employees you employ, you have very little control over the conditions of the service of these employees, you have virtually no control, by the nature of it, of your physical facilities that you are compelled to use — all of which adds up to a staggering amount of "no control" in terms of the duties you have to perform. . . .

> Mr. O'Brien: Mr. Chairman, I would have to generally agree with your prem-
> ise . . . that is a staggering list of "no control." I don't know [whether] it has
> ever been put more succinctly to me. If it had been at an appropriate time,
> perhaps I wouldn't be sitting here. (House Subcommittee on Departments of
> the Treasury and Post Office and Executive Office of the President, February 27,
> 1967: 27–28)

As frequently occurs with disputed public problems, a Presidential commission was formed to investigate the state of the Post Office and to recommend solutions. The Chairman of the Commission, which was formed in the
spring of 1967, was Frederick R. Kappel. Kappel was former Chairman of the
Board of AT&T and had served in numerous government advisory positions.
More important, he had just completed work on the Ash Commission, whose
task had been to make recommendations on the modernization of the entire
federal structure. Kappel was joined by eight members of the business and
educational world,[1] and George Meany, President of the AFL-CIO, to which
most unionized postal employees belonged.

The Kappel Commission agreed that reorganization was overdue and
considered five structural alternatives: maintaining the Post Office as a
Cabinet department but with improved management techniques; a sub-Cabi-
net government agency insulated from some political interference; a government corporation; a government corporation with strong influence from the
private sector, called variously a "mixed" or "conglomerate" corporation; and
a regulated private corporation (Kappel Commission, Annex I, 1968: 181–
220). In its June 1968 report, *Toward Postal Excellence,* the Commission, with
a dissent from Meany,[2] gave its support to a government corporation with a
formal structure very much like a regulated public utility but wholly owned
by the federal government. Of the five alternatives considered, the government corporation gave the most power to the Postmaster General with the
least interference from external agents.

Richard Nixon, elected President in 1968, appointed wealthy businessman
Winton Blount as Postmaster General and charged him with guiding the
corporate reform proposals through congressional hearings. The postal corporation movement survived despite protest from large mailers, postal unions,
the postmasters' and supervisors' organizations, and rural citizens. Perhaps
the most important reason for the corporation's survival is that Congress had
tired of the great patronage ordeal of appointing postmasters and rural
carriers, a chore that many felt was not worth the advantages.[3] Too, Congress
was pleased to have a popular bipartisan issue like better mail service during
the divisiveness of the Vietnam War.

With reform a certainty, opposition groups developed their own legislative
proposals, but the bill that passed in the summer of 1970, and became effective
on July 1, 1971, was much like the original Kappel Commission proposal with

some changes that reflected political lobbying. By then it had the support of the publishers and other large mailers who were promised improved service, but the unions were still reluctant. George Meany gave his support only after the inclusion of a 14 percent pay hike for workers into the bill and the promise of the AFL-CIO's exclusive right to represent unionized mail employees at the bargaining table (House Committee on Post Office and Civil Service, April 22, 1970: 2–4).

In addition to a nine-member Board of Governors which appoints the Postmaster General, the bill established an independent Postal Rate Commission, gave the unions the right to bargain for wages, removed all postal positions from the patronage system and largely from the control of the Civil Service Commission, authorized the new United States Postal Service to borrow up to $10 billion for long-term capital improvements and removed control over postal funds from the Treasury Department. The Postal Service was given until 1984 to break even. In the interim, Congress would appropriate enough money to pay for the difference between costs and revenues (Title 39, U.S. Code, 1970).

In this reorganization, much of the new formal structure was imposed by a law that also destroyed the former structure and codified the defeat of opposition groups. The destruction was incomplete, however, as the internal structure of the organization was not mentioned in the legislation.

This was one of the first tasks that Blount and his staff attacked in the transition year before the legislation became effective. Blount's strategy reflected the model favored by the Ash Commission: he retained what policy-making authority had traditionally existed at the top and added new offices to reflect the increased authority of the Postal Service in areas such as planning and research and decentralized all operating authorities to the field. The Postmaster General became the Chief Executive Officer and the Deputy Postmaster General became the Chief Operating Officer. The regional offices were reduced from 15 to 5 and they reported to the Deputy Postmaster General. The Deputy Postmaster General also had Headquarters offices that reported to him, but these were largely field support groups. The regions became independent subunits and to cope with the increased span of control, they were subdivided into metro areas and districts, which were further divided into sectional centers. Blount sought support for the new structure among the still reluctant postal supervisors by denouncing the former organization and appealing to their pride:

> There is a need for a basic change in our entire approach to management. The structure we have lived with for years is a civil service-style hierarchical organization. What a man earns is measured by how many people he supervises. People look to the book to tell them what they are supposed to be doing. And we spend a lot of time filling out forms. We need to shift to a new orientation....

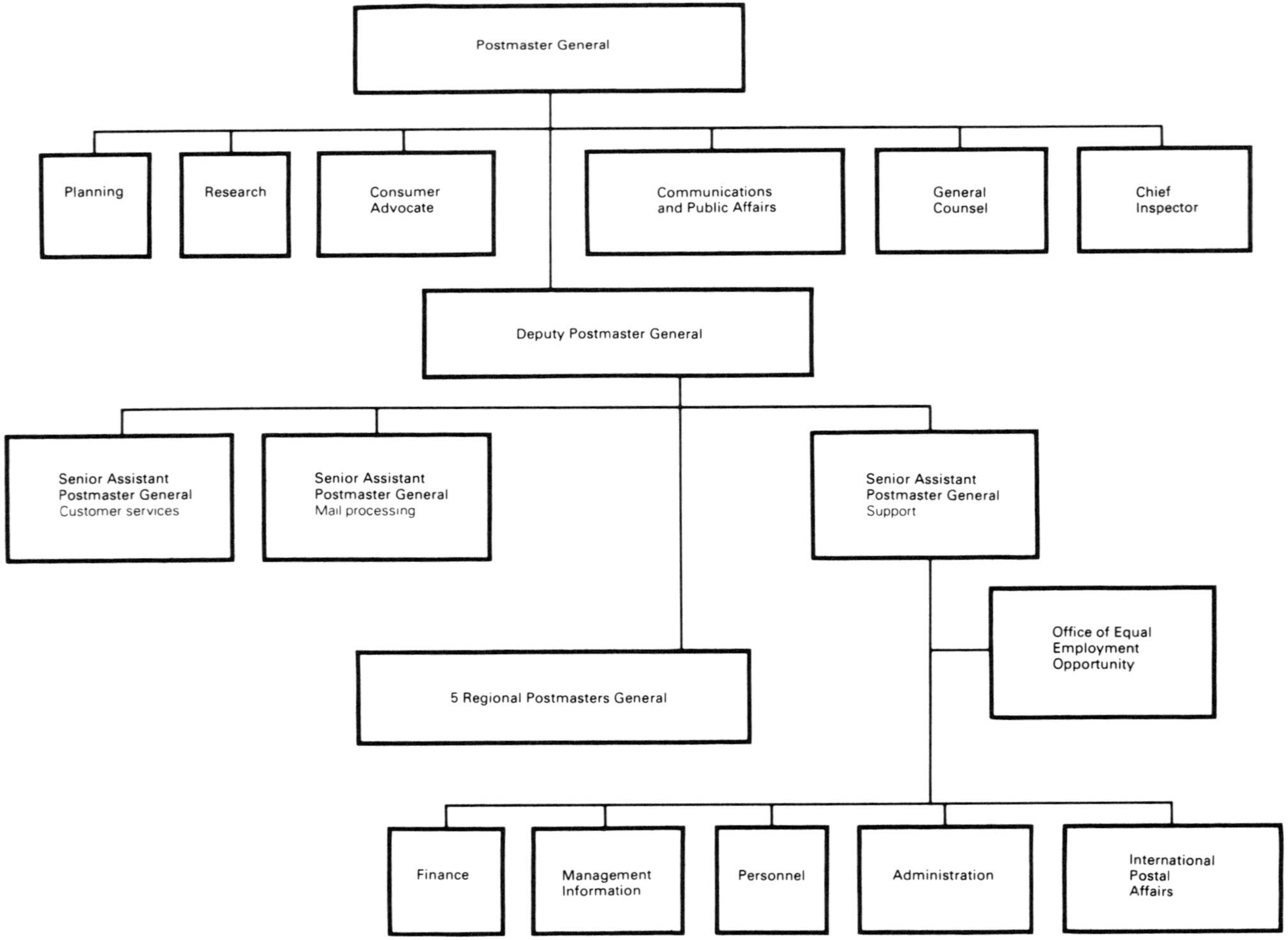

Figure 10.2 U.S. Postal Service, 1971

> It [decentralization] will get away from the straitjacket of the past, whereby the postal system was run by the book and the book was written in Washington. We want to give managers a chance to manage, to innovate and initiate — and even to make mistakes. . . . Treating our service people in the field like messengers guarantees an experienced, well-trained staff of messengers, but it doesn't breed managers. (*Postal Leader,* June 1971: 1)

The formal structure of an organization is usually what is most easily changed in a reorganization, and the act of imposing a new structure effectively destroys the former in most instances. In the case of the Post Office, the destruction was completed by law after considerable struggle; in most other organizations it is decreed by top management and reflects management's philosophy. Unwilling subordinates usually have little choice but to accept the change. In retaliation, they erode its effects by re-establishing informal networks that approximate old lines of authority. Erosion was a secondary concern, however, for the new postal structure. Blount was quick to recognize that the legislation had many enemies and the new structure could be destroyed by Congress as readily as Congress had destroyed the POD should any dissident groups gain power. The most potentially powerful enemies were his own employees—the postmasters, supervisors, and postal union members —who had established contacts in Washington, represented a great many votes, and controlled one of the largest contribution funds in Washington. The fact that postal employees contact nearly every household in the United States six days a week gives them a great opportunity to influence others as well. Another influential group of adversaries were the organized postal customers, such as publishers, mail order firms, the greeting card industry, and institutional mailers. The Post Office's competitors, express companies, package delivery firms, and courier services, were newly alert to the aggressive action of a formerly pas- sive rival as well. They lobbied to raise postal rates before the Postal Rate Commission.

Blount was correct in his estimation of the tenuous position his organization faced. In the spring of 1973, less than two years after the reorganization took effect, over 70 bills were entered in Congress to modify the legislation or to return postal management to Congress (Myers, 1975: 127). Although this case is extreme, other organizations face the same conditions. "The single most important determinant of whether a bureau can establish autonomy (and how fast it can do so) is the character of its power setting. If its suppliers or beneficiaries are strong and well organized in comparison with its rivals and sufferers, then it will quickly gain a clearly autonomous position" (Downs, 1967: 10). The new U.S. Postal Service quickly destroyed the former ideology, power alliances, and leadership in order to impose new ones favorable to the new structure and neutralize opposition.

IDEOLOGY

Ideology is usually associated with political parties, social classes, and advocacy groups, but rarely with businesses. This seeming oversight is because the profit ideology, widely shared throughout capitalist industries, is considered a given by most organizational analysts. Until reorganization, the ideology behind the POD was service, service at all costs. It gave logic to the POD's operating methodology, sustenance to the entwined power relations among mailers, postal employees, and Congress, and even support to such economically debilitating policies as subsidized rates and rural post offices.

Dependable public service is a noble ideology and gives a sense of purpose to employees in routine jobs in factory-like conditions. The fact that the POD was not in business for profit elevated the workers' positions in the minds of many employees. Phrases such as the "sanctity of the mails" and the "mails must go through" reified the postal mission. Calling mailers "patrons" and workers "civil servants" emphasized the subservient relationship that existed between the POD and the general population. Postmasters had to reside in the town in which they worked so that they could be accountable to the citizens there (Kappel Commission, 1968: 41).

The almost exclusive preoccupation with this concept of service was expressed in the absence of financial and cost data, even for processing activities. In its investigation, the Kappel Commission found "postal financial management concentrates on acquisition and control of the input side of postal operations," and information about costs was "inadequate or nonexistent" (Annex I, 1968: 89). Postmasters were given "budgets" of man hours, not dollars, and were paid according to the number of employees they supervised. There was no incentive to be efficient; rather, the incentive was to use as many workers as possible and elaborate justification procedures grew up around requests for more workers. The best justification was that service would suffer.

This ideology of good mail service uncompromised by considerations such as cost, competition, and even market demand had considerable emotional appeal even if, objectively, service was deteriorating with increasing volume and outdated methods. Such traditional values were held most tightly by the senior employees who had the greatest personal investment in them. There was no doubt that change was coming with the recruitment of younger employees in the 1960s as volume soared, but the senior employees still held power as supervisors and in the unions, where they largely determined the posture of employees on issues before Congress.

The POD was what Downs calls a "non-market" organization, where "there is no direct relationship between the services a bureau provides and the income it receives for providing them" (1967: 30). The service-at-all-costs ideology was congruent with this organizational form but posed a fundamental threat to the new "quasi-market" government corporation. The ideology of service gave reason to the non-rational and justification to the inefficient. Unless challenged and destroyed, the old ideology would be the foundation for the new business-like structure. The Postal Service management used a four-fold strategy to discredit the old ideology and implant a new one supportive of the new regime: symbolic reorientation, internal communications, external communications, and training and indoctrination.

Symbolic Reorientation

Whatever image citizens, employees, and customers had had of the POD, it was severely damaged in the fight over the reform legislation. This had the additional effect of demoralizing employees and, in some instances, predisposing them to opposing the new regime. Discrediting the POD was followed by removing the signs of its existence.

The first and most obvious move was retiring the 200-year-old name of the organization. Only federal cabinet agencies are called departments and the name change symbolized its removal from a political status to that of an independent agency. It also dissociated the new organization from the old.

Postal management hired the industrial design firm of Loewy/Snaith to develop new symbols and perform a corporate "make-over." They designed a new logo; chose a modern type face for all publications, stationery, and contracts; and selected bright new postal colors. Thousands of olive green postal trucks and mailboxes were painted a patriotic red, white, and blue. Loewy/Snaith also chose a series of color schemes for repainting lobbies and a new sign system for post offices to replace the largely hand-lettered signs.

The new image was developed during the transition year between passage of the bill and the effective date of July 1, 1971. Burnaford and Company, a promotion firm, was hired to link the new symbols with the occasion of the reorganization. A birthday party theme was chosen to symbolize the death of the POD and the birth of the USPS; parties were held in every post office in the United States on July 1. The USPS issued a stamp of the new logo on that day and gave free commemorative covers to the public. Post offices were open to the public and tours were given of the processing facilities. In many areas there was a symbolic removing of the old POD seal of a colonial rider and its replacement by the new USPS eagle poised for flight.

Internal Communications

Internal communications, that is, the formal communication network within the postal organization, are forms of symbolic reorientation but they are separated in this study because they were directed exclusively at employees and included substantive as well as symbolic content. The internal communications effort was aimed at both preaching the new ideology and counteracting opposing efforts by employee unions and supervisory organizations. The POD's Office of Public Information was reorganized into the Department of Communications and Public Affairs and included a new Office of Internal Communications whose mission was to formulate policy for explaining corporate decisions to employees, create house organs for disseminating information and act as a clearinghouse for offices wishing to communicate with employees through mass publications. The highly dispersed workforce placed unusual burdens on printed communications as a medium of information. Eventually, videotape equipment supplemented printed publications as a method of communicating with middle-level managers.

The POD had initiated a fairly professional employee house organ, *Postal Life*, in the mid-1960s that was issued bimonthly and sent to the homes of all employees. It was a generally innocuous compendium of human interest stories and bits of information about postal history and lore. After the reorganization it became an important medium for disseminating management's point of view on automation, labor negotiations, work conditions, and other issues of importance to management-union relations. It also served as a way of breaking down the former ways of thinking of employees used to the previous ideology and noncompetitive posture of the POD. Articles praised post offices that were meeting new efficiency standards—"What Makes Ft. Worth No. 1," May-June 1971: 8—encouraged employees to become aggressive in their selling of postal products—"Little Stamps, Big Business," March-April 1972: 17—and even sought to instill some fear of competition, something postal workers never considered when Congress appropriated funds— "That Other Package Service and How It Succeeded," November-December 1972: 12.

Middle-level management was perhaps the most important target of top management: without convincing them to support the system there would be no way to control the rank and file employees. In 1971 the Internal Communications staff initiated a monthly management newsletter, *Postal Leader*, that denigrated former policies—"Small P.O. Inspection No Longer Nit-Picking," "Postmasters Get Freedom to Move," May 1971—and praised new ones— "Promotions Open to All in Seattle Region," January 1971. The Postmaster General held unprecedented management briefings staged by Burnaford and Company for field managers all over the country to make them feel part of the "team," and managers were flown to Washington to contribute their ideas for the new organization (Meyers, 1975: 158). The contrast with the formerly highly structured and authoritarian system was striking. Certainly, much of it was for effect, but it aimed at dividing supervisors from any opposition to the USPS and neutralizing their associations in Washington.

External Communications

External communications are here meant to include those activities directed at influencing the USPS's supporters and enemies, especially Congress and customer groups. Large mailers, just as employees, had industry groups with lobbyists in Washington representing their interests before Congress. The USPS attempted to keep these ties broken by winning their customers to their side. Unable to grant favorable rates to mailers, the USPS established a national sales force and customer service representatives to help large mailers improve the efficiency of their mailing operation and to thereby save money with in-house mailing systems. But the eventual need to increase rates and reduce subsidies made the publishers one of the most active opponents of a self-sufficient Postal Service (Myers, 1975: 132-145).

Although individual mailers had little organized influence, disgruntled mailers have always represented a large portion of the complaints congressmen receive and are a large source of annoyance to congressional staff. By keeping congressmen undisturbed by complaints about the mail, USPS management hoped to smooth over relations with Congress. A consumer advocate was appointed to act as a funnel for complaints (*Postal Life,* November-December 1971: 6). The USPS also established the Office of Advertising and began its first paid advertising campaign to put forth its new businesslike image and to win acceptance for its new position in the marketplace. When criticism of the USPS grew, top-level Washington executives were dispatched around the country on "media tours" to hold briefings with the press and appear on radio and TV talk shows.

Training and Indoctrination

Faced with a managerial staff that was selected for its seniority and which embraced the former service-at-all-costs ideology, the training and indoctrination of supervisors became a top priority to USPS management. Indoctrination is perhaps an extreme concept but it is appropriate to the extent that the training often focused on unlearning old habits of relating to work, employees, and customers, and relearning new businesslike orientations.

The Postal Service Management Institute (PSMI) in Bethesda, Maryland, was the center for these efforts. Blount, and especially his successor in 1972, Elmer T. Klassen, encouraged the growth of PSMI's staff, which became a 75-member faculty of professional trainers, organizational development specialists, and numerous others with technical and academic expertise. About 20,000 supervisors a year were sent through PSMI's extensive courses, which included data management, customer services, and cost-benefit analysis (PSMI Catalog, 1971). During their often intensive training, managers were housed on campus in dormitories for a week or more. In addition, the PSMI staff went into major post offices and conducted lengthy on-site management training called the TEAM program (Team Effectiveness Approach to Management); managers were forced to play decision-making games together to break down years of authoritarianism. Correspondence courses, a technical training school at the University of Oklahoma, and regional training centers supplemented the effort. Blount also took the entire top staff in Washington to the Harvard Business School for a week-long management course.

Destroying the "service-at-all-costs" ideology and replacing it with a businesslike, efficient service ideology was most critical to accomplish among the employees, particularly the supervisory workers. If supervisors did not make their decisions on the basis of costs, the new organization could not survive. Hence, the heavy reliance on resocialization activities for supervisors. The organization's ideology-changing activities were most successful, as one would expect, among the junior supervisors who had least commitment to the former system and the most to gain by expanded promotional opportunities for those that could demonstrate new efficiencies.

The superficial image-changing activities can only be seen as strategies to forestall the enemies of the reorganization. By appearing new and forward looking, top management hoped to convince the public that substantive changes were taking place within that would soon be evident in improved service and new products. Destruction and replacement of the ideology and its trappings enabled Blount and Klassen to modernize with more immediate impact.

LEADERSHIP

Although the younger career supervisors were reasonably willing to change with the new organization, there were relatively few of them, especially in the regional offices and in Washington. Although the top positions in Washington were occupied by political appointees, almost all of whom were from industry, the newly important field management and technical positions near the top were filled primarily by people with enough seniority to have worked up from the bottom. In May 1971, the Postmaster General, in a sweeping move to purge these older postal officials, gave regional and headquarters employees a one-time bonus of six months' pay if they would leave immediately. "A dramatic, and some say heartless move, to point up the reorganization and cut away senior officials," a total of 2,099 "took the bait" *(Business Week, May 13, 1972)*. About 4,000 employees were left in the five regions and Washington. Klassen reorganized the remainder and then used 14 professional recruiters to seek people from industry. The USPS was able, in one stroke, to destroy much of the former leadership, replace some of it with people already embracing the new ideology, and serve notice to those who had not been purged that the USPS did not operate on the same basis as the POD.

In order to assure a steady supply of leaders loyal to the USPS the organization had to dismantle the former management recruitment system. It did this in four ways. First, it weakened the seniority system by making clerks and carriers almost immediately eligible for supervisory positions *(Postal Bulletin,* August 8, 1970: 2) and encouraged more ambitious persons to stay in the postal system. Second, it allowed supervisors to compete for promotions outside their own post office for the first time, thus promoting loyalty to the larger organization at the expense of loyalty to the workers or management of any one office *(Postal Leader,* January 1971: 1). Third, it subverted the former "up the ladder" promotion system by establishing management trainee programs that recruited college graduates, especially those with an MBA, for middle-management positions *(Postal Life,* November-December 1971: 2). The trainees were relatively few in number, two or three hundred, but they had substantial impact because they were young and, after relatively little time, were allowed to manage the previously sacrosanct operations activities. Finally, the former postmaster and rural carrier positions were removed from politics and filled by disinterested parties. Postmasters were selected by the recommendation of Postmaster Advisory Selection Boards, which were interview committees composed of postal managers and local business leaders. Furthermore, postmasters were no longer required to reside in the town in which they worked *(Postal Bulletin,* April 8, 1971: 1).

Power Bases and Alliances

The internal struggles for change, difficult as they might have been, were more effectively controlled than struggles with external agents. The legislation defined new relationships between the USPS and Congress and the USPS and the employees but left open to question exactly what those relations would be. In addition, the new position of competitors, customers, and other government agencies to Congress and the USPS were not defined. All of these groups had stakes in the former alliances and were threatened by the new situation. The Post Office had to support helpful alliances and destroy or cripple relationships between external agents that had a stake in the failure of the USPS.

An interesting example of how the USPS attempted to break the long-standing relationship between unionized employees and Congress was the gag rule ordered by Blount. When, predictably, the unions complained to Congress over drastic job cutbacks instituted by Blount during the reorganization, Blount issued an order that all communication between the Post Office and Congress would go through his office *(Postal Bulletin,* January 21, 1971).

Both Congress and the unions, and many postmasters as well, balked and charged Blount with denying them basic freedoms.

In an effort to increase its ability to exercise control over its operations, the Post Office attempted to cut itself from its sister agencies. A number of federal agencies perform work for other agencies and, indeed, depend on business from them to survive. Because of its size, the Post Office was one of the largest consumers of federal services. To assert its independence, the USPS did such things as issue bonds on the open market, despite the fact that it could have received money interest free from the Treasury Department (Myers, 1975: 82), and install a new personnel system not compatible or comparable to the one administered for other agencies by the Civil Service Commission (*Postal Bulletin,* February 4, 1971: 1).

Economic factors generally determined how successful the USPS was in developing new ties. It was somewhat successful with employees at the expense of generous wage increases and relatively unsuccessful with customers because of the rising rates needed to pay the new salaries.

CONCLUSIONS

The reorganization of the U.S. Postal Service unleashed incredible forces both in and out of the organization; the forces were aimed at protecting or consolidating the power of interest groups. In the sense that all organizations are distributions of power and that these subunits of power compete or cooperate depending on their interests at the time, they are political systems (Harvey and Mills, 1970: 185). As polities, organizations have supporters, enemies, and neutral observers. Political parties engage in competition for control of the resources and their allocation in the political state. In a similar fashion, unions, management, and departments compete for the allocation of organizational resources. As nations battle to impose their will and protect their own economic interests in the world economy, so too do competing businesses, opposing agencies, and consumer groups struggle to protect their own economic interests. Certainly, the analogy of the organization as a political state does not extend to all spheres, but it is a useful model for understanding the process of organizational change.

Students of organizations will recognize that political systems are in a continuous fight for survival, but that this survival process is muted in "mature" states which have established alliances and substantial means for maintaining independence. It is in new states in their early days, following political coups, that control is most vulnerable to upset and that successful revolutionaries seek to stabilize their positions by forming coalitions and destroying the previous regime. Downs recognizes that an organization expresses the same needs as a new political regime as it attempts to reach an "initial survival threshold." Before then "it has not yet generated enough external support to resist severe attack" (1967: 9). Hence, it is only in the birth of a new organization or in a reorganization of revolutionary proportions that routine survival processes are revealed fully. These processes are clearly seen in the case of reorganization of the Post Office, in which the beneficiaries of the former status quo had nothing to risk by declaring a challenge and everything to gain by successful opposition.

The newly restructured organization, faced with attack in its unstable youth, retaliated by destructive actions against what it perceived to be the most debilitating aspects of the former organization: the formal structure, the ideology, the leadership, and opposing alliances and power bases. Destruction took place at the same time the new organization was engaged in the constructive activities of creating new work methods, building new facilities, developing technological improvements, and creating alliances. Destruction is an inherent part of successful change; without destroying competing forms the organization allows its competition to flourish unimpeded.

To extend the analogy of organizations to political systems, political leaders who seize power through revolutionary means recognize that they must destroy enough of the opposition's leadership, ideology, and organization to give the new regime an opportunity to develop supporters. As Mao said, "Before a brand new social system can be built on the site of the old, the site must be swept clean" (1967: 18). Destruction is never total, but must be enough to weaken the opposition without incurring the wrath of potential supporters. This process is not analytically neat; there are many restrictions on the actions an organization can take, and rarely will it be able to act, even in extreme circumstances, in the most effective way possible. Certainly its enemies can thwart its efforts and force it to change tactics. Nor will all organizations seek to destroy the same structures. Targets will be those that pose the greatest threat to the organization and can be part of the formal structure, decision-making model, loyalty system, technology, or leadership, or a combination of such factors.

The methods an organization will employ will be based on the resources available to it. For example, the most effective way to remove former opposing leaders is by annihilation, but this is not usually acceptable or necessary in organizational struggles. Removal from the organization is the usual recourse if sufficient power exists. If, as is the case in many government organizations, this is not possible, removal from positions of importance is the next choice. Each of these "less destructive" alternatives poses some threat to the organization, as with a former leader still in the organization commanding loyalty among sympathetic subgroups.

To destroy or replace a competing ideology, the organization can move in several directions: remove and replace employees embracing the competing ideology; resocialize its employees, but this requires substantial time and expense; or changing employee behavior without changing their commitments. From the organization's point of view, total removal of opposition would be best, but since this is not realistic, most organizations settle for changing employee behavior. This method reduces, but does not eliminate, the threat to the organization.

As students of organization have recognized, change is a continual process of adaptation to new demands and changing environments. What must be recognized, however, is that change is not just the reaction of organizations to such unitary and abstract phenomena as leadership style and management philosophy, but rather a dynamic push and pull between contradictory forces that reside within and without the organization and constantly struggle for domination. Change is a complex and multidimensional process that destroys as it creates. These processes are least evident in organizations that have developed an equilibrium between opposing interests and most apparent when the balance is upset in times of revolutionary birth or reorganization, when survival is paramount.

NOTES

1. Other members of the Kappel Commission were: George P. Baker, Dean, Harvard University Graduate School of Business Administration; David E. Bell, Vice President, The Ford Foundation; Fred J. Borch, President, General Electric Company; David Ginsburg, Partner, Ginsburg and Feldman; Ralph Lazarus, Chairman, Board of Directors, Cummins Engine Company; W. Beverly Murphy, President, Campbell Soup Company; Rudolph A. Peterson, President, Bank of America.

2. Meany's dissension reads, "I agree with the goal of modernizing the postal system. . . . However, the status of the Post Office as a Cabinet Department has a positive value that should not be discarded lightly" (Kappel Commission Report: 2).

3. Congress held hearings in 1968 before the release of the Kappel Commission findings on the subject of removing politics from postal appointments; there was support for this independent of postal reorganization. See hearings before the House Subcommittee on Postal Operations February 6, 7, 8 and March 26, 28, 1968.

REFERENCES

Postmaster General. 1969. *Annual Report*. Washington, DC: U.S. Government Printing Office.

———. 1972. *Annual Report*. Washington, DC: U.S. Postal Service.

Bell, Daniel. 1973. *The Coming of Post-Industrial Society*. New York: Basic Books.

Benson, James. 1973. "The analysis of bureaucratic-professional conflict: Functional versus dialectical approaches." *Sociological Quarterly*, 14: 376–391.

Business Week. 1972. "Postal Service: The talent hunt." May 13: 115.

Committee on Post Office and Civil Service, U.S. House of Representatives. 1970. *Hearings: Postal Reform.* Washington, DC: U.S. Government Printing Office.

———. 1971. *Hearings: Briefings by Postmaster General and Postal Rate Commissioner.* Washington, DC: U.S. Government Printing Office.

Cullinan, Gerald. 1968. *The Post Office Department.* New York: Praeger.

Downs, Anthony. 1967. *Inside Bureaucracy.* Boston: Little, Brown.

Fowler, Dorothy Ganfield. 1967. *The Cabinet Politician.* New York: AMS Press.

Golembiewski, Robert T., and Alan Kiepper. 1976. "MARTA-toward an open, effective giant." *Public Administration Review,* 36: 46–60.

Harvey, Edward, and Russell Mills. 1970. "Patterns of organizational adaptation: A political perspective." In Mayer N. Zald (ed.), *Power in Organizations:* 181–213. Nashville: Vanderbilt University Press.

Hummon, Norman P., Patrick Doreian, and Klaus Teuter. 1975. "A structural control model of organizational change." *American Sociological Review,* 40: 813–824.

Labovitz, Sanford, and Jon Miller. 1974. "Implications of power, conflict and change in an organizational setting." *Pacific Sociological Review,* 17: 214–239.

Mao Tse-Tung. 1967. Stuart R. Schram (ed.), *Quotations from Chairman Mao Tse-Tung.* New York: Bantam Books.

Mazmanian, Daniel A., and Mordecai Lee. 1975. "Tradition be damned! The Army Corps of Engineers is changing." *Public Administration Review,* 35: 166–172.

Meyer, Marshall W. 1975. "Leadership and organizational structure." *American Journal of Sociology,* 81: 514–542.

Myers, Robert J. 1975. *The Coming Collapse of the Post Office.* Englewood Cliffs, NJ: Prentice Hall.

PSMI Catalog. 1971. Washington, DC: U.S. Postal Service.

Postal Bulletin. 1990. Washington, DC: U.S. Government Printing Office.

———. 1971. Washington, DC: U.S. Postal Service.

Postal Leader. 1971. Washington, DC: U.S. Postal Service.

Postal Life. 1971. Washington, DC: U.S. Government Printing Office.

———. 1972. Washington, DC: U.S. Postal Service.

President's Commission on Postal Organization (Kappel Commission). 1968. *Toward Postal Excellence, and Annex I.* Washington, DC: U.S. Government Printing Office.

Sherwood, Frank P. 1976. "The American public executive in the third century." *Public Administration Review,* 36: 586–589.

Subcommittee on Departments of the Treasury and Post Office and Executive Office of the President, U.S. House of Representatives. 1967. *Hearings: Appropriations, 1968.* Washington, DC: U.S. Government Printing Office.

Subcommittee on Postal Operations, U.S. House of Representatives. 1968. *Hearings: Taking Politics Out of Postmaster and Other Appointments and Promotions in the Postal Service.* Washington, DC: U.S. Government Printing Office.

U.S. Code, Title 39. 1970. Washington, DC: U.S. Government Printing Office.

PART IV

STUDIES OF
THE SOCIETAL AND
INSTITUTIONAL ENVIRONMENT

A good deal of organizational theory and research since the heralded but belated discovery of the environment—an honor usually given to Paul Lawrence and Jay Lorsch for their justly famous 1967 work, *Organization and Environment*—is devoted to defining, characterizing, and categorizing certain alleged features of the social and institutional domains within which organizations, as human creations, operate. This taxonomic focus is hardly surprising. Organizational environments are sprawling conceptual fictions that cannot be put under bell jars to have their physical features observed, probed, tested, and measured. Their being is not obvious, their features are not given, but assigned. Still, there is no shortage of students willing and eager to take up the naming and framing tasks necessary to conceptualize and textualize the domain. Moreover, empirical studies of organizational environments have grown by leaps and bounds since 1967. Many of these are qualitative, focusing on such matters as how ritual practices spread from organization to organization, how clusters of organizations form and shape and are shaped by markets, or how broad cultural understandings of proper form and action influence the structural arrangements and socioeconomic fortunes in and among organizations.

Studies like these require a variety of empirical materials, ranging from economic indicators to government reports, industry statistics, organizational histories, informant interviews, company records, field visits, and so on. In general, written and credible secondary data sources assume prominence over research materials collected firsthand. Considerable time is spent cataloging, summarizing, and even customizing written materials. Then, of course, the environment, in a pinched or expansive form, must be communicated to readers. Quasi-historical narratives are most often created to provide meaning and texture to supposedly descriptive but not so easily defined environmental constructs like industries, states, organizational fields, and institutions. These are, of course, conceptual entities but, as theorists are quick to point out, they are as real in their consequences as air quality on health. How such entities form and assert force in the world, however, is the kind of study in which absolute objectivity is a chimera and absolute relativity is self-defeating. Good studies do not choose between absolutes. Three carefully balanced studies are presented in this section.

The first study, by Paul Hirsch, examines the performance of organizations in two industries. This insightful 1975 study relies on company records and industrial statistics to locate and help classify materials gleaned from extensive interviews and fieldwork. "Organizational Effectiveness and the Institutional Environment" begins with a deceptively simple question: Why is the typical pharmaceutical company far more profitable than the typical phonograph record company? The question is made sociologically interesting when Hirsch argues that the firms in both industries are strikingly similar in a number of important ways, including their manufacturing methods, broad marketing strategies, and critical dependence on new products. Hirsch locates the answer to his opening question in the different political and economic rules of the game that have emerged in each industry. The story of how such rules developed over time and how they operate takes up most of the chapter. The logical next question of why firms in the pharmaceutical industry were able to establish and sustain a favorable environment is left rather open. Thus, a decoding neatly turns into an encoding, and new research questions replace the old.

The second chapter presents a highly structured comparative case study of three religious organizations operating in two culturally distinct societies. "Authority, Organization, and Societal Context in Multinational Churches" pushes Weber's familiar ideal types of authority—rational-legalistic, traditional, charismatic—into unfamiliar territory. Reed Nelson frames his 1993 study as exploratory, but it is an exploration guided by a confessed institutional theorist with Weberian interests. Substantively, Nelson wonders, first, what forms of authority characterize each studied church and, second, how these forms of authority are received in particular cultural contexts. His methods are basically literary. He read everything he could find about the three churches and only contacted selected church leaders for additional information when the literature came up short. From textual encounters come sketches of the authority base in each church and an assessment of how well such a form of authority works for each church in Brazil and the United States. This is an armchair study, but a convincing one. It may also remind readers that qualitative work does not always come drenched in personal experience.

Finally, the last study in this section, and this collection, takes us to Norway to examine the rise and fall of an institutional device initially created to aid fishermen (and the nation's economy) faced with serious, various, and always shifting market difficulties. "The Dynamics of Institutionalization" is a story told in 1995 to complicate institutional theory. Petter Holm, bothered by studies that treat institutions as if they were timeless, static, and invulnerable, develops an empirical counterexample. The case history of a collective sales arrangement in Norwegian fisheries unfolds as an institutional change story taking place across sixty-plus years. The instigators of change, however, are the very actors that are said, paradoxically, to be under the spell of the institution itself. Resolving this paradox without doing away with the notion of an institution altogether is tricky. Holm looks to conflict and concerns himself mostly with the recorded political and practical actions of institutional movers and shakers. It is quite clearly a top-down case selected to illustrate the particular theoretical move Holm wishes to make. It is a good move, a clever one, and, at least for the moment, satisfying.

The three studies are theoretically tight but methodologically loose. No boilerplate format appears. Each is organized and presented in a rather unique and stylish way. Yet none of the authors have much to say about how they came to fashion their tales. They tell us the sources they used, but not how they sorted out and drew on these sources. A good deal of silent selectivity stands behind each writer's decisions about what plot to follow, what details to include in the story, what organizing concepts to use, what events to highlight, and so forth. And as we all know, the facts do not speak for themselves but must be given significance and weight by interpretive nerve and sharp argument. The craft of qualitative work is thus apparent in these studies. It is a writer's craft, which is learned but not taught. One thing is certain, however. No one ever managed to write a strong qualitative study without reading one first. Three exemplary ones follow. Read on.

11

ORGANIZATIONAL EFFECTIVENESS AND THE INSTITUTIONAL ENVIRONMENT

Paul M. Hirsch

One of the most widely discussed and least studied concepts in the field of organizational analysis is the institutional environment. As originally conceived by Parsons (1956a, 1956b) and elaborated by others (Dill, 1958; Thompson, 1967; Evan, 1966, 1972), organizations interact with elements in their institutional environment whenever decisions must be made about issues concerning both the organization and the community of which it is a part.

REVIEW OF LITERATURE

A major task for high-level administrators is to reduce or neutralize threats to organizational stability resulting from dependence on the environment

AUTHOR'S NOTE: This analysis is drawn from a far more extensive study, reported in Hirsch, 1976. For helpful comments and suggestions, I wish to thank Howard Aldrich, Selwyn Becker, Max Heirich, Edward Laumann, Stephen Magee, Peter Pashigian, Richard Peterson, J. B. Richie, David Segal, Ross Stolzenberg, Stephen Withey, Mayer Zald, and an anonymous reviewer. As author, I remain solely responsible for any conclusions drawn. This research was supported by NIMH Grant No. 1-Fol-MH48847-01 and by a small grant from the National Association of Broadcasters. Reprinted from *Administrative Science Quarterly*, 20 (Sept. 1975): 327–344.

(Aldrich and Pfeffer, 1975), and an important aim of trade associations is to enable members to collectively manage and negotiate the outcome of such dependency. Katz and Kahn (1966) described these efforts as political and linked organizational effectiveness explicitly to an external referent and efficiency to internal activities more easily controlled by the organization. Zald (1970), in his political-economy framework for organizational analysis, further divided each of these internal and external dimensions of organizational behavior into political and economic components.

It follows that a fruitful way to study how the external political and economic environments of organizations engaged in similar activities affect their performance is to examine the interaction of sets of organizations with agencies in their institutional environments (Evan, 1972). The unit of analysis would be an entire industry (or its nonprofit analog), whereas the study of efficiency would focus on the analysis of individual organizations.

A few studies have tried to specify components of the institutional environment and follow their interaction with a class of organizations (Ridgeway, 1957; Pfeffer and Leblebici, 1973; Epstein, 1969, 1973a, 1973b; Wilson, 1973; Allen, 1974; Benson, 1975; Wamsley and Zald, 1973). The finding of Lieberson and O'Connor (1972) that leadership succession in large corporations bore only a limited relation to the performance of large corporations further suggests that much of the unexplained variance in present research on organizational success may be due to the complex web of institutional processes still largely unexplored by students of organizations. For example, a useful extension of the study by Lawrence and Lorsch (1967) would be to examine more closely the institutional environment in which each of the three industries studied had been operating over the last 20 years. If it were found that the rate of return to the worst-performing container manufacturer sampled were higher than that of the best-performing plastics manufacturer, then it might not be simply that the internal organization of the container manufacturer was inappropriate (relative to better-performing organizations in the same industry), but also that the institutional environment of these two industries was so different that the best-performing plastics manufacturer could not overcome external constraints placed upon the entire plastics industry. Yet, the relative performance of the industries from which samples are drawn is not examined in most studies of organizational effectiveness, largely because their environments are often defined as beyond the scope of measures used to assess the major components of each organization's task environment (Hirsch, 1975).

This article compares the organizational effectiveness of the phonograph record industry and the ethical pharmaceutical industry (that is, requiring a doctor's prescription, about 60 percent of all drug sales) to explore the collective interaction of organizations in each industry with their institutional environment. Special note is taken of specific institutional mechanisms that influence the context for industry profitability (that is, the upper and lower limits on profit for individual organizations in any given industry), and of specific rules and procedures negotiated between government agencies and industry trade associations for their members. Finally, a study is made of how events at the institutional level influence decisions within industries and organizations about which types of new products to sponsor and promote, decisions that often result in further interaction and negotiation with the institutional environment.

Operation and Criteria for Comparison

Phonograph record and ethical pharmaceutical manufacturing are both process production industries (Woodward, 1965: 152). Both employ highly mechanized and relatively simple batch production technologies, which come at the end of the manufacturing cycle: record manufacturing entails stamping vinyl from sounds; pharmaceutical manufacturing involves tableting drugs according to standardized procedures.

Both industries are strikingly similar in other ways. Both are dependent on external gatekeepers (physicians and radio station personnel) to introduce their products to consumers. They also derive the greatest percentage of profits from the sale of new products and, therefore, place a high premium on product innovation, for new products become rapidly obsolescent and experience unstable consumption patterns. Both have been stimulated by important technological inventions since World War II and experienced growth and expansion well above average for most manufacturing industries. Both also exist in legal environments predicated upon patents, trademarks, and/or copyrights and their administration by the United States Patent Office. Both industries entail a long chain of organizational stages at which decisions on new products must be made. Finally, both actively project an image of high risk and attendant uncertainties about profits.

Particular care was taken to hold constant the effect of production technology on organization structure and performance. Marketing, described by Woodward (1965) as the critical function for pharmaceutical manufacturers, is also the most uncertain task faced by record manufacturers; in general, most of the uncertainty occurs on their research and marketing, and regulatory boundaries. For example, both, in addition to requiring capital and raw materials, depend on independent organizations and individuals in the technical subsystems of their industries for many of their product innovations. Both use boundary-spanning representatives to direct a flow of new product ideas to their employers for possible sponsorship: in record manufacturing, seeking and signing new musical groups to exclusive recording contracts with their organizations; in pharmaceutical manufacturing, doing research on in-house projects, sponsoring basic research by outside investigators. Pharmaceutical manufacturers are also on the alert for exclusive patent rights or licenses to develop and manufacture newly discovered drugs, for instance, the Salk vaccine.

Although new products may be discovered by smaller organizations, marketing them on a large scale generally falls to the leaders of each industry. The stratification of organizations in such distribution industries is often based on the ability of each organization to market items (within product categories) that are essentially indistinguishable to consumers. At the output boundary of these organizations, massive advertising campaigns narrow the distance between manufacturers and consumers. For the industries studied, most advertising must be directed to doctors and disk jockeys, the gatekeepers and opinion leaders for mass constituencies. Hollander (1970) has suggested that as societal complexity increases, the roles of professional opinion leader and purchasing agents may merge in a wide variety of consumer-oriented industries. Here, such institutional regulators of innovation are required by law (the Food and Drug Administration and the Federal Communications Commission) to be independent of the producer organizations at the technical and managerial levels of the industry, so that the success of new drugs and records depends primarily on the reception of each product innovation by doctors and disk jockeys, who may choose among the wide selection released by many organizations. Where direct advertising is prohibited (prescription drugs) or economically unfeasible (records), only a few new products will become known or available to the general public. Therefore these two industries require contact men to coopt the opinion leaders whose allegiance cannot be purchased legally and who are delegated the task of screening out inferior candidates: record companies use regional promoters; pharmaceutical houses detail the physician. The power of role occupants in the system (such as talent scouts, disk jockeys, record reviewing wholesale buyers, doctors, hospital pharmacy committees, and government regulatory agencies) to influence the success or failure of a given product innovation increases largely as a function of their temporal position in the processing sequence outlined. The resulting power differential, in turn, has produced a variety of strategies and tactics by manufacturing organizations to influence or coopt doctors and disk jockeys and thereby reduce their level of marketing uncertainty (Hirsch, 1972).

Retail outlets and ultimate consumers comprise the societal subsystem that rewards the preceding subsystems through purchase and other positive feedback (legitimation) and also regulates their activities by supporting legislation designed to prohibit the marketing of goods and other practices judged harmful by public representatives.

The focal organization in each system, at the managerial level of organization, is the manufacturing organization engaged in locating, developing, producing, promoting, and distributing new drugs and recordings.[1]

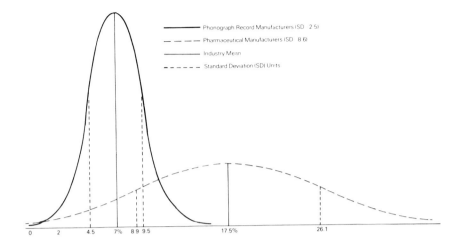

Figure 11.1 Reported rates of return in the pharmaceutical[a] and recording[b] industries
a. From Conrad and Plotkin, 1967. This study follows the practice of the United States Census of Manufactures in combining data from both ethical and over-the-counter drug manufacturers. If this has any biasing effect, it is likely to understate the profitability of the ethical pharmaceutical industry.
b. Adopted from Glover and Hawkins, 1965.

Differential Profitability

Between 1950 and 1965, pharmaceutical manufacturing was one of the most profitable of all industries in the United States, and phonograph-record manufacturing one of the least. Reported mean annual rates of return on investment for all pharmaceutical manufacturers between 1956 and 1966 ranged from 16.7 to 20.3 percent (Mueller, 1969). For 29 publicly held organizations between 1950 and 1966, Conrad and Plotkin (1967) found an average rate of return of 17.5 percent, with a standard deviation of 8.6. Using this estimate, it appears that for the industry as a whole, roughly two-thirds of all pharmaceutical manufacturers realized rates of return from 8.9 to 26.1 percent, assuming a normal distribution. In contrast, the record industry's reported rate of return between 1955 and 1964 was about 7.0 percent, with a standard deviation of 2.5 (Glover and Hawkins, 1965); roughly two-thirds of the organizations in this industry had rates of return ranging from 4.5 to 9.5 percent. As shown in Figure 11.1, the best-performing record company, within one standard deviation of the average, therefore, exceeded the worst-performing drug manufacturer's rate of return by less than 1 percent.[2] Although industry concentration seldom is associated with low profitability, concentration ratios reported in the United States Census of Manufactures (1971) showed that in 1967, the four-firm concentration ratio was higher (58 percent) for record manufacturers than for drug companies (24 percent, combining ethical and over-the-counter manufacturers). How can one best account for the differential performance of the two industries?

Differences between Industries

These industries differ in (1) demand elasticity, (2) the absolute dollar amount of sales, (3) scale of capital investment (in absolute dollars), (4) the percentage of sales invested in research and development, and (5) relative prestige. Pharmaceutical manufacturers are favored by more stable demand patterns and repeat sales than are recording manufacturers. Although both industries rely upon a few best sellers to offset losses on product failures or those with small volume, once a pharmaceutical manufacturer succeeds in promoting a successful new drug or trademark, the product will, in turn, contribute to the firm's profitability for a longer period than the hit record or popular recording artist of a record manufacturer. The likelihood of a positive serial correlation between individual firms' rates of return in the drug industry, and a negative serial correlation in the record industry, would account in part for the smaller variance in record industry profits, once these are averaged over time.

The record industry is also substantially smaller than the pharmaceutical industry: in 1969, retail sales at list prices were slightly over $3 billion for ethical pharmaceutical manufacturers and under $1 billion for record manufacturers, and with the latter and their retailers engaged in far more price discounting. Although in percentage each industry invests approximately the same proportion of its sales on capital expenditures, the amounts spent by pharmaceutical manufacturers are higher in absolute dollars. Large pharmaceutical manufacturers also invest substantially in research and development, while in the recording industry, many analogous expenditures of this type are borne by the musical groups themselves, and not by the manufacturer. Finally, the social value of pharmaceuticals to society in prestige and functional importance tends to be substantially higher than that of records; for example, in a national survey, Siegel (1970) found that pharmaceutical manufacturers ranked third in 23 industries (which did not include the record industry, however). While such a prestige differential might lead to the speculation that a corresponding difference in rewards (profitability) should be expected (Davis and Moore, 1945), the primary aim of this study is to find out how and which institutional mechanisms worked in favor of one industry and against the other.

These differences between the two industries should be borne in mind, for they are difficult to control and are not factored into the analysis. One can fairly assume, however, that more detailed study of differences in internal efficiency in manufacturing and administrative operations, among the organizations in the two industries, would add little light on the overall discrepancy in profitability between the industries. For example, manufacturing costs in both industries have declined since World War II, and in the pharmaceutical industry, the economic performance of individual manufacturers has not been associated with the use of project or disciplinary teams in research, nor with the role accorded manufacturing departments in new product development (Hirsch, 1973: 217–220). At the industry level of analysis, organizational effectiveness encompasses the relative success of each industry in handling: (1) uncertainties inherent in market mechanisms, (2) the selection of new products by external gatekeepers, and (3) the persuasion of government agencies that the public interest is best served by special concessions in the development and interpretation of statutes relating directly to industry profitability.

METHOD

Personal interviews were conducted between 1969 and 1972 with 53 executives and managers, consisting of 23 from the pharmaceutical industry, 21 from the recording industry, and 9 in radio broadcasting. Respondents from the most and least successful organizations in each industry were included. Field work also included attendance at six trade meetings, such as the National Association of Broadcasters, American Medical Association, and Pharmaceutical Advertising Club. Over 30 volumes of congressional hearings on the pharmaceutical industry were also consulted, as were published industry biographies and other secondary material.

INSTITUTIONAL MECHANISMS AFFECTING INDUSTRY PROFITABILITY

Profitability of both the pharmaceutical and record industries has also been strongly affected by three aspects of their institutional environment: (1) degree of control over the distribution and wholesale price of their products, (2) patent and copyright statutes and their administration, and (3) predictability of adoption behavior by independent gatekeepers and opinion leaders.

Control over Distribution and Prices

For consumer goods, wholesale and retail distribution is often a difficult and complex boundary contingency. Classes of new products must be presold to the salesmen of the organization, enthusiasm and/or financial incentives offered to national or regional distributors, and requests for shelf space from the retailer must be justified by the promise of consumer demand (Moller and Wilemon, 1971). For new products, especially, the manufacturer tries to retain autonomy over decisions about both channels of distribution and prices charged. The pharmaceutical and record industries are typical in this regard.

Shortly after World War II, both industries were engaged in the development and marketing of highly innovative products: antibiotics and other "wonder drugs," and unbreakable long-playing and 45 rpm records. Because prescription drugs are so central to health and had to be sold through licensed pharmacists, the pharmaceutical industry had little likelihood of its products being sold at retail through alternative channels. However, competition was increasing among manufacturers as a growing number of national, regional, and local organizations began to market more chemically equivalent ("generic") drugs. Such interchangeable products did pose a threat to many of the larger manufacturers, whose pricing policies and market shares could be affected, and in 1954, they formed a trade association, the National Pharmaceutical Council (NPC). Its major achievement was a successful campaign before state boards of pharmacy to redefine the meaning of substitution at the retail level. Whereas the traditional definition of the term had been the provision of a different *type* of drug from that prescribed by the physician, the proposed redefinition prohibited the druggist's substitution of one manufacturer's *brand* of a specific drug for another's (United States Congress, Senate, 1961). For example, if buffered aspirin were a prescription drug, the Rexall or Norwich brands of buffered aspirin could not be substituted for Bufferin if the prescription read Bufferin.

Within eight years, at least 38 state boards of pharmacy had adopted the proposed redefinition of substitution at the retail level, and hospitals, whose pharmacies routinely practice substitution, had to devise legal arguments to protect their formulary procedures. While any medical judgment on the merits of this change is beyond the scope of this article, it is important to note that major manufacturers collectively moved rapidly and effectively to protect themselves through the formation of a trade association and succeeded in stabilizing this aspect of their market by altering their institutional environment. Quite likely one reason for the absence of organized opposition by retail pharmacists to the resultant change was that prescriptions were filled on the basis of markups, not fee-for-service. Consequently, if this definition increased the cost of retail prescriptions, the druggist's income would increase correspondingly.

Upon the invention of the long-play (33 rpm) record by the Columbia Broadcasting System, RCA launched a competing (45 rpm) record. Apparently as an inducement to manufacturers of record players to produce machines that could play these recordings, both firms freely licensed patents to these inventions to all competitors, including new entrants, so that the new speeds would become standard throughout the industry (Gelatt, 1965). Since United States copyright law already required the compulsory licensing of all songs (by their owners) to all manufacturers wishing to record them—in direct contrast to the awarding of exclusive patents in the pharmaceutical industry—conditions were ripe for record manufacturers to find it increasingly difficult to differentiate their records from one another's (Peterson and Berger, 1975).

With the adoption of the long-playing record during the 1950s, the industry experienced unanticipated challenges in distribution, since the new type of unbreakable record proved highly attractive to mail-order businesses (such as the Book-of-the-Month Club) and to mass merchandisers with central purchasing offices, ranging from department stores to supermarkets. High-volume purchasers obtained quantity discounts from new entrants into manu-facturing (having free access to its technology) and also circumvented local full-line distributors in favor of direct purchase of specific ("hit") records from their producers (Gelatt, 1965). Within a short time, the efforts of major manufacturers to continue selling only to authorized dealers through fran-chised distributors failed: their autonomy over both the price of the product and its distribution was greatly diminished. As sales rose, margins and profits fell, and industry leaders soon spoke of experiencing a "profitless prosperity," as illustrated in the questions addressed to a spokesman for the industry by a member of the House subcommittee holding hearings on copyright-law revision (United States Congress, House, part 2, 1965: 898):

Q. At the top of the chart, with the heading "typical margins on a $3.98 list price monaural longplaying record," do I understand correctly that the margin for the independent distributor which you have listed at 15 percent, would be 60 cents on that record?

A. No sir. . . . The average price here is . . . about $2.83.

Q. Well, the chart says $3.98.

A. This is what it is called, sir. It is called a $3.98 record, but nobody pays it.

Q. Is the independent distributor's margin calculated on the $3.98 selling price?

A. No, sir; it is calculated on the $2.83.

Q. Well, what does $2.83 represent?

A. His actual selling price.

Q. Is $3.98 the consumer price?

A. No.

Q. Is it the consumer listed price?

A. Yes.

Q. It is the consumer listed price. Now what is the selling price from the record company or the wholesaler, and will you describe the term and fit it to that chart, so that we can understand it?

A. . . . To answer Mr. Tenzer's question, . . . on this so-called $3.98 record. This is very misleading, because . . . scarcely ever does anyone now pay $3.98. . . . There are all kinds of prices for the so-called $3.98 record.

During this time period, major manufacturers took little or no concerted action, partly because there was no legal basis for restricting competition or sales to qualified retailers and collective measures to do so may well have violated United States antitrust laws. The movement of Columbia Records and other manufacturers into direct mail-order sales, and, later, into the retail field through wholly-owned chain record stores, illustrate two adaptations to these changes in their marketing environment. To further recapture control over the distribution and price of their records, large manufacturers have also belatedly followed the example of drug manufacturers by setting up wholly-owned distribution operations and adhering more closely to posted wholesale prices.

Patent and Copyright Protection

Pharmaceutical Manufacturers

Patent, trademark, and copyright legislation make up an important aspect of the legal and economic environment of many American industries. The individual or company awarded the patent may legally enforce a monopoly right to be the sole producer of the invention registered with the United States Patent Office. Prior to World War II, no "naturally occurring" substances (for instance, most antibiotics) were patentable according to the Patent Office. Beginning with the discovery of penicillin (unpatented), the pharmaceutical industry became more seriously involved in research and development. Ease of entry into antibiotic production, encouraged by government tax incentives and the potential for further therapeutic advances, led to many sellers with excess capacity and severe price-cutting by manufacturers of the new drug. Between 1945 and 1955, bulk prices per billion units fell from $6,000.00 to $35.00, and in seven years the wholesale cost of a single vial of procaine penicillin had dropped to less than 6 percent of its original price. By 1950, manufacturers referred to unpatented antibiotics as "distress merchandise" and a Pfizer Company executive stated (United States Federal Trade Commission, 1958): "If you want to lose your shirt, start making penicillin or streptomycin."

Contending that an extension of patent protection to all new drug discoveries was necessary to stimulate further investments in research, industry representatives pressed successfully in the late 1940s for a relaxation of the traditional interpretation (United States Task Force on Prescription Drugs, 1968), and the industry did subsequently step up research for patentable new drugs. The industry was substantially restructured as manufacturers integrated forward and backward to reap the benefits which would accrue to those organizations successful in the ensuing competition to discover effective new drugs. For example, by 1956, four patented broad-spectrum antibiotics accounted for 50 percent of all antibiotic sales in dollars, but only 24 percent of all antibiotics prescribed; although three of the newer drugs were manufactured by the same process utilized in penicillin production, the price differential between patented and unpatented antibiotics produced by the same firms yielded a gross profit of 75 percent or more on patented products, but only 20 percent on the others (United States Federal Trade Commission, 1958).[3] Thus an important change in the industry's context for profitability—at least for the short run—was effected by a change in policy followed by an organization in its institutional environment, that is, the Patent Office. By 1950 it was clear that unpatented products were poor investments, but that patents on new drugs and on minor variations or combinations of existing drugs could be obtained, if adequate resources for research, advertising, promotion, and possible lawsuits by competitors were available. To minimize litigation, a long-standing and occasionally controversial practice of the Patent Office has been to promote a private settlement, in which those competing for the same patent decide among themselves which one will become the sole applicant. Typically a winning pharmaceutical manufacturer would then grant exclusive production or marketing licenses to the "losers," whose applications would be withdrawn, and reject applications from all other organizations for the same privileges. Between 1950 and 1958, nearly 2,000 patents on antibiotics produced by new molds had been awarded, though many would not be produced commercially by the owners of the patents, and an unprecedented total of 6,107 new prescription drug products had been introduced by American pharmaceutical manufacturers.

Changes in Promotion

Trademarks are awarded for a period of 40 years, patents for 17 years. Since 1948, most pharmaceutical products have been identified by both an official chemical ("generic") name, which includes a description of the drug's active chemical ingredient, and by one or more brand names (trademarks), which are registered with the Patent Office by the manufacturer(s). In the advertising and promotion of most drugs to the medical profession, the brand name is more prominently featured. Since the manufacturer is usually accorded the right to provide both of the names for each new drug, brand names are nearly always shorter and simpler than their generic equivalents, an outcome often discussed in the course of congressional hearings. For example (United States Congress, Senate, Part 2, 1967: 764):

> **Senator Nelson:** "You did not happen to bring along a list of generic names supplied by the brand name companies that are shorter than the brand names they created for themselves, did you?"
>
> **Commissioner of Food and Drug Administration (Goddard):** "That would be a very short list, Senator."

During the early 1950s, pharmaceutical promotion shifted from using the manufacturer's trade name in association with the generic name of a drug (for example, Bayer Aspirin) toward using a brand name, which referred neither to the generic or chemical contents nor to its manufacturer (for example,

Excedrin, Miltown). This strategy, employed by many of the largest firms in the industry, would increase in effectiveness once physicians could be persuaded to remain loyal to brands and once antisubstitution laws were modified to prevent the pharmacist from treating generically equivalent drugs as identical.

The increased access to patents, combined with a new reliance on brand names and new laws against substitution, comprise two aspects of the pharmaceutical industry's institutional environment which were effectively combined to prestructure a more favorable context for high profitability.

Phonograph Record Manufacturers

Record manufacturers are similarly affected by laws on copyright protection. All musical compositions less than 100 years old are subject to copyright protection, and manufacturers must pay a fixed royalty to the copyright holder on every recorded version of the selection sold. The United States Copyright Act of 1909, however, requires the publisher of a song to grant all manufacturers the right to record any composition on equal terms, once it has been licensed to a single organization. This foreclosed the possibility that a single manufacturer might obtain an exclusive license to record and promote a particular song for a period of time—in contrast to the pharmaceutical industry, where it is precisely the possession of exclusive licenses or patents which came to differentiate the major organizations from each other and from all others. Corry (1965: 250–251) has assessed the impact of the copyright act on the record industry as follows:

> A . . . major determinant of conditions in the record industry . . . is the statutory requirement of compulsory licensing. The availability of musical compositions for recording to all who pay the mechanical royalties has affected the record industry since its inception. . . . It has largely eliminated competition for composition recording rights since they are openly available. Competition in the record industry has instead focused on such other elements as the recording artist, promotion, and pricing. . . . Entry into the industry is easier since even the newest, smallest firm has access to copyrighted compositions. Conversely, large companies with extensive artist rosters and financial resources may release recordings of compositions popularized by small firms. Although there are some differences in the mechanical royalties paid, authors and composers generally receive a set royalty rather than one established by market conditions. Both the relative bargaining strength of the music publisher and the record company and the interownership now prevalent in the industry would be more significant if there were no compulsory licensing.

General

Relations among organizations in both industries have been substantially altered and determined over time by the changing language and administration of American patent and copyright law. In this respect, and in terms of the broader class of institutional arrangements encompassing statutes and administrative law on taxes, tariffs, and labor relations as well, they are hardly unique. In each of these arenas, industries have been differentially successful in negotiating favorable institutional arrangements which, in turn, feed back onto the range of potential profits to be realized by their member firms (Hirsch, 1975). For both industries studied, patents and copyrights, as aspects of their legal environment, seem crucial to an evaluation of organizational performance and to an understanding of the choices made by manufacturers in selecting product innovations. If, for example, proposals in Congress to require compulsory licensing of patents and the abolition of brand names after a specified time period in the pharmaceutical industry are enacted, the broadened access to new chemical compounds would be roughly equivalent to the compulsory licensing of musical compositions mandated by the copyright act. Most economic analyses of the pharmaceutical industry agree that this would alter the structure of the industry, lower profitability, and affect product innovation (Walker, 1971), so one can expect that such an institutional change would also affect the day-to-day operations and performance of individual manufacturers.

In general, patent arrangements have influenced the structure and profitability of industries in which technological change or product innovations are important factors, ranging from refining gasoline, manufacturing automobile and aircraft parts, and photographic, telephone, and electrical equipment, to manufacturing eyeglass frames, bathtubs, dry ice, and fire alarms (Vaughn, 1956; Bowman, 1973; Stocking and Watkins, 1968). Copyright law and its administration, while affecting a smaller number of industries, is especially important to organizations and individuals engaged in the production, processing, or dissemination of information, ranging from writers and publishers, computer programmers, and copymachine makers, to movie production companies, cable television operators, and broadcasting organizations. Many American industries are similarly built around the fragile structure of these and other negotiated institutional mechanisms and arrangements (Scherer, 1970; Stigler, 1968; Kahn, 1971; United States Congress, House, 1965).

In the record industry, since neither performers nor manufacturers were afforded protection for their products by the early legislation, both subsequently lobbied unsuccessfully for an extension of the coverage of the copyright law. Historically, both argued that the law did not envision the development of radio and the jukebox, and that they were entitled to a performance fee or royalty for the public performance of their product by other profit-seeking organizations. The radio medium is an especially important aspect of the environment, for it is the most important means by which consumers hear new records (Hirsch, 1969, 1972). Since managers of radio stations have no vested interest in promoting or selling records, however,

executives of the record industry argue that they have to adapt their produc-
tions to whatever will be played on radio stations directed to teenagers, who
account for the majority of record purchasers. While it is difficult to assess
the following claims in economic terms, it is especially interesting that some
major spokesmen for this industry have attributed both its major emphasis on
rock music and recurrent profit squeezes to the absence of copyright protection. For example, an executive of Capitol Records has argued (United States
Congress, House, 1965: 951–956):

> A radio station takes our product, and performs it on the air, and sells the time
> to reach an audience with that performance, but does not have to pay for that
> performance. They are reusing the product as a business . . . without our being
> able to control it. . . . [Radio] has a wide listening audience who do not buy
> records. Why should they? It is cheaper and easier to turn on the radio and get
> it for nothing. . . . In spite of an extensive catalog of standard recordings in all
> fields built up over a period of 25 years . . . , 70 percent of [our] sales are on
> new records released in the last three months. . . . If performance fees were to
> go to the record company and the performer, the frantic concentration on
> teenage rock and roll in the search for fast and large sales and quick returns
> would stop. Sales are the only means of profit for the performer and record
> company right now, so all music must be designed . . . to get records
> played . . . on that one radio station in each market that plays the so-called top
> 40 records. . . . Let us be compensated for the use of our records on [all radio
> stations] and we can record for the benefit of the vast listening audience who
> want good music, but do not necessarily buy records.

One can see that in the control over distribution and access to increased patent
or copyright protection, the record industry has been much less successful
than the pharmaceutical industry.[4] Both outcomes, however, stem from a set
of similar strategic problems and negotiation processes, with each industry
seeking gains through use of the same mechanisms. The comparative effectiveness of the pharmaceutical manufacturers vis-à-vis these aspects of their
institutional environment helps to account for the wide profit differential
between the comparable manufacturers in the two industries.

Cooptation of Institutional Gatekeepers

The final component of the institutional environment studied was the
degree of success in reducing uncertainty about new product selection by
powerful gatekeepers and opinion leaders on each industry's marketing
boundary. Before 1950, the American Medical Association (AMA) was the
major organizational gatekeeper mediating between the pharmaceutical
manufacturer and the consumer. No drug could be advertised to doctors in
any of the Association's 12 journals, unless it had been evaluated and approved
as safe and effective by the AMA's own Council on Drugs. When a new drug
was accepted only its originator was permitted to advertise the product by a

brand name; all other versions could be advertised by their generic name only, accompanied by the trade name of the manufacturer. The association also published an annual volume, *Useful Drugs,* with a critical evaluation of pharmaceutical products. The *Journal of the American Medical Association,* during the late 1940s, also rebuked the industry (in editorials such as "Silly Names for Penicillin") for confusing physicians by its adoption of brand names as a promotional device, and discouraged their inclusion in its advertisements (United States Federal Trade Commission, 1958). During the early 1950s, relations between the organized profession and the industry underwent a dramatic change. The AMA adopted policy changes permitting advertisements by brand name for any drug certified as safe by the United States Food and Drug Administration; it transferred authority to screen advertisements to a new committee with more lenient standards than the Council on Drugs. It also halted the publication of *Useful Drugs*, creating a vacuum filled by *Physician's Desk Reference,* an industry-produced volume comprised of copy submitted by manufacturers. Between 1953 and 1960, the income of the AMA from advertisements tripled, while revenues from membership dues and subscriptions increased 20 percent; as a proportion of total revenues, income from advertising rose from less than one-third to approximately one-half. For the pharmaceutical industry, this represented an eightfold increase in advertisements solely in AMA journals, from \$11.5 to \$88.5 million by 1966, by which time the number of pages of advertising in the *Journal of the American Medical Association* alone exceeded both *Time* and *Life* (Mintz, 1967). These policy changes were also accompanied by an unusual degree of job mobility between the AMA and the Pharmaceutical Manufacturers Association, a trade group formed in 1958. About this time, the AMA also began lobbying against federal legislation to require proof of a new drug's effectiveness for premarket clearance from the Food and Drug Administration. In effect, passage of the 1962 Kefauver-Harris amendments to the Pure Food and Drug Act transferred to the government the regulatory function which the Council on Drugs of the AMA had performed prior to the Association's internal policy changes.

In organizational terms, it is clear that the medical profession was effectively co-opted by the drug industry. Barriers to the promotion of new and duplicative or combination drugs were removed, and much of the subsequent political controversy over increased government regulation of the industry can be traced back to the deregulation in the private sector. James Burrow (1963) suggests that during the early 1950s, the priorities of the AMA were primarily the defeat of a growing number of proposals to establish national compulsory health insurance and any incursion of the federal government into the health care field. Among the objectives he reported, the evaluation of new drugs received no mention; the Council on Drugs was only one of a multitude of committees, councils, and bureaus comprising the AMA's organizational structure. When a management consultant was asked to suggest new sources of revenue from advertising, an obvious answer lay in displacing the Council's goals and tapping the potential revenue from advertisements promoting more trademarked products (Burack, 1967). A reasonable inference is that the association altered its standards on drug advertising in order to realize higher priority goals. Although the industry's strategy of brand names preceded its unrestricted access to physicians through the Association's journals, the combination of increased access with the cessation of routine and well-publicized evaluation of new drugs further increased the economic incentives and rewards to manufacturers for releasing a multitude of new products and dosage forms. While these were promoted as medical advances, many were also publicly criticized as of undetermined therapeutic value by independent authorities, whose disapproval was one of the stimuli for the series of governmental inquiries initiated shortly thereafter.

In sum, much of the organizational effectiveness of the pharmaceutical industry as measured by the economic success among its member organizations from 1950 to 1965 has been attributed to (1) increased access to patents, (2) its brand name strategy, and (3) a dramatic reversal of policy by the American Medical Association toward the regulation and promotion of new drugs. Each instance highlights changes in the institutional environment of the industry, which provided the context in which many of its member organizations were able to achieve higher profits than their counterparts in the recording industry.

In the record industry's attempt to coopt professional gatekeepers, nearly an opposite set of events occurred. Traditional patterns of promotion were disrupted by radio's loss of audience to the emerging television industry. Between 1949 and 1959, for example, advertising revenues realized by four national radio networks declined from $128 to $35 million. Radio station managements undertook a major search to locate new audiences, markets, and advertisers; they also looked to record companies to produce records to attract new listeners. For a short time, access to having records played by radio (a functional equivalent to free advertising), became far easier for all record producers: many new manufacturers entered the industry, and gradually the market share of the eight largest firms dropped from 87 percent in 1947 to 67 percent in 1967 (United States Census of Manufacturers, 1971). By 1963, however, fewer than 25 percent of all singles records released were played by radio stations in any American city (Shemel and Krasilovsky, 1964). As competition increased and the new radio formats stabilized, organizations wanting to have their records played by radio resorted to outright bribes on an unprecedented scale. In organizational terms, they became both more dependent and less effective vis-à-vis this aspect of their marketing environment. Efforts to coopt mass-media opinion leaders did not succeed.

Three significant aspects of the record industry's external environment help to explain its organizational ineffectiveness as measured by its characteristically low rate of return during the time period covered in this article: (1) the loss of control over price and the channels through which records are distributed, (2) the decrease in the predictability of decisions taken by programmers of radio stations, and (3) the failure to effect legislation granting full copyright protection to recordings. Each instance highlights elements in the institutional environment which provided the context in which major firms lost a significant share of the market and experienced declining rates of profit, in contrast to pharmaceutical manufacturers, whose efforts to control analogous aspects of their environment were far more successful.

DISCUSSION

In this article, we have explored the interface between constraints imposed by the environment of two industries and the comparative effectiveness of the industries in shaping and reaching accommodations with market mechanisms controlled by institutional agencies. The analysis provided an illustrative example of the utility of taking whole industries as units of analysis to better specify concrete institutional mechanisms and their relation to organizational performance. While no claim of proof is offered regarding these specific instances, the comparison also suggests that the examination of industry biographies can uncover institutional arrangements that significantly influence the collective performance of organizations engaged in similar activities.

The question remains as to why the pharmaceutical industry was the more successful at influencing the operation of these institutional mechanisms. Functional theory would stress prestige and societal importance. Conflict theory suggests that its greater profitability could follow from its larger size, which should enable an industry to better marshal the resources needed to recruit better lawyers, lobbyists, and other skilled professionals to manage contingencies posed by regulatory agents in its environment; furthermore, that an industry's degree of prestige in society is itself another institutional level variable—the outcome of a negotiated process, subject to revision, and often entailing advertising and related campaigns to raise or maintain existing levels of legitimacy.

While these competing causal explanations may be empirically testable over a large sample of industries, neither interpretation is sufficiently persuasive in this instance to warrant the rejection of its alternative. For example, although the recording industry is smaller than the pharmaceutical, many of its major organizations are subsidiaries of large entertainment or broadcasting conglomerates well versed in the skills of collective action in other fields where their interests are at stake (such as obtaining passage of legislation to extend

the duration of broadcasters' licenses from the FCC). Similarly, the functionalist interpretation is weakened by the observation that since 1960, the
pharmaceutical industry has come under considerable political pressure to
reduce or better justify its high profitability. It has been forced to struggle hard
to retain the legitimacy and prestige which, the theory would argue, once
established would easily be retained. Concerning prestige and profitability
differentials more generally, the broad functional interpretation may serve as
a good point of departure from which to explore (1) the strategies and tactics
employed by industries to ensure or overcome the mean rates of return that
functionalist theory would roughly project for them; (2) the processes and
institutional mechanisms involved in negotiations over industry-wide profitability contexts, often entailing hard-fought battles among competing sets of
organizations; and (3) the economic and sociological bases of differences
between observed and expected rates of return among industries, given some
initial ranking of their respective prestige scores and contribution to society.
For example, while the prestige of pharmaceutical manufacturers has probably
risen along with earnings since the advent of "wonder drugs," this correlation
in itself would be an unlikely (and at best insufficient) explanation for the
comparatively higher returns reported by some ultimate consumer-oriented
industries (such as soft drinks, confectionary, and cosmetics), relative to others
(such as textile manufacturing, food products).

Changes in the internal organization of each industry's typical firm have
not been reported here, nor have variations in the structure and performance
of individual companies. That events at the institutional level have influenced
their operations, however, is evidenced in the pharmaceutical industry by (1)
a substantial increase in funds allocated to research and development after the
liberalization of patent restrictions; (2) by a steep increase in the cost of
clinically testing new drugs in order to conform to new FDA standards
mandated by passage of the Kefauver-Harris Amendments to the United States
Pure Food and Drug Act; and (3) by the growth in size and stature of the
Office of Legal Counsel, as the enforcement of government regulations has
become stricter. In the record industry, (1) the organization of (artistic)
production became debureaucratized (Peterson and Berger, 1971), (2) contracts with musicians and independent producers came to delegate to them
an unusual degree of artistic control over the final product, and (3) promotion
and distribution became centralized functions (Hirsch, 1972). Each of these
changes constitutes an adaptation to new conditions imposed on the typical
firm by the dependence of the industry on radio and the inability to effect
changes in wholesale distribution. Since 1960, the record industry has been
the object of new investigations into bribery, and recent reported rates of
return (where available) suggest that it also continues to be more volatile and
less profitable than average for American manufacturing industries. Government inquiries into pharmaceutical industry profitability have continued to

focus on its success in dealing with the institutional mechanisms we have discussed (Silverman and Lee, 1974). Although profit rates have not declined, the expiration of key patents, a government ruling that reimbursements to Medicare patients for prescriptions be limited to generic drugs wherever possible, and repeal of antisubstitution laws in at least one state contribute to what *Business Week* (1974) recently called the "clouded future" of the pharmaceutical industry.

Of course, among the set of companies within an industry, there is a clear range of variation in performance, and a detailed analysis of such differences often does yield insights and findings that distinguish the high and low performers in terms of their internal organization and management styles. We have not dealt with these questions here. Rather, emphasis has been placed on the stratification of whole industries interacting with their institutional environment, utilizing readily available data, accessible and highly relevant to many current propositions and hypotheses of organization theorists.

Chandler (1962: 492) has addressed the divorcement of environmental issues from organizational analysis and noted an important consequence of this problem:

> That the expansion and government of industrial enterprises in a market economy should be closely related to the changing nature of the market seems obvious enough. Yet many writers dealing with business administration often discuss leadership, communication, and structure with only passing reference to the market. On the other hand, economists, antitrust lawyers, and other experts on market behavior have said little about the impact of the market on corporate administration.

In this context, the boundaries of research and theory on organizations and administrative science might well be expanded to account better for organizational effectiveness and to integrate processes at the institutional level of organization.

NOTES

1. Some manufacturers depart from this pattern by concentrating only on the production of finished and semifinished goods, on contract for private-label merchandisers.

2. The studies from which these estimates are derived (Conrad and Plotkin, 1967; Glover and Hawkins, 1965) were commissioned by each industry's trade association for presentation before congressional committees. Both industries are portrayed as subject to high risks and uncertainty, and if there is any bias in reporting profitability it is likely to be downward in each case. In this connection, the possibility of slight distortions in reporting, as well as the pharmaceutical industry's custom of expensing research and development costs (which *grew* rapidly during the period covered here), have been considered. Of primary interest is the *magnitude* of the difference in reported rates of return, which is sufficient for this analysis to assume that it could not be due solely to measurement error. Rather, the differential between the two industries is taken to

illustrate the central point for students of organizations, that is, that the performance of individual firms and the range of choices available to organizations is linked to industry characteristics and the larger institutional environment. For a comparison of the pharmaceutical and aluminum industries based on reported rates of return, see Mueller (1969).

3. High profit margins on the most successful of these, tetracycline, were a stimulus for later congressional hearings, and a major antitrust suit resulting in one of the largest court-ordered settlements in United States history. One reason for high rates of return during this time period could be that most of the newer drugs had been available only a short time, and it is during the first several years of release that returns to newly patented products should be highest. Although economic theory is beyond the scope of this article, an economist might suspect entry barriers, high concentration, or measurement error as the basis of sustained high rates of return for an industry. Telser (1974) has presented an interesting model suggesting that high seller concentration within therapeutic categories does not mean that entry barriers have prevented new firms from coming into the drug industry. Economic theory also predicts that unusually high rates of return for an industry should be short-lived, as they serve to attract new entrants, thus increasing competition and pushing profits down, closer to more normal levels.

4. In 1970, Congress finally did award record manufacturers limited copyright protection, largely to reduce the incidence of unauthorized copying of records for resale (McCaghy and Denisoff, 1974). Subsequently, the House of Representatives passed a copyright bill permitting record manufacturers to negotiate performance fees, but broadcasters objected to the royalty provision and predicted that it would be struck from later versions (Hall, 1971, 1972).

REFERENCES

Allen, Michael P. 1974. "The structure of interorganizational elite cooptation: Interlocking corporate directorates." *American Sociological Review*, 39: 393–406.
Aldrich, Howard, and Jeffrey Pfeffer. 1975. "Organizations and environments." Unpublished paper, New York State School of Industrial and Labor Relations, Cornell University.
Benson, J. Kenneth. 1975. "The interorganizational network as a political economy." *Administrative Science Quarterly*, 20: 229–249.
Bowman, Ward S. 1973. *Patent and Antitrust Law.* Chicago: University of Chicago Press.
Burack, Richard. 1967. *The Handbook of Prescription Drugs.* New York: Pantheon.
Burrow, James. 1963. *AMA: Voice of American Medicine.* Baltimore: Johns Hopkins University Press.
Business Week. 1974. "The drug industry's clouded future." November 23: 64–73.
Chandler, Alfred D. 1962. *Strategy and Structure: Chapters in the History of the American Industrial Enterprise.* Cambridge: Massachusetts Institute of Technology Press.
Conrad, Gordon R., and Irving H. Plotkin. 1967. *Risk and Return in American Industry: An Econometric Analysis.* Cambridge: Arthur D. Little, Inc. In United States Congress, Senate, Select Committee on Small Business. "Competitive Problems in the Drug Industry," part 5. Hearings before the Subcommittee on Monopoly. 90th Congress, First and Second Sessions. Washington, D.C.: U. S. Government Printing Office.
Corry, Catherine S. 1965. *The Phonograph Record Industry: An Economic Study.* Washington, DC: The Library of Congress Legislative Reference Service.
Davis, Kingsley, and Wilbert E. Moore. 1945. "Some principles of stratification." *American Sociological Review.* 10: 242–249.
Dill, William. 1958. "Environment as an influence on managerial autonomy." *Administrative Science Quarterly*, 2: 409–443.
Epstein, Edwin M. 1969. *The Corporation in American Politics.* Englewood Cliffs, NJ: Prentice Hall.
———. 1973a. "Dimensions of corporate power—I." *California Management Review*, 16: 9–23.

———. 1973b. "Dimensions of corporate power—II." *California Management Review,* 16: 32–47.

Evan, William. 1966. "The organization set: Toward a theory of interorganizational relations." In James D. Thompson (ed.), *Approaches to Organizational Design:* 173–191. Pittsburgh: University of Pittsburgh Press.

———. 1972. "An organization set model of interorganizational relations." In Matthew Tuite, Roger Chisholm, and Michael Radnor (eds.), *Interorganizational Decision-Making:* 191–200. Chicago: Aldine.

Gelatt, Roland. 1965. *The Fabulous Phonograph From Edison to Stereo,* rev. ed. New York: Appleton-Century.

Glover, John D., and David Hawkins. 1965. *Economic Analysis of the Proposal to Increase Copyright License Fee for Phonograph Records.* In United States Congress, House, Committee on the Judiciary. Copyright Law Revision, part 2. Hearings before Subcommittee No. 3 on H.R. 4347, H.R. 5680, H.R. 6831, and H.R. 6835: 771–888. 89th Congress, First Session. Washington, DC: U.S. Government Printing Office.

Hall, Mildred. 1971. "A view of the copyright copout—stall, separatism and standoff." *Billboard* (January 16): 3, 90.

———. 1972. "Lawmakers in for hectic 12 months." *Billboard* (January 8): 1, 5.

Hirsch, Paul M. 1969. *The Structure of the Popular Music Industry: An Examination of the Filtering Process by Which Records Are Pre-selected for Public Consumption.* Ann Arbor: University of Michigan Survey Research Center.

———. 1972. "Processing fads and fashions by cultural industry systems: An organization-set analysis." *American Journal of Sociology,* 77: 639–659.

———. 1973. "The organization of consumption." Unpublished doctoral disertation, University of Michigan.

———. 1975. "Organizational analysis and industrial sociology: An instance of cultural lag." *American Sociologist,* 10: 3–12.

Hollander, Stanley. 1970. "She 'shops for you or with you': Some notes on the theory of the consumer purchasing surrogate." In George Fisk (ed.), *Essays in Marketing Theory.* Boston: Allyn and Bacon.

Kahn, Alfred E. 1971. *The Economics of Regulation: Principles and Institutions.* Volume 2 (Institutional Issues). New York: Wiley.

Katz, Daniel, and Robert L. Kahn. 1966. *The Social Psychology of Organizations.* New York: Wiley.

Lawrence, Paul, and Jay Lorsch. 1967. *Organization and Environment.* Cambridge: Harvard University, Graduate School of Business Administration.

Lieberson, Stanley, and James O'Connor. 1972. "Leadership and organizational performance: A study of large corporations." *American Sociological Review,* 37: 117–130.

McCaghy, Charles, and R. Serge Denisoff. 1974. "Pirates and politics: An analysis of intergroup conflict." In R. Serge Denisoff and Charles McCaghy (eds.), *Deviance, Conflict, and Criminality.* Chicago: Rand McNally.

Mintz, Morton. 1967. *By Prescription Only,* 2d ed. Boston: Houghton Mifflin

Moller, William, Jr., and David Wilemon (eds.). 1971. *Marketing Channels: A Systems Viewpoint.* Homewood, IL: Richard Irwin.

Mueller, Willard F. 1969. "Profitability in the drug industry: A result of monopoly or a payment for risk?" In *United States Federal Trade Commission, Economic Papers by the Staff of the Bureau of Economics, 1966–1969.* Washington, DC: U.S. Government Printing Office.

Parsons, Talcott. 1956a. "Suggestions for a sociological approach to the theory of organizations—I." *Administrative Science Quarterly,* 1: 63–85.

———. 1956b. "Suggestions for a sociological approach to the theory of organizations—II." *Administrative Science Quarterly,* 1: 225–239.

Peterson, Richard A., and David G. Berger. 1971. "Entrepreneurship in organizations: Evidence from the popular music industry." *Administrative Science Quarterly,* 16: 97–106.

———. 1975. "Cycles in symbol production: The case of popular music." *American Sociological Review,* 40: 158–173.

Pfeffer, Jeffrey, and Huseyin Leblebici. 1973. "Executive recruitment and the development of interfirm organizations." *Administrative Science Quarterly,* 18: 449–461.

Ridgeway, Valentine P. 1957. "Administration of manufacturer-dealer systems." *Administrative Science Quarterly*, 1: 464–483.

Scherer, Frederick. 1970. *Industrial Market Structure and Economic Performance*. Chicago: Rand McNally.

Shemel, Sidney, and M. William Krasilovsky. 1964. *This Business of Music*. New York: Billboard Publishing.

Siegel, Paul M. 1970. "Prestige in the American occupational structure." Unpublished Ph.D. dissertation, University of Chicago.

Silverman, Milton, and Philip R. Lee. 1974. *Pills, Profits, and Politics*. Berkeley: University of California Press.

Stigler, George. 1968. *The Organization of Industry*. Homewood, IL: Richard Irwin.

Stocking, George W., and Myron Watkins. 1968. *Monopoly and Free Enterprise*. New York: Greenwood Press (reprint of 1961 Report of the Twentieth Century Fund).

Telser, Lester. 1974. "The supply response to shifting demand in the ethical pharmaceutical industry." Paper presented at the Conference on Drug Development and Marketing. Washington, DC: American Enterprise Institute.

Thompson, James D. 1967. *Organizations in Action*. New York: McGraw-Hill.

United States Bureau of the Census. 1971. *1967 Census of Manufactures*. Industry Statistics, Volumes 1 and 2. Washington, DC: U.S. Government Printing Office.

United States Congress, House, Committee on the Judiciary. 1965. Copyright Law Revision, parts 1–3. Hearings before Subcommittee No. 3 on H.R. 4347, H.R. 5680, H.R. 6831, H.R. 6835, Bills for the General Revision of the Copyright Law. 89th Congress, First Session.

United States Congress, Senate, Committee on the Judiciary. 1961. Administered Prices: Drugs. Report of the Subcommittee on Antitrust and Monopoly. 87th Congress, First Session.

United States Congress, Senate, Select Committee on Small Business. 1967–1971. "Competitive problems in the drug industry," parts 1–20. Hearings before the Subcommittee on Monopoly. 90th Congress, First and Second Sessions, 91st Congress, First and Second Sessions, 92nd Congress, Second Session.

United States Federal Trade Commission. 1958. *Economic Report on Antibiotics Manufacture*. Washington, DC: U.S. Government Printing Office.

United States Task Force on Prescription Drugs. 1968. *The Drug Makers and the Drug Distributors*. Washington, DC: U.S. Government Printing Office.

Vaughn, Floyd L. 1956. *The United States Patent System*. Norman: University of Oklahoma Press.

Walker, Hugh D. 1971. *Market Power and Price Levels in the Ethical Drug Industry: A Critical Analysis*. Bloomington: Indiana University Press.

Wamsley, Gary, and Mayer N. Zald. 1973. *The Political Economy of Public Organizations*. Lexington, MA: Lexington Books.

Wilson, James Q. 1973. *Political Organizations*. New York: Basic Books.

Woodward, Joan. 1965. *Industrial Organization: Theory and Practice*. London: Oxford University Press.

Zald, Mayer N. 1970. "Political economy: A framework for analysis." In Mayer Zald (ed.), *Power in Organizations*. Nashville, TN: Vanderbilt University Press.

12

AUTHORITY, ORGANIZATION, AND SOCIETAL CONTEXT IN MULTINATIONAL CHURCHES

Reed E. Nelson

Authority as a source of compliance and a determinant of organizational form merits study in its own right, but particularly as a phenomenon whose manifestations and implications vary across societies. Weber's original work on authority was eminently comparative, integrating exhaustive historical research from four continents. Moreover, his writings make it clear that the exercise of domination and the nature of society are not only closely related but inseparable. Unfortunately, the field of organization studies has made rather inconsistent use of the Weberian legacy generally and of his work on authority particularly.

Although Weber posited three pure types of authority—rational-legal, traditional, and charismatic—the bulk of the literature has implicitly or explicitly assumed rational-legalism as the principal foundation for most organizations. Perrow (1979), for example, has vigorously championed the notion that complex organizations by their very nature are bureaucratic. Institutional theorists posit the hegemony of bureaucratic forms through coercion and imitation (Meyer and Rowan, 1977; DiMaggio and Powell, 1983). Less

AUTHOR'S NOTE: Thanks are due to Thomas Burger, Cindy Lindsay, Monty Lynn, William McKinley, William McCusker, Charles Stubbart, Charles Vance, Rys Williams, and the reviewers for their helpful comments. Reprinted from *Administrative Science Quarterly*, 38 (Dec. 1993): 653–682.

explicitly, but equally important, research on organization structure uses measures derived from the dimensions of rational-legal bureaucracy, such as formalization, specialization, and hierarchy (e.g., Pugh et al., 1963; Blau and Schoenherr, 1971; Meyer, 1972; Pugh and Hickson, 1976). Even those who propose nonbureaucratic paradigms tend to ignore Weber's other two authority types as a basis for organization (Ouchi, 1979; Witt, 1979; Scherer, 1988).

Neglect of traditional and charismatic authority and of the interrelations among society, authority, and organization may stem in part from Weber's own emphasis on rationalism in the modern world (Mitzman, 1969; Glassman, 1984). More important, I believe, is a long-standing neglect of the type of comparative research that gave rise to Weber's original insights. The great bulk of empirical research on organizations is carried out in industrial concerns and government agencies of developed Western countries, where the "iron cage" of bureaucratization has held sway for many decades. Of the comparative research that has been done, much comes from industrial settings and follows the basic pattern of the Aston studies by focusing on interrelations between bureaucratic structural dimensions (Maurice, 1979). This reliance on the Aston methodology makes even comparative research insensitive to the presence of nonbureaucratic elements in organizations (e.g., Inkson, Pugh, and Hickson, 1970; Glaser, 1971; Heydebrand, 1973; Hickson et al., 1974), although there are some exceptions to this trend (see Lammers and Hickson, 1979).

In recent years management scholars have rediscovered charisma and tradition in organizations, but in a rather limited way. Those who write about charisma tend to focus on the attributes, techniques, and strategies of charismatic leadership and its aftermath (e.g., House, 1977; Trice and Beyer, 1986; Conger and Kanungo, 1988). Most references to tradition are associated with the content and transmission of organization culture (Clark, 1970; Pettigrew, 1979; Deal and Kennedy, 1982; Wilkins and Ouchi, 1983; Schein, 1985; Dyer, 1986). In both cases, authority type is examined in relative isolation from societal context. This contrasts sharply with Weber's original work and subsequent sociological research in the Weberian tradition, which views authority as interacting intimately with institutional form and social context (Schweitzer, 1984; Biggart, 1989; Schluchter, 1989; Lindholm, 1990). These limitations in attention and sample selection ignore possible variability in the type of authority used in organizations and may obscure linkages among society, authority, and organization. Such inattention is particularly undesirable in an increasingly interdependent international community where multinationals are major players.

To broaden the focus of attention on authority, this article reviews the experience of three churches operating in the U.S. and Brazil as a means of inductively exploring the relationship between authority type, societal environment, and organizational outcomes. The article has two goals. First, and most important, I attempt to establish the fact that three large denominations based on three different authority types coexist and even compete in two very different societal contexts. This point is important because of the aforementioned paucity of studies of charisma and tradition-based organizations, but it is especially important because the Weberian opus is generally not concerned with multiple authority systems in a single society; Weber is much more preoccupied with the transformation from one authority type to another. The coexistence of church organizations characterized by diverse authority types is also germane to current issues in organization theory because it runs counter to the affirmation of institutional theorists that organizational fields tend to be homogenous bodies populated by similar organizational forms (Meyer and Rowan, 1977; DiMaggio and Powell, 1983, 1991).

Weber developed a detailed and systematic portrait of the rational-legal bureaucracy that has been widely used in organization studies. His ideas on tradition and charisma, however, have not been systematically applied to the morphological analysis of complex organizations. Therefore, to substantiate the traditional and charismatic nature of the organizations studied, it is necessary to systematize and extend Weber's ideas on how tradition and charisma can be expressed in concrete organizational forms. The resulting ideal-typical description of competing bureaucratic, traditional, and charismatic organizational forms is an ancillary but useful outcome of this article.

The second goal of this article is to develop exploratory propositions about the comparative performance of authority systems in diverse host societies. Weber says little about comparative performance of authority types across different contexts. Yet if diverse authority systems do indeed survive within a single organizational field across different societies, the dynamics influencing their growth and perpetuation would be of practical and theoretical interest. Moreover, studying cross-national performance of organizations with different authority bases should be of particular relevance to institutional theory, because it affords an opportunity to see how similar institutional forms fare in national contexts that logically would generate different isomorphic pressures.

Churches and Organization Studies

There are several reasons why religious organizations should provide a particularly promising setting for the comparative study of authority, organization, and society. First, because churches are generally exempt from the technological and many of the capital constraints of other types of organizations, they are unusually expressive of, although not invariably isomorphic with, the sociocultural environment. This freedom makes religious organizations a particularly good vehicle for capturing interactions between societal context and authority in organizations. Second, the social and cultural function of churches, what Parsons and Smelser (1956: 18) referred to as "pattern maintenance," suggests that there will be a link between religious organizations' ability to relate successfully to the social environment and their organizational performance. Third, in the absence of financial, coercive, or other utilitarian motives (Etzioni, 1961; Schluchter, 1989) for compliance in religious organizations, one can expect the exercise of legitimate authority to be of central importance.

Finally, churches, particularly multinational churches, merit study in their own right yet have been neglected in both the fields of organization studies and international management. Churches are big business, one of the biggest, if one considers the number of employees and members of religious organizations. An average Sunday finds some 80,000,000 Americans in church (Jacquet and Jones, 1991). The Mormon Church, a medium-sized denomination by Baptist or Catholic standards, has an approximate annual income of around $2 billion and holds close to $8 billion in assets (Heinerman and Shupe, 1985)—more than many *Fortune* 500 corporations. Moreover, churches are multinational businesses. Religious organizations were really the first multinationals, and by almost any measure, many are still among the largest. All major world religions at one time or another have expanded by moving across national and cultural boundaries, and many, if not most, still compete worldwide. By generally ignoring churches, organization theorists neglect a significant proportion of all organizations, both nationally and cross-nationally.

Weber's Ideal Types of Authority

Although Weber posited several types of authority (Murvar, 1985), most attention has focused on the pure or ideal-typical categories of charismatic, traditional, and rational-legal. Rational-legal authority rests on the "belief in the 'legality' of patterns of normative rules and the right of those elevated to authority under such rules to issue commands" (Weber, 1947: 329). Intentionally established abstract rules that are universally applicable make the exercise of rational-legal authority possible. Rational-legal was the latest authority form to develop and is fundamental to the theories of bureaucracy and capitalism (Parsons, 1947; Collins, 1980). In Weber's (1947: 333) writings, the bureaucratic organizational form is a straightforward extension of rational-legal authority: "The purest type of exercise of legal authority is that which employs a bureaucratic administrative staff."

The other two pure types of authority are traditional and charismatic. Although traditional authority contains many subtypes, their legitimacy is based on "the sanctity of the order and the attendant powers of control as they have been handed down from the past" (Weber, 1947: 334). While traditional authority can generate personal loyalty to the ruler, the source of this loyalty is social category or type, not personal attributes. Unlike rational-legal and traditional authority, which derive from abstract principle and longstanding practice, respectively, charisma emanates from the extraordinary personal qualities of individuals. Weber (1947: 329) defined charisma as "resting on devotion to the specific and exceptional sanctity, heroism or exemplary character of an individual person, and of the normative patterns or order revealed or ordained by him." Because it derives from personal idiosyncrasies and creativity rather than rationality or established practice, charismatic authority is frequently a source of revolutionary change and the disruption of established institutional forms. One important difference be-tween the three authorities lies in the degree of latitude or caprice afforded individual leaders. In the bureaucracy, jurisdiction is carefully defined and circumscribed, while the charismatic leader enjoys unlimited discretion. Tra-dition represents a midpoint on this continuum; leaders have arbitrary control in areas not bound by tradition. It is probably possible for organizations to use more than one authority type simultaneously (Knoke and Prensky, 1984), or a mixture of authority types, but the emphasis in this article is on more or less pure examples of single authority institutions.

Gaps in the Study of Authority and Complex Organization

Many, if not most, Weber scholars, with the exception of Parsons (1947), believe that the major unifying theme of Weber's work is the inexorable development and ultimate triumph of formal rationality over other principles of social and economic organization (e.g., Bendix, 1962; Nelson, 1974; Tenbruck, 1975; Cassanova, 1984; Glassman, 1984; Swatos, 1984; Schluchter, 1989). Hence in Weberian thought, the ascetic rationalism of Calvinism (Weber, 1948; Mitzman, 1969), the calculable rationality of West-ern legal and accounting schemes (Weber, 1927; Collins, 1980; Langton, 1984), and the technical and control efficiencies of the rational-legal bureau-cracy (Weber, 1968; Perrow, 1979) overcome traditional systems and emas-culate charisma.

Both Weber's personal experience (Mitzman, 1969) and the social context of fin de siècle Europe and Wilhelmian Germany reinforce a vision of triumphant rationality. Rapid industrialization and urbanization were sweep-ing away the last holdouts of traditional social organization and positivistic technocracy, and science demonstrated the seemingly unerring strength of rationalism. The backlash of charismatic movements that preceded and precipitated World War II was still decades away. The mass technologies that facilitate the manufacture of charisma (Glassman, 1984) were in their infancy, and the durability of traditional religion both in the West and in the Islamic countries was likewise not yet visible. Weber did have occasion to observe charismatic leaders in operation in American and German religious, political, and artistic circles and noted the propensity of rapidly changing social systems to generate charisma, but he believed that economic and political pressures would lead to rapid routinization (Weber, 1968). In Weber's time, it was not yet apparent that rationalized technology, the bureaucratic enterprise, and even mass markets could diffuse across nations rapidly without occasioning the same destruction of traditional institutions that the slow but thorough gestation of rationalized capitalism had caused in the West (Farao, 1958; Organski, 1965; Guerreiro Ramos, 1968; Richmond and Copen, 1973; Collins, 1986). As a result, Weber tended to view rationalism as an irresistible, all-transforming force, tradition as historically important but ultimately doomed, and charisma as potent but ephemeral and short-lived in its pure form. Given Weber's historical vantage point and his belief in the hegemony of rationality, it is not surprising that his work generally does not explore the dynamics of diverse authorities within the same society, nor how rational-legal, traditional, and charisma-based authority systems might fare across different societies.

There are other reasons why Weber is mute on the subject of the coexistence of organizations employing diverse authority systems and their comparative dynamics across societies. To a large degree, the societies that serve as a context for Weber's discussion of traditional and charismatic authority ante-date the advent of complex organizations with identifiable boundaries inter-acting with other institutions in dense organizational fields, as is the case in most societies currently. Hence, he would have had minimal opportunity to observe or analyze the coexistence of organizations employing diverse types of legitimate authority.

There is also the simpler matter of research focus. Weber's concern with the defining features of modern occidental civilization, in conjunction with his methodological strategy of formulating pure or ideal types, involved a certain underemphasis of the typologically mixed, although this strategy presupposes the existence of nonideal phenomena. Hence, Weber's preoccupation with the significance of rational bureaucratic organization tended to push to the sidelines the study of charisma and tradition in modern society.[1]

Finally, in the particular case of charismatic authority, it is unlikely that Weber would have classified any enduring organization as charismatic. Students of Weber's work have struggled with the ambivalence in Weber's thought on charisma and institutions (e.g., Parsons, 1947; Eisenstadt, 1968; Glassman, 1984; Swatos, 1984; Schluchter, 1989). On one hand, Weber (1968: 363) affirmed that "in its pure form charismatic authority has a character specifically foreign to everyday routine structures." On the other hand, he spoke of hereditary charisma and charisma of office (Parsons, 1947; Weber, 1947) and suggested that charisma and patrimonial domination can evince very similar social structures.

In contradiction to Weber's original formulations, recent work suggests that permanent institutions based on charisma can indeed survive largely free of bureaucratic or traditional encumbrance (Carmic, 1980; Zablocki, 1980; Miyahara, 1983; Schweitzer, 1984; Biggart, 1989; Schluchter, 1989; Lindholm, 1990). With the exception of Biggart's comparison of bureaucratic and charismatic organization, however, the authors of this work do not contrast organizations using different authority types. Thus, even intelligent theory generation must begin with new empirical data, beyond what is available in the current Weberian literature. By examining the cross-national experience of contemporary churches employing three diverse authority types it should be possible to generate theory that extends Weber's original thinking on *herrschaft* and human institutions.

Denominations Studied

The three religious bodies studied are the Christian Congregation in Brazil and its American branch, the Christian Congregation in the United States; the Assemblies of God; and the Church of Jesus Christ of Latter Day Saints (the LDS or Mormon church). These three churches share important similarities that hold constant several extraneous variables and make comparative study feasible and meaningful. All three are growing rapidly and attract a lower- and middle-class clientele. All three lie somewhat outside of mainline denominational tradition and seek the same kind of conservative, religiously committed converts. All three have been operating in the U.S. and Brazil for at least five decades and have developed stable, recognizable strategies and practices. Despite their similarities, each of the three churches has its own unique strategy and organizational form, and as I demonstrate below, each is controlled and legitimized by different types of authority.[2] The U.S. and Brazil provide contrasting societal contexts, particularly in indices of industrialization and modernization, variables with broad social and economic consequences (Riesman, 1950; Rowstow, 1961; Organski, 1965; Berger, 1979).

Three organizations addressing similar populations through very different approaches in two countries should provide requisite variability for "local" (Glaser and Strauss, 1967) or exploratory theory generation, if not for more general insights. My purpose is to generate grounded theory, not to test a priori hypotheses (Glaser and Strauss, 1967; Campbell, 1988, 1991). The bulk of the information used in the descriptions below comes from published studies of the three bodies. Occasionally, when published information was vague or questions arose that were not answered in written sources, I contacted church leaders in Brazil or the U.S. with specific questions. Where I have used these people as sources, I have cited them as references, and listed them in the reference section, labeled "personal communication."

TRADITIONAL AUTHORITY AS A BASIS FOR COMPLEX
ORGANIZATION: THE CHRISTIAN CONGREGATIONS

The great spiritual awakening of the early twentieth century spawned dozens of pentecostal denominations within a period of ten years or so. The Christian Congregation (CC) is one of the most prosperous of the early movements. The CC's founder, an Italian immigrant named Luigi Francescon, was at the same time passionately opposed to strong individual leadership in the movement and adamantly opposed to formal organization on the grounds that they limited the workings of the Holy Spirit and promoted inequality among the faithful (Ottolini, 1945; De Caro, 1977), an aversion reflected in the original name of the body he founded: "the Unorganized Christian Churches of North America." Francescon and his followers broke away from other early pentecostal bodies again and again over his aversion to individual influence and formal organization. Ultimately, he withdrew from the very fellowship he had founded, now the Christian Church of North America, over his opposition to the development of a formal denominational structure.

A number of congregations accompanied Francescon when he left the original movement. These became known as the Christian Congregations (CCs), and they have retained much of the character of the earliest churches founded by Francescon. In the absence of bureaucratic or charismatic mechanisms, the Christian Congregations are governed by oral traditions imputed to the original believers and interpreted and enforced by the most senior members, elders, of the church—in sum, by traditional authority.

The Christian Congregations have no paid clergy and eschew most trappings of formal organization (Erutti, n.d.; Ottolini, 1945; Francescon, 1952; De Caro, 1977). They have no membership records, no operating manuals or similar documents, and no paid officials of any kind. They deny the existence of any hierarchy, prohibit public proselytizing, distribute no pamphlets, levy no tithing, and have only a few official positions. There is only one kind of devotional meeting, and it is totally improvised except for a basic sequence involving hymns, prayers, testimonials, and impromptu preaching (Nelson, 1988a).

Internal homogeneity appears to be very high, despite the Congregations' apparently loose organization. All of the 5,000-plus congregations adhere to the same austere behavioral standards, including strict monogamy, prohibition of television, radio, movies, makeup, smoking, alcohol, and gambling. Although there are no Sunday schools, retreats, or similar mechanisms to transmit doctrine, member beliefs, while very simple, are remarkably uniform throughout the body (Leonard, 1963; Nelson, 1978). The religious vocabulary of members varies little from place to place, as does church decor, meeting format, clothing, and personal lifestyles of the faithful.

Part of the Congregations' ability to survive with minimal formal structure and professional leadership doubtless stems from the reduced number of activities the church conducts. As mentioned before, worship services are improvised, obviating any planning or liturgical functions. No codified doctrine is promoted, outside of a few basic and noncontroversial beliefs long accepted in evangelical Protestantism. Moreover, the CCs have no ancillary social or educational functions, except for charitable activities carried out by individual congregations. Still, the church obviously carries out a number of tasks that permit survival and even growth. Although a lack of formal documentation and protocol makes it difficult to learn exactly how the Christian Congregations fulfill basic organizing functions, field studies of the body (Leonard, 1963; Hollenweger, 1972; Nelson, 1978, 1984, 1988a, 1989) provide some idea.

Oral tradition, seniority, precedent, and social networks appear to provide the principal organizing tools in the CCs. The CCs are, above all, a story-telling church. Hollenweger (1972: 85) calls the CCs' approach "religion by word of mouth." Testimonies and sermons drive home the church's world-view in countless anecdotes that are broadcast by constant traveling and visiting between members of different congregations. A visiting brother or sister will invariably receive free lodging at the house of a local member and may be invited to preach if he or she does not volunteer a testimony. Frequently, members suffering affliction will make a vow to tell the story of their deliverance "to all the congregations [they] are permitted to visit," ensuring the propagation of miraculous events (Nelson, 1985: 118).

Members of many years develop an impressive repertory of sayings and stories that help them socialize younger members. The absence of written sources of church history and doctrine makes seniority an important asset, and seniority rather than charisma or competence is the only recognized basis for selection of leaders in the church: The most senior male member of any congregation is automatically the leader or "elder" of the congregation. Other males, in descending order of seniority may be chosen to assist as "cooperators" or deacons. Routine decisions are made by this group of senior males according to oral church tradition. Nonroutine or problematic decisions may be checked with the elders of the oldest congregation in the city or with the oldest congregation in the country, if the matter is weighty (Francescon, 1952; Hollenweger, 1972; personal communication, Dos Santos, 1989). This scheme virtually eliminates ambiguity over leadership and succession, matters that tend to be problematic in religious movements generally, and especially in Protestantism. Possible deficiencies in leadership that might result are probably attenuated by the very small number of administrative tasks undertaken in the church and by the fact that the improvised meetings provide ample opportunities for more charismatic members of the church to participate. Some elders seldom preach, deferring to more loquacious members of the congregation, and the extensive traveling members do spreads around the talents of gifted speakers.

If oral tradition, precedent, and seniority provide the soul of the church, the social networks of its members provide its body. Because the CCs actually prohibit public proselytizing, almost all new converts are introduced to the church through contacts with current members (Nelson, 1989). This recruitment strategy has several likely consequences. It assures that new members will have at least one friend in the church to mentor them and monitor their behavior. In a denomination with no formal rules, written catechisms, or membership records, interaction between members likely supplies the principal means of socialization and control.

Recruitment by network probably provides some winnowing out of and protection from dishonest, unstable, or highly aggressive individuals who would prove disruptive to the organization. More subtly, recruitment by networks probably populates the organization with people of similar social origins and worldviews, if not similar personalities. This homogeneity in turn reduces the need for internal processing and control mechanisms, contributing to the great uniformity observed in the Christian Congregations despite their having little formal structure.

Traditional Authority in the CC

The three organizations studied can be meaningfully compared by contrasting their attributes to the elements of Weber's (1968) bureaucratic ideal type, which is more detailed and complex than most summaries of it in the literature. This affords an opportunity both to demonstrate the nonbureaucratic nature of the CC and confirm its traditional nature by identifying the traditional mechanisms that fulfill important organizing functions.

Clear "specification of spheres of competence" (Weber, 1968: 218) is a fundamental attribute of Weberian bureaucracy. This includes the assignment of obligations according to a formal division of labor, the formal provision of incumbents with authority for specific functions, and a clear definition of the "means of compulsion" (Weber, 1968: 218) available to a given incumbent. In the CCs, duties are minimally defined, very general in nature, and specific roles in the worship service tend to rotate from one individual to another. The head of the congregation has veto power rather than proactive authority, and "the means of compulsion" appear to take the form of generalized peer pressure rather than defined sanctions assigned to specific office holders. Hence, instead of the bureaucratic principle of "specification of spheres of competence," the CC may be said to function according to the principles of "generalized spheres of action and rotation."

The bureaucracy consists of offices arranged in a scalar hierarchy with a system of appeals running from one level to the next. In one of few official documents (Congregacao Crista no Brasil, 1962), the CCs deny the existence of hierarchy but affirm that they "respect seniority in the ministry." Important or controversial decisions are made by consensus in a council of the most senior members of a congregation. This is similar to what Weber described as the purest or most primitive administrative arrangement for traditional authority, the gerontocracy. Hence, instead of hierarchy and appeals, the CCs use the principles of sequential seniority-based statuses and consensus.

A third component of the bureaucratic form as described in Weber (1968: 218) is the "rational application of technical rules and norms." The application of these rules requires specialized training, and incumbents are "subject to strict and systematic discipline and control in the conduct of office" (1968: 221). As described, formal rules and norms applied by trained administrators in a systematic, disciplined fashion are almost absent in the CCs. To be sure, social control is paramount in the CCs, but this control is accomplished through pressure from peers and elder members who have absorbed and mastered acceptable behaviors through long, generic experience in the church. No formal training is available, and minimal formal oversight is exercised. Hence, instead of rational application of technical rules and norms, the corresponding principle of organization in the CCs is control through intense socialization. In the bureaucracy, administrative acts, decisions, and rules are formulated and recorded in writing. In the CCs, written codes of behavior, membership records, receipts for contributions, minutes of meetings, and other written records are conspicuously absent. An annual balance sheet and directory of congregations and meeting times is published, and a circular indicating dates of upcoming baptisms is distributed (one to a congregation), but files appear to have a negligible role in the organization's memory. Rather, oral tradition diffused by frequent visiting between units appears to fulfill that function. In the bureaucracy, individuals are selected and promoted on the basis of their technical qualifications. In the CCs, ascriptive criteria, such as age, gender, seniority, kinship, and membership in social networks, are major determinants of membership and position. This parallels Weber's observations of the importance of inheritable and ascriptive roles and statuses in the makeup of many traditional authority systems (Weber, 1968).

The position of the individual vis-à-vis the organization is scrupulously defined and limited in the bureaucracy, but less so in the CCs. In the bureaucracy, members are "separated from the ownership of the means of administration and production," and there is no private appropriation of position by the incumbent (Weber, 1968: 219). The official's position in the bureaucracy is typically his or her primary occupation, providing a fixed money salary and a predictable career path. In the CCs, most congregations begin in private residences and move to rented or purchased buildings as space needs require. The founding head of the household is by definition the most senior male, and as a matter of course, he becomes the head of the congregation, a position occupied for life. In this regard, young congregations are an extension of the founder's household, and a special status is permanently appropriated by the founder. This institutional extension of the household is the rule under Weber's patriarchicalism, an early traditional authority system (Weber, 1968; Murvar, 1985). No position in the CCs is remunerated, so no salaries or careers are available.

Although no member in the CCs can appropriate church resources for private benefit, the different statuses afforded by age, gender, and foundership attach to individuals, not office. Hence, instead of a clear separation between individual and office, the CCs feature overlap between individual status and organizational office.

CHARISMATIC AUTHORITY: THE ASSEMBLIES OF GOD

The Assemblies of God (AG) resulted from the cooperative association of several pastors who were prominent in the early pentecostal movement (Nichol, 1966; Graver, 1971; Hollenweger, 1972; Blumhofer, 1985, 1989). By the time the first convention of what was to become the Assemblies of God met in 1914, a number of gifted pentecostal preachers had founded large congregations and developed widespread followings. From its inception, the Assemblies of God have struggled to foster a semblance of homogeneity and stability without losing the strong-willed, popular pastors who control the largest congregations and account for the bulk of the membership (Bloch-Hoell, 1964; Poloma, 1989). This has resulted in a loose confederation of clergy supporting a very small central office and an amorphous statement of beliefs. The Assemblies held national conventions for over 40 years before they approved their first bylaws.

Despite doctrine, clientele, and historical roots that are similar to the Christian Congregations, the organization of the Assemblies of God assumes a form that is almost an inverse image of the Christian Congregations. In the Christian Congregations, the individual is lost in the interstices of highly connected social networks, ascriptive categories (particularly age, gender, and kinship), homogeneous oral tradition, and improvised meetings that tend to put a succession of different faces before the congregation each week. In the AG, by contrast, a coherent movement is hardly visible because of the emphasis placed on individual gifts and mobility, and individual congregations are as different one from another as the personal styles of their charismatic pastors. Persons of both genders, almost all ages, varied theologies, and myriad social and ethnic backgrounds have become AG pastors. Thus, the variability that the Christian Congregations eschew is tolerated, if not embraced, by the Assemblies of God.

Individual inspiration and charismatic leadership are the basic organizing principles of the AG approach. Individual inspiration and prophecy are welcome, even critical in the Christian Congregations. Individuals take turns as the charismatic mouthpiece of the congregation during regularly scheduled public meetings, but individual charisma has virtually no role in influencing the structure or agenda of a CC congregation. In the Assemblies, however, individual spiritual gifts, particularly those of the pastor, are given the freest of hands.

Of the relatively few formal requirements for ordination as a pastor in the AG, previous charismatic experience (i.e., speaking in tongues) is obligatory (Assemblies of God, 1982). Pastoral charisma appears so fundamental that Poloma (1989) found a strong association between the charismatic experience of the pastor and the frequency of charismatic manifestations in congregations. Individual pastors have tremendous influence in the life of the congregation. Meeting format and content, doctrinal matters (except for a very few general guidelines), finances, and outreach are all determined by the pastor with varying degrees of input from the congregation. Moreover, many congregations were founded by a charismatic pastor who attracted most members to the church by virtue of his or her personal appeal and who has played a personal role in many conversions (Willems, 1967; De Souza, 1969; Blumhofer, 1985; Nelson, 1988a).

There are almost no limits on the size, scope, tone, and management of the ministries an enterprising pastor may undertake. The besmirched empires of ex-Assemblies of God pastors Jim Bakker and Jimmy Swaggart are examples. People who have never heard of the AG have heard of, and possibly sent money to, one of these men, yet the church made no effort to regulate or rein in either of them until sexual offenses made them subject to formal repeal of credentials (Hadden and Swann, 1981; Hadden and Shupe, 1988). The highly divergent doctrinal initiatives, and the intense competition and enmity, of Bakker and Swaggart are indicative of the variability tolerated in the denomination at large. Swaggart preached a highly conservative doctrine repudiating dancing, movies, rock and roll music, and the like, while the Bakkers espoused a much more accommodative gospel permitting all of the above.

If the Assemblies give their pastors considerable free reign, they are also quite liberal with members and with other denominations. Although both members and pastors may be disciplined for moral failings, considerable diversity in belief is tolerated, and the Assemblies have been reluctant to elaborate and codify doctrine and practices binding on all believers (Assemblies of God, 1976, 1982; Poloma, 1989). A basic statement of beliefs exists, but its tenets are quite general, and the church explicitly rejects the idea that that statement represents a creed. Church officials and historians (Assemblies of God, 1982; Blumhofer, 1985, 1989) have even been reluctant to accept the label "church" or "denomination," preferring the title "movement" or "cooperative fellowship."

The Assemblies of God have been quite active in ecumenical activities and permit people of any denomination to participate fully in church activities indefinitely with little or no pressure to become members of the AG (Menzies, 1971; Assemblies of God, 1982). This contrasts to both the Christian Congregations and the Mormon church, which reject all external institutional contact and stress unequivocally the importance of receiving the denomination's baptism, independent of prior religious experience (Leonard, 1963; Nelson, 1984; Shipps, 1985).

Over time, a certain degree of bureaucratization and patrimonialism has arisen at the regional and national levels, but individual AG churches are quite autonomous, and the officers and policies of the national organization are subject to approval by the direct vote of pastors and congregational representatives (Menzies, 1971; Poloma, 1989). In actuality, the "congregational representative" in voting is the pastor's wife more often than not, further enhancing the already considerable dominance of pastors. Popular pastors who have attracted large followings, founded large churches, or developed large ministries have a dominant influence over decisions made at the regional and national levels (Poloma, 1989; personal communication, Braithwaite, 1993). Thus, although some patrimonial or bureaucratic mechanisms can be found, they are largely subject to the inclinations of individual pastors whose personal charisma has attracted large followings and contributions.

The same individualism and charisma that reign inside the AG also mark recruitment strategies. While appeals to friends and family are doubtless an important source of converts for the AG, as for any religious movement, mass appeals to the general public seem to be the dominant approach. Radio and television programs, heavily advertised public revivals and healing campaigns seem to be vehicles of choice (Harrell, 1975; Hadden and Swann, 1981). And as would be expected, individual charismatic figures provide the main appeal for all of the above. People tune into a program or attend a meeting not so much because of its subject matter or doctrine, but because of a specific individual's appeal.

Although the internal dynamics of AG churches doubtless vary to a greater degree than CC or LDS (Mormon) bodies, descriptions of the ministries of several well-known AG pastors suggest a common pattern that I believe is often found in congregations. While the pastor can and frequently does intervene in the details of church administration that interest her personally, she typically has a number of intensely loyal personal favorites to whom very broad prerogatives, with minimal oversight, are given. Personnel who find favor with the charismatic are frequently rewarded with spontaneous bonuses, gifts, expense accounts, or discretion over resources, like the interior decorator for Jim Bakker's ministry who received a $600,000 bonus one year. Responsibilities and compensation may change rapidly for staff as different personalities and projects wax and wane in favor. Conflicts between lieutenants of the charismatic are frequent as they vie for attention and favor, and occasionally a charismatic member of the pastor's staff may even rebel and start a rival ministry or unseat the charismatic founder (Harrell, 1975; Barnhart, 1988).

Ministries often change direction radically according to perceived changes in the environment or whims of the pastor. Fundraising tends to focus on gifts or offerings for specific needs and projects rather than budgeted requirements, although actual use of funds tends to be very flexible, following the needs and pressures of the moment (Harrell, 1975; Bakker, 1976; Barnhart, 1988).

Charismatic Authority in
the Assemblies of God

The Assemblies of God exhibit many attributes that contrast sharply with both bureaucracy and the traditional form incorporated by the Christian Congregations. Again, by contrasting the Assemblies to the ideal-typical bureaucracy and identifying its major organizing mechanisms we can establish its charismatic nature. This is particularly important because of Weber's ambivalence about the existence of permanent charismatic institutions.

In the bureaucracy, discrete spheres of competence are specified. In the CCs (traditional authority), there are generalized spheres of action that frequently overlap due to rotation of tasks. In the AG, there is a tendency toward the development of semiautonomous domains of action that are not clearly defined and that may change with the fortunes of the charismatic's disciples. These domains may be the subject of intense competition between staff members. Weber noted the tendency for broad but fluctuating responsibilities in the followings of charismatic leaders but did not stress the propensity toward competitive domain development among lieutenants. Other observers of charismatic movements, notably of national socialism, however, have observed this tendency (Lacouture, 1970; Fest, 1973; Haffner, 1979; Goff, 1988).

The bureaucracy uses a scalar hierarchy with provisions for appeals as a principal means of decision making and control. The Christian Congregations appear to use graduated ascriptive statuses and consensus for the same purpose. In the AG, personal proximity to the charismatic leader seems to be the major means of stratification, with the possibility that a relatively unknown follower may succeed in attracting the attention of or making a direct appeal to the charismatic leader.

In the bureaucracy, the means of compulsion are specified for each position, while in the traditional Christian Congregations, compulsion is accomplished by general and unrestricted peer pressure. Weber makes clear that in the charismatic situation, compulsion is ultimately vested in the charismatic leader and is exercised according to the leader's caprice. This appears to be the case in many churches of the AG also. Again, however, competition between members of the charismatic leader's staff and between congregations and ministries leads to ambiguities implied in Weber's work and observed by other students of charisma. In the Assemblies and in other charismatic situations, competition between charismatic figures or lieutenants means that directives, controls, and punishments are applied differentially, depending on the political or social dynamics of each situation. This phenomenon is especially pronounced in the denomination's uneven and frequently impotent attempts to discipline its pastors and in frequent schisms within congregations and within the denomination at large (see Poloma, 1989).

Rational, universalistic application of technical rules and norms under the supervision of specially trained administrators provides control in bureaucracies. Intense socialization and peer pressure appears to serve the same purpose in the tradition-based Christian Congregations. Neither detailed rules nor extensive socialization appear to be central in the AG. Instead, it is likely that loyalty to the charismatic and obedience to her lieutenants as legitimate representatives provide some degree of control. Careful oversight of responsibilities is rare, but sudden promotion to or removal from duties is possible if the interests of the charismatic are involved or competing lieutenants clash over the specifics of performance. Similarly, rewards and punishments for specific behaviors may occur, but these tend to be administered by caprice rather than systematically, as in the bureaucracy.

The bureaucracy has files and rulings, while the Christian Congregations have visits and oral tradition as retention devices (Aldrich, 1979). In many AG congregations and ministries, the unique vision and charismatic personality of the leader provide what little organizational memory exists. The importance of the leader's personality and unique Weltanschauung in providing identity and direction for the charismatic movement has been noted by Weber and others (Weber, 1968; Eisenstadt, 1968; Trice and Beyer, 1986).

Selection and promotion in the bureaucracy is by universalistic means. In the CCs it is by ascription. As Weber would predict, in the AG, selection is by response to the idiosyncratic "call" of the charismatic leader, and promotion is a function of an individual's proximity to the leader.

The bureaucracy rigorously separates individual and office, providing a fixed salary and distinguishing between organizational and personal resources. In the CCs, there is overlap between individual status and office, but no payment for services. In the AG, the concept of office is of relatively little importance. The organization is often an extension of the charismatic leader, and frequently, little distinction is made between organizational resources and personal budgets. Although fixed salaries may be stipulated for pastors, it is not uncommon for significant portions of compensation to come from spontaneous offerings, royalties, special collections, and fundraising campaigns. This is reminiscent of the provision of needs by begging, gifts, or booty that Weber associates with charisma.

RATIONAL-LEGAL AUTHORITY: THE LDS CHURCH

The Church of Jesus Christ of Latter Day Saints (LDS or Mormon) was founded in 1830 by a semiliterate frontiersman named Joseph Smith. Early in the development of the church, Smith received a series of revelations establishing a differentiated organization legitimized by a legalistic priesthood. As a result, formal bureaucratic administration was established early on. This has increased in refinement and complexity over the years (Barrett, 1979; Shipps, 1985).

The highly formalized, bureaucratic approach of the LDS church stands in stark contrast to both the Christian Congregations and the Assemblies of God. Highly detailed manuals formulated at church headquarters determine every aspect of the local congregation's operations, right down to who sits on the stand at meetings (Heinerman and Shupe, 1985). A multilayered hierarchy runs from members to "home teachers" to "quorum presidents" to "bishops" to "stake presidents" to "regional representatives" to "area presidencies" to "the quorum of the seventy" to the "presidency of the 1st quorum of the seventy" to "the quorum of the twelve" to the "first presidency" to the president of the church (Gottlieb and Wiley, 1984). The operation of LDS congregations is virtually identical the world over, and all units in all countries are linked directly to church headquarters in Salt Lake City through a functional chain of command.

Not only is there great vertical differentiation, but horizontal differentiation is also very high in the LDS, despite the fact that congregations average about 450 members and almost never exceed 2,000 (O'Dea, 1957; personal communication, Scofield, 1993). Each standard congregation or "ward" staffs as many as 200 different administrative positions that support a plethora of activities, including regular worship services, genealogical research, missionary activity, choir, nursery, child and youth programs, Cub and Boy Scout troops, employment placement assistance, separate women's and men's organizations, comprehensive charitable activities, singles activities, youth and men's sports teams, a library, teacher training, periodical subscription drives, monthly visits to all church members of record, two types of introductory classes for new church members, promotion of food storage and emergency preparedness, homemaking classes, member contributions to church maintenance, daily early morning religion classes for youth, and occasional church socials, dances, and conferences (Arrington and Biton, 1979). As if this were not enough, Mormonism includes detailed, standardized rituals performed in special buildings called temples. These rites surpass the Catholic liturgy in complexity (O'Dea, 1957; Gottlieb and Wiley, 1984; Shipps, 1985).

Recruitment is not accomplished principally by social networks (although this is undoubtedly an important source of new members), nor through charismatic appeals, but through methodical door-to-door canvassing by volunteer missionaries, buttressed with small amounts of institutional advertising in mainline media like the *Reader's Digest* and network television. The church currently has some 40,000 volunteer full-time personnel fulfilling two-year missions.

New converts to the church are baptized after taking a series of seven short doctrinal lessons from missionaries and agreeing to conform to church behavioral standards, including a 10 percent tithe, strict monogamy, and abstinence from tobacco, coffee, alcohol, and drugs. Detailed records of the member's age, number of children, marital status, financial contributions, and office in the LDS priesthood are kept (personal communication, De Oliveira, 1993). A formal interview with the head of the congregation ascertains the member's worthiness to participate in temple ordinances. Members who conform to the behavioral standards listed above are issued a document called a "temple recommend," which permits entrance into the temple and indicates good standing in the church. Active members who commit adultery, have abortions, or are convicted of felonies are usually excommunicated after a formal disciplinary council meets (Arrington and Biton, 1979; Gottlieb and Wiley, 1984).

The similarity between the above description of the LDS church and Weber's ideal-typical bureaucracy is so great that little would be gained from a detailed comparison of specific elements. The only substantive divergence from the pure Weberian model is the relative dearth of full-time salaried administrators in the church; most positions rely on volunteer labor.

Table 12.1 summarizes the elements of Weber's three authority types as typified by the three churches. It also contrasts the organization form found under traditional authority in the CCs, which is similar to Ouchi's (1979) clans, with bureaucracy as described in Weber (1968). The clan organization is clearly an expression of traditional authority, and many of its attributes can be derived from Weberian theory.

At this point, the first objective of this article has been largely fulfilled. The fact that three organizations using fundamentally different authority bases coexist in the same organizational field in two different societies should be apparent. I now examine the comparative performance of these churches in two nations in an attempt to generate theory about the growth and perpetuation of authority systems across societies—the second and most ambitious goal of the article.

COMPARATIVE PERFORMANCE

Aspects of performance of the Assemblies of God, Christian Congregations, and LDS church vary as dramatically as do their organizational forms.

TABLE 12.1 Organizational Attributes of Diverse Authority Systems

Rational-Legal (LDS)	Traditional (CCs)	Charismatic (AC)

I. Specification of spheres of competence
  A. Formal division of labor
  B. Authority for specific functions
  C. Specific means of compulsion
	I. Generalized spheres of action and rotation
	  A. Competitive accumulation
	  B. General veto power of elder
	  C. Generalized peer pressure
		I. Semiautonomous fiefs
		  A. Rotation of tasks
		  B. All actions subordinate to charismatic
		  C. Distribution of means of compulsion subject to dispute and constant reformation

II. Scalar hierarchy
  A. Appeals
	II. Sequential statuses
	  A. Consensus
		II. Influence determined by proximity to charismatic
		  A. Direct appeal to charismatic possible

III. Rational application of technical rules and norms
  A. Specialized training
  B. Systematic control of office
  C. Rules applied by trained administrators/vertical networks
	III. Control through socialization
	  A. intense, prolonged contact with peers and seniors
	  B. Minimal oversight of office
	  C. Peer pressure enforces desired behaviors; strong social networks
		III. Control problematic emulation of founder and her vision
		  A. Intense dedication toward charismatic
		  B. Minimal oversight of office duties and status may change suddenly
		  C. Charismatic's rewards and punishment enforce behavior, weak networks

IV. Files record rules, decisions	IV. Oral tradition and visits founder between units provide organizational memory	IV. Emulation of charismatic
V. Selection and promotion by competence	V. Selection and promotion by ascription (age, seniority, networks)	V. Selection by response to "call" of charismatic, promotion by individual charisma and by proximity to charismatic

VI. Separation between individual and office
  A. Separation of individual and means of production
  B. Nonappropriation of positions
  C. Full-time, salaried career
	VI. Overlap between individual status and office
	  A. Organization begins as extension of household
	  B. Founder appropriates leadership of congregation
	  C. Uncompensated, honorific positions
		VI. Concept of office under-developed
		  A. Organization is extension of individual
		  B. Founder appropriates leadership and often resources
		  C. Tendency toward gifts, booty, campaigns, irregular compensation

Moreover, the same denominations differ radically in their performance between nations. While there are doubtless a number of factors unrelated to authority type and its organizational correlates that influence the growth and stability of the churches discussed, the comparative performance of the organizations discussed varies in ways that are intuitively consistent with the observations made about authority type and organization and that have clear theoretical implications. Below, I briefly describe the performance of the three churches in the U.S. and Brazil. Under the rubric "performance" I have included the organizational outcomes of growth, uniformity both within and between national movements, and the frequency of disruptive events, specifically schisms and scandals. These outcomes are included because they are frequently sought (or avoided) by many organizations, especially churches. For churches, growth and uniformity are two of the most universally sought-after outcomes (Niebuhr, 1929; McKinney, 1979; Wagner, 1979). Growth is also central to the system-resource model of effectiveness (Yuchtman and Seashore, 1967). Schisms and scandals appear to be particularly traumatic to churches and injurious to their legitimacy (Niebuhr, 1929; Takayama, 1980).

The Christian Congregations

The Christian Congregations have united impressive growth with harmony and institutional stability in Brazil. They have generated no major splinter groups, despite a notorious propensity toward schism in Latin American Protestantism (Willems, 1967; De Souza, 1969; LaLive, 1970; Flora, 1977; Perreira, 1979; Nelson, 1988b). There is also great uniformity in church practices and member behaviors throughout the denomination. Meeting format does not vary; preaching styles, vocabulary, and content are similar; the architecture and layout of churches are similar; meetings begin and end punctually; and buildings are kept spotlessly clean. Very little deviation from church mores regarding extramarital sex, tobacco and alcohol, and dress and grooming occurs among practicing members. This uniformity is found not only among the Brazilian congregations but extends to the North American churches, which are almost indistinguishable from the Brazilian churches except for the language used.

In Brazil, growth has been impressive. The Christian Congregations are the second largest Protestant body in Brazil, with about 2.5 million members (Assembleias de Deus, 1982). Over the last decade, the CCs have added between 40,000 and 60,000 new members yearly (Congregacao Crista no Brasil, 1982, 1991). This is particularly impressive when one considers that the Christian Congregations have no paid clergy and sponsor no formal proselytizing.

The experience of the Christian Congregations in the U.S. has been less enviable. After founder Francescon and his churches parted ways with other pioneers of the pentecostal movement in Chicago, the Christian Congregations suffered three major schisms. The first and largest separated Francescon's original congregation from the rest of the movement he founded. The larger movement, from which Francescon withdrew, became known as the Christian Church of North America, a highly amorphous federation of pentecostal churches now totaling about 12,000 members. It bears little resemblance to the original churches. Francescon's original congregation, now called the Christian Congregation Church, suffered two additional schisms. Both schisms, as well as Francescon's exit from the present-day Christian Church of North America arose from proposals to change the body to be more in line with American cultural patterns and bureaucratic organizing principles (Christian Church of North America, 1977; personal communication, Episcopo, 1992). In the last split, the Brazilian congregations undertook the sponsorship of dissidents from the original congregation who resisted changes in church practices. The dissidents built their own church some two miles from the original congregation. This body, called the Christian Congregation in the United States, is identical to the Christian Congregation in Brazil.

The original body (the Christian Congregation Church) has dwindled to about 250 active members, a majority of which are children of the original Italian immigrant founders. The Christian Congregation in the U.S. has about 500 members scattered across some 20 locations around the United States (personal communication, Spina, 1992). At least half of the membership is Hispanic, including many recent immigrants from Latin America. Brazilian immigrants are the senior elders of the oldest congregation in Chicago and numerous other congregations.

The Assemblies of God

The Assemblies of God have experienced extremely rapid growth in the U.S. and extraordinary growth in Brazil. The AG have been the United States' fastest growing denomination for several years running (Jacquet and Jones, 1991), and in Brazil, the AG have been the fastest growing church for at least a decade (Read, 1973; Assembleias de Deus, 1982). American membership now stands at about 2.2 million (Jacquet and Jones, 1991). In Brazil, the Assemblies are the country's largest Protestant denomination, with 7.5 million, about three times the size of the Christian Congregations, which hold second place.

Much AG growth may likely be attributed to the motivation and charisma of their pastors. Observers of Protestantism in the U.S. and Latin America have noted the resourcefulness and entrepreneurial genius of many AG pastors (Harrell, 1975; Hadden and Swann, 1981; Stoll, 1990). For years, the two most-watched American televangelists were AG pastors, and the two largest single congregations of any denomination in Brazil are churches founded by AG pastors (Hadden and Swann, 1981; personal communication, Braithwaite, 1993). Ministries undertaken by AG pastors without denominational impetus or support include orphanages, retirement centers, theme parks, periodicals, publishing houses, foreign missions, traveling revivals, radio and TV stations, patriotic rallies, gospel talk shows, retreats, schools, and seminaries (Harrell, 1975; Bakker, 1976; Stoll, 1990).

The dynamism and growth of the AG have been accompanied by heterogeneity, conflict, schism, and frequent scandals in both the U.S. and Brazil. In Brazil, two major denominations, Brazil para Cristo and Deus e Amor, are breakaways from the Assemblies, and a recent conflict has resulted in two national conventions, each using the name "Assemblies of God." Many smaller splinter groups have also come about from frequent conflicts within and between churches (Martin, 1990). In the U.S. a whole branch of American pentecostalism (the "oneness" denominations) resulted from an early theological disagreement in the Assemblies (Bloch-Hoell, 1964; Nichol, 1966; Anderson, 1979). In addition, several churches left the AG because their pastors had disagreements with the denomination or because they felt no need for further denominational affiliation, and there is a marked tendency for the AG's most famous clergy to leave the church. Nationally known evangelists who have severed association with the AG over the years include Aimee Semple McPherson, A. A. Allen, Kenneth Hagin, David Wilkerson, David DuPlessis, and Jack Coe.

There is almost no formal coordination and little uniformity between the AG in the U.S. and Brazil (Vingren, 1970; Poloma, 1989; Martin, 1990; Stoll, 1990). Some American pastors provide specialized ministries to Brazil, but their role is purely advisory and their services are rendered to specific churches, not to the denomination as a whole (personal communication, Braithwaite, 1993; personal communication, Harrison, 1993). Aside from limited cooperation and the general tenets of pentecostal ideology, the national bodies have little in common.

Within nations, individual churches share some commonalities and are connected by informal and some formal contacts, but congregations vary extensively in their worship practices, doctrine, administration, and theology. Many AG churches do not even include "Assembly of God" in their titles. And as mentioned before, acrimonious public disputes between pastors and informal rivalries between churches are not uncommon (Harrell, 1975; Anderson, 1979; Goff, 1988; Poloma, 1989).

Scandals involving AG ministers are endemic. Throughout denomination history, numerous cases of misappropriation of funds, fraudulent miracles, illicit sex, and substance abuse have caused embarrassment and defections. At least 20 of the prominent AG pastors listed in the *Dictionary of Pentecostal and Charismatic Movements* (Burgess and McGee, 1988) have been implicated in one type of indiscretion or another. Although other denominations have had problems in this regard, the AG seems to have been particularly afflicted. By contrast, the Christian Congregations and LDS churches seem to have been relatively free of scandal.

The Latter Day Saints

Like the Christian Congregations in Brazil, the LDS church in the U.S. has combined rapid growth with uniformity and stability. Since the succession crises incident to the death of Joseph Smith in 1844, no major schisms have developed. U.S. membership currently stands at about 4.3 million, and the church consistently ranks among the fastest growing U.S. denominations (Jacquet and Jones, 1991). Although Mormonism was founded some 80 years before the AG and CCs, the fact that most of the growth in all three bodies has come since World War II makes current membership figures somewhat indicative of comparative growth rates.

Units are rigorously uniform in structure, functioning, theology, and practice in the U.S. and Brazil, and strict adherence to LDS behavioral standards is required of active members in all congregations in both the U.S. and Brazil. As with the CCs, scandals involving LDS leaders have been very rare in either country.

LDS growth in Brazil has been slow compared with the other two bodies. In 1992, there were some 400,000 on church membership rolls in Brazil (Ensign, 1993), about a sixteenth of the membership of the CCs, and less than 6 percent of AG membership in that nation. Moreover, this growth was achieved with the help of literally tens of thousands of volunteer American missionaries over the years. The CCs and AG in Brazil have been largely independent of foreign financial and human resource contributions. Furthermore, retaining converts to the LDS in Brazil is more problematic than in the U.S. It is not uncommon for congregations with 500 members of record to have average worship attendance of less than 150, while an American congregation of the same size would tend to have average attendance of around 250 (Read, 1973; personal communication, De Oliveira, 1993). Table 12.2 summarizes the performance dimensions discussed for the three bodies in the U.S. and Brazil. Below, I explore theoretical explanations for these performance differences and inductively develop specific propositions about authority type, organizational performance, and societal context.

AUTHORITY, PERFORMANCE, AND SOCIETY

The nature and performance of the churches studied have implications for existing theory and suggest propositions that go beyond current theory. For Weberian theory, the discovery of organizations using different authority bases

TABLE 12.2 Performance Attributes of Three Churches Studied

Performance	Growth	Uniformity	Schisms	Scandals	International uniformity
Christian Congregations (traditional)					
In U.S.	Very low	High	Moderate	Few	Uniform
In Brazil	Very high	High	Low	Few	
Assemblies of God (charismatic)					
In U.S.	Very high	Low	High	Many	Minimal uniformity
In Brazil	Extremely high	Low	High	Many	
LDS (legal-rational)					
In U.S.	Very high	High	Low	Few	Uniform
In Brazil	Low	High	Low	Few	

and competing in the same organizational field has several implications. First, it demonstrates that even in highly rationalized, capitalistic societies like the U.S., charismatic and traditional authority can offer viable alternatives for legitimizing complex organizations. Thus the door of the "iron cage" has remained ajar through the years. The survival and prosperity of the charisma-based Assemblies of God also suggest that permanent institutions can be based on unroutinized charisma, a conclusion that Weber himself might question but that students of Weber's thought seem to accept (Schweitzer, 1984; Biggart, 1989; Schluchter, 1989).

At the same time, the fortunes of the three churches in these two nations suggest that while societies are not rigorously homogeneous in the authority types that support their institutions, the social environment can favor one authority type over another. Thus, the bureaucratic LDS church has grown rapidly in the bureaucratic U.S. and slowly in more traditional Brazil, while the traditional Christian Congregations have grown rapidly in Brazil and slowly in the U.S. Such isomorphism is posited both in Weber's original work and its derivatives (Stinchcombe, 1965; Langton, 1984) as well as in modern institutional theory.

Weber associated charisma with change and stress in social systems (Eisenstadt, 1968; Weber, 1968; Bensmen and Givant, 1975), so the extraordinary growth of the Assemblies of God in Brazil seems logical, given the rapid industrialization, urbanization, and social dislocation that have characterized that country from midcentury on (Smith, 1963, 1972; Guerreiro Ramos, 1968). The vigorous but more modest growth of the AG in the U.S. might similarly be attributed to lesser but significant social upheavals in this country. The almost pandemic incidence of charismatic movements and leaders around the globe, however (Lacouture, 1970; De Queiroz, 1977; Lindholm, 1990), leads one to suspect that Weber was overly pessimistic about the long-term prospects of charisma in the modern age.

The study of these three churches also has implications for institutional theory. The comparative performance of the churches in the U.S. and Brazil suggests that isomorphism does not automatically favor the propagation of increasingly bureaucratic organizations. This assumption is implicit in the institutional literature generally (a possible exception being Orru, Biggart, and Hamilton's 1991 work) but is contradicted by the prosperity of the Christian Congregations in Brazil. More important, insofar as traditional and charismatic organizations share fields with bureaucratic organizations, they likely provide resistance to isomorphic pressures and reduce the homogeneity of organizational fields. This suggests a connection between institutional theory and sociology of religion that has not been exploited. Classical church-sect theory (Niebuhr, 1929; Troeltsch, 1931; O'Dea, 1957) suggests that religious organizations bureaucratize as they grow and age. This is a concept familiar enough to organization theorists (e.g., Blau and Schoenherr, 1971; Kimberly and Miles, 1980). What is unique about church-sect theory is its observation that bureaucratization alienates portions of the church clientele, resulting in schismatic pressures that create nonbureaucratic (probably charismatic or traditional) organizations. It is possible then, that the internal dynamics of churches generate resistance to bureaucratic isomorphism. Independent of the specific mechanism, however, the experience of the churches studied suggests that institutional theorists may need to pay more attention to the sources of resistance to isomorphism in addition to factors that favor isomorphic response.

At the same time that the study of these churches suggests factors that may resist isomorphism and introduce heterogeneity, their performance across nations reinforces the contention of both Weberian and institutional theory that isomorphic pressures influence the fortunes of organizations, and it offers clues as to how these pressures play out across nations and different authority types. Not only do isomorphic pressures appear to differ by nation, but organizational susceptibility to these pressures seems to vary by authority type.

Judging from its performance in Brazil and the U.S., the traditional Christian Congregations would appear to be most susceptible to isomorphic pressures. In Brazil, which still retains a relatively stable core of traditional values (Smith, 1963, 1972; Guerreiro Ramos, 1968; DaMata, 1978) the CCs have attained wide acceptance, while their appeal in the U.S. has been limited largely to small numbers of Latin immigrants. Schisms in the American congregations that have arisen over issues of secularization and bureaucratization also suggest susceptibility to isomorphism. The few American congregations that emerged from the schisms unaltered, however, are identical in almost all particulars to the Brazilian congregations. Thus, it may be possible that even in adverse environments, traditional organizations can develop a small core of faithful followers that is capable of resisting isomorphic pressures.

The attenuation of extended family and neighborhood social networks through affluence, mobility, and the institutionalization of society (Lemasters, 1954; Schwartzweller, 1964; Berardo, 1967) has probably deprived the American congregations of their major recruitment and control mechanism. This attenuation, along with the role of modernization in eroding the acceptance of any homogeneous set of traditional values (Riesman, 1950; Durkheim, 1951; Berger, 1979), may do more than impair the functioning of traditional social forms. It might also create a "social vacuum" to be filled by bureaucratic institutions. It is possible, therefore, that isomorphism is effected not only by the "push" of mimetic, coercive, and normative pressures but also by the "pull" of eroding institutions.

The bureaucratic LDS church follows a growth pattern that is almost the exact inverse of the Christian Congregations: rapid growth in the U.S. versus stunted growth in Brazil. This is consistent with my assumption that the vigor of traditional institutions in Brazil favors the growth of tradition-based churches, while the density of bureaucratic forms in the U.S. favors the growth of bureaucratic churches here.

By contrast, the absence of schisms in either country and the procedural and structural homogeneity of the LDS church in both countries suggest that the bureaucratic form may be more resistant to centrifugal forces from the social environment than traditional organizations. The internal logics of bureaucratic versus traditional organization summarized in Table 12.1 provide reasons why this may be the case. The centrality of socialization as the principal means of control and the overlap between individual status and office probably make the traditional organization rather permeable to the social norms and institutional patterns of the host society. The bureaucracy, with its unambiguous written codes, systematic oversight of office, and universalistic controls should be much more resistant to environmental pressures toward deviation. This property probably makes it easier for bureaucracies to maintain homogeneity across units in different nations.

The charismatic AG appears to be equally immune to the bureaucratic isomorphism of the U.S. and the traditional isomorphism of Brazil. The body has grown rapidly in both countries without wholesale incorporation of either traditional or bureaucratic elements in its design. This is consistent with Weber's writings, which portray charisma as independent of if not opposed to rational-legal and traditional authority. It would appear, however, that the independence of the AG has been purchased at the cost of internal uniformity and control both within and between nations. Still, the fact that the AG continues to survive and grow as a recognizable entity, despite its schisms, scandals, and lack of uniformity, suggests that unroutinized charisma can provide a viable basis for ongoing organizations in different societies.

Neither Weberian nor institutional theory has articulated specific predictions about the comparative performance of diverse authority systems across nations. In closing, I suggest several propositions about the organizational outcomes of bureaucratic, traditional, and charismatic organizations as they diffuse across national boundaries. These propositions are straightforward extensions of the discussion above and might provide hypotheses for future confirmatory research on *herrschaft* and complex organizations:

Charismatic churches will (1) have broad appeal across a variety of cultures; (2) have particular appeal in periods of rapid social change or stress; (3) attract talented but individualistic leaders; (4) generate many of their own competitors through schisms; (5) experience difficulty maintaining a consistent image, ideology, and internal control; and (6) be almost incapable of implementing uniform policies across nations.

Bureaucratic churches will (1) grow more rapidly in post-traditional societies than in traditional or transitional societies; (2) be capable of maintaining a consistent image, ideology, and control independent of the host culture; (3) attain greater uniformity cross-nationally than either charismatic or traditional churches; (4) experience fewer schisms than charismatic churches generally; (5) experience fewer schisms than traditional churches operating in post-traditional societies; and (6) dedicate proportionately greater resources to explicit administrative control mechanisms than traditional or charismatic churches.

Traditional churches will (1) grow more rapidly in traditional or transitional societies than in post-traditional societies; (2) experience more schisms in post-traditional societies than in traditional societies; (3) be capable of maintaining a consistent image, ideology and control with a minimum of formal administrative mechanisms; (4) experience less internal conflict and fewer succession disputes than bureaucratic or charismatic churches; (5) experience easier recruitment and less member deviance in host societies with dense social networks; and (6) maintain cross-national uniformity across nations at the expense of growth in post-traditional countries.

CONCLUSIONS

The theoretical discussion and subsequent propositions above are drawn from the interchange of relevant Weberian thought and descriptions of three churches in two countries. Only future research can assess the generalizability of these findings to other churches or for other types of organizations in other countries. The very factors that make churches a good site for exploring linkages between authority, organization, and society make it somewhat difficult to apply the insights gained to other organizational fields. The propositions advanced here will probably be more useful for the study of clubs, labor unions, political parties, charities, and other normative (Etzioni, 1961) bodies to a much greater degree than for utilitarian or coercive organizations, although one dissertation (Reiss, 1979) has identified traditional, charismatic/patrimonial, and bureaucratic firms among Brazilian industrial concerns.

Probably the most logical next step in studying *herrschaft* and organization is to estimate the comparative frequency of authority types in specific organizational fields. The generalizability of the propositions advanced is of limited interest if charismatic and tradition-based organizations are an anomaly found only in a few religious organizations. By the same token, the consequences of different authority types will be of greater importance in fields that are not populated by one predominant authority system. Assuming the attributes of charismatic and traditional organizations identified in Table 12.1 are an accurate depiction of organizational forms that accompany different authority types, they could serve as a guide to research on the distribution of authority types in organizational fields.

Similarly, the template developed in Table 12.1 could be used to ascertain the degree to which diverse authority types coexist within organizations. In the same way that Weber was mute about the possible coexistence of diverse authority types within societies, he did not elaborate how complex organizations might employ multiple authority systems. Yet just as the ideal-typical bureaucracy probably does not exist in reality, it is likely that some organizations, whether successfully or dysfunctionally, contain multiple or hybrid authority systems. The study of authority and organization will remain in its infancy until this question is studied also.

Another area that will require further study is possible variation within authority types. Weber's treatment of bureaucracy and charisma suggests that the institutional forms they produce are rather homogenous, while traditional authority would appear to produce a fairly broad range of institutional arrangements. One major axis of differentiation in traditional authority is the degree of caprice afforded traditional leaders. Under patrimonialism, one major subtype, the leader frequently holds almost unlimited power (Murvar, 1985). Under feudalism, another important category, traditions constrain the leader's caprice in important ways, despite the nominal obligation of personal loyalty on the part of followers. In the CCs, personal arbitrariness appears to be highly limited, but more patrimonial forms are certainly conceivable. Further work needs to ascertain the degree of variation within authority types and to catalogue specific institutional manifestations associated with authority types or subtypes. Such work, like the other research proposed here, would probably best be done on individual organizational fields. Traditional and charismatic authority may not be important sources of legitimation for all, or even a majority of organizations, but, if we ignore the richness and power of Weber's theory of *herrschaft* and its cross-national implications, we are likely to understand little about the many organizations that are not based on rational-legal principles.

NOTES

1. I am indebted to Thomas Burger for this point.

2. Because these bodies (particularly the Assemblies of God) vary in their degree of interunit control and cohesion, particularly at the strategic apex, one reviewer has suggested that the term "denomination" rather than "church" is most appropriate. Accordingly, excepting in passages in which such usage proves excessively repetitive, I use the term "denomination" or "body" when referring to the movement as a whole. All three denominations, however, satisfy Aldrich's (1979) definition of organizations as "goal oriented, boundary maintaining, activity systems."

REFERENCES

Aldrich, Howard E. 1979. *Organizations and Environments*. Englewood Cliffs, NJ: Prentice Hall.

Anderson, Robert Mapes. 1979. *Vision of the Disinherited: The Making of American Pentecostalism*. New York: Oxford University Press.

Arrington, Leonard J., and Davis Biton. 1979. *The Mormon Experience*. New York: Knopf.

Assembleias de Deus. 1982. *A historia das Assembleias de Deus*. Rio: Casa Publicadora das Assembleias de Deus.

Assemblies of God. 1976. *Qualifications and Responsibilities of Deacons and Trustees*. Springfield, MO: Gospel Publishing.

———.1982. *Who We Are and What We Believe*. Springfield, MO: Gospel Publishing.

Bakker, Jim. 1976. *Move That Mountain*. Charlotte, NC: PTL Television Network.

Barnhart, Joe E. 1988. *Jim and Tammy: Charismatic Intrigue Inside the PTL*. Buffalo, NY: Prometheus Books.

Barrett, Ivan J. 1979. *Joseph Smith and the Restoration*. Provo, UT: Brigham Young University Press.

Bendix, Reinhard. 1962. *Max Weber: An Intellectual Portrait*. New York: Anchor.

Bensmen, Joseph, and Michael Givant. 1975. "Charisma and modernity." *Social Research*, 42: 570–614.

Berardo, Felix M. 1967. "Kinship interaction and communications among space age migrants." *Journal of Marriage and the Family*, 29: 541–544.

Berger, Peter L. 1979. *The Heretical Imperative*. New York: Anchor-Doubleday.

Biggart, Nicole Woolsey. 1989. *Charismatic Capitalism: Direct Selling Organizations in America*. Chicago: University of Chicago Press.

Blau, Peter M., and Richard A. Schoenherr. 1971. *The Structure of Organizations* New York: Basic Books.

Bloch-Hoell, Nils. 1964. *The Pentecostal Movement: Its Origin, Development, and Distinctive Character*. Copenhagen: Universitetsforlaget.

Blumhofer, Edith Waldvogel. 1985. *The Assemblies of God: A Popular History*. Springfield, MO: Gospel Publishing.

———.1989. *The Assemblies of God: A Chapter in the Story of American Pentecostalism*. Springfield, MO: Gospel Publishing.

Braithwaite, Bruce. 1993. Assembly of God missionary to Brazil. Personal communication.

Burgess, S. M., and G. B. McGee (eds.). 1988. *Dictionary of Pentecostal and Charismatic Movements*. Grand Rapids, MI: Zondervan.

Campbell, Donald T. 1988. *Methodology and Epistemology for the Social Sciences*. Chicago: University of Chicago Press.

———.1991. "Coherentist empiricism, heremeneutics, and the commensurability of paradigms." *International Journal of Educational Research*, 15: 587–597.

Carmic, Charles. 1980. "Charisma: Its varieties, preconditions and consequences." *Sociological Inquiry,* 50: 5–23.

Cassanova, Jose V. 1984. "Interpretations and misinterpretations of Max Weber: The problem of rationalization." In Ronald M. Glassman and Vatro Murvar (eds.), *Max Weber's Political Sociology:* 141–154. Westport, CT: Greenwood Press.

Christian Church of North America. 1977. Stephan Galvano (ed.), *Fiftieth Anniversary Book.* Sharon, PA: General Council, CCNA.

Clark, Burton R. 1970. *The Distinctive College: Antioch, Reed, and Swarthmore.* Chicago: Aldine.

Collins, Randall. 1980. "Weber's last theory of capitalism: A systematization." *American Sociological Review,* 45: 925–942.

———.1986. *Weberian Sociological Theory.* Cambridge: Cambridge University Press.

Conger, Jay A., and Rabindra N. Kanungo. 1988. "Behavioral dimensions of charismatic leadership." In Jay A. Conger, Rabindra N. Kanungo, and Associates (eds.), *Charismatic Leadership: The Elusive Factor in Organizational Effectiveness:* 78–97. San Francisco: Jossey-Bass.

Congregacao Crista no Brasil. 1962. *Fe, doutrina, e estatutos.* Sao Paulo: Congregacao Crista no Brasil.

———.1982. *Enderecos e Informacoes Estatisticas.* Sao Paulo: Congregacao Crista no Brasil.

———.1991. *Enderecos e Informacoes Estatisticas.* Sao Paulo: Congregacao Crista no Brasil.

DaMata, Roberto. 1978. *Carnavais, malandros e herois.* Rio: Zahar.

Deal, Terrence E., and Allan Kennedy. 1982. *Corporate Cultures.* Reading, MA: Addison-Wesley.

De Caro, Louis. 1977. *Our Heritage: The Christian Church of North America.* Sharon, PA: General Council, CCNA.

De Oliveira, Saul Messias. 1993. Personal communication, former regional representative of the quorum of the twelve, LDS church.

De Queiroz, Maria Isaura Perreira. 1977. *Messianismo no Brasil no mundo.* Sao Paulo: Edicoes Alpha-Omega.

De Souza, Beatriz Muniz. 1969. *A experiencia da salvacao.* Sao Paulo: Duas Cidades.

DiMaggio, Paul J., and Walter W. Powell. 1983. "The iron cage revisited: Institutional isomorphism and collective rationality in organizational fields." *American Sociological Review,* 48: 147–160.

———. 1991. "Introduction." In Walter W. Powell and Paulo J. DiMaggio (eds.), *The New Institutionalism in Organizational Analysis:* 1–40. Chicago: University of Chicago Press.

Dos Santos, Ubirijara. 1989. Personal communication, Christian Congregation member of Sorocaba, Brazil.

Durkheim, Emile. 1951. *Suicide.* New York: Free Press.

Dyer, Gibb W., Jr. 1986. "The cycle of cultural evolution in organizations." In Ralph H. Kilmann, Mary J. Saxton, Roy Serpa, and Associates (eds.), *Gaining Control of Corporate Culture:* 200–229. San Francisco: Jossey-Bass.

Eisenstadt, S. N. 1968. "Introduction." In *Max Weber on Charisma and Institution Building.* Chicago: University of Chicago Press.

Ensign of the Church of Jesus Christ of Latter Day Saints. 1993. "Burgeoning Brazil: The blessings and challenges of growth." January: 79–80.

Episcopo, Joseph. 1992. Personal communication, elder of the Christian Congregation Church, Chicago, IL.

Erutti, Leonard. n.d. *The Life and Mission of Peter Ottolini.* St. Louis, MO: Italian Evangelical Church.

Etzioni, Amatai. 1961. *The Comparative Analysis of Complex Organizations.* New York: Free Press.

Farao, Roberto. 1958. *Os donos do poder.* Porto Alegre: Editora Globo.

Fest, Joaquim C. 1973. *Hitler, eine biographie.* Frankfurt am Main: Verlag Uhlstein.

Flora, Cornelia Butler. 1977. *Baptism of Fire and of the Spirit: Pentecostalism in Colombia.* Cranbury, NJ: Associated University Presses.

Francescon, Louis. 1952. *Testimentary Document.* Chicago: Christian Congregation Church.

Glaser, Barney G., and Anselm L. Strauss. 1967. *The Discovery of Grounded Theory: Strategies for Qualitative Research.* Chicago: Aldine.

Glaser, W. A. 1971. "Cross-national comparisons of the factory." *Journal of Comparative Administration,* May: 83–117.

Glassman, Ronald M. 1984. "Manufactured charisma and legitimacy." In Ronald M. Glassman and Vatro Murvar (eds.), *Max Weber's Political Sociology:* 141–154. Westport, CT: Greenwood Press.

Goff, J. R. 1988. *Fields White unto Harvest: Charles F. Parham and the Missionary Origins of Pentecostalism.* Fayetteville, AR: University of Arkansas Press.

Gottlieb, Robert, and Peter Wiley. 1984. *America's Saints: The Rise of Mormon Power.* New York: Putnam.

Graver, J. R. 1971. *Pentecostalism.* New York: Award Books.

Guerreiro Ramos, Alberto. 1968. *Administracao e estrategia de desenvolvimento.* Rio de Janeiro: Fundacao Getulio Vargas.

Hadden, Jeffrey K., and Charles E. Swann. 1981. *Prime Time Preachers: The Rising Power of Televangelism.* Reading, MA: Addison-Wesley.

Hadden, Jeffrey K., and Anson Shupe. 1988. *Televangelism.* New York: Henry Holt.

Haffner, Sebastian. 1979. *The Meaning of Hitler.* Cambridge, MA: Harvard University Press.

Harrell, Richard. 1975. *All Things Are Possible.* Bloomington, IN: Indiana University Press.

Harrison, David. 1993. Personal communication, Assemblies of God missionary to Brazil.

Heinerman, John, and Anson Shupe. 1985. *The Mormon Corporate Empire.* Boston: Beacon Press.

Heydebrand, Wolf V. 1973. *Comparative Organizations: The Results of Empirical Research.* Englewood Cliffs, NJ: Prentice Hall.

Hickson, David J., C. R. Hinings, C. J. McMillan, and J. P. Schwitter. 1974. "The culture free context of organizational structure: A tri-national comparison." *Sociology,* 8: 59–80.

Hollenweger, Walter J. 1972. *The Pentecostals.* Minneapolis: Augsburg Publishing.

House, Robert J. 1977. "A 1976 theory of charismatic leadership." In James G. Hunt and Lars L. Larson (eds.), *Leadership: The Cutting Edge:* 189–273. Carbondale, IL: Southern Illinois University Press.

Inkson, J., Derek S. Pugh, and David J. Hickson. 1970. "Organizational context and structure: An abbreviated replication." *Administrative Science Quarterly,* 15: 318–329.

Jacquet, Constant H., and Alice M. Jones (eds.). 1991. *Yearbook of American and Canadian Churches,* vol. 59. Nashville: Abingdon Press.

Kimberly, John R., and Raymond Miles. 1980. *The Organizational Life Cycle: Issues in the Creation, Transformation and Decline of Organizations.* San Francisco: Jossey-Bass.

Knoke, David, and David Prensky. 1984. "What relevance do organization theories have for voluntary associations?" *Social Science Quarterly,* 65: 3–20.

Lacouture, Jean. 1970. *The Demigods: Charismatic Leadership in the Third World.* New York: Knopf.

LaLive, Christian D. E. 1970. *O refugio das massas.* Rio: Paz e Terra.

Lammers, Cornelis J., and David J. Hickson. 1979. *Organizations Alike and Unlike: International and Interinstitutional Studies in the Sociology of Organizations.* London: Routledge and Kegan Paul.

Langton, John. 1984. "The ecological theory of bureaucracy: The case of Josiah Wedgwood and the British pottery industry." *Administrative Science Quarterly,* 29: 330–354.

Lemasters, E. E. 1954. "Social class mobility and family integration." *Journal of Marriage and the Family,* 16: 226–232.

Leonard, Emilio. 1963. *O Protestantismo Brasileiro.* Sao Paulo: ASTE.

Lindholm, Charles. 1990. *Charisma.* Oxford: Basil Blackwell.

Martin, David. 1990. *Tongues of Fire: The Explosion of Protestantism in Latin America.* Oxford: Basil Blackwell.

Maurice, Marc. 1979. "For a study of the societal effect: Universality and specificity in organization research." In Cornelis J. Lammers and David J. Hickson (eds.), *Organizations Alike and Unlike:* 42–60. London: Routledge and Kegan Paul.

McKinney, William J., Jr. 1979. "Performance of United Church of Christ congregations in Massachusetts and in Pennsylvania." In Dean R. Hoge and David A. Roozen (eds.), *Understanding Church Growth and Decline: 1950–1978:* 224–247. New York: Pilgrim Press.

Menzies, William W. 1971. *Anointed to Serve: The Story of the Assemblies of God.* Springfield, MO: Gospel Publishing.

Meyer, John W., and Brian Rowan. 1977. "Institutionalized organization: Formal structure as myth and ceremony." *American Journal of Sociology,* 83: 340–363.

Meyer, Marshall W. 1972. *Bureaucratic Structure and Authority: Coordination and Control in 254 Government Agencies.* New York: Harper and Row.

Mitzman, Arthur. 1969. *The Iron Cage: An Historical Interpretation of Max Weber.* New York: Knopf.

Miyahara, Kifiro. 1983. "Charisma: From Weber to contemporary sociology." *Sociological Inquiry,* 53: 368–388.

Murvar, Vatro. 1985. "Patrimonialism, modern and traditionalist: A paradigm for interdisciplinary research on rulership and legitimacy." In V. Murvar (ed.), *Theory of Liberty, Legitimacy and Power:* 40–86. London: Routledge and Kegan Paul.

Nelson, Benjamin. 1974. "Max Weber's author's introduction (1920): A master clue to his main aims." *Sociological Inquiry,* 44: 269–278.

Nelson, Reed E. 1978. "Cultural environment and organization design in a Brazilian pentecostal sect." Unpublished M.A. thesis, Brigham Young University.

———. 1984. "Analise organizacional de uma igreja brasileira: A Congregacao Crista no Brasil." *Revista Eclesiastica Brasileira,* 44: 544–558.

———. 1985. "Funcoes organizacionais do culto numa igreja anarquista." *Religiao e Sociedade,* 12 (1): 112–126.

———. 1988a. "Five principles of indigenous church organization." *Missiology,* 17: 40–51.

———. 1988b. "Organizational homogeneity, growth and conflict in Brazilian protestantism." *Sociological Analysis,* 48: 319–327.

———. 1989. "Organization-environment isomorphism, rejection, and substitution in Brazilian protestantism." *Organization Studies,* 10: 207–224.

Nichol, John Thomas. 1966. *Pentecostalism.* New York: Harper and Row.

Niebuhr, H. Richard. 1929. *The Social Sources of Denominationalism.* New York: Henry Holt.

O'Dea, Thomas. 1957. *The Mormons.* Chicago: University of Chicago Press.

Organski, A. F. K. 1965. *The Stages of Political Development.* New York: Knopf.

Orru, Marco, Nicole Woolsey Biggart, and Gary G. Hamilton. 1991. "Organizational isomorphism in East Asia." In Walter W. Powell and Paul J. DiMaggio (eds.), *The New Institutionalism in Organizational Analysis:* 361–389. Chicago: University of Chicago Press.

Ottolini, Pietro. 1945. *Storia dell'opera italiana.* Trenton, NJ: Merlo's Publishing.

Ouchi, William G. 1975. "Markets, bureaucracies, and clans." *Administrative Science Quarterly,* 24: 570–581.

Parsons, Talcott. 1947. "Introduction." In *Max Weber, The Theory of Social and Economic Organization:* 1–86. New York: Free Press.

Parsons, Talcott, and Neil J. Smelser. 1956. *Economy and Society: A Study in the Integration of Economic and Social Theory.* Glencoe, IL: Free Press.

Perreira, Jose Reis. 1979. *A historia dos batistas no Brasil.* Sao Paulo: Casa Publicadora Batista.

Perrow, Charles. 1979. *Complex Organizations: A Critical Essay,* 2d ed. Glenview, IL: Scott, Foresman.

Pettigrew, Andrew M. 1979. "On studying organizational cultures." *Administrative Science Quarterly,* 24: 570–581.

Poloma, Margret M. 1989. *The Assemblies of God at the Crossroads: Charisma and Institutional Dilemmas.* Knoxville: University of Tennessee Press.

Pugh, Derek S., and David J. Hickson. 1976. *Organizational Structure and Its Context: The Aston Programme I.* Lexington, MA: Heath, Lexington Books.

Pugh, Derek S., David J. Hickson, C. R. Hinings, K. M. Macdonald, C. Turner, and T. Lupton. 1963. "A conceptual scheme for organizational analysis." *Administrative Science Quarterly,* 8: 289–315.

Read, William. 1973. *Brazil 1980: The Protestant Handbook.* Grand Rapids, MI: Erdmans.

Reiss, Gerald. 1979. "The development of Brazilian industrial enterprise: A historical perspective." Unpublished doctoral thesis, University of California at Berkeley.

Richmond, Barry, and Melvyn Copen. 1973. "Management techniques in developing nations." *Columbia Journal of World Business,* 8: 49–58.

Riesman, David. 1950. *The Lonely Crowd*. New Haven, CT: Yale University Press.

Rowstow, W. W. 1961. *The Stages of Economic Growth*. Cambridge: Cambridge University Press.

Schein, Edgar H. 1985. "The role of the founder in creating organizational culture." *Organizational Dynamics*, Summer: 13–28.

Scherer, Ross P. 1988. "A new typology for organizations: Market, bureaucracy, clan and mission, with application to American denominations." *Journal for the Scientific Study of Religion*, 27: 475–498.

Schluchter, Wolfgang. 1989. *Rationalism Religion and Domination: A Weberian Perspective*. Berkeley: University of California Press.

Schwarzweller, Harry K. 1964. "Parental family ties and social integration of rural to urban migrants." *Journal of Marriage and the Family*, 29: 662–670.

Schweitzer, Arthur. 1984. *The Age of Charisma*. Chicago: Nelson-Hall.

Scofield, Monte. 1993. Personal communication, Bishop of Marion, IL, Ward of the LDS Church.

Shipps, Jan. 1985. *Mormonism: The Story of a New Religious Tradition*. Urbana, IL: University of Illinois Press.

Smith, T. Lynn. 1963. *Brazil: People and Institutions*. Baton Rouge: Louisiana State University Press.

———. 1972. *Brazil: Portrait of Half a Continent*. Westport, CT: Greenwood Press.

Spina, Joel. 1992. Personal communication with an elder of the Christian Congregation in the United States.

Stinchcombe, Arthur. 1965. "Social structure and organizations." In James G. March (ed.), *Handbook of Organizations*: 142–193. Chicago: Rand McNally.

Stoll, David. 1990. *Is Latin America Turning Protestant?* Berkeley, CA: University of California Press.

Swatos, William. 1984. "Revolution and charisma in a rationalized world: Weber revisited and extended." In Ronald M. Glassman and Vatro Murvar (eds.), *Max Weber's Political Sociology*: 141–154. Westport, CT: Greenwood Press.

Takayama, K. Peter. 1980. "Strains, conflicts, and schisms in Protestant denominations." In Ross P. Scherer (ed.), *American Denominational Organization: A Sociological View*: 298–329. Pasadena, CA: William Carey Library.

Tenbruck, F. H. 1975. "Wie gut kennen wir Max Weber." *Zeitschrift fur Statswissenschaft*, 131: 719–742.

Trice, Harrison M., and Janice Beyer. 1986. "Charisma and its routinization in two social movement organizations." In Barry M. Staw and L. L. Cummings (eds.), *Research in Organizational Behavior*, 8: 113–164. Greenwich, CT: JAI Press.

Troeltsch, Ernst. 1931. *The Social Teachings of the Christian Churches*. New York: Macmillan.

Vingren, Gunnar. 1970. *Diario de um pioneiro*. Rio: Casa Publicadora das Assembleias de Deus.

Wagner, C. Peter. 1979. "Church growth research: The paradigm and its applications." In Dean R. Hoge and David A. Roozen (eds.), *Understanding Church Growth and Decline: 1950–1978*: 270–287. New York: Pilgrim Press.

Weber, Max. 1927. *General Economic History*. New York: Greenberg.

———. 1947. *The Theory of Social and Economic Organization*. New York: Free Press.

———. 1948. *The Protestant Ethic and the Spirit of Capitalism*. New York: Scribner.

———. 1968. *Economy and Society*. New York: Bedminster Press.

Wilkins, Alan L., and William G. Ouchi. 1983. "Efficient cultures: Exploring the relationship between culture and organizational performance." *Administrative Science Quarterly*, 28: 468–481.

Willems, Emillio. 1967. *Followers of the New Faith*. Nashville: Vanderbilt University Press.

Witt, Joan Rothschild. 1979. "The collectivist organization: An alternative to rational bureaucratic models." *American Sociological Review*, 44: 509–527.

Yuchtman, Ephraim, and Stanley Seashore. 1967. "A system resource approach to organizational effectiveness." *American Sociological Review*, 32: 891–903.

Zablocki, Benjamin. 1980. *Alienation and Charisma: A Study of Contemporary American Communes*. New York: Free Press.

13

THE DYNAMICS OF INSTITUTIONALIZATION
Transformation Processes in Norwegian Fisheries

Petter Holm

INTRODUCTION

What are institutions? How do they work? Are they created intentionally, or do they come about as unintended by-products? When and why do they change? Despite the renewed interest in institutions across the social sciences during the last decade or so, no consensus has emerged on these questions. There are basically two ways of thinking about institutions. From a rational perspective, institutions are perceived as efficient solutions to predefined problems (Olson, 1965; Williamson, 1975). Institutions are instruments and they can be understood in the context of the tasks for which they were created.

AUTHOR'S NOTE: The article was written with support from the John D. and Catherine T. MacArthur Foundation Grant No. 91-16567A and Norwegian Research Council Grant No. 1301-500.136. For helpful comments and suggestions, I wish to thank Richard Apostle, Hans Kristian Hernes, Svein Jentoft, Eva Munk-Madsen, Leigh Mazany, Knut H. Mikalsen, Arthur L. Stinchcombe, and two anonymous *ASQ* reviewers. Reprinted from *Administrative Science Quarterly*, 40 (Sept. 1995): 398–422.

This view may contribute insights about the function of institutions and why they change but is still problematic. It disregards an important aspect of what institutions are, namely, frameworks for action and, as such, outside the scope of strategic manipulation. The second way of thinking about institutions, represented by the new institutionalists in organizational theory (Meyer and Rowan, 1977; DiMaggio and Powell, 1983), focuses particularly on the aspects of institutions that are ignored by the rational school. The new institutionalists define institutions as "socially constructed, routine-reproduced, program or rule systems" (Jepperson, 1991: 149). The study of institutions is the study of norm-governed behavior. In this perspective, the processes by which institutions are formed and reformed, which tend to be interest-driven and highly political, have been ignored. The result is an institutional theory that cannot explain how institutions are created and how they change (DiMaggio and Powell, 1991).

I remain sympathetic to the new institutionalism in organizational theory. I believe, however, that institutionalists should not focus exclusively on situations that are ignored by rationalists, i.e., those in which actors do not see or are prevented from pursuing their interests (DiMaggio, 1988). Institutionalist analysis must include all types of behavior, including those driven by interests and power (DiMaggio and Powell, 1991). This can be achieved if we take seriously the insight that institutions, while they are products of action, also constitute action. To handle both sides of this equation, I propose that institutions be seen as nested systems, drawing a distinction between actions guided by the established institutional order, on the one hand, and actions geared toward creating new or changing old institutions, on the other. This perspective makes it possible to retain the insight that institutions are products of action, and therefore constructed for some purpose, without giving up the notion that institutions are frameworks for action, and therefore taken for granted.

Theoretical Issues

From a rational perspective, institutions help align individual and collective interests. When a group of interdependent rational individuals act independently and with regard to their own interests, and the pay-off structure is a prisoner's dilemma, the best option for each individual produces a suboptimal solution for the group as a whole. In this situation, the group may establish an institution in the form of an agreement that aligns individual and collective interests. The institution is the solution to the collective-action problem. For instance, each member of a village knows that a wall around it would make everyone more secure. Each also knows that if the others fail to contribute to the wall, it will not be built, and his or her contribution will be wasted. Since all of them prefer to free-ride, the wall will not be built. They therefore might agree to form an institution that compels everyone to contribute (Bates, 1988).

From a rational perspective, then, an institution is a means to reconcile the inherent contradiction between individual and collective interests. This way of thinking about institutions has been influential in rational choice theory (Elster, 1979; Taylor, 1987), agency theory (Alchian and Demsetz, 1972; Libecap, 1989), economic history (Chandler, 1962; North and Thomas, 1973), and institutional economics (Olson, 1965; Williamson, 1975) as well as in organizational theory (Thompson, 1967).

While this model can explain how institutions work, it cannot serve as an explanation for their creation. It ignores the second-order collective-action problem that arises in the attempt to solve the original problem. Even if every member of the group in question realizes that the original problem, the building of a wall, can be solved by some institution, the same incentive problem occurs in the institutional project itself. Each member prefers the others to take on the cost to initiate, construct, and monitor the institution. Since all members think this way, the institution will not be established (Olson, 1965; Bates, 1988; Ostrom, 1990). This conclusion, which is somewhat problematic, since institutions in fact are established, stems from the implicit assumption that the structures of the first-order and second-order collective-action problems are identical. The underlying frame of reference is the image of a society constituted by presocial, autonomous, and rational individuals.

Institutionalists do not confront this problem. From their perspective, the individual, rational actor is not regarded as a universal constant but as a social construct defined within a particular set of institutions (Thomas et al., 1987). New institutions are not created from scratch but are built upon older institutions and must replace or push back preexisting institutional forms. There is no problem of infinite regress here. The question of the first institution has no meaning within institutional theory, since neither society nor individual actors can exist without institutions. Instead of the theoretical problem of the first institution, institutional theory must handle the empirical problem of describing and analyzing the institutional structure within which action takes place.

Nested Systems. In a nested-systems perspective, a distinction is made between action guided by institutions, on the one hand, and action aimed explicitly at manipulating institutional parameters, on the other (Ciricay-Wantrup, 1985; Ostrom, 1986, 1990). It is useful to think of these two modes of action as hierarchically ordered. The institutional arrangements at one level constitute the subject matter of an institutional system at a higher level (Burns and Flam, 1987; Jepperson, 1991). Professional soccer, for instance, is played by rules set down by the international soccer federation, FIFA. Players might be unhappy with the rules. To change them, however, they must engage in a rather differently structured game than soccer, i.e., that of influencing FIFA's policy-making bodies. While the mode of action at the first level can be characterized as practical, the mode of action at the second level is political.

When first-order institutions are defined by second-order institutional systems, institutional change may originate at either of the two levels. An event at the first-order level, for instance if technological change has undermined established institutions, may set off corrective actions at the second-order level. How this comes about depends on the relationship between the two levels of action. First, there is a qualitative break between levels: The pattern of practices at the first level cannot be completely defined at the next (Parsons, 1960). This means that substantial disturbances at the first-order level may be absorbed at that level. It also means that there sometimes will be institutional drift, such that institutions at the first-order level can be modified without this being noticed or sanctioned at the second-order level (Zucker, 1988). Institutional change may also originate at the second-order level (or higher). Sometimes an institution that is regarded as legitimate and efficient by its primary user groups is swept away by more general institutional reforms. Sometimes an institutional innovation that has been unsuccessfully promoted for an extended period of time suddenly becomes possible because of shifts within the larger field of power and social structure (Starr, 1982; Brint and Karabel, 1991). Second, although the two levels of action are qualitatively different and should be kept analytically distinct, there are interconnections between them. The relationships between levels are structured. This means that there will be rules defining what type of problems at the first-order level of action can legitimately be considered at the second-order level, the proper procedures for doing that, who can participate in decision making, and so on. It also means that there will be rules defining and limiting the authority of the second-order level toward the first-order level. Hence, whether a "problem" at the first-order level of action will trigger institutional change depends on the ease with which it can be translated to the second-order level, if it can be attached to a "solution" there, and whether this "decision" can be translated back to the first-order level (March and Olsen, 1976).

Institutionalization as a Dynamic Process. It has been argued that the stability of an institution will increase with its interconnectedness to other institutions (Zucker, 1988). While not disputing this, I will add that such interconnectedness in nested systems sometimes can produce dynamic change patterns. Depending on the degree of coupling, changes in one part of an institutional system may have repercussions in other parts. In addition to the mechanism of negative feedback, implying that a new balance will be established quickly when the system is disturbed, we should allow for the possibility of positive feedback and path dependence. A seemingly insignificant event can then set off chain reactions and generate cumulative effects (Boudon, 1981; David,

1986; Arthur, 1990). An institutional modification—for instance, a new regulation of competitive practices that allows a previously fragmented interest group to organize—can affect the relative capacity for political mobilization among groups. In this way, new practices at the first-order level of action can be converted to a new power constellation at the second-order level and thereby establish a foundation for further institutional change. Institutional change means that organizational fields are restructured (DiMaggio, 1991) and that new relationships between the different levels of action are established. A nested-systems perspective therefore relies more on endogenous processes than exogenous forces in explaining institutional change. Although institutional change often will be triggered by external events, such change impulses will often be redirected in internal processes and end up in quite unexpected places (Thelen and Steinmo, 1992).

Institutionalization and Ideology. Institutions come with rationalized myths that make sense of their establishment and existence (Jepperson, 1991). When they are attacked, there are readily available accounts for the way things are and why they should remain that way. Those affected by an institution will be committed to it by the resources they have invested in its reproduction. In this way, institutions are stabilized by mutually reinforcing systems of practices, interests, and ideas. While this makes sense of how institutions work, it leaves open important questions as to their origin. What is the relationship among practices, interests, and ideas in the institutionalization process? Should institutional change be explained with reference to overarching ideological trends or with reference to shifts in underlying power structures?

From within a nested-systems perspective, the problem of institutional creation can be placed at the second-order level of action, regarding institutions as human products, created for some purpose. Institutional projects are political projects. In these projects, however, there is interaction between interests and ideas (Thelen and Steinmo, 1992). On the one hand, ideas are formed by interests. Replacing one institution with another means that income, power, and status will be redistributed. To succeed, an institutional entrepreneur must mobilize external and internal constituents behind his or her project. One instrument for doing that will be the construction of accounts that make sense of the proposed institutional project and discredit the alternatives. On the other hand, interests are formed by ideas. Actors will often find themselves in situations in which it is not obvious what their interests are or how they can be realized (March and Olsen, 1976). New ideas can make actors see the situation and their own place in it from a new angle. In this way, ideas constitute interests. A nested-systems perspective will pay attention to the ways practices, interests, and ideology interact in processes that are structured by institutions (Thelen and Steinmo, 1992).

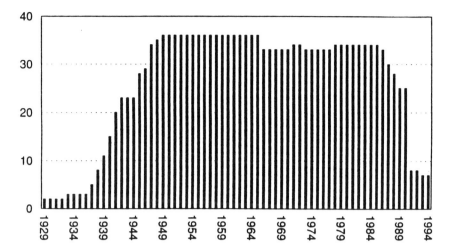

Figure 13.1 The number of MSOS in Norwegian fisheries, 1929–1994
SOURCE: See Appendix.

I demonstrate the relevance of the nested systems view in the area of economic institutions by focusing on the creation, legitimation, and decline of the mandated sales organization (MSO) of Norwegian fisheries. Although the MSO form may not warrant much interest in its own right if you are not a Norwegian fisherman, it highlights important general themes of economic organization. A law-sanctioned cartel, it is but one example of an institutional form that can be found throughout Europe (Streeck and Schmitter, 1985) and that reflects a general European tendency of lenience toward cartellization, as opposed to the hard-nosed antitrust policy of the U.S. (Fligstein, 1990). The MSO form, furthermore, is a corollary of European neocorporatism which, in contrast to U.S. pluralism, is characterized by close institutionalized ties between economic and political organization (Streeck, 1992).

THE RISE AND FALL OF THE MANDATED
SALES ORGANIZATION, 1930–1994

The MSO system of Norwegian fisheries was built up of legally protected organizations with monopoly control over closely defined segments of the fish trade. The economic value of the trade flow controlled by individual MSOs varied. In the heyday of the MSO, however, they collectively dominated Norwegian fisheries. Figure 13.1 shows the number of MSOs in Norwegian fisheries from 1929 until 1994. During the first decade of this period, the MSO form was created, in a highly conflictual process. During the next decade, the MSO form gained legitimacy and proliferated rapidly throughout the sector. Between 1950 and 1980, the MSO form was institutionalized and remained a taken-for-granted part of the sector. Then, during the 1980s, the MSO form lost legitimacy, and the number of MSOs rapidly declined.

Norwegian Fisheries

Norway is located adjacent to two of the world's most productive oceans, the North Sea and the Barents Sea. Fishing has traditionally been an important part of the Norwegian economy and formed the basis for the settlement of western and northern Norway. In the 1930s, when the institutional transformation of the industry started, the total number of fishermen peaked, reaching 125,000 in 1938. In that year, fish and fish products accounted for 15 percent of the total value of Norwegian exports (Central Bureau of Statistics, 1978). The basic organizational problem facing the industry was—and still is—large and unpredictable fluctuations, both on the input and output sides. On the resource side, these fluctuations are an inherent trait of the ecosystems on which the fisheries rely. On the market side, the major source of uncertainty was lack of a domestic market. Roughly 90 percent of the Norwegian production of fish was exported. The traditional solution to the problem of environmental fluctuations was to maintain flexibility. Those who made a living from the sea had alternatives if fishing failed or fish prices slumped. Most fisher households kept a cow and some sheep. This adaptation went together with simple technology and low investment. In this system, efficiency was sacrificed for flexibility. Put under pressure by declining catches or weak market prices, the typical fisherman's response was to retreat to alternative means of subsistence rather than collective mobilization to solve the problems within the sector.

By the time our story begins, at the end of the 1920s, a process of technical and organizational change had been going on for some time. The fishing fleet had been motorized. New technology had transformed fish processing. Extension of transportation networks had drastically lowered transportation costs. These developments had made the industry more efficient but also less flexible, as more capital was tied up in specialized equipment and alternative means of subsistence fell into disuse. The new vulnerability was revealed by the international recession following the crash on Wall Street in October 1929. The demand for fish in international markets dwindled. This happened not only because of shrinking purchasing power in the markets. Several of the major fish-importing nations increased trade barriers to protect their own industries. At the same time, the supply of fish in international markets had reached an all-time high due to the introduction of new technology (trawling), new operational models (year-round deep-sea fishing), and new participants (Faroe Islands, Iceland) (Gerhardsen, 1949). The intersection of structural change, swelling supply, and weak demand created a major crisis in international fish trade (Norway, Ministry of Commerce, 1937).

Institutional Creation in Nested Systems

The first two sales organizations within the Norwegian fishery sector were authorized by the government in 1929. With this decision, which was sanctioned by the Parliament when the Herring Act was formally adopted the following year, two legal monopolies in the herring trade had been established. Both organizations had been formed by herring fishermen in western Norway. I concentrate here on Storsildlaget, which at the time it was authorized had been in operation for two years and was the true pioneer. Storsildlaget was formed in response to the difficult market situation for herring. The herring fishery was seasonal. Large quantities were landed during a few winter weeks. At the beginning of the season, the fishermen usually would get a fair price. When the fishery peaked, however, the bottom would fall out of the market. At this point, the firsthand price no longer stood in a reasonable relation to the price in the export market. In the atomized market system, the merchants had the upper hand vis-à-vis the fishermen. This was the problem the fishermen's sales organization was formed to solve. While the fishermen could not stand up to the merchants individually, they could collectively. The organization would negotiate firsthand herring prices and regulate the supply of herring to the best-paying market segments. Each fisherman would receive an average price, whatever the price his particular catch obtained. This constituted the greatest obstacle for the project. Would individual fishermen resist the temptation to sell outside the organization when the merchants offered more than the average price (Hallenstvedt, 1982)?

The first-order collective-action problem here, the hardship facing a group of fishermen acting individually in market structure, is a version of the prisoner's dilemma. The fishermen's common interest lay in restricting the supply of herring, which would bring better prices. As long as they acted individually, this option was not available. To solve their dilemma, the fishermen had to set up a rule system that allowed them to market the herring collectively. This institutional project represents the second-order collective-action problem. If we simply assume that the fishermen in this situation were rational and acted individually, we cannot account for the fact that Storsildlaget was established and successfully organized the herring trade for two years without legal protection. To explain this, we must look into the pattern of interaction among the fishermen. The herring fishery in question was concentrated both in time and geographically, and the fishermen largely came from the same area, had the same social background, and operated the same type of technology. Such factors created favorable conditions for collective identification and mobilization among the fishermen and had led to the formation of an interest organization as early as 1915 (Hallenstvedt and

Dynna, 1976). During the market crisis of the late 1920s, the fishermen from within this organization were able to establish the sales organization (Christensen and Hallenstvedt, 1990).

The example shows how the second-order collective-action problem was handled in an arena structured by the herring's migration pattern, technological conditions and social and institutional factors. A consideration of the process through which the fishermen campaigned to have their sales organization protected by law expands this point. A rule making all fishermen sell their catch through the organization, enforced by the police and the legal apparatus of the Norwegian state, would immediately solve the free-rider problem. Mobilizing the state's power behind the fishermen's institutional project in this way was not a simple matter, however. It would require, first, that the fishermen's problem could be made so important that it warranted a place on the political agenda; second, that the fishermen's solution would survive through the various stages of the decision-making process; and third, that the required number of votes would be cast in their favor. The fishermen did succeed in persuading the Norwegian government and Parliament that the Herring Act was a good idea. This can be explained partly by a well-organized lobbying effort, partly by the west-coast fishermen's close affiliation to the Liberal party, which was in power at the time (Christensen and Hallenstvedt, 1990).

The account of the creation of the very first MSO in this way connects the market crisis, the relative bargaining position of fishermen and merchants, the condition for collective action among fishermen, and the access structure of the Norwegian political system. The account of the next phase of the MSO reform involves the same factors, but in a different constellation. The herring fishermen's successful mobilization of the Norwegian state behind Storsildlaget had structured the general problem of fish trade and placed it firmly in the political arena. The main questions no longer concerned whether cartels would be viable or if the state would support them but, rather, which interest groups would benefit from them. In this process, the adoption of the 1932 Salt Fish Act and the 1938 Raw Fish Act were crucial events. The former protected the merchants' interests; the latter the fishermen's. The two acts were based on radically different conceptions of the sector's basic problem and its core client group. The explanation for this inconsistency lies not primarily in the fishery sector but in a more general development process within Norwegian politics, which is evident in the main controversies surrounding the organization of the fish trade in the 1930s.

The train of events that ended with the adoption of the Salt Fish Act started in the export market. Under the pressures of large supplies of fish and weakening demand, the conditions in core export markets quickly deteriorated. The decreasing price trend led to short-sighted competitive practices as exporters started underbidding each other. The complaints against the lack of organization in fish exports mounted. Opportunism, disloyalty, and cut-throat competition among Norwegian exporters flourished. The result of all this was that the prices fell even more than they should have according to the laws of demand and supply (Giske, 1978; Hallenstvedt, 1982).

This analysis of the situation was itself controversial at the time. Its strongest supporters were the fishermen. The free market, they argued, was the fundamental problem. In its place they wanted a system of centralized fish export under government control (Christensen and Hallenstvedt, 1990). The fish exporters opposed this vehemently. The problem, they claimed, was international in character. There simply was no internal Norwegian cause for or solution to the crisis. In the absence of international agreements, government intervention in Norwegian fish exports could only magnify the problems. Any restraints on the Norwegian fish exporters would advantage their foreign competitors (Norway, Director of Fisheries, 1928). Both these accounts of the situation were carefully constructed as part of the battle over the further implementation of the MSO form conducted within the framework of Norwegian political institutions. This phase of the MSO process differed markedly from that preceding the adoption of the Herring Act, which in comparison had the character of cool problem solving. This time, heavy mobilization occurred on both sides, and it came to heated confrontation over general principles.

The Salt Fish Act, adopted by the Norwegian Parliament in 1932, was the outcome of this conflict. According to the act, the government could decide that the export of dried salted fish would be permitted only for members of an officially recognized organization of fish exporters. The Salt Fish Act applied at first only to exports of dried salted codfish. Later in the decade it was extended to dried unsalted fish (stockfish). The act thereby applied to the bulk of Norwegian fish trade in the codfish sector. On the face of it, the Salt Fish Act was a compromise. On the one hand, the fishermen's faction was accommodated, inasmuch as the act imposed some organization on the salt fish trade. On the other hand, the professional fish exporters were satisfied, since no significant reins on competitive practices had been introduced (Hallenstvedt, 1982). In practice, however, the exporters had won the battle. They could proceed as before but, now, shielded from competition. Instead of being put under government control, as the fishermen had wanted, they had gained government protection.

This outcome is explained by the class bias of Norwegian politics at the time. The merchants were core constituents of the ruling liberal-conservative coalition, while fishermen, peasants, and workers were but marginal groups within the Norwegian polity. The heavy bias in favor of merchants' interests in public administration pulled in the same direction (Hallenstvedt, 1982). Had this class bias remained, the Raw Fish Act would not have been adopted. This act, modeled on the 1930 Herring Act, was a direct response to the problems of north Norwegian cod fishermen. During the depression, they found themselves at the losing end in the marketplace.

The prices were dropping more in the firsthand markets at home than in the export markets abroad. The merchants, claimed the fishermen, saved themselves at the fishermen's expense (Norway, Ministry of Commerce, 1937; Giske, 1978; Christensen and Hallenstvedt, 1990). The rationale behind the Raw Fish Act, then, was to compensate for the fishermen's difficult position in the firsthand market. Mandated sales organizations formed by fishermen constituted the basic mechanism of the act. The MSOs were granted legal monopoly in firsthand sales of fish and could, if the negotiations stalemated, unilaterally set firsthand prices. The Raw Fish Act also allowed them to license and control fish buyers and to regulate the supply of fish by catch restrictions (Hallenstvedt, 1982). With these prerogatives, the MSOs had a strong bargaining position vis-à-vis the buyers.

While the 1932 Salt Fish Act catered to merchants' interests, the 1938 Raw Fish Act was the answer to problems as defined by the fishermen. This shift occurred as the fishermen gained better access to the Norwegian political system. One reason for this was the improved organization of fishermen during the 1930s. The Norwegian Fishermen's Association (Norges Fiskarlag) had been established as early as 1926 but did not become an effective political force until the latter half of the 1930s (Hallenstvedt and Dynna, 1976). More important still was the general redistribution of political resources in Norwegian politics. The balance tipped in 1935, when the Labor party came into power. Because of the close ties between the Fishermen's Association and the Labor party, the Social Democratic government quickly made its mark in the fishery sector. The 1938 Raw Fish Act, which established the fishermen as the dominant interest group within the sector, was but one expression of a new political order.

Whereas the MSO form was an answer to the market crisis, the process in which it was created was structured by institutional forces. In the first phase of the MSO reform, Storsildlaget solved the collective-action problem facing the fishermen in a fragmented marketplace. The fishermen were able to overcome the free-rider problem because of a preexisting institution, a fishermen's organization, which made it possible to bind individual fishermen to a common cause. During the next phase of the MSO reform, the herring fishermen sought legal protection for their sales organization. To achieve this, their problem had to be accepted as legitimate and pressing in the core political arenas of the Norwegian state. In the third phase of the reform, leading from the Salt Fish Act to the Raw Fish Act, the MSO reform activated the basic lines of conflict in the Norwegian polity. The Conservatives sided with the merchants, while the Social Democrats stood up for the fishermen. In this way, the fishery crisis was channeled through the political system and was defined and redefined along the way. The outcome of this process, the MSO form, cannot be seen as a rational response to an externally defined problem. Instead, it was the result of how lines of conflict were activated, how other issues tied in, what actor groups became involved, and which solutions were available (March and Olsen, 1976). This, to a large extent, had to do with the institutional structure of the arena in which the new institution gradually took form.

Institutional Creation as a Dynamic Process

At the same time that the MSO model was adopted in the fishery sector, a reform along similar lines happened in Norwegian agriculture (Furre, 1971). Parallel reforms also appeared in other North Atlantic fish-exporting nations, in Newfoundland (Alexander, 1977), Iceland (Joónsson, 1980), and the Faroe Islands (Toftum, 1994b). This reform wave must be understood on the backdrop of the international recession, which had undermined the belief in free-market solutions (Furre, 1971). In accord with the cooperative ideology (Carlsson, 1992), new faith was invested in organization building. In Norway, the incorporation of the labor movement in the Norwegian polity was an important inspiration. This happened during the 1930s and paved the way for interest organization in itself as a legitimate tool of social engineering. As the government-appointed task force appointed to sort out the fishery crisis explained:

> As a part of all work to increase profitability, organization has proved to be an invaluable tool. Organization has not only caused, for instance, wages to increase and thereby lead to a higher standard of living and higher labor productivity, organization has also forced firms, branches, and industries as a whole to leave the road of chance and instead work more systematically from the first to the last link of the industry, from production to marketing. These results have not only been productive for the individual firms but also for society as a whole. (Norway, Ministry of Commerce, 1937: 52; my translation)

These observations, suggesting that the MSO reform in Norwegian fisheries was a reflection of a broad ideological shift at the international level, conform nicely to new institutionalist expectations. Within this perspective, new organizational forms are adopted as the rationalized myths on which their legitimacy rests proliferate through society (Meyer and Rowan, 1977; DiMaggio and Powell, 1983). While general cultural and ideological trends certainly influenced the MSO process, however, this perspective leaves important questions unanswered. A significant example is the thoroughly different outcomes of the reform activities in different North Atlantic fishery nations in the 1930s. In Norway, the MSO reform completely rearranged the fisher sector and turned the traditional power structure upside down. In Iceland and the Faroe Islands, the MSO form gained considerable importance in fish exports but never dominated the sector (Toftum, 1994a, 1994b). In New-foundland, the modest organizational efforts along MSO lines during the 1930s quickly foundered in the postwar period (Alexander, 1977).

While ideas or events in external environments can set things in motion, such change impulses will be shaped by processes and will often generate unexpected outcomes through feedback processes. One example from the MSO reform is the connection between the 1932 Salt Fish Act and the adoption of the Raw Fish Act six years later. As I have already argued, this represented a shift of priorities that primarily can be explained by the turn toward social democracy in Norwegian politics. But, in addition, the Raw Fish Act was a direct response to the Salt Fish Act. An important argument in the Parliament's debate over the Raw Fish Act was that, since the merchants had MSOs, the fishermen should have them too. This argument of fairness was reenforced by the claim that the Salt Fish Act, contrary to the Parliament's intention, had shifted the distribution of power and revenues in the sector even further in favor of the merchants (Christensen and Hallenstvedt, 1990). The example shows how the outcome of an institutional project, in this case the Salt Fish Act, sometimes can be fed back into the political process in which it was created. In the following I concentrate on one important class of such feedback processes, namely, those in which the institutional project creates new political actors. This was clearly the case with the MSO reform. The sales organizations' entry into the fisheries changed the relations between and the relative influence of the major interests in the sector and restructured the relationship between sector groups and the authorities. Maybe it is an exaggeration to say that the MSO reform created a sector-political system in the fisheries, since organizations with explicit political functions were present before 1930, but the reform certainly expanded the sector interests' capacity for political mobilization.

In 1949, 36 MSOs of varying scale and scope had been authorized within Norwegian fisheries (see Appendix). Although both fishermen and merchants had been allowed to form such cartels, they had very different consequences for the political effectiveness of the two groups. While the MSO reform propelled the fishermen to a dominant position within the sector, it left the merchants fragmented and weak. This had to do with differences in the MSO form between harvesting and trade and must be understood against the background of the specific organizational sequence in each segment.

In the harvesting segment, a general interest organization, the Fishermen's Association, existed before the sales organizations were created and had played an important role in the MSO reform during the 1930s. The presence of a general and relatively unified interest organization for fishermen meant that the sales organizations could stay out of sector politics and concentrate on the technical task of regulating firsthand trade of fish. The creation of sales organizations, furthermore, solved the association's financial problems. After the MSO reform, its main source of income was a 1 percent levy on the catch, collected by the sales organizations as one of their legally defined prerogatives. Every Norwegian fisherman was in this way obliged to contribute to the association in proportion to his catch, regardless of his position on the organization's policies. The MSO reform hence solved the notorious problems of a voluntary organization in an economically weak field. In the harvesting sector, then, the reform established a tidy division of labor, in which a diverse set of economic organizations backed up one relatively strong political organization.

In the processing and export segment, in contrast, no general interest organization existed before the adoption of the Salt Fish Act. This meant that the first systematic organizational effort among the merchants occurred in direct response to the international market crisis of the 1930s and was directly tied to the possibility of legal protection. This had important consequences for the organizational pattern that resulted. The export MSOs became cartels as well as general interest organizations. Since they as cartels were defined according to specific market segments, the fragmentation of the fish markets spilled over to the merchants' political organization. While the MSO reform had created a unified political apparatus for the fishermen, the organizational mix of economic and political issues in processing and exports left the merchants hopelessly fragmented and unable to define common interests (Hallenstvedt, 1990).

The MSO reform was a path-dependent process, in which a small variation in initial conditions had important consequences. No one could foresee this outcome, but when it happened, it left the fishermen in an ideal position to consolidate their position and dominate the further development of the sector. The sector system that grew out of the MSO reform was one in which fish processing and export were defined as auxiliary functions necessary to realize the market value of the fishermen's catch. The core sector institutions were in particular committed to the interests of the predominant type of fishermen in the 1930s, engaged in small-type, seasonal fishing from peripheral communities scattered along the Norwegian coast. The system of fishermen's sales organizations was constructed to end the merchants' traditional exploitation of fishermen (Holm, 1993b). This commitment was reinforced by the 1939 Trawler Act, which severely restricted the use of trawler technology (Sagdahl, 1982), and the legal protection of an owner-operated fishing fleet (Mikalsen, 1982). In this way, the MSO reform constituted a sector system in which the fisherman was the core client.

Because of the way the MSO reform came about, born out of the particular problems and considerations of the 1930s, it tied the government's hands in the area of fishery policy after World War II. Based on their previous successes, the fishermen in the postwar period started out with grand ambitions. They now wanted to finish what had been started in the 1930s, creating a cooperative sector model with the fishermen in complete control, not only in harvesting but also in fish processing and exports (Sagdahl, 1973). This was rejected by the Labor government, which had other plans for the sector. To the Social Democrats, the end of the war represented the beginning of a new era; they embarked on an ambitious project to transform Norway into a modern welfare state. Structural change and industrialization on a large scale were at the core of this plan. Such ideas also informed the government's fishery policy. This meant that the Social Democratic government now actively promoted the very sector model it had helped block out with the Raw Fish Act and the Trawler Act before the war.

In line with the industrialization doctrine, considerable amounts of political prestige and money were invested in the attempt to modernize the fisheries. Large freezing plants were established in northern Norway, aided by generous government grants (Lien, 1975; Hersoug and Leonardsen, 1979). The legal restrictions on who could own fishing vessels were relaxed (Mikalsen, 1982). So were the restrictions against trawlers (Sagdahl, 1982). Funds for building off-shore fishing vessels were made available through the State Fisheries Bank (Handegård, 1982). While these measures in the long run did have structural effects, they did not lead to substantial modification of the sector system created by the MSO reform. The traditional, small-scale, and labor-intensive fishery of the 1930s was gradually replaced with a modern, high-tech, capital-intensive industry, but the MSO system with its commitment to coastal fishing and coastal communities remained intact.

The best illustration of the fishermen's ability to subvert government policy is the fate of the Main Agreement. This agreement, signed by the government and sector interests in 1964, regulated the conditions for state subsidies to the sector. In line with the industrialization doctrine, the government had intended the Main Agreement as a program for structural rationalization, with investment support and buy-back programs as main instruments. In practice, however, it became an income support scheme. During the 1964–1990 period, the subsidies amounted to 19 percent of the value of the catch, of which nearly 80 percent was allocated to income support. In this way, the Main Agreement established a system in which the state buffered the fishery sector from fluctuations in resources and markets. Instead of being an instrument for rationalization and industrialization, as the government had intended, the Main Agreement had been turned into an economic safety net for the fishermen (Holm, 1991).

Although several factors explain this outcome (Holm, 1991), the most important is the dominant position of the fishermen, as established by the MSO reform. Taking existing power structures into account, the Main Agreement had been signed by the government and the Fishermen's Association. The Fishermen's Association was also appointed the exclusive representative for the sector to the yearly subsidy negotiations. Because the association had strong commitments to small-scale fishermen and coastal communities, this built strong resistance points into the subsidy system and hence rendered it virtually useless as an industrialization device. Furthermore, the Main Agreement continued on the course set out by the MSO reform. The agreement immediately consolidated the association's position within the sector, as formerly independent groups, such as the Fishing Vessel Owners Organization, joined in order to influence the subsidy negotiations.

The MSO reform was influenced by strong ideological currents of the 1930s, including the receding faith in free-market solutions, the new legitimacy of organization, and the cooperative movement. Still, such factors alone could not explain the outcome of the reform. To do that, we also had to consider how the initial modest institutional innovations of the MSO process caught on and, through feedback processes, eventually led to a complete restructuring of the sector system. This happened because of slight variations in the condition surrounding the implementation of the MSO form in harvesting and trade, respectively, which translated to a shift in the political capacity of fishermen and merchants. The fishermen became the dominant interest group, and they could set out to consolidate their position in new institutional projects. At the same time, the reform had established new resistance that made it more difficult for authorities to have it their way. The MSO reform thus established a new self-reproducing power structure within the field, which with inevitable logic pushed toward increasing interconnectedness and consistency.

Institutional Change and Legitimation

At the beginning of the 1990s, a new reform wave swept over the fishery sector. First, the subsidy practices were severely restrained as a result of the 1992 agreement on a European Economic Area (EEA) between the European Free Trade Association (EFTA) and the European Community. Although no formal changes were made, the Main Agreement's most important mechanism, direct income support, was no longer allowed (Holm and Johnsen, 1990). Second, a new Fish Export Act was adopted in 1990. All the MSOs in fish exports were replaced by one fish export council (Norway, Ministry of Fisheries, 1989). As a result of this, it became possible to establish a single interest association for processors and exporters, the Federation of Norwegian Fishing Industry (Fiskerinæringens Landsforening) (Moxnes, 1990). Third, the legally defined prerogatives of the fishermen's sales organizations were weakened in the 1992 adjustment of the Raw Fish Act (Norway, Ministry of Fisheries, 1992). Fourth, new restrictions on the transfer of money from the sales organizations to the Fishermen's Association weakened the association's financial basis (Norwegian Fishermen's Association, 1993). With these changes, the MSO model had been pushed from the center to the periphery of Norwegian fisheries. Given the heavy institutionalization of the MSO model, how could this happen?

One explanation, from the new institutionalist perspective, is that the reform wave in the fisheries coincided with a new ideological climate. During the 1980s liberalist ideas gained new legitimacy in many Western nations. Deregulation and privatization were at the center of the "new right" movement. The state should be rolled back and market principles given more space (Marchack, 1991). From this perspective, the fishery sector—infused with privileged organizations, state subsidies, and legally protected monopolies— was an obvious target (Hernes and Trondsen, 1986). Agency was also a factor, as liberalist ideas informed the creation of a single European market, the cornerstone in the revitalization of European cooperation (Cecchini, 1988), and the Norwegian Labor government's primary goal from the late 1980s was joining the European Community. In the Norwegian context, hence, the new legitimacy of liberalist ideas was closely tied to the process of European integration.

The result of the November 1994 referendum was negative, however, and Norway did not join the European Union (EU). Still, Norway has come a long way in adapting to the EU, in particular through the EEA agreement (Norway, Ministry of Foreign Affairs, 1992). In the fisheries, this process was a direct pretext for the changes in the subsidy system and some of the modifications of the Raw Fish Act. It is only a small exaggeration to say that the reform process in the fisheries preempted most of the institutional changes that would have been necessary if Norway had joined the EU (Holm, 1993a; Norway, Ministry of Foreign Affairs, 1994).

While the new ideological climate and the EU are important factors in explaining the demise of the MSO system, they do not tell the whole story. The EU question activated a basic theme in Norwegian politics: the resistance against central authority. The strength of this resistance must be understood in the intersection of a territorial conflict between center and periphery: a sociocultural conflict between the urban elite and the rural commoners and an economic conflict between the merchants and the primary producers within agriculture and fisheries (Rokkan, 1966). The lines of these conflicts cut across another important area of conflict in the Norwegian polity, that between labor and capital. In the EU question, the Labor party as well as the national labor organization were split. While the elite members of the labor movement sided with the government to have Norway join the Union, a large minority of the lay members fought vigorously against it. Together with the Socialist party, the Agrarian party and the Liberals, they succeeded in mobilizing a small majority against EU membership.

Ironically, the very same coalition that kept Norway outside the European Community had made the MSO system invulnerable to the government-sponsored industrialization project during most of the postwar period. Why were these forces, strong enough to stop EU membership, no longer able to prevent the destruction of the MSO system? This question must be answered with reference to a parallel institutional change process within the fishery sector. At the core of this change process was the idea of fishery resource management, an idea that contradicted basic conceptions, values, and procedures within the established sector system. The MSO system had been created as if there were no limits to fish resources. The sales organizations were a response to the market crisis of the 1930s, in which the main problem was too much fish. The Main Agreement was supposed to create efficiency through subsidization, with no reins on total harvesting capacity. But the fishery is based on a limited and vulnerable natural resource. As any textbook of fishery economics will point out, subsidization will reinforce the inherent tendency toward overexploitation in a free-access fishery and will therefore create inefficiency (Hannesson, 1994).

Starting from the premise of fish as a limited and vulnerable resource, the MSO sector system was highly problematical, if not irrational. Until the 1970s, however, this idea had but limited access to the sector. This was not because of ignorance about the dangers of overfishing. Instead, it was a direct result of an oceans regime based on the principle of "Mare Liberum": that the riches of the sea outside a narrow coastal band were open to all. Conforming to the logic of "The Tragedy of the Commons" (Hardin, 1968), this led to virtually unrestrained international competition and a fishery policy that proceeded as if fish stocks were unlimited (Colombos, 1967; Ulfstein, 1982). Only with the new oceans regime, established during the late 1970s, when 200-mile extended economic zones (EEZ) became internationally accepted, could the resource management idea be implemented at the level of practical policy. Only from January 1, 1977, the date the Norwegian EEZ was established, could the slow process of building up a resource management system in the fishery sector commence.

This is not the place to analyze how the new oceans regime was created, nor describe how the Norwegian management system was built. Suffice it to report the outcome of these processes: a centralized, bureaucratic resource management system. The core concern within this system is to adjust fishing intensity to available fishery resources. The basic input is science-based recommendations of a total allowable catch (TAC) for each of the most important commercial fish stocks. These recommendations, which are certified by the International Council for the Exploration of the Sea (ICES), are transformed to specific fish quotas and other catch restrictions through a cumbersome negotiations process involving, among others, representatives from neighbor states over the allocation of shared stocks and representatives from the sector interests over distribution of quotas between different groups of fishermen (Hoel, Jentoft, and Mikalsen, 1993). The final regulations, sanctioned by the government, are enforced through explicit systems of monitoring and control (Hallenstvedt, 1993).

In this way, the focal point of the fishery sector has gradually moved from the sales system to the resource management system. This has also meant a power shift within the sector. The positions within the MSO system from which the fishermen could dominate the sector, in particular the Main Agreement, have been undermined. At the same time, processors and exporters have escaped from the fine-meshed system of regulations in which they were entangled. The organizational arrangements that fragmented them were abandoned with the new Fish Export Act in 1990. The rule systems that subordinated them to the fishermen, the Raw Fish Act and the Main Agreement, have been weakened. It is no coincidence that the Fishermen's Association, under the zero-sum game imposed by resource management, is paralyzed by internal conflicts, while the new processor organization, the Federation of Norwegian Fishing Industry, is about to take over as the dominant interest organization within the sector.

Institutional theory holds that institutions can be accounted for. When institutions are challenged, good reasons can be given for their existence (Jepperson, 1991). From such propositions one would expect that the sector changes described here would be accompanied by an ideological shift, including the acceptance of new accounts of the fundamental situation of the fishery, what its basic problems are, and how they can be solved. The MSO reform was legitimated with reference to the story, carefully constructed by the fishermen and the Labor party, about how the merchants within the free-market system could save themselves at the fishermen's expense. In this situation, the Raw Fish Act would restore order and justice. Moreover, the act would force the merchants to make their money in the export markets abroad instead of exploiting the fishermen at home. This would improve the economic return of the sector as a whole (Hallenstvedt, 1982). In the postwar period, this account formed the core of a mythology in which the Raw Fish Act took on the status of the fishermen's constitution, the savior from chaos and oppression, the very foundation for the settlement along the Norwegian coast (Norges Råfisklag, 1963). The traditional fishery, as defined and protected by the established institutional order, with the fishermen in core positions, represented the good life in small coastal communities. This idyll of independence and equality was contrasted to the ugly features of large-scale industrial capitalism, which represented dependency, hierarchy, and centralization (Brox, 1966).

The emerging resource-centered sector system is legitimized with reference to a mythology that has been most forcefully expressed by Garrett Hardin (1968) in "The Tragedy of the Commons," the tale of the inevitable tragedy facing rational men exploiting common property resources, for instance, a fish stock. The logic of the situation creates a conflict between individual and collective interests. Since each fisherman will gain the full value of the fish he can catch, there is no incentive for him to save a fish for tomorrow or next year. It might have grown larger. But since he cannot trust that others will not catch it before him, that is immaterial. By themselves, rational fishermen are therefore locked into a system that compels them to increase their effort while there are fish to be had, even when they know that this will deplete the stock. To avoid the tragedy, the system itself must be changed through privatization or state management.

The two accounts cast the actors involved in very different roles. In the MSO myth, the basic problem is too much fish. In the resource management myth, the basic problem is stock depletion. In the former, the fisherman is the vulnerable hero, while the merchant represents the evil oppressor. In the latter, the main threat comes from the rapacious fisherman. The two tales also cast the state in different roles. In the MSO story, the state merely provides assistance to the fishermen for them to restrain the merchant. In the resource management story, the state, assisted by science, must play a much more active and autonomous role if the tragic relationship between fishermen and fish is to be transformed into a sustainable and happy one.

The enormous legitimizing power of the tragedy-of-the-commons myth does not primarily hinge on its correspondence to facts. Its core assumptions, that common property equates with free access, that fishermen by themselves are unable to prevent overfishing, and that common property resources with inevitable necessity are overexploited, have all been refuted (McCay and Acheson, 1987; Berkes, 1989; Feeny et al., 1990; Bromley, 1992). Instead, its wide acceptance at the level of national policy making must be understood with reference to its institutionalization at the international level where, in the context of the UN Conference on the Law of the Sea, it provided the rationale for the new oceans regime. The new regime, which represented a large-scale redistribution of global fishery resources—from a few industrial nations engaged in industrial distant-water fishing to a multitude of coastal states—could only be legitimized with reference to the promise of better resource management, as explicated in the tale of the tragedy of the commons (Copes, 1981; Ulfstein, 1982; Dahmani, 1987; Sanger, 1987).

The collapse of the MSO form happened in the context of external pressures and ideological change. Now these forces pulled in the opposite direction from that of the 1930s. Liberalist ideas again were in demand. Instead of market collapse and protectionism, market extension and dismantling of trade barriers had top priority. While such factors certainly contributed to the demise of the MSO form, they became influential primarily because the integrity of the MSO system already had been eroded. This happened as resource management was gradually institutionalized as the core concern within the sector. The emerging sector system has brought new practices, new power structures, and new ideologies. Where practices are concerned, the fish trade has been deregulated, while harvesting must face new constraints. The processors have been let loose to compete in international markets. To prevent them from destroying the resource base, the fishermen have been surrounded by strict bureaucratic controls. Where power structures are concerned, the coastal fishermen have been dethroned and have lost most of their privileges. The processors, liberated from the tight reins imposed by the MSO system, have become more influential. But the new sector system has also created important power positions for previously marginal actors, in particular the state and the scientific community. Where ideology is concerned, the MSO myth has given way to the tragedy of the commons. The image of the vulnerable fisherman exploited by the merchant has been replaced by the image of the rapacious fisherman who must be restrained by science and bureaucracy.

Both the birth and the death of the MSO system were informed by ideological trends. But understanding why the new ideas became so influential in the Norwegian fishery required an examination of how they were connected to problems, issues, and conflicts within the sector, in the political system, and at the international level. While both the triumph of the MSO form in the 1930s and its defeat 50 years later happened as some actors gained and others lost influence, the ideological shifts that accompanied these changes could not be explained as reflections of shifts in an underlying power constellation. To some extent, the new power constellations were constituted with reference to the new ideology. From an institutional perspective, neither underlying power structures nor overarching ideologies are the primary explanations. The core institutional insight is that of interaction between practices, interests, and ideas.

CONCLUSION

The analysis of institutional change that I have pursued here only covers part of the institutionalist agenda. Even the most fundamental of transformations will not affect all institutions. The more institutionalized forms will easily escape our attention because they remain taken for granted, but they are no less a part of the subject area of institutionalist analysis. The social practices that show themselves as technical, natural, and self-evident are the most heavily institutionalized and should therefore take center stage in institutional analysis (Zukin and DiMaggio, 1990; Powell, 1991), but there is a tendency within institutionalist thinking to exclude them from analysis. This is done through the division between "technical" and "institutional" environments. The former refers to rational, market-like phenomena, in which efficiency considerations have primacy, while the latter refers to the realm of rules, regulations, and rituals, in which legitimacy considerations dominate (Meyer and Rowan, 1977; Meyer and Scott, 1983; Scott and Meyer, 1991). This division of the world into one "hard" and one "soft" part excludes some of the most important phenomena in modern societies—market forces, competition, professionalization, and science—from institutional analysis. It also opens institutionalist analysis to an underlying assumption that ideas, rituals, and symbols are empty and decoupled from the hard facts of efficiency considerations and power politics. Instead of constituents of action, institutions are then reduced to surface phenomena, and institutional changes become as ephemeral and short-lived as fads and fashion.

The new institutionalism in organization theory is a part of the "cognitive revolution" in the social sciences (DiMaggio and Powell, 1991). It is influenced by phenomenology, for instance, through Berger and Luckmann's (1967) sociology of knowledge and Garfinkel's (1967) ethnomethodology. Within the phenomenological tradition, social structures are not granted separate ontological status but exist only in the minds of people. It therefore primarily lends itself to the study of society as seen from the perspective of the individual (Burrell and Morgan, 1980). While the new institutionalists readily acknowledge their inspiration from phenomenology, they do not take it all that seriously in their practical analyses of institutional processes. Instead, institutions tend to be accepted as hard facts that can be studied with positivist methods. Institutional analysis then runs the opposite risk of reifying social structures instead of exposing them as socially constructed phenomena (Silverman, 1970). In this article, I have tried to show how this trap can be avoided without a retreat to the subjectivist perspective. Drawing on a nested-systems perspective, I have focused on the processes through which institutions get to be taken for granted and stop being taken for granted. This position does not entail a rejection of the cognitive foundation of institutions. Rather, it complements the institutionalist perspective so as to be able to include power processes, much in the spirit of Powell and DiMaggio (1991). The nested-systems perspective, which distinguishes between action guided by institutions and action aimed at changing or defending institutions, allows us to sort out the double nature of institutions, as both frames for action and products of action. This is an analytical distinction. In practice, the "practical" and "political" modes of action are not completely separate. On the contrary, much of the dynamics of institutional processes can be traced to the interconnections between these two levels of action: the ways in which an innocent event at one level, through feedback processes through the next level, can generate completely unexpected results. Together with the double-edged relation between ideas and interests, in which interests form ideas and ideas constitute interests, this means that a nested-systems perspective leaves much room for endogenous change. While institutional change may be triggered by external events, the outcome will be shaped through internal processes structured by the institutions themselves.

REFERENCES

Alchian, Armen A., and Harold Demsetz. 1972. "Production, information cost, and economic organization." *American Economic Review,* 62: 777–795.

Alexander, David. 1977. *The Decay of Trade: An Economic History of the Newfoundland Saltfish Trade, 1935–1965.* St. John's: ISER Books.

Arthur, W. Brian. 1990. "Positive feedbacks in the economy." *Scientific American,* 262(2): 80–85.

Bates, Robert H. 1988. "Contra contractarianism: Some reflections on the new institutionalism." *Politics & Society,* 16: 387–401.

Berger, Peter, and Thomas Luckmann. 1967. *The Social Construction of Reality.* New York: Doubleday.

Berkes, Fikret (ed.). 1989. *Common Property Resources: Ecology and Community-based Sustainable Development.* London: Belhaven Press.

Boudon, Raymond. 1981. *The Logic of Social Action: An Introduction to Sociological Analysis.* London: Routledge and Kegan Paul.

Brint, Steven, and Jerome Karabel. 1991. "Institutional origin and transformations: The case of American community colleges." In Walter W. Powell and Paul J. DiMaggio (eds.), *The New Institutionalism in Organizational Analysis:* 337–360. Chicago: University of Chicago Press.

Bromley, Daniel W. (ed.). 1992. *Making the Commons Work: Theory, Practice, and Policy.* San Francisco: SCS Press.

Brox, Ottar. 1966. *Hva skjer i Nord-Norge? En studie i norsk utkantpolitikk.* Oslo: Pax.

Burns, Tom R., and Helena Flam. 1987. *The Shaping of Social Organization: Social Rule System Theory with Applications.* London: Sage.

Burrell, Gibson, and Gareth Morgan. 1980. *Sociological Paradigms and Organizational Analysis.* Hants: Gower.

Carlsson, Alf. 1992. *Cooperatives and the State: Partners in Development? A Human Resource Perspective.* Stockholm: Institute of International Education.

Cecchini, Paolo. 1988. *Studies on the Economics of Integration: The Cost of Non-Europe.* Brussels: Commission of the EC.

Central Bureau of Statistics. 1978. *Historisk statistikk.* Oslo: Central Bureau of Statistics of Norway.

Chandler, Alfred D. 1962. *Strategy and Structure: Chapters in the History of the American Industrial Enterprise.* Cambridge, MA: MIT Press.

Christensen, Pål, and Abraham Hallenstvedt. 1990. *På første hånd: Norges Råfisklag gjennom femti år.* Tromsø: Norges Råfisklag.

Ciricay-Wantrup, S.V. 1985. *Natural Resource Economics: Selected Papers.* Boulder, CO: Westview Press.

Colombos, C. 1967. *The International Law of the Sea.* London: Longman.

Copes, Parzival. 1981. "The impact of UNCLOS III on management of the world's fisheries." *Marine Policy,* 5(July): 217–228.

Dahmani, M. 1987. *The Fisheries Regime of the Exclusive Economic Zone.* Dordrecht: Martinus Nijhoff.

David, Paul A. 1986. "Understanding the economics of QWERTY: The necessity of history." In W. Parker (ed.), *Economic History and the Modern Economist:* 30–49. London: Blackwell.

DiMaggio, Paul J. 1988. "Interest and agency in institutional theory." In Lynne G. Zucker (ed.), *Institutional Patterns of Organization: Culture and Environment:* 3–21. Cambridge, MA: Ballinger.

————. 1991. "Constructing an organizational field as a professional project: U.S. art museums, 1920–1940." In Walter W. Powell and Paul J. DiMaggio (eds.), *The New Institutionalism in Organizational Analysis*: 267–292. Chicago: University of Chicago Press.

DiMaggio, Paul J., and Walter W. Powell. 1983. "The iron cage revisited: Institutional isomorphism and collective rationality in organizational fields." *American Sociological Review,* 48: 147–160.

————. 1991. "Introduction." In Walter W. Powell and Paul J. DiMaggio (eds.), *The New Institutionalism in Organizational Analysis:* 1–38. Chicago: University of Chicago Press.

Elster, Jon. 1979. *Ulysses and the Sirens: Studies in Rationality and Irrationality.* Cambridge: Cambridge University Press.

Feeny, David, Fikret Berkes, Bonnie J. McCay, and James M. Acheson. 1990. "The tragedy of the commons: Twenty-two years later." *Human Ecology,* 18(1): 1–19.

Fligstein, Neil. 1990. *The Transformation of Corporate Control.* Cambridge, MA: Harvard University Press.

Furre, Berge. 1971. *Mjølk, bønder og tingmenn: Studiar i organisasjon og politikk kring omsetninga av visse landbruksvarer 1929–30.* Oslo: Det Norske Samlaget.

Garfinkel, Harold. 1967. *Studies in Ethnomethodology.* Englewood Cliffs, NJ: Prentice Hall.

Gerhardsen, Gerhard Meidell. 1949. *Salted Cod and Related Species. FAO Fisheries Study 1.* Washington, DC: Food and Agriculture Organization of the United Nations.

Giske, Anders. 1978. "Klippfiskomsetninga i støypeskjeia." Unpublished Master's thesis in history, University of Bergen.

Hallenstvedt, Abraham. 1982. *Med lov og organisasjon: Organisering av interesser og markeder i norsk fiskerinæring.* Tromsø: Universitetsforlaget.

————. 1990. "Fiskeindustriens organisering." In Einar Moxnes, *Fiskeindustriens organisering og rammevilkår*: 101–127. NOU 24. Oslo: Ministry of Fisheries.

————. 1993. Ressursforvaltning og kontroll—kontrollpolitikk i fiskeriene i de nordiske land og i EF. *Nordiske Seminar og Arbejdsrapporter 1993*: 583. København: Nordisk Ministerråd.

Hallenstvedt, Abraham, and Bjørn Dynna. 1976. *Fra skårunge til høvedsmann.* Trondheim: Norwegian Fishermen's Association.

Handegård, Odd. 1982. "Statens Fiskarbank— administrasjon og klientideologi." In Knut H. Mikalsen and Bjørn Sagdahl (eds.), *Fiskeripolitikk og forvaltningsorganisasjon:* 61–100. Tromsø: Universitetsforlaget.

Hannesson, Rögnvaldur. 1994. *Bioeconomic Analysis of Fisheries.* Oxford: Fishing News Books.

Hardin, Garrett. 1968. "The tragedy of the commons." *Science,* 162: 1243–1248.

Hernes, Gudmund, and Torbjørn Trondsen. 1986. *Fast i fisken?* Oslo: FAFO.

Hersoug, Bjørn, and Dag Leonardsen. 1979. *Bygger de landet?* Oslo: Pax.

Hoel, Alf Håkon, Svein Jentoft, and Knut H. Mikalsen. 1993. *User-group Participation in Norwegian Fisheries Management.* Tromsø: NFH.

Holm, Petter. 1991. "Særinteresser versus allmenninteresser i forhandlingsøkonomien." *Tidsskrift for Samfunnsforskning,* 32(2): 99–119.

————. 1993a. *Et marked for fisk? Om EFs fiskeripolitikk og norsk fiskerinæring.* Oslo: Kystnæringen.

————. 1993b. "Fra hushondsøkonomi til blandingsøkonomi: Institusjonelle endringsprosesser i norsk fiskerinæring." In Petter Holm (ed.), *Et marked for fisk? Om EFs fiskeripolitikk og norsk fiskerinæring:* 163–192. Oslo: Kystnæringen.

Holm, Petter, and Jahn Petter Johnsen. 1990. *Hovedavtalen for norsk fiskerinæring ved en EF-tilpasning.* Tromsø: Fiskernes EF-utvalg.

Jepperson, Ronald L. 1991. "Institutions, institutional effects, and institutionalism." In Walter W. Powell and Paul J. DiMaggio (eds.), *The New Institutionalism in Organizational Analysis:* 143–163. Chicago: University of Chicago Press.

Jónsson, Sigfús. 1980. *The Development of the Icelandic Fishing Industry 1900–1940 and Its Regional Implications.* Reykjavik: Economic Development Institute.

Libecap, Gary D. 1989. *Contracting for Property Rights.* Cambridge: Cambridge University Press.

Lien Børre. 1975. "Findus og norsk fiskeripolitikk 1943–1956." Unpublished Master's thesis in history, University of Tromsø.

March, James G., and Johan P. Olsen. 1976. *Ambiguity and Choice in Organizations.* Oslo: Universitetsforlaget.

Marchack, M. Patricia. 1991. *The Integrated Circus: The New Right and the Restructuring of Global Markets.* Montreal: McGill-Queen's University Press.

McCay, Bonnie J., and James M. Acheson (eds.). 1987. *The Question of the Commons: The Culture and Ecology of Communal Resources.* Tucson: University of Arizona Press.

Meyer, John W., and Brian Rowan. 1977. "Institutionalized organizations: Formal structure as myth and ceremony." *American Journal of Sociology,* 83: 340–363.

Meyer, John W., and W. Richard Scott (eds.). 1983. *Organizational Environments: Ritual and Rationality.* Beverly Hills, CA: Sage.

Mikalsen, Knut H. 1982. "Lovgivning, eiendomsrett og næringspolitikk." In Knut H. Mikalsen and Bjørn Sagdahl (eds.), *Fiskeripolitikk og forvaltningsorganisasjon:* 174–201. Tromsø: Universitetsforlaget.

Moxnes, Einar. 1990. *Fiskeindustriens organisering og rammevilkår. NOU 24.* Oslo: Ministry of Fisheries.

Norges Råfisklag. 1963. *Norges Råfisklag 25 års beretning.* Tromsø: Norges Råfisklag.

North, Douglass C., and Robert P. Thomas. 1973. *The Rise of the Western World: A New Economic History.* Cambridge: Cambridge University Press.

Norway, Director of Fisheries. 1928. *Torskefiskeriene og handelen med klippfisk og tørrfisk. Årsberetning Vedkommende Norges Fiskerier II.* Bergen: John Griegs Boktrykkeri.

Norway, Ministry of Commerce. 1937. *Innstilling om fiskerienes lønnsomhet. Instilling VIII (hovedinnstilling) fra Komiteen til behandling av forskjellige spørsmål vedrørende fiskeribedriften.* Oslo: Ministry of Commerce.

Norway, Ministry of Fisheries. 1989. *Ot.prp.nr.90 (1988-89) Om lov om regulering av eksporten av fisk og fiskevarer.* Oslo: Ministry of Fisheries.

———. 1992. *Ot.prp.nr.61 (1991–92) Om endringer i fiskerilovgivningen.* Oslo: Ministry of Fisheries.

Norway, Ministry of Foreign Affairs. 1992. *St.prp.nr. 100 (1991–92) Om samtykke til ratifikasjon av Avtale om Det europeiske økonomiske samarbeidsområdet (EØS), undertegnet i Oporto 2. mai 1992.* Oslo: Ministry of Foreign Affairs.

———. 1994. *St.meld.nr.40 (1993–94) Om medlemskap i Den europeiske union.* Oslo: Ministry of Foreign Affairs.

Norwegian Fishermen's Association. 1993. *Norges Fiskarlag: Framtidige arbeidsoppgaver, struktur, organisering.* Trondheim: Norwegian Fishermen's Association.

Olson, Mancur. 1965. *The Logic of Collective Action: Public Goods and the Theory of Groups.* Cambridge, MA: Harvard University Press.

Ostrom, Elinor. 1986. "An agenda for the study of institutions." *Public Choice,* 48: 3–25.

———. 1990. *Governing the Commons. The Evolution of Institutions for Collective Action.* Cambridge: Cambridge University Press.

Parsons, Talcott. 1960. "Three levels in the hierarchical structure of organizations." *Structure and Process in Modern Societies:* 59–69. New York: Free Press.

Powell, Walter W. 1991. "Expanding the scope of institutional analysis." In Walter W. Powell and Paul J. DiMaggio (eds.), *The New Institutionalism in Organizational Analysis:* 183–203. Chicago: University of Chicago Press.

Powell, Walter W., and Paul J. DiMaggio (eds.). 1991. *The New Institutionalism in Organizational Theory.* Chicago: University of Chicago Press.

Rokkan, Stein. 1966. "Numerical democracy and corporate pluralism." In R. A. Dahl (ed.), *Political Opposition in Western Democracies:* 70–115. New Haven, CT: Yale University Press.

Sagdahl Bjørn. 1973. "Trålpolitikk og interessekamp." Unpublished Master's thesis in political science, University of Oslo.

———. 1982. "Teknologisk endring og interessekonflikt—trålfiskets innpasning i torskefiskeriene." In Knut H. Mikalsen and Bjørn Sagdahl (eds.), *Fiskeripolitikk og forvaltningsorganisasjon:* 141–173. Tromsø: Universitetsforlaget.

Sanger, Clyde. 1987. *Ordering the Oceans: The Making of the Law of the Sea.* Toronto: University of Toronto Press.

Scott, W. Richard, and John W. Meyer. 1991. "The organization of societal sectors: Propositions and early evidence." In Walter W. Powell and Paul J. DiMaggio (eds.), *The New Institutionalism in Organizational Analysis:* 108–140. Chicago: University of Chicago Press.

Silverman, David. 1970. *The Theory of Organizations.* London: Heinemann.

Starr, Paul. 1982. *The Social Transformation of American Medicine.* New York: Basic Books.

Streeck, Wolfgang. 1992. *Social Institutions and Economic Performance: Studies of Industrial Relations in Advanced Capitalist Economies.* London: Sage.

Streeck, Wolfgang, and Philippe C. Schmitter (eds.). 1985. *Private Interest Government: Beyond Market and State.* London: Sage.

Taylor, Michael. 1987. *The Possibility of Cooperation.* Cambridge: Cambridge University Press.

Thelen, Kathleen, and Sven Steinmo. 1992. "Historical institutionalism in comparative politics." In Sven Steinmo, Kathleen Thelen, and Frank Longstreth (eds.), *Structuring Politics:* 1–32. Cambridge: Cambridge University Press.

Thomas, George M., John W. Meyer, Francisco O. Ramirez, and John Boli (eds.). 1987. *Institutional Structure: Constituting State, Society, and the Individual.* Newbury Park, CA: Sage.

Thompson, James D. 1967. *Organizations in Action.* New York: McGraw-Hill.

Toftum, Jens Helgi. 1994a. *Institusjoner i fiskeomsetningen på Island—stabilitet og endring. Prosjektrapport NFR 1300—500.136 Institusjonene i fiskeomsetningen—stabilitet og endring.* Tromsø: Norges fiskerihøgskole.

———. 1994b. *Institusjoner i fiskeomsetningen på Færøyene—stabilitet og endring. Prosjektrapport NFR 1300—500.136 Institusjonene i fiskeomsetningen—stabilitet og endring.* Tromsø: Norges fiskerihøgskole.

Ulfstein, Geir. 1982. *Økonomiske soner—hva nå? Om folkerett og fiskeriforvaltning.* Tromsø: Universitetsforlaget.

Williamson, Oliver E. 1975. *Markets and Hierarchies: Analysis and Antitrust Implications.* New York: Free Press.

Zucker, Lynne G. 1988. "Where do institutional patterns come from? Organizations as actors in social systems." In Lynne G. Zucker (ed.), *Institutional Patterns of Organization: Culture and Environment:* 23–49. Cambridge, MA: Ballinger.

Zukin, Sharon, and Paul J. DiMaggio (eds.). 1990. *Structures of Capital: The Social Organization of the Economy.* Cambridge: Cambridge University Press.

APPENDIX   MSOs in Norwegian Fisheries, 1929–1994

Organization (name)	Type	Authorized	Authorization Cancelled
Storsildlaget	Firsthand sales	1929	1936
Stor- og Vårsildlaget	Firsthand sales	1929	1936
De Norske Klippfiskeksprtørers Landsforening	Exports	1933	1991
Noregs Sildesalslag	Firsthand sales	1936	1989
Håbrandfiskernes Salgslag	Firsthand sales	1936	1988
Notfiskarsamskipnaden	Firsthand sales	1937	1949
Brislingsfiskernes Landslag	Firsthand sales	1937	1949
Islandsfiskernes Forening	Firsthand sales	1938	1987
Nordsjøsildfiskernes Salgslag	Firsthand sales	1938	1939
Saltsildeksportørenes Landsforening	Exports	1938	1991
Norges Tørrfiskeksportørers Landsforening	Exports	1939	1991
Norges Råfisklag	Firsthand sales	1939	In operation
Norges Makrellag	Firsthand sales	1939	1989
Norges Levendefisklag	Firsthand sales	1939	1973
Eksportutvalget for Tørrfisk	Exports	1940	1991
Eksportutvalget for Klippfisk og Saltfisk	Exports	1940	1991
Eksportutvalget for Fiskemel	Exports	1940	1991
Hermetikkfabrikantenes Eksportutvalg	Exports	1940	1991
Eksportutvalget for Sildemel og Olje	Exports	1941	1991
Eksportutvalget for Fetsild	Exports	1941	1986
Eksportutvalget for Saltet Småsild og Skjærsild	Exports	1941	1966
Eksportutvalget for Tran	Exports	1941	1991
Norges Feitsildeksportørers Landsforening	Exports	1941	1991
Norges Saltrogneksportørers Landsforening	Exports	1942	1991
Eksportutvalget for Saltet Rogn	Exports	1942	1991
Eksportutvalget for Saltet Storsild og Vårsild	Exports	1942	1966
Eksportutvalget for Saltet Islandssild	Exports	1945	1966
Eksportutvalget for Fersk Sild	Exports	1945	1987
Eksportutvalget for Fersk Fisk	Exports	1945	1991
Eksportutvalget for Frossen Fisk og Filet	Exports	1945	1991
Eksportutvalget for Frossen Sild	Exports	1945	1987
Sunnmøre og Romsdal Fiskesalgslag	Firsthand sales	1946	In operation
Rogaland Fiskesalgslag	Firsthand sales	1947	In operation
Skagerakfisk	Firsthand sales	1947	In operation
Sogn og Fjordane Fiskesalgslag	Firsthand sales	1947	1988
Hordafisk	Firsthand sales	1947	1988
Fjordfisk	Firsthand sales	1947	1989
De Norske Saltfiskeksportørers Landsforening	Exports	1948	1991
Feitsildfiskernes Salgslag	Firsthand sales	1949	1989
Sild- og Brislingsfiskernes Salgslag	Firsthand sales	1949	1966
Islandssildeksportørenes Landsforening	Exports	1949	1987
Eksportutvalget for Saltet Sild	Exports	1966	1991
Fiskeprodusentenes Fellessalg	Processed fish	1971	1993
Fiskeoppdretternes Salgslag	Firsthand sales	1978	1991
Eksportutvalget for Fersk og Frossen Sild	Exports	1987	1991
Vest-Norges Fiskesalgslag	Firsthand sales	1988	In operation
Norges Sildesalgslag	Firsthand sales	1989	In operation
Eksportutvalget for Fisk	Exports	1991	In operation

SOURCE: The sources for the table are different types of government documents. An Odelstingsproposisjon (Ot.prp.) is a government proposal on legislative matters that was prepared for the Odelsting, which is a chamber of the Parliament involved in creating legislation. A Stortingsmelding (St.meld.) is a document in which the government provides information to the Parliament (Stortinget). Both are printed documents available in any Norwegian library. The specific sources used are as follows: Ot.prp.nr.7.1930; Ot.prp.nr.58.1932; Ot.prp.nr.57.1935; Ot.prp.nr.1.1936; Ot.prp.nr.48.1937; Ot.prp.nr.52.1937; Ot.prp.nr.53.1938; Ot.prp.nr.59.1938; Ot.prp.nr.55.1940;   St.meld.nr.3.1948;   Ot.prp.nr.63.1948;   Ot.prp.nr.63.1951;   Ot.prp.nr.30.1955; Ot.prp.nr.85.1969–70; Ot.prp.nr.90.1988–89; St.meld.nr.41. 1989–90; Ot.prp.nr.61.1991–92.

Index

347

About the Contributors

Patricia A. Adler is Associate Professor of Sociology in the Department of Sociology, University of Colorado, Boulder. Her research interests include deviance and drugs, socialization and child development, interpretive theory and social psychology, and work and occupations. Previous studies have focused on the social organization and subcultures of upper-level drug traffickers, elite college athletes, and preadolescents. Her current work looks at the sociology of resorts, examining occupational careers, lifestyles, seasons and temporality, tipping and service, the simulacrum of nature, different subcultures, and the leisure-work nexus in a destination Hawaiian resort.

Peter Adler is Professor of Sociology at the University of Denver. His research interests include social psychology, qualitative methods, sociology of sport and leisure, and deviant behavior. Recent publications include *Peer Power*, with Patricia A. Adler (1998), a study of preadolescents. He is currently involved in a project on the occupational culture of resort workers. Together with Patricia A. Adler, he served as editor of the *Journal of Contemporary Ethnography* for eight years and was the founding editor of *Sociological Studies of Child Development*, a research annual.

James R. Barker is Assistant Professor of Organizational Theory and Strategy in the Department of Management at the U.S. Air Force Academy. His research interests focus on the development and analysis of control practices in technological and knowledge-based organizations. His recent projects include collaborative research with scientists at the Los Alamos and Sandia

National Laboratories. He is also collaborating with colleagues in Australia to study the consequences of concertive control environments. He won the 1993 Outstanding Publication in Organizational Behavior Award from the Academy of Management for his research on self-managing teams.

Nicole Woolsey Biggart is Professor of Management and Sociology at the Graduate School of Management, University of California, Davis. "The Creative-Destructive Process of Organizational Change," written as a graduate student, was her first publication. Since then, she has written extensively about the social bases of economic activity, including *Charismatic Capitalism: Direct Selling Organizations in America* (1990) and *The Economic Organization of East Asian Capitalism*, with Marco Orru and Gary G. Hamilton (1997). At present, she is working on a comparative analysis of rotating savings and credit associations, a type of informal capital market found among poor people around the world.

Robert E. Cole is Professor of Business and Sociology at the University of California, Berkeley. He is a long-term student of Japanese work organization and is the author of the forthcoming book, *Managing Quality Fads: How American Business Learned to Play the Quality Game* (1998). He is also co-editor, with Ikujiro Nonaka and David Teece, of *Knowledge and the Firm* (Oxford University Press, forthcoming). His most recent work focuses on strategies for the transfer of knowledge in multidivisional firms. He is the co-director of the Management of Technology Program at Berkeley, a joint effort of the Haas School of Business and the College of Engineering.

Burton R. Clark is Allan M. Cartter Professor Emeritus of Higher Education and Sociology in the Graduate School of Education and Information Studies, University of California, Los Angeles. His recent books are *Places of Inquiry: Research and Advanced Education in Modern Universities* (1995) and *Creating Entrepreneurial Universities: Organizational Pathways of Transformation* (1998).

Richard M. Cyert is the Richard M. and Margaret S. Cyert Professor of Economics and Management in the Graduate School of Industrial Administration at Carnegie Mellon University. His interest has been in decision making under uncertainty, and that remains a major interest. He is the author of *Bayesian Analysis and Uncertainty in Economic Theory* (1987), with Morris H. De Groot, and remains interested in that area.

William R. Dill has been dean of the Schools of Business at New York University, president of Babson College, and interim president of two other schools (Anna Maria College and Boston Architectural Center). His books include *The New Managers* (1978), *The Organization World*, and *Running the American Corporation* (1962). His interest in organizational issues